LEAPING LIFE'S

PAT SMYTHE

LEAPING LIFE'S FENCES

•THE•
SPORTSMAN'S
PRESS
LONDON

Published by The Sportsman's Press 1992

A catalogue record for this book
is available from the British Library

ISBN 0–948253–59–2

Photoset and printed in Great Britain by
Redwood Press Limited, Melksham, Wiltshire

Contents

List of Illustrations

Facing page 51

Signing copies of *Jump for Joy* in Exeter, 1954.
The late Marquis and Marchioness of Exeter, when he presented me with the Sports-woman of the Year trophy in 1952.
Sir Harry Llewellyn gives me a bite of his ice cream during Rotterdam Horse Show.

Facing page 66

Prince Hal beat the best in the world for the gold buttons with the Championship of Algiers, 1955.
Sam Koechlin jumping the final cross-country fence on Goya, for the Swiss team in the Olympic Three-Day Event, Stockholm 1956.

Facing page 67

Stockholm, 1956: the first time a lady received an Olympic medal for show-jumping.
Flanagan clears the parallel bars at the Stockholm Olympics.

Facing page 82

Serenading Flanagan with the guitar.
A different sort of mount: a white racing camel at El Golea in Algeria, 1956.
With Colonel Gordon Smythe, Uncle Gordon (Dad's older brother), at Buckingham Palace 1956.
A sporting encounter with Danny Kaye.

Facing page 83

Tosca with her second foal, La Favorita, 1958.
Mr Pollard, who won me my only Queen's Cup at White City, 1958.

Facing page 98

Scorchin' winning his first *Daily Mail* Cup with me at White City, 1960.
White City, 1961. The Queen presents me with the first John Player Trophy that Scorchin' won.

Facing page 99

General Franco presenting the European Showjumping Trophy, Madrid 1962.
Laurie Lee with his daughter Jesse came to open our Miserden Church Fete in 1965.
Flanagan eating his laurels after winning the Hickstead Derby, 1962.

Facing page 114

Paul helped Flanagan to dress for our wedding reception at Sudgrove in September 1963.
Monica's christening at Miserden Church in 1966. With Sam, Sibylle, Dominik and Catherine.

Facing page 115

I am mounted on Bayridge, with Lucy in front of me; Monica is on Dimple.
Lucy, on Dimple, giving Gordon Richardson, now Lord Richardson of Duntisbourne, some useful banking tips.
Sam and I watching Monica and Lucy playing ball with Tiggy, the cairn.

Facing page 146

Family jump! Lucy on Twinkle, Monica on Man Friday, Pat on Legend and Sam on Springtime (hidden) at Steinacker, August 1975.
Our one-handed helicopter pilot who took us to Ujung Kulon in 1977, and on the way back ran out of fuel.

Acknowledgements

The author and publisher would like to thank the following for the use of their photo-
graphs: Associated Press, Michael Charity, Cheltenham Newspaper Company, Rex
Coleman, *Daily Express, Daily Mirror, Evening Standard, The Field,* Fox Photos, Keystone
Press Agency Ltd, L'Année Hippique, S.B. & B. Mallett.

Foreword by Colonel Sir Harry Llewellyn, BT, CBE

As far as the ladies are concerned, Pat Smythe must stand out, in my opinion, as an all time great. She was tremendously determined to win and had a tough, virile approach. I remember once when I beat her in New York by a tenth of a second she stumped away after the competition and never even congratulated me. I mentioned this to her the next day, and she replied, 'I was so cross at being beaten – even by you!' She was a *winner*.

I think Pat was the best lady rider I have ever seen. Oddly enough, she was more of a hand rider. She liked to have a horse taking a light hold of her in order to ride it. She did not use her legs much but she had a wonderful sense of balance and timing and was a beautiful natural horsewoman with tremendous guts. What more can I say?

In 1953 she took Prince Hal to America and this coincided with Foxhunter's last visit there. Unfortunately he had had a fall at Harringay and jumped with little confidence in Harrisburg where Pat brought out Prince Hal to win five events in consecutive days. Although Tosca had been a big winner in England it was really this performance with Prince Hal that brought her to the top internationally.

Reading her account brought back many happy memories of visits abroad with British teams to the winter shows in Paris, Brussels and Geneva. On these trips, Pat's desire to find out what she could about life led to visits to the museums and historic buildings in Rome, Paris and Madrid. These gave her an appreciation of so many facets that it led her to having a very full life. With my wife Teeny, she was able to get away from our horses as both had a great appreciation of art in many forms. Nobody filled her time more profitably than Pat. She married a successful horseman and leading industrialist, Sam Koechlin, with whom she settled in Switzerland where she brought up her two charming daughters.

We have both always had a consuming interest in wildlife but it was not until the seventies that Pat was to visit reserves all over the world as a very active Trustee of the Worldwide Fund for Nature. Her contribution to equestrian events and wildlife operations has been immense and greatly appreciated all over the world. She has put so much into the lives of so many and this book is a record of her outstanding achievements.

Foreword by Lady Philippa Scott

Pat Smythe's name will always be associated with showjumping. What is not perhaps so well-known, except among her friends, is her interest in the natural world and her concern for the conservation of the environment. Like so many millions of people her inspiration came from my husband, the late Sir Peter Scott. A near neighbour, we had first met over ponies with my step-daughter who had insisted that I approach this celebrity at a local horse show.

Pat's life has been full of fences of all kinds which she has negotiated with tremendous skill and determination. The move to Switzerland when she married Sam Koechlin brought her nearer to the headquarters of the World Wildlife Fund, as it then was, and she was to become more and more involved with their work. Her travels with Sam brought her into contact with wildlife all over the world and she has been and continues to be an untiring ambassador for the many conservation organisations with which she is associated.

1

'Thursday's child has far to go':
The Early Years

'Thursday's child has far to go', as the birthday rhyme lays down. There was certainly a spirit of adventure born with me on that Thursday morning of 22 November 1928. I was delivered at 24, Shotfield Avenue, East Sheen, to join my brother Ronald, already three and a half, and almost as a replacement for our elder brother Dickie, who had died of a heart complaint two years and a day before. In a matter-of-fact way, my Dad noted, 'Patricia born 10.05 a.m. Monique [mother] splendid! Dull wet morning. To office after lunch. Aunt Isobel died today.'

As soon as I could toddle, wanderlust lured me through the garden gate and out into the suburbs. The next time I was 'delivered' to Mother was when I disappeared one day. She dashed outside, found the gate unlatched and rushed down the road. A butcher's boy on his bicycle saw her distress and hauled me out of his basket, shouting 'Hey Miss, this your baby?' He had rescued me as I was about to cross the Upper Richmond Road.

Grandfather Frank Curtoys had been the Rector at Cromhall in Gloucestershire for thirty-three years where Mother was born and brought up with her three elder brothers. Frank was also a scholar and fond of music, probably far better suited to Academic surroundings than a quiet country parish. The Curtoys family was descended from a knight who had come over with William the Conqueror, which brought some Norman blood into the entangled Smythe line.

The name is associated with Curt Hose, short stockings, the name of Robert Duke of Normandy, the eldest son of William the Conqueror, whose thirteenth-century effigy lies on his tomb in Gloucester cathedral. Poor Robert ended his days in Cardiff Castle, imprisoned by his younger brother Henry IV. The tomb of another victim of those days, murdered at Berkeley Castle was Edward II, the Confessor, who is placed on the opposite side of the choir.

Charlotte, our Granny, was a character who coped with Grandpa's depression and lameness from his damaged hip, and the boisterous boys always getting into trouble, especially the middle one, Hugo. Granny always gave Hugo hell in return for the trouble he caused with his high spirits. I was impressed in later years that Hugo, on his visits to England, was the son that took the most trouble with Granny when she was old and causing quite a bit of mischief amongst other old ladies, in order to amuse herself. Mother was always very good with Granny and I tried to visit the old lady in Bath as often as I could after Mother was killed.

Grandpa Frank and Charlotte celebrated their Golden Wedding in 1947 in Bath a year before he died at eighty-nine.

Country life had suited mother well as a child, she used to ride the neighbouring farmer's hunters and point-to-pointers whenever she got the chance. She loved sport and during her time at St Swithin's School, Winchester, she was Captain of the cricket XI and the head of High House.

All four children left home at Cromhall Rectory before they were twenty. Mother married at just nineteen, meeting my father Eric at the wedding of her older brother Ollo, where Eric was best man and she was bridesmaid. Very soon afterwards they got engaged while following the Beaufort Hounds at Leighterton near Badminton. They were hunting in Dad's three-wheeled car, the Flying Bug, not on horses!

Eric had been through the Great War while Mother was at school. He was the descendant of a family that came from Rosedale Abbey, in the North Riding of Yorkshire. They left this mountainous area of wild sheep moors and fertile valleys, famed for quarries of building blocks and iron-stone, to settle in Ireland in 1630. The family home of Barbavilla in Co. Westmeath, was built by William Smythe and was where his descendants lived until the last war.

Dad's mother Alice, was petite, fun and rode horses, while his father Arthur had played the cello with their family orchestra, before becoming a distinguished electrical engineer and consultant to the firm responsible for the electrical grid of Preston, Bath and Cardiff, where my Dad was born, the second of two sons. He and his brother Gordon were taken to Switzerland when their father contracted tuberculosis, as the pure mountain air of Davos was then one of the few known aids in dealing with the deadly disease. Arthur retired to bed for eighteen months before gradually becoming the 'Davos miracle' as he improved and became his old self again. Meanwhile the boys were brought up speaking the local Swiss dialect in primary school, then going to the *Gymnase Scientifique de Lausanne* where Eric passed his *Certificat de Maturité* before going to Heidelberg University in Germany, leaving him fluent in German, French and English, as well as the Swiss dialect, which is not an officially written language.

Qualified as a Civil Engineer, A.M.I.C.E., he joined the service of the Honorable Artillery Company from 1909–1913 and was awarded a whip as wheeler driver. On the outbreak of the Great War he was in the Intelligence Corps of the 4th Army. His four years in France gained him three mentions in Despatches, with the M.C. and bar, together with the French Cross of the Legion d'Honneur. The languages learnt during his Swiss education enabled him to become the youngest staff officer in British Intelligence and he was in the party which attended the signing of the Armistice Agreement of 11 November 1918 at the final surrender.

Mother was always the attractive and vivacious centre of the family. Although she seldom drank alcohol, she would be the first to be dancing on the table at a party. In adversity during the war, while nursing father and keeping the family going then and after he died, she was always outwardly optimistic with faith in the future. In her company everyone felt the fun and true sense of gaiety, as her

(*above left*) Patricia Rosemary Smythe, aged about three with Raider as a pup. He was my companion until he died in 1939. (*above right*) My father, Eric Hamilton Smythe, 1886–1945. (*below left*) Royal Richmond Horse Show, 1933. I am leading my brother Ronald on Bubbles. (*below right*) Mother on Malamra at Ferne Gymkhana, 1939.

(*above*) With Mother and Ronald. (*left*) On Pixie, winning equal first prize at the Richmond Horse Show 1939, my first big win. (*below*) On Fireworks, 1941. My Uncle Gordon gave me this polo pony when he joined the Pioneer Corps. I taught her to gymkhana and jump with great success locally, while she gave me the link between riding ponies and horses.

birth on a Sunday denotes that, 'the child that is born on the Sabbath Day is bonny and blythe and good and gay', the latter being the original meaning of the word.

I hope that I absorbed some of this joyous part of her character by observation because I took life very seriously. My first joke I made unintentionally was when I was five. Mother teased me saying 'If you do that I'll only feed you on a banana.' I came back with, 'If you do that I'll give you a raspberry.' In the silence that followed, and then the ripples of laughter from Mother, I suddenly realised that I had made a joke, surprising myself.

One of Mother's disruptive traits was that she was always late for everything. The result of the panic I felt when we arrived late for appointments, trains and especially horse shows is that I have always been super punctual. As most horse shows had their events running late, Mother could not understand my nervous frenzy. There were a few times when I had to ride a horse or pony into the arena, without having had time to hammer in the frost nails (used instead of studs during the war) to stop it slipping, and with no time to supple the animal or jump a practice fence. Hurrying straight into the ring, sometimes, the horse would go clear and Mother would smile benignly. My habitual punctuality stood me in good stead in my married life, as Sam's crowded programme had to be run to a precise time table.

Ollo, Mother's elder brother Oswald, born just before the turn of the century, passed out of Sandhurst near the top of the list. In the Indian Army he fought on the North West Frontier and got on well with the tribesmen while learning their language. He had a bad smash with an American vehicle in Italy at the end of the last war. For two weeks he was left for dead in the American field hospital, when suddenly he sat up and began to command the tactics for a tank battle. His smashed legs were quickly set by the hospital staff and he came back into the land of the living and in due course he was brought back to England.

His widow, Lini, who was brought up in Austria, and was his second wife, lived in Sudgrove Cottage. She had helped his first wife with their three children; they and their offspring came to visit her, as our Gloucestershire house has always been a centre for the family when they come to England.

Hugo, the mischievous brother when a boy, also had to find his way in the world from his teens. After adventures and various jobs in Canada and America he started work with Reyrolles as a civil engineer. His work took him from Shanghai and points East to Buenos Aires and points West. The few times he visited home were always exciting, we would learn naughty phrases in kitchen Chinese or Spanish and one time he arrived with a black and swollen face and damaged arms and legs. He had climbed a telephone pole in his car and broken the pole near the top, we were told. His sense of humour helped him through his life, even when he was interned in Changi jail all through the war, when the Japs took the peninsula of Singapore while he was working on the power station. He somehow survived, although he lost ten stone in camp; many of his friends died just after their release as their condition was too bad for recovery.

Hugo's daughter Sheila by his first wife Elsie, is four years younger than myself and lived with us during the war. His second wife Evelyne had just produced their son Jeremy before she escaped from Singapore in a convoy sailing to South Africa, where they waited, wondering if they would ever be together again. Jeremy came to stay with us when he went to school first in Cirencester and then at Kelly College, Tavistock, so our families were closely involved.

Nicco, the third brother, went to sea before farming sheep in South Africa. During the war he became a Naval Commander in the South African Navy Reserve at the ports of Walvis Bay, Port Elizabeth and Durban. He and Mary his wife had two daughters, Sue and Barbara, who are good friends and make our home a port of call with the rest of the family, just as I visit the clan in other continents.

My earliest memories include Ronald rolling on the nursery floor while nanny rained blows at whatever part of his anatomy was uppermost, while I howled for his discomfort in the conflict. He usually emerged unscathed while nanny probably suffered from his bright ideas and endless initiative. A more unusual memory occurred in the early 1930s when Mother excitedly showed us from the nursery window, a zeppelin slowly flying up the Thames. It was the R101, a ship that was later abandoned after the disaster to her sister zeppelin that flew into a French hillside, killing all on board. It was not until 1938 that the Germans produced their Graf Zeppelin, which they flew on a promotion tour all around the British coast, taking photos of harbours and military sites, which would stand them in good stead while they planned for the coming war.

Another memorable prewar event was the night that the Crystal Palace burnt down. I was grabbed out of bed, wrapped in a blanket, and Daddy drove us in the car to a hill in Richmond Park where we could watch the terrifying blaze and flames making the night sky glow red.

I do not remember my first ride, because from earliest days I was popped onto a sheepskin without stirrups when my brother's pony Bubbles was around, or on one of the Argentinian polo ponies that Mother helped to school and exercise in Richmond Park. My children started like this too. A woolly sheepskin is very comfortable and warm to sit in 'as snug as a bug in a rug', with the sheepskin and the neckstrap or pony's mane to grab, which helps children on a leading rein to feel secure before they graduate to holding reins.

The legs of a child hang down naturally in the correct position while they have no stirrups; sitting up with a straight back the child is in harmony with the pony's movements. We used a saddle for shows, but usually rode on a sheepskin or bareback. Sometimes a polo pony had a prominent backbone, so a rug and padding was essential if one did not want to be cut in two.

Schooling polo ponies was a great lesson in discipline, teaching the ponies balance and obedience, with the lightest touch on the rein. The reins are held in the left hand so that the right arm is free to carry a polo stick. Turning the pony is called neck reining, because the outside rein is against the pony's neck, with the reins held in one hand. As a child, I jumped my pony with only the left hand on the reins, as one rides a polo pony. On turning a corner the pony was trained to do a flying change at the canter, so that the same fore leg and hind leg would be leading in balance on the turn. The aim of training for polo is that with minimum pressure on the reins, the pony is balanced, and able to stop and start again from a halt to a canter, in control and comfort. The rider should have light hands, with movements helped by their body balance to gain obedience and accuracy from their mount. When this goal of harmony is achieved, the partnership of horse and rider produces a delightful spectacle.

Naturally for normal training of horses for all the other disciplines and equestrian training, the principles of harmony without obvious domination should be apparent. The top riders give the least obvious signs of intervention with their horses during a round, because they know how to get the horse balanced with impulsion well before each jumping effort. This takes patient work on the flat, teaching the horse obedience and sensitivity to the rider's hands, legs and balance in the saddle. At a later stage the horse's muscles can be built up by working over trotting poles, to make it supple and footsure in its work. Each stage should be understood and learnt by the horse while the muscles are being formed and strengthened for progressive stages of work.

It has always sickened me to see the Germanic trend, copied by some of our riders, of using the bit in the horse's mouth as a saw, pulling its head from side to side while entering the ring, in order to impose domination on the animal. It is even worse when they go through the same sawing motions when leaving the arena, often after the horse has jumped a clear round. This is the time when the animal deserves praise and relaxation on a long rein as a reward for its good work.

My balance when riding on a sheepskin was severely tested when I was four. I was not too confident and always held onto the sheepskin and pony's mane with both hands. It was in Richmond Park when mother's nightmare happened. Her highly strung young polo pony, Ñata, was frightened by some people jumping out of the bracken, and she suddenly shied and started to buck. I was trotting beside mother on Bubbles, and my leading rein was pulled out of her hand. Bubbles, Ronald's pony, bolted back across the park towards his stable with me on top without reins saying 'Whoa, Bubbles, whoa', but he didn't listen. Mother quietened the frightened Ñata and came back to the stables with dread in her heart. Miraculously I was still sitting on Bubbles, who was standing there with the dragging leading rein. I told her proudly 'I can gallop all by myself'.

I certainly needed this new found confidence when we bought Pixie home from Dartmoor. We had gone for our summer holidays to the West Country and had found 'my' pony. She was a chestnut mare, just over 13 hh, and bred on the Prince of Wales' farm at Tor Royal. She had the Prince of Wales' feathers branded on her near side shoulder. She turned out to be a real character, aged four to my five years. The times she bucked me off or jumped me off, because she jumped so high over any obstacle, were beyond the records. This early training may have given me a very secure seat for later experiences in point-to-pointing and jumping, making sure that I would 'stay put' if possible.

A disruption to my pony riding also happened when I was four. I contracted diphtheria while we were on holiday at Burnham-on-Sea. I was rushed to Axbridge Isolation Hospital, where I was segregated from the family for the first time; their only contact with me could be through the closed window. It was an awful experience, but perhaps I became interested in sheep farming from watching the sheep on the Mendips from my bed. I felt imprisoned there on my own; it was a long drive for Father to come down from London, but when he came he noted in his diary, 'Pat wonderfully composed' and another time 'Pat very merry bless her!', so I must have learnt to act well during this frustrating time. Mother came many times and was very distressed that she could only wave through the window. After ten weeks in hospital, although some of the swabs were still positive, mother took me home. I had learnt to dread those words from the doctor, 'Positive again', meaning that I could not leave the hospital. When mother spirited me away after ten weeks in bed I was very weak and had to learn to walk again. My poor Rupert Bear was even worse off, because he was baked and fumigated so he became a well-scorched and hairless Teddy, the penalty for coming back with me. My infection immediately cleared with home and fresh air.

I had heard that the illness might affect my heart, and therefore never complained or worried when later my heart gave me trouble during heavy physical work. It was only discovered that I had a congenital heart disease after my husband Sam died when I was already fifty-six years old. Meanwhile my heart had survived the toughest assignments that I had demanded of it for over half a century.

I was soon back in the saddle, and having grown during the weeks in bed, I had longer legs for riding the bigger polo ponies. These were Argentinian ponies shipped over unbroken by Johnnie Traill, the international polo player. He kept the ponies in stables built on Ham Common in a yard run by Billy Walsh, a genial Irishman. Mother was delighted to be asked to ride the ponies, although she had one or two bad falls off the green, half-broken ponies of the Argentinian Pampas. Once, when Johnnie lassoed her, pinioning her arms to her side, the rope got under the pony's tail, and as it clamped down its tail in fear, it bucked and ran away towards a road crossing the Park. An extra buck and twist sent Mother into orbit, with her arms still pinioned and no hard hat; she hit the ground head first and Johnnie thought she had broken her neck. After catching her horse he came back to her as she came to, although she remembered nothing later. A chastened Johnnie let her ride back to the stables, with her thumb dislocated and a badly bruised neck.

Father was working hard and did not approve of Mother risking her life with cowboy antics, especially when he was away. That day he had gone to Newcastle to see a new industrial plant, and he, too, had a miraculous escape. An explosion in the works happened seconds after he passed by. The accident in the factory kept him up North for a week, while Mother, to her relief, had time to get her neck treated. On Dad's return he quickly guessed that a horse escapade had caused her trouble.

On my fifth birthday, my father's diary noted that he had to arrange a £2000 mortgage for Beaufort, a nice house in the cul-de-sac off Gipsy Lane. It was just by Barnes Common, with the station nearby for him to catch the train to Victoria, close to his office, where he was the director of Electrical Improvements Ltd and consultant to Babcock and Wilcox. After we moved in, I was thrilled to have a bigger garden, where I could keep my rabbit, Snow White. We made a goldfish pond and a sandpit. The lawn was big enough, too, to put up my home-made jumps for me and my friends and the dog to jump. Raider our Cairn terrier learnt to jump through my bicycle as I put my feet up. Snow White had a course of obstacles down her run to her feeding place and the coloured mice, Tim and Tiddler, had a scenic garden of obstacles to negotiate in their pen. I used a stop watch to time myself and my friends jumping around a course of deck chairs and garden obstacles, long before time became an element of success in show jumping.

Beaufort gave us the freedom of Barnes Common where I could roam with Raider. My favourite stop was in the goods yard of Barnes Station where the coalman had built himself a little hut, with his horse tethered outside contentedly munching the feed in its nosebag. In the hut, a pot of stew for dinner was always kept warm on the small stove, as well as the kettle brewing at all hours. The stove was kept burning with coal dust, so quite a taste of coal impregnated the filling stew which I can still smell in my imagination, along with the special waft of scent from the unclipped heavy horse, its wavy coat mixed with working sweat and coal, covered by a sack protecting its back and loins.

Usually I would put my 6d a week pocket money into the Post Office Savings Bank, but occasionally I would get some carrots for the horse and the coalman's pot, as we were the best of friends. Before the war, we could buy my favourite fruit water ice from the chap on the Wall's tricycle for one copper penny.

Riding in Richmond Park on Pixie, was a constant battle of wits with the keepers, as Pixie and I loved jumping the park benches. I was forbidden to jump the polo ponies in case they then tried to jump the polo ball. In those days there was no riding track to keep on so we could take the ponies for picnics and hobble them, letting them graze while we played in the bracken, although at rutting time in the autumn we learnt to be careful to keep away from the mating stags, with their huge antlers; they were terrifying if they charged.

Another advantage of our new home was its proximity of the Roehampton Club, where there were polo matches, tennis courts, a golf course and a roller skating rink. We also were allowed to use the wooden horse, which we sat on to practise polo strokes. I learnt to swim in the pool and practised golf with cut down clubs and hit tennis balls against the practice boards. Mother and father were good tennis and golf players, so we could improve our skills while they played in matches. One popular evening at Roehampton was Guy Fawkes night with a superb display of fireworks. I have never liked loud noises and I would firmly block my tender ears, putting a rug over my head saying 'I don't mind them, if I can't hear them'!

Another real fear, when I was little, was to hear wood being cut with electric saws. I would listen before I set off for a ride, to hear if the saws were working in the Park that day. If they were, I would go in another direction while my tummy turned at the distant whine of the blade sawing through those trees. Perhaps it was a premonition of the present destruction of rain forest and the great tropical forest habitat around the world. The crash and rumble of thunder frightened me too, but having seen the damage that lightning can do this fear is justified. We lost a pony once; she had been grazing in the middle of a field away from trees, but had metal shoes on and was killed instantly.

At Christmas time we used to leave London and drive to the Cotswolds where we visited my Uncle Gordon, Dad's elder brother and Aunt Dorothy at Swindon Manor near Cheltenham. They had bought the Manor when he retired from the Army as Regimental Colonel having served with the Burma Rifles. He kept a few polo ponies and played during the polo season in the West Country. He also hunted with the Cotswold Hounds and so my Pixie came to visit, too, on occasions. My excitement before these holidays usually made me run a tempera-ture, but bundled up in the car, I would soon be cured by hilarious stops for picnics on the Cotswolds, where Mother 'baa'd' to the sheep, bringing them crowding around us. The old Manor House with a mud and wattle wall in one of the oak panelled rooms, was full of exciting nooks and secret crannies which made a blissful playground for our games and adventures. It was also the link to the future, when our London life changed to the Cotswolds during the war.

The Pony Club played a part in my competitive riding, but I had to ride a long way to the Mid-Surrey Pony Club. The route would lead down the Kingston Bypass while I followed mother driving the car; she would wait for me to catch up. Nowadays road traffic would make that impossible. We kept Pixie in a paddock by Ham House on Ham Common. Sometimes a neighbour would tip his lawn mowings over the fence, which Pixie tucked into with relish, probably eating the lot before it got a chance to ferment. It is not a recommended food for ponies but we fed her hay regularly and she thrived.

Home-made fences were put together in our little paddock, the first one being a hedge. Pixie was never careless when jumping, in fact she hardly touched a fence in her life, which is why she was so difficult to sit on. The kind helper who had made the hedge topped it with a piece of prickly gorse off the common, where we always jumped the gorse bushes. The first time I faced the new jump with trepidation, Pixie stopped at the hedge, picked off the topping of gorse with her teeth, and then jumped the fence from a standstill with a huge leap that sent me flying. We did not replace the gorse.

In the next field the great rider Paul Rodzianko used to school the horses that he was showing and jumping for their owners. He was a brilliant horseman and cavalryman of the old school. He had come to Olympia in London before the Great War with the Russian showjumping team, and became the first triple winner of the King's Cup, then known as the King Edward VII Cup, in the years 1912, 1913, 1914, the only rider to have won in three consecutive years. The cup vanished during the Great War when Paul took it back to Russia, and the competition was later replaced by the King George V Cup. Paul had studied under James Fillis, the Englishman who became the *Ecuyer en Chef* at the Russian Cavalry School and a master of High School work. He then had the chance to go to the Italian Cavalry School to learn cross-country riding with Fred Caprilli, profiting from both these great riding Masters.

Paul joined the British Army during the Great War and became a nationalised British subject between the wars. The excellent Irish team of Fred Ahearne, Jed O'Dwyer, Dan Corry and Jack Lewis were trained by him before he came back to England where one of his best pupils was Mike Ansell.

I met him often during my jumping days and his sometimes incorrigible behaviour impressed and amused me. He was any man's equal, and once he was dining with important people when he made an outrageous statement. His wife must have reprimanded him with her foot under the table. He turned to her and said loudly with his Russian accent, 'Vife, Vife, for vhy do you kick me? I never let my vives keek me!'

Other people's ponies were sometimes sent to Mother to school and to improve their mouths. We used the gaucho method of tying a soft strip of rawhide around the pony's lower jaw, under the tongue, so that the bars of the mouth could not be hurt while the pony was being re-schooled or broken in. The reins to the 'bocado', the strip around the lower jaw, were also of soft rawhide and mother was lightweight with very good light hands.

The ponies would improve quickly under her tuition. However, one of the visiting ponies did not approve of Pixie's company in the paddock, and one morning we found that Pixie had been kicked above the eye, which was very swollen. In spite of constant treatment for her poor eye, I was heartbroken when the vet told me that the eye had gone blind. At first I thought that she would die and certainly never jump again, but Pixie decided otherwise and jumped as well and higher than ever.

Mother was very ambitious when she entered Pixie in the under 13.2hh pony jumping at the Richmond Royal Horse Show in June 1939. We had jumped in a few pony competitions at Pony Club rallies and country shows when on holiday, but Richmond was the goal for all the top riders, children with ponies that had won at the horse show meccas of Islington and Olympia.

Pixie had not been jumped for the week before the show, because I had been in bed with a high temperature and 'flu. I got up shakily on the morning of the show, but I was determined to make it. Riding across Richmond Park, I found one or two benches which I jumped when the keepers were not looking, and Pixie was pleased to be jumping again. We were both nervous when we arrived among the crowds. Horses of all types and sizes were beautifully turned out and many had smart rugs with the horse's name on each side. I had not plaited Pixie's mane and tail, but I made a pledge to learn how to do this in the future and to sew the plaits so that they stayed neat and tidy for the day. I felt out of my depth with so many experienced little riders, all seeming to be very sure of themselves. Just before it was my turn to jump my knees went weak and I asked 'Mummy, can you give me something like aspirin to stop my knees trembling?' She told me it would not help, but I need not jump if I didn't feel well enough. That was the challenge I needed as the solid wooden doors to the arena swung open and No. 13 was called. I was going to make 13 my lucky number. Pixie blew her nose with a snort as we saw the coloured jumps around the arena with the green cricket pitch roped off in the middle. We started a little stickily as both Pixie and I were very impressed and I was not feeling very strong. At a high red plank with ROAD CLOSED painted on it, Pixie hesitated as though reading the order, but some enthusiastic chap in the crowd shouted 'Hup' and over the plank Pixie soared, while I grabbed her unplaited mane, which may have saved the day. Our enthusiasm swelled as we turned for home, and with the reins held in my left hand in polo pony style, we finished clear.

We still had work to do as several other ponies were clear too, and the fences were put up for us to jump again, as results were not decided on time then. The ponies kept going clear over higher and higher fences. Finally after three of us jumped four clear rounds, the fences were already higher than for the Open Jumping Class for grown-ups. It was decided that we three riders would divide the first prize. The other two child riders were Douggie Bunn, now known as the Master of Hickstead, the superb jumping arena in Sussex, and Fred Winter, the famous jockey and trainer, who so sadly had a fall at home that has now curtailed his activities. That day in June 1939 may not have rated as 'red letter' in their diaries, but for me it was the first big step.

2

Farming, Ferreting and Finality: The War Years

My riding activities were never allowed to interfere with school and I could hardly wait for weekends and holidays. My school at Oakhill in Wimbledon had a small bus that did the round to pick up several girls in the morning and return them in the evening. It was a great relief to me that I could live at home, as I missed my brother when he was sent as a boarder to Fonthill preparatory school at the age of seven. I was excited by the occasional weekend visits to his school where I met his friends, one being John Severne who much later flew the Royal Family in the Queen's Flight. We would go and have picnics on the East Grinstead rocks, and invent many climbing games.

I was not exposed to the shattering experience of boarding school until we had no home at the beginning of the war. I then promised myself that I would never submit my children to the misery that I felt. Schools have changed since then, and many friends' children now enjoy boarding. In Switzerland my girls went through the State school system, so they never had to leave home. Swiss children only go to boarding school if they need cramming or if their parents are abroad.

Father's rheumatoid arthritis worsened and began to curtail his activities and sports. I would listen to him painfully coming down the stairs, then one day he came down with a rapid rhythm. I ran to the hall to see the miracle, but this one good day was not repeated. The doctor advised him to get a cure in the dry and warm climate of North Africa.

The way of life was about to change forever. War was on the way. That summer Ronald and I were staying at Swindon Manor, where I was enjoying my holiday riding Fireworks, my favourite of Uncle's polo ponies. The anxious talk was of Nazi Germany, Hitler's threats of invasion and war. On the fateful day of 3 September 1939 we all went to Tewkesbury Abbey, instead of our normal Sunday worship in St Lawrence, the charming old Church with its unusual octagonal tower standing next to Swindon Manor. The solemnity of the occasion is imprinted on my mind, as the Dean came to announce, during the service, the news that war had been declared. Mother, like myself in 1939, had been ten years old at the outbreak of the Great War. I wondered if God was also shocked at the news and I felt older as we returned glumly to the Manor.

The change came immediately, with Mother joining the Red Cross in London and my school moving to Seaford into a house near the Downs School. Gresham's, Ronald's public school moved from Holt, Norfolk to Newquay, while the arrangements for Dad's journey to Biskra, for his cure in North Africa went ahead for after Christmas. It seems crazy now that a sick man should travel in war time, but even Dad had no qualms about going to North Africa, as he had spent his four years fighting in France, where the Great War, in spite of the massacre of men, had remained fairly localised. Beaufort, our home, would have to be let.

Mother was working in the Red Cross when I visited her on the way to school. I slept in her camp bed in London, while she was on night duty. Her first casualty of the blackout was a man who had gashed his forehead by walking into an air raid warden wearing a tin hat. Compared with the events later in the Blitz, this was light relief, except for the man with the headache. I learnt all the bandaging and first aid from Mother's manuals, which stood me in good stead through life, while looking after animals and people needing care or when dealing with wounds and casualties.

In school at Seaford, I felt homesick and insecure. We had no home and father was far away, as the war came closer with the Luftwaffe over Britain. I had a fellow feeling for Dorothy Tutin, who was in my dormitory and although younger than me, she was a sweet and popular girl but still succumbed to the grief of being away from home. When she was acting in London years later, I went backstage and we had a giggle about those days. I was not in favour with my contemporaries, who were mostly related to each other, as I was ambitious in sport, and always came back first in the early morning run. I enjoyed distance running, but success was interpreted as 'swanking' and the 'gang' of eleven year olds made me more of a loner.

I took the chance to learn something new, tap dancing, and playing lacrosse with the Down's School, but my greater pleasure was to escape to the sea and the cliffs of the Seven Sisters Downs where I could bird-watch and observe the wild life undisturbed by noise or people. The plants of the shore line fascinated me and the chalk downs grew wild flowers that I had not seen in the Cotswolds or the lush Severn valley. Once I found a guillemot that could not fly due to the oil clogging its wings. I risked taking it back to school to clean it before releasing the elegant black and white auk with its white feathers restored to their natural colour. No questions were asked at school about how I had found the unhappy guillemot, because everyone wanted to save its life and were indignant about the effects of the oil.

The South Coast was an easy target for the Luftwaffe, so the school packed up. Mother had gone to rescue Father from France, where he had arrived in Aix les Bains from Biskra. Italy was in the war, so France had the Wehrmacht converging from the frontiers. Father was crippled and the collapse of France was imminent.

Mother had arranged that Pixie, my pony and I would be rescued by our friends, the Drummond-Hay family. Lady Margaret and Lady Jean were daughters of the Duchess of Hamilton, who started a school for her grandchildren, during the emergency, at Ferne House, her Dorset home. I knew her grandchildren Sheena, Vora, Douglas and Charloch who were Chris Mackintosh and Jean's children, and Jane, Malcolm and Anneli, the children of Jimmy Drummond Hay and Margaret. The three older girls were about my age and Mother had got to know the family through playing polo at Ferne. We had stayed with them when both Mother and I had ridden and competed in the Ferne Gymkhana, where my triumph aged nine, had been in the Apple Bobbing Event, when I plunged straight to the bottom of the bucket to secure the apple and finished the dripping victor, while Pixie deservedly got my apple as a reward for our win, an event recorded by a photo in the *Tatler*!

Ferne was amazingly relaxed compared with my normal school discipline. The grandchildren of Nina, Duchess of Hamilton had not had to suffer the rigours of ordinary school. School days were cheerfully based on the League of Health and Beauty, and we only wore clothes and shoes when they were necessary. Prunella Stack was the charming wife of Nina's son, Lord David, with their two infant sons, Diamid and Ian. The war became reality for us all when Lord David was killed, and the little boys and Prunella were left alone. At that time we did our best to help Prunella with the boys. Ian is now one of the experts on elephants; he and his wife Oria live for much of their time in Kenya, studying these wonderful animals.

Nina, the Duchess, was a Christian Scientist, and deeply devoted to animal salvation. The lovely stables were filled with fierce stray dogs, and the field that we had to ride through to Cranbourne Chase was a hazard as dangerous as the African bush. The wild and shaggy unkempt broncos, remnants of Buffalo Bill's rodeo on his English tour, would attack us and our ponies with hooves flying and teeth bared.

We were usually up to the challenge, riding bareback and using cowboy tactics. A greater hazard to our ponies and traps when we drove them on the narrow lanes between Ferne and Dennis Farm in Wiltshire, where the Drummond Hays lived, were the Army vehicles that scared the ponies, making them try to pivot round between the banks of the narrow lanes away from the mechanical giants. Sometimes, I would wake before the others and take Pixie for a bareback dawn ride up on Wynn Green and along the Cranbourne Chase. I learnt later that a Chase was common hunting land for all, whereas a Forest like Sherwood was reserved as a King's hunting ground. School was so informal that I could slip back in without a question. Music was a welcome challenge as the academic standard was not taxing, and the piano teacher, an Austrian refugee, a charming lady, taught me a great deal, especially on Beethoven. I appreciated these lessons when I was fifteen and a friend at St Michael's fell ill and gave me her ticket to hear Lamond performing an unforgettable Beethoven concert at Cheltenham. I returned to Cirencester by train that night, before Dr Beeching cut this old Roman town off the rail network.

One evening, Sheena, Vora and I were in the bath together, making our five inches of water ration come a bit higher with the bulk of our small bodies. The water level increased with our tears when Sheena told me that they were being evacuated to Canada. To my relief, the Drummond-Hays stayed in England, so I was able to join them in their charming thatched home at Dennis Farm. Ferne has since been demolished and no souvenirs are left of the lives of the Duke and Duchess of Hamilton and their family.

I was in my element with Jane Drummond-Hay, as we were responsible for the ponies and polo ponies. We went to school at Fonthill Abbey, where among the pupils were the daughters of Lord Portal. Jane and I used to ride and lead sometimes five ponies each from Semley Common to Fonthill for the riding lessons. It was exhausting but fun, although once I was reduced to tears when the two ponies that I was leading on each side, crossed in front of me as I was cantering on the verge on my way back to the common. I ended up in a tangle of five ponies in the middle of the road. A big black car hooted behind me. I tried to sort the ponies out as quickly as I could, the car passed me followed by a few army cars, then I soberly trotted on to catch up with the others. 'Did you see the King?' they shouted. No, I had not. I was furious. King George VI had been reviewing the troops stationed near Fonthill. I did so want to see him and had missed the chance of a lifetime, while he had waited for me to clear the road! Black Pet was the large animal that I was riding and she had a bad temper. 'Pet' had caused my trouble. She did compensate later for letting me down on this occasion, by jumping superbly for me, especially as she did not approve of other jockeys.

I had seen King George V and Queen Mary in an open carriage when Dad took Ronald and me to see the Jubilee parade before the war. The ceremonial procession with the glorious turnout of horses, carriages and the pageantry of the occasion, had impressed me deeply. Another sharp memory was imprinted when I heard the austere music played on the wireless, as I got ready to go to school one day, that was mourning the death of the King. Mother quickly helped me to sew a black band on the arm of my coat, before I ran to catch the school bus.

Although I was very happy with the horsey and fairly chaotic life at Dennis farm, Ronald had a nasty shock when he arrived there for the school holidays. We had nowhere else to go as Uncle Gordon had closed Swindon Manor when he joined the Pioneers for the war and was sent to North Wales. Lady Margaret Drummond Hay had a full house with her three children, myself, her husband Jimmy and his friends from the army dropping in to stay when on leave. Margaret was not to be defeated and had a brilliant idea about how to provide extra accommodation. Malice, the stallion was turned out in the field for his summer holiday together with some of his wives, and the stallion box was turned into a special bedroom for Ronald or other guests. Over the door the plaque of Malice, written in large white letters, welcomed my brother as he reluctantly entered the box. There were two doors to the box, with the second door leading to the stallion paddock. The rain was teeming down and neither of the doors were draught proof so Ronald had to sleep with his clothes in his bed to keep them dry enough for the morning. I had taken over the horsey side of our lives while he had been away at school. My bohemian existence depended entirely on horse trans-port, while his holiday in Malice's box extinguished any sparks of enthusiasm he had left for a horsey life, especially when he had to borrow the stable broom to sweep the flood water from around his bed back to the yard.

Meanwhile we were waiting news from Mother, who had hurried to Aix les Bains during the collapse of France, with the Germans and Italians advancing rapidly. She had to rescue poor crippled Father, but with that country in turmoil, we had no word of what was happening to them. Mother's tenacity and courage would not let her admit defeat. She found a bicycle and pedalled twenty-five miles to Chambery where the officials were about to send their passports to England. She managed to seize them off the desk and rushed back to get Father on a packed train across France, which took two and a half days, without food or drink or access to the toilets. They arrived at Bordeaux with no way to get down to the quay at Le Verdon where there was still one boat, the SS *Madura*.

They were strafed by German planes while waiting for a friendly Frenchman to get them to the boat. 'Lie down', said Father to Mother as the bullets rained down. 'No,' said Mother, 'this is my only skirt, you lie down.' 'No,' replied Dad as the unfriendly planes came over, 'I'll never be able to get up.'

Mother then donned her Red Cross uniform and miraculously someone helped them to the ship. She had been nursing sick children on the terrible train journey, and now she was going to be the only Red Cross nurse on the boat. For twenty-eight hours they were intermittently bombed and machine gunned while they waited for more refugees. The escort ships had left and the boat with its normal capacity of 160 people, already had over 1000 extra people and still more were arriving, with only standing room on the deck available.

Mother did her best to feed starving and sick children and over 250 babies under two years old with soup from bouillon cubes that she had brought along. Everyone wanted her help while the boat was a sitting target for the German bombers. She nearly lost hope of seeing us again or of Daddy coming home alive. Father could not move, but he was furious that he had to be carried by some French marines onto the boat to be put in a bunk that a fit passenger vacated for him. He wanted to be back in the fray, actively helping in the evacuation and confounding the enemy. With life saving equipment for 200, they finally had 1,666 people on board. By the Grace of God they arrived thankfully in Falmouth, to find the local people having tennis parties! The refugees were soon looked after and they had cheered to see three French Curtis fighters as they approached the Cornish coast, the first friendly planes they had seen since crossing France on land and the sea from Bordeaux to Falmouth, continually harassed by German and Italian aircraft. The French pilots of the Curtis planes had probably just got out of France too, so that they could join the Free French, flying with the RAF.

I have read Mother's account of this escape that she wrote in the *British Red Cross Review* in October 1940. There had been no supplies or nursing aids for her in the ship, but she had improvised and given help to everyone possible. The part she played in saving many lives was deeply appreciated, and the Captain insisted that she took Daddy off the boat first. She had miraculously brought Father back to Britain, but we were shocked when we saw how frail and ill he had become.

They were to stay at Ferne, while Dad had a course of gold injections at Shaftesbury. Meanwhile, Nina, Duchess of Hamilton decided that she could give further help to Dad, who seemed at death's door. She held his hand, assuring him that she would make him better. Daddy was hardly fit enough to resist this kindness.

'I've never felt it so strong before,' she told him in ecstasy, 'Can you feel it, Eric?' 'No,' said Father.

'It's so strong! I feel it passing to you from me, you must feel it Eric.' 'No,' said Father thoughtfully. 'Perhaps its coming from me to you.' There ended the session, to Father's relief. Nina was an unforgettable character from another age.

One day we heard a huge volume of noise in the sky. We rushed out and saw the sky black with German bombers flying over us. We watched in horror, no-one seeking cover. The news filtered through the next day that Coventry had been flattened with many women and children lost in the rubble of the city.

My diary shows an active time at the end of September 1940, when on Friday 13th: 'bombs were dropped on Buckingham Palace and the invasion is expected this weekend.' The 15th: '185 German bombers brought down'. The 17th: 'Ron has got school cert. 7 credits, 2 distinctions, super'. The 27th: 'big air battle, 133 planes brought down'. 2nd October: 'Sheila and I, Jane and Malcolm to Fonthill school. Miss René Ironside, nice Headmistress. Johnnie Traill visits Ferne and breaks arm on bolting pony'. 16th October; 'direct hit on 14 Melbury Road, all Merz family killed except Coz Bob. Coz Charles was my Godfather'. 25th November, 'Tea with the Iky Bells, winner of the Fastnet Race.'

We left our good friends the Drummond Hays, who had made a safe haven for me, and moved back to Swindon Manor for Christmas. Cheltenham, with our contacts there through Gordon, was where we settled while Mother went house hunting. I went to Pate's Grammar School, before we found Crickley Lodge. Our new home nestled on the edge of the Cotswolds, below the ancient British Camp and Devil's Table Rock on Crickley Hill. The house belonged to Mrs Butt-Miller, who had won the Derby with her horse Mid-day Sun. I had to bicycle to the grammar school in Cheltenham, but I cheerfully put up with pushing my bike up Crickley Hill in the morning and up Leckhampton Hill in the evening, because I was at a day school. On the steep fields or 'banks' of the Cotswolds we kept our ponies with Uncle Gordon's polo ponies, and we acquired a Guernsey cow called Delphine, who was in my charge. I did the feeding, care of the cow, milking, also skimming the milk and butter making, so that Father could supplement his wartime rations and also we needed to have a few paying guests to help with the upkeep of the house.

Pixie started war work pulling the trap, and the other ponies had to go in harness too. Harrowing the fields, tedding the hay (the tedder tossed the cut grass to help it to dry), and bringing up the hay cocks to the rick, were all jobs for the ponies. We made the wine cocks by hand, forking the hay into pyramids so the rain would drip off, then when the hay was dry enough, we would put a chain around the bottom of the hay cock and attach the pony to the chain. With a mighty heave, the pony would put its weight in the breast harness and the pyramid of hay would move gracefully, like magic, following the pony to the hay rick, where we would add it to the growing stack. When we needed to use the hay in the winter time, I would cut it with a two-edged blade that needed some strength to wield, and then carry the loose hay to the cowshed or stable.

In the holidays, I worked on farms for fivepence an hour. At one dairy farm there were eighty cows to be milked by hand twice a day, mucked out and fed with hay from the rick. That took myself, an old man of eighty and a disabled boy, twelve hours to accomplish. I was twelve years old and before I left home and when I returned at night, I had our horses and cow to care for. Harvest was really tough, as we used to stook the sheaves of corn, for them to dry out, and then load them on horse drawn wagons before stacking the corn in a rick. That was an itchy time, when the harvest bugs bit around one's middle, and the thistles in the corn left their prickles everywhere.

We were also growing cabbages and lettuces in our garden, not only for us, but to sell in Cheltenham to the hotels. I would drive Pixie into town in the Ralli trap, with a load of vegetables. I'd get out and push the trap up Crickley Hill to help Pixie. On top we'd trot happily along while I sang songs and looked at the view over the Severn Vale to the Malvern Hills beyond, and get out again to hold the trap back as we descended the steep pitch of Leckhampton Hill. Pixie would wait patiently, tied to a lamp post, in Cheltenham, while I found out which hotel would give the best price for our greens. With money in hand, I would spend it on our rations and return home with the groceries.

Horse shows and gymkhanas were a highlight of the holidays, if I could organise a Saturday free from farming. Gymkhana events were a prime necessity, as I could enter for half a crown, and get £1 if I won. I needed the £1 to enter for the jumping, which was my aim and *raison d'être*. My experience in schooling and training polo ponies made them ideal for Musical Sacks, Potato races or any gymkhana events needing a handy and fast pony. I could usually hold my own in the Under-16 events, but I needed to win some open gymkhana events too. Here I came up against the top 'pros' like Wally Biddlecombe, father of the jockeys Terry and Tony, who lived down below us in the Vale. Other horsemen and farmers fancied their chances in the gymkhana circus, so I learnt early to compete against men. This initiation was a good preparation for standing up for myself when I started to compete in International jumping, where girl riders were few and far between.

I soon became adept at ferreting, in order to supplement our meagre meat ration. If the line ferret slipped its collar and went to sleep in the burrow while we were getting soaked in the rain, we would burn salt and paraffin to smoke it out and back into our special care. From our willow trees, called 'pollards' because the head was pruned to produce young branches, I made clothes pegs and catapults to give me a little pocket money. I learnt water divining too, from an old man, when our water supply was cut off from our well by an American Army Camp being built above us on the hill at Ullenwood.

Our charity work was mainly organising Red Cross Gymkhanas and events where friends would perform with me, usually on our ponies, in some fun displays. I had taught myself and the ponies to do Cossack trick riding and the ponies had learnt individual tricks like shaking hands and bowing. I always loved the circus and the patience of good circus people in their training methods. There is much to learn, from the hard working and gifted circus families, about empathy with animals and the psychological approach to each character to produce its individual skills and talents.

I needed all the experience that I had learned the hard way when Finality joined the ponies. She was a three-year-old mare, by a Thoroughbred stallion and out of Kitty, a milk cart pony. Kitty had been 'honourably retired to stud' after kicking her milk float to pieces in Tunbridge Wells High Street. Her foal developed her mother's sense of humour.

She arrived in the middle of the night at Cheltenham Station, where Mother had to ride on Fireworks the nine miles to fetch her in the blackout. She had had a tough day, apart from nursing Father at night, but the final straw was when the wild young mare broke away from her as she came up Leckhampton Hill in the dark past the haunted house. A murder with the body dismembered and part of the torso never found, had happened there a year or two before, and the bad spirits always frightened the horses as they passed that spot. Dawn was breaking as Mother got both horses home and the young 'Late Night Final' became Finality.

She was no athlete when I started to ride her. She was unbalanced and would fall over her feet but she could buck! As her muscles developed with steady work, she got stronger and I would have to sit tight in case she started her rodeo act. I had already been initiated into the skills of sitting on a bucking pony with Pixie. Sometimes I would return home feeling very sore, and I am reminded of the multiple times that I 'bought a piece of ground' as one calls falling off, with the aches and twinges from falls that damaged joints and muscles during my career.

My parents got a chance to send me and my cousin Sheila to a Church School, St Michaels at Cirencester. The classes were much smaller than the grammar school, and the School Certificate exam loomed on my horizon. A lady called Miss Simpson from Gibraltar unravelled the maze of mathematics for me, a subject that had left me baffled in our big classes at grammar school. I heard that I could do Art for School Certificate if my Latin results were below 20% so I made sure of achieving 13% and happily took up Art. Credits in all subjects gave me matriculation when I was fifteen, although my brother had anxious letters from me, dreading the results of the exams. He was up at Queen's College, Oxford as a History Scholar, the scholarship gained before his seventeenth birthday. He had many activities while busy composing music and as well as joining the RNVR.

At home we had often had musical evenings. Mother could play the piano and violin, we all sang, but Ronald could compose on the spot and could even play my moods on the piano. I could neither compose music nor was I gifted in playing like Ronald, although later I took up the guitar and amused myself with friends playing Spanish and South American songs, also picking up folk songs in many other languages. This pastime made me happy but it frustrated me that I did not have extra talent for either music or art. Although I could do both, neither was at the standard that could give me satisfaction. I knew my limitations and was disappointed that I did not have that touch of genius.

Lonely journeys driving the Horse Box or car, even now, can be usefully employed learning words of songs or foreign languages. It also compensates for

(*left*) On Prince Hal at Miserden, 1950.

(*below*) Finality qualifying for the final of the King George VI Cup at White City 1948. This was the last time that ladies could compete in this trophy.

(*right*) Relaxing in White City collecting ring, with Paula holding Tosca and Mary Whitehead, who had lent me her Nobbler to win the Bruxelles Grand Prix in 1949, on the bonnet of the Jeep with me.

(*below*) Chatting with Sam at Badminton, 1950.

(*below*) The last fence at the Berkeley Hunt Point-to-Point in 1950, going on to win with Only Just, a horse that I hunted, trained and raced.

the fear of letting one's brain atrophy while coping with a necessary but dull activity.

Our guests used to join in and it was always a cheerful household in spite of illness, anxiety and the war. Down below us was Brockworth and we sometimes had test pilots, who were working for Gloster Aircraft, and their families to stay. The balloon barrage would go up to protect Brockworth when enemy aircraft came our way. Crickley Lodge had a roof pinnacle knocked off by a whistle of a whistling bomb, which exploded in a field below us, while the empty whistle cannister was found on the lawn.

Gerry Sayer flew the first ever jet in this country, the Gloster E28, but he was killed flying a Typhoon in collision with another Typhoon in cloud cover, before the Gloster Meteor had been ready for testing; he was the first of our friends to go. Michael Daunt then took over as principal test pilot and did the first tests on the Meteor. He survived many close shaves especially while sorting out the Meteor's teething troubles. On one occasion, when standing too close to one of the Meteor's air intakes, he was sucked into the jet engine. Luckily, he was a big man and his bulky shoulders stuck and the engine stopped before he was asphyxiated. Another Meteor had an impeller disintegrate in mid air, but he crash-landed it successfully. Once, while flying a different aircraft, the tail snapped off in mid air; the sudden dive down threw him out of the cockpit and somehow the rip cord opened his parachute, although he had passed out and remembered nothing later. A kind parson, who saw the accident, crossed the potato field to see if help was not too late. As the parson crouched over the prostrate 'corpse' it lashed out catching the parson on the nose, as Michael came to and realised that the harness around his neck was suffocating him.

A friend, Tony Frenkel was sent to take up another job, and by coincidence he and Marjorie his wife became our next door neighbours when we moved to Miserden and he farmed at Edgeworth. They came to dinner with us the night before mother was killed. Our churches were run together, by our Miserden vicar, and I became godmother to their second daughter Jocelyn, while later Marjorie was godmother to my second daughter, Lucy.

Peter Cadbury and Ben his wife, who was a great friend of Mother's, used to call in; I stayed with them in Ascot twenty years later when competing at the Ascot Horse show run by Lavinia, Duchess of Norfolk and her daughter. We were always intrigued, as children, in how these tall test pilots could fit in the small cockpits. One of the tallest, Michael Warren, was sadly another who was killed over Minchinhampton Common near Aston Down, the place the pilots nicknamed Aspirin Down, a place of refuge in an emergency.

Our great friends were John and Brownie Grierson, who rented a house in Painswick as a base for their two small children. After the war they went to live in Guernsey, so that John could keep a Czechoslovakian plane there. When John flew into Staverton he would come and visit us at Sudgrove after Sam and I were married. He rarely told of his lifetime of adventures since his birth in 1909, the same year as Sir Peter Scott, but he was a tough pioneer of flying through an incredible span of development in aircraft design and potential.

Sir Malcolm Campbell, who had flown his own machine in the year of John's birth, helped him in 1932 to fight for permission to fly to Samarkand. John was also helped by George Bernard Shaw, the only man in England who had any influence with the top people in Moscow at that time. I was to meet Sir Malcolm's son Donald at the Bertram Mills luncheon, a yearly event then which is sorely missed, before the première of the Christmas Circus at Olympia. John became a member of the Council of the Royal Geographical Society, and a committee member of the Scott Polar Research Institute. While at school he took his first flying lessons at Brooklands in 1926, the time that Byrd successfully flew to the North Pole and which may have started John's fascination with flying. He entered the Royal Air Force College at Cranwell, before becoming interested in long distance flying after an unauthorised flight home from India in 1931. The following year he decided to investigate for himself what was going on in the USSR. He bought third hand a four-year-old Gipsy Moth which he called *Rouge et Noir*, because one side was black and the other red. The solo flight to Samarkand with the 85hp de Havilland plane, stood the test over 9,300 miles through every weather, steered by a compass in the open cockpit of the biplane. He was a sick man when he returned, but undaunted, set off the following year flying from England to Canada over Greenland. In Iceland he met Charles and Anne Lindbergh, becoming close friends with them. John died suddenly when he was sixty-eight, while giving the Lindbergh lecture in Washington's Air and Space Museum. I heard this sad news on Swiss radio, while I was driving the children to Sunday school at the Basel Munster.

We had fun trips with John; he flew me over Sudgrove, from Staverton, and also our Swiss home at Burg on the edge of the Jura mountains, on visits to Basel, when I could take unique photos from his plane. We had one scary flight from Torino where I had been jumping, when he and a navigator said they would drop me off in Geneva, as I wanted to ski nearby for a couple of days. Fierce storms drove us back from the pass by Mont Blanc, with the plane dropping dangerously down towards jagged rocks and peaks protruding from snowfields below the air pockets. He said we would have to turn back, but as we approached the Valais with the Matterhorn, the wind was calmer so we found a way over the Petit Combin, which I recognised from a two-day skiing trip from Verbier. We flew under the Dents du Midi and along the French side of Lac Leman and gratefully into Geneva. Another time Sam and I flew with John and Brownie from their Guernsey home to Deauville; while Sam worked in a seminar, we could visit the Normandy studs and Honfleur, the charming little port from where the French sailors set out to discover Canada.

Roland Beamont was already a keen fisherman when we met in August 1938 at Fordingbridge; he had just passed his driving test, while I was on holiday with my family and Pixie, riding at local shows. The rosettes that Pixie won in the gymkhanas pleased me, but my greatest thrill was to be taken fishing by Roland. Dad noted, 'Pat goes fishing with Rollo and catches tiddlers only', but I was happy with my bent pin fishing for tiddlers and with luck a perch or two, while he fly-fished for trout.

During the years we remained in touch and I had written to him from school asking him for his Air Force rank. He had replied, 'I am a Pilot Officer until I get my promotion to Air Vice Marshal!' I kept his letter and wrote to congratulate him for his award of a Bar to the DFC in early 1943.

The Gloster Meteor, being tested at Brockworth, entered service in July 1944 with 616 squadron at Manston. My fishing friend 'Bee' had the chance to fly one, by private arrangement with the Squadron's CO. He preferred his Tempests at neighbouring Newchurch, but the Meteor was improved later. During the war his 609 squadron of Typhoons had been in combat with FW 190s when covering Peter Scott's motor torpedo boats, the MTBs. He then commanded the first Wing of Tempests, which were operational by April 1944 and flew over the invasion fleet on the night of D-Day. The Tempests were also used to shoot down the VIs bombarding London, and accounted for 630 out of the 1800 that were shot down by the RAF, Roland's personal tally being 32.

A mishap after Arnhem while leading a squadron of his Tempest Wing from the front line in Holland, came when a pot shot from the ground scored a hit and caused his Tempest to crash land in Germany; he was captured while trying to escape and did not enjoy the last months of the war. On becoming Chief Test Pilot for English Electric after he had left the RAF in peacetime, he flew the Canberra which became the first plane to fly the Atlantic twice in one day in 1952 with him at the controls. He was testing Britain's first supersonic aircraft, the PI Lightning, in 1954 and four years later flew it at twice the speed of sound. Progress in aircraft design was so rapid that the TSR 2 supersonic strike aircraft which he flew in 1964 was decades ahead of its time and had proved its ability and worth, when the Wilson Government cancelled it in 1965, and with it went the hopes of the Royal Air Force of benefiting from this far-reaching British technical achievement in supersonic flight. We were able to celebrate the fiftieth anniversary of our first fishing together, catching rainbow trout on the Sweatfordwater not far from the Avon that flows through Fordingbridge. The quiet stretch of the river where nightingales and blackcaps sing their serenade in spring make a haven for musing over the memories of half a century.

Mother never seemed to go to bed, she was nursing father at night where she had a bed in his study room downstairs. I would take turns in helping him dress and undress and washing him, but his condition was deteriorating. We had Christmas 1944 together, but he died within a month, early on 19 January. It happened to be the week that Sam was to die, exactly forty years later. They both succumbed to heart failure, after living for four years, without complaining, in constant pain.

While my Father was ill, he would talk to me of his love of climbing during his upbringing in Switzerland. I heard fearful stories of electrical storms while making bivouacs on high mountains and of having to abandon the ice axes which could attract lightning in unfriendly weather. Edward Whymper and A. F. Mummery became my heros. I mourned the fate of Hudson, Hadlow, Michael Croz and Lord Francis Douglas after their fatal fall whilst descending the Matterhorn with Whymper, after the first successful ascent to the summit.

Mummery, who disappeared on Nanga Parbat in the Himalayas, had made his name in the Alps, having climbed the Zmutt and Furggen ridges of the Matter-horn. Dad had achieved the summit without a guide in the early 1900s.

I studied the books of Guido Rey and Frank Smythe, learning the names of the peaks, dreaming of a chance to go abroad after the war. One of Eric's climbing friends was Captain John Noel, who has died recently aged ninety-nine. He was the last survivor of the Mount Everest Expeditions of 1922 and 1924, and one of the last surviving officers of the British Expeditionary Force of 1924. We had been in correspondence about the climbs that Eric and John had done together in Switzerland before the Great War.

Early on the morning of the day he died, my father Eric had an hallucination that he was climbing the Matterhorn. Mother was holding his hand as he called, 'Monique, Patling, come on quickly, we're nearly at the summit'. Two days later I tolled the bells at St Peter's Church, Bentham at the Sunday Service, as I was the only one of the local kids who could ring both bells. 'Come on, come on' they echoed up to Crickley Lodge, where Daddy lay.

Religion, in the form of simple faith in the immense capacity of God, has been a mainstay through my life. I believed, but found it difficult to express the reason why I had this belief in God. Ronald, who was brilliant and a superb debater, could disprove with assurance any subject that I believed in implicitly. He was going through a stage of atheism, with life at Oxford having been a disrupting experience. At home, I had become the farmer, and we did not tune into the same wavelength.

At St Michael's School, Sister Rosalys, the head nun belonging to the Sister-hood of the Holy and Undivided Trinity, had a great sense of humour and gave the school a secure basis for the girls, in worship and discipline.

A wise and understanding vicar, the Reverend Ronald Sutch, prepared our class for confirmation at Cirencester Parish Church. He had a great empathy with people, so nearly twenty years after my confirmation, when he was Arch-deacon in Cheltenham, I turned to him for advice and help before Sam and I were married.

In school we had chapel every evening and learnt the round of jobs, ringing the chapel bell, serving at communion, and reading the lesson. I was very nervous of reading in front of everyone, and my voice would tremble and I would feel close to tears of relief when it was over. The effort to conquer my nerves paid off later, when I had to make speeches at Guild Hall functions, or lecture to large audiences. I enjoyed singing and church music gave me an excellent training in sight-reading and descant singing. Mother and I used to sing part songs together during the long hours driving the trailer to horse shows, as there was no radio in our old American army jeep.

I had left St Michael's after Matriculation to help Mother with the guests at Crickley Lodge while she nursed Father. I was sixteen when he died, and the older cousin 'Bob', Stella Merz, offered to pay my school fees at Talbot Heath, Bournemouth, for two years further study. Her two grown up children and husband, Charles, who was my godfather, had been wiped out in 1940 when a land mine fell on their house in Melbury Road, London. She had been buried for forty-eight hours under a beam that had saved her life, although her arms were badly broken.

We had to move from Crickley Lodge, and Mother was going to Bath, where her parents were retired. She intended to set up a riding establishment with our ponies, so that they would pay their way, and eventually we settled in one room of the Blathwayt Arms on Lansdown, where we cleaned out and repaired the racehorse stables by the abandoned race course.

The responsibility I felt towards Mother and our existence made me resent going back to the confined atmosphere of a girls' boarding school. I took the chance of studying the piano and music again, neglected since my days at Ferne in 1940 with the Austrian lady, which gave me an emotional outlet but not much satisfaction due to my lack of talent. I applied myself to science and studied farming from set books that I had been lent by an agricultural student friend in Gloucestershire, which took up more time and concentration than the curriculum of school subjects. It was a lucky chance for me, when I was told at school to debate against the nationalisation of agriculture!

May 8th 1945 came and was celebrated at school. As a new girl, I was busy marking my clothes, and included that date of VE day along with my name. It was sad that Father had not lived to see that second victory in Europe. Pixie my pony, had her first foal on that day, and Vicky, for Victory Day, her skewbald filly, stayed with us until her last days at Sudgrove.

My bicycle provided my great escape and I explored the New Forest to the Isle of Wight, but I could not wait for half term or the holidays to get back to Bath and continue training Finality and the other horses. At school I was Games Secretary, in charge of the organisation of home and away games matches and transport. I had been doing the entries and transport of my horses since I was aged eleven, a more complicated business when I had to finance it myself, and a win could mean a comfortable ride home in a lorry or train, while losing might mean a long trek home in any weather.

Finality nearly died when she was moved from Crickley. She was always greedy, as she had been hand-reared when her mother died, so she expected food to be provided. In her new field on Lansdown she thought that the corn on the other side of the rusty barbed wire looked better than her paddock grass. With no one around, she jumped the wire and waded through the corn, getting all the best bits. Full of corn and wanting to return to the other horses, she got tangled in the wire and stood torn and shivering. Ronald happened to be visiting Granny in Bath that day and was told about the emergency by a farmer. Mother was away for the day, moving our belongings and I was at Bournemouth in school. The vet was contacted by Ronald and when Mother returned she heard that the mare might have to be put down, but certainly would never jump again.

My heart was torn by that wire too, Final caused me almost the most heart-break of any animal that I've cared for. Our despair turned to hope when the accident-prone mare decided that she would jump again, and with Mother's expert nursing of her wounds she had recovered enough for me gratefully to get

her fit for jumping when I got back at the end of term. Previously, at Crickley, we
had nursed her back to health from a terrible stake wound in her shoulder.

At Bath Show in 1945 Mother and I won the Musical Chairs in pairs for a ten
shilling first prize! Finality was second in the open and won the bareback
jumping. At Box, Final won the open and I won the pony jumping on my
gymkhana pony, who also won three gymkhana events, but Mother put me in my
place by winning the open musical chairs. My highlight came at Melksham when
Final beat Tankard and Brian Butler, but Tankard, who was to win the King's
Cup and the Daily Mail Cup twice at the White City, won the high jump. Two
years later we were in the British Team together for Ostend and Le Zoute, but
that dream then was beyond my imagination.

Bad news of Final came to me again that winter; she had caught strangles, like
diphtheria in a human, and was desperately ill. Again the tough mare, nursed by
Mother, pulled through. She took all the spring to get fit but by August she was
jumping well and we heard of the Victory Show being held at the White City
Stadium for the first post-war national championships. We ambitiously entered
Finality, but a third stroke of trouble knocked this test of her ability on the head
when a loose horse at a local show galloped into her leaving her with a gashed
fetlock. She stayed at home with a compress on the wound, while I miserably
watched at the White City, feeling mad at this latest mishap that forced me to be
an unwilling spectator.

My ambition was fired further by watching horses, some of them old international jumpers, over an attractive variety of coloured fences, with bushes
decorating the wings. We had been used to the old-fashioned type of fences
consisting of a hedge, a post and rails, a stile, a gate, a triple bar, a wall,
with occasionally a double, often built with single poles, and the last fence at a
bigger show would be the water jump in the middle of the arena. Sometimes
the old riding pros would lean down and undo the standing martingale, to
give their horse's head more freedom as they galloped down to clear the water.
Time did not count and one could circle between the fences if the stride was not
just right, clear rounds had endless jump offs and the spectacle was slow and
monotonous.

At White City the horses were jumping these new impressive fences well, and
the horses, needing more impulsion for the spreads, were being ridden forward,
rather than always being checked back. Ted Williams, a top rider before and after
the war, for more decades than anyone can remember, was the best in the
competition with only half a fault for a slat until the last horse to go. National
jumping had the sliver of wood or 'slat' on all the fences, which made half a fault if
the horse knocked it off with its hind legs, or one fault if it was its fore legs.
Likewise the pole down was four faults when hit in front and two faults behind,
the theory being that a horse would be more likely to fall when jumping out
hunting if it hit the fence with its fore legs.

Colonel Mike's prisoner-of-war friend Colonel Nat Kindersley was last in the
ring. His wife had bought his horse Maguire for £40 from the army, after Nat had
ridden him in the winning British team in London in 1939. Although Nat had

been away in a German prison camp for so long, the pair rallied to jump the only clear round.

I felt increasingly confined at school again while my favourite sport of show jumping was beginning to flourish. The Headmistress at Talbot Heath, Miss Freda Stocks, a daunting and respected leader of her flock, was not pleased when I told her that I would leave school after five terms. I had won the biology prize, a preparation that helped my future work with the World Wide Fund for Nature, and gave me an understanding of conservation and ecology. She thought I was throwing away the possibility of a scholarship to university but I knew that I must care for Finality full time if I wanted us to make our mark. It seemed then almost beyond our reach to jump for Great Britain, in that first post-war year of our team being sent to compete abroad. There were all the experienced Army riders who had returned from the war with some good horses and their style was more forward and fluent than our local riders.

Finality caught the public's eye at the Bath and West Show, held at Cheltenham that year. I was the local girl and had been in the Young Farmers' Club that held meetings in the Cheltenham Boys' Grammar School, so the support helped Final to rise to the occasion and she won both competitions, coming second in the Championship. We were mentioned in *The Times*'s sports column, as a 'refreshing performance, with style and pace worthy of an international event'. We had moved back to Crickley, in the terrible snows of early 1947, but 'home again' for us lasted only a few months.

These happy months prepared us for the first International Horse Show at White City and after a set back from a sore heel, Finality was sound in time to jump. I was thrilled to compete with Harry Llewellyn, who I'd seen winning the Victory Cup at the National Show there the year before on Kilgeddin. He had not entered Foxhunter, the horse he had just bought. I had admired this handsome bay horse at the Beaufort Show with his Norfolk owner, Norman Holmes.

The King's Cup was won in a rain storm by the Frenchman, Pierre Jonquères d'Oriola on Marquis III. The weather was appalling, but Finality was used to the West Country and her consistency was noticed. I could hardly believe it possible when I was invited to join the British Team travelling to Ostend and Le Zoute International Shows in Belgium.

I had been abroad once in my life, when the Mackintosh family, safely back from their evacuation in Canada, had invited me for the New Year of 1947 to Zermatt in Switzerland, Dad's climbing paradise. By then my pocket money saved from my weekly sixpence since well before the war had accumulated in the Post Office Savings Bank to £25, which saw me through an unforgettable holiday. I had arrived, after sleeping in the luggage rack of the train across France, to see the New Year in with a hilarious fancy dress party, joining the Mackintosh and Drummond-Hay children, friends and some Edinburgh medical students for a real Scots evening.

In daylight I saw the unique and impressive Matterhorn, the Monte Rosa, the twin peaked Dom and the famous mountains arising around Zermatt. Everyone seemed to be able to ski, so I went along too, without any preparation or teaching and not even waterproof ski trousers or jacket. In spite of falls and learning to ski the hard way, I had attained a dream in coming to the mountains that Dad had known so well. Five years went by before I had the chance to ski in the Alps again.

I had not had time for holidays or boyfriends until I went to Zermatt but there I fell for a medical student with a respected Scots name. (It wasn't the ginger-headed Scot who skied with a tin leg that he had acquired during the war, who sometimes, as he hurtled down the mountain, would disappear into a cloud of powdered snow from which his tin leg, still attached to the ski, would appear alone to continue the crazy descent without its owner, leaving the mountainside strewn with sportsmen who had fainted at the sight of the truant leg, skiing off by itself.) My friend came to stay for the Cotswold Hunt Ball when we returned home and also rode a horse, then our ways parted. I had better luck with Sam in 1950, when he came to the Hunt Ball, because although he never attended another one, our paths crossed again more than a decade later with more permanent consequences.

In 1948 the three sons of Captain Webber, the Secretary General of the BSJA, took me to Epsom for the Derby. We were on the Downs side and I put my money, the little I had, on My Love. He duly won, and while we were throwing our hats in the air and cheering, we noticed that our 'Bookie', a doubtful-looking character, was beatling off across the Downs. The boys hared after him, caught him and somehow extracted our winnings, which we spent on a good dinner at a pub on the way home.

My second journey abroad was to Belgium with Finality. Foxhunter was to make his international debut with us at Ostend at the start of a unique show-jumping partnership, with his great personality making a perfect match for 'Sir Harry', as we know him now. Ruby Holland-Martin who lived in the Evesham vale at Overbury, where he had his stud, had raced and had his own show jumper, High Jinks, with one of Harry's horses Tallycoed. Ruby was to breed Grundy, the winner of both the 1975 Derby and the King George VI and Queen Elizabeth Diamond Stakes where he beat the four-year-old Bustino by a whisker in an epic 'classic of the century', which was a unique achievement for Ruby and his small stud. The other two team riders were Brian Butler with Tankard and Toby Robeson, the father of Peter, who in 1956 was to ride in our Bronze medal team at the Stockholm Olympics.

I had no groom, so I drove Finality to Tilbury docks where I met the team grooms who kindly agreed to look after Final while travelling over in the boat with all the horses. I watched the horses being loaded, which was a horrifying experience. Finality was put into an open crate on the dockside, chains were attached as the scared mare was swung off the ground over our heads and the high side of the boat before being lowered onto the deck. She whinnied to me as she soared up, while I prayed that she would not try to jump out. Travelling with horses was fairly primitive at that time, and we learned from experience that many foreign shows expected the horses to be tied in lines, where there was a great risk of your horse being kicked or bitten by the next horse. We took along with us spare poles to sling between the horses and wooden blocks to put on the end of their halter ropes, so that they could lie down without getting a leg over the rope. Nowadays no one would risk a valuable show jumper under these conditions, but at that time we had no choice.

Finality was 'in the money', only a token offered, at both Ostend and Le Zoute, with a medal in a Light Weight Hunter Class, an event I entered because girls were not allowed to jump in the Nation's Cup Team. Her best result, as the only British clear round in the Grand Prix du Zoute, was literally crowned for me in the final speed event when she came to the last fence with the fastest time, but jumping into the setting sun she turned a somersault. I was knocked out and carried off on a stretcher.

As I regained consciousness, I found that I was lying on my hotel bed, clad in my navy blue school knickers and white school shirt. Mother's hunting breeches and hunting stock had been removed. As I focussed on the team members who had come to commiserate with me, they started to giggle over my attire. I felt as sensitive as a Scot about his kilt. I remembered how I had giggled when Mother scorched her frilly panties while drying them under the grill, on our only hotplate for cooking and warming our room at the Blathwayt Arms during the bitter month of February. Clothes were rationed and coupons were in short supply. Finality and I were just fit enough the next day to take our bruises and headaches home, together with a lot more experience.

Johnnie Traill, the international Polo and Golf Pro, had paid half the cost of Finality with Mother, probably about £40 each in 1943, but now that she was jumping well he wanted to sell her for £1500. Half of that would go to Mother, but we had fed and trained the mare for four years. I managed not to sell her in Belgium where our final fall was to me a blessing in disguise, delaying her sale.

I had suffered some crippling falls when she bucked me off. Back pains were a legacy of those falls, and once I had to get her home with the trailer, returning from a show, driving most of the way in second gear, because my back stopped me from changing gear. I spent a week flat in bed when I eventually got home, while the gear box needed most of that time to cool down.

In England one of the top owners of show jumpers was Tommy Makin, himself a great winner in his day. He had an excellent Irish rider, Seamus Hayes, who rode Tommy's string of horses brilliantly but sometimes Finality managed to beat them and I feared that he had an eye on the mare.

Finality and I had a new experience when we went to the Bath and West Show at Cardiff in 1948, the same show held at Cheltenham the year before which had drawn attention to the mare's ability. I managed to hitchhike to Cardiff with Francis and Beryl Doney from Minchinhampton in their cattle lorry full of horses. Rachel Carpenter, who was working for them, came from Gloucester, and she would ride anything she was offered for gymkhanas, jumping and pony racing. I was slightly her senior and we had competed together as children. Finality was piled in with the other horses as there were no partitions, while we were crouched in the bay over the cab, sitting among the rugs and tack, so that we didn't get squashed by the horses.

It was wet in Cardiff, but as I was warming up I could find no practice jumps. Suddenly I espied Seamus jumping a pole that Tommy had put up beside his lorry. When he had jumped it, I politely asked Mr Makin, if I could pop Finality over the pole too. He kindly told me to 'Come along quick'. As we jumped, Tommy took a long stick with a hedgehog skin tied on the end and touched Final's fore legs and hind legs with it while we were in the air. It was an automatic movement of his, one that his own horses were used to. I had not practised 'rapping' as it was called, because I had no help and Finality was so careful that she did not need to jump any higher. After this surprise encounter with a hedgehog she jumped the highest clear round of the competition. Mr Makin must have regretted his spontaneous action, but later when he owned the mare she made it clear that she would not jump if she received that treatment. I knew now why some horseboxes stopped on the roads where a hedgehog had crossed at the wrong moment.

At the end of the show, we wet riders rubbed down our soaking horses and loaded them into the box, where they soon generated their own heat and began to steam. Francis Doney, being a born and bred West Country man from Cornwall, had many friends who ran some of the pubs along the Welsh side of the Severn, before we could cross the river at Gloucester. I was shivering in the back when eventually he ground the lorry up Crickley Hill and, to my concern, he forgot to stop and let me out at the Dryhill lane home. 'Never mind,' said Rachel, 'you can sleep in my bed at Amberley, and we will find a corner for Final.' Reassured, I relaxed and at 3.00 a.m. we unloaded, fed the horses, and piled into Rachel's bed together with young Ann, who had come along to ride the Doney ponies.

I had to wear my still damp show clothes for the long hack back to Crickley next morning. Mother was relieved when Final and I arrived home safely, and Rachel is still one of my best friends, after our crowded night with three exhausted girls in a single bed.

3

Post-War Triumphs and Tragedies

Great Britain was to host the Olympic Games of 1948; as girls were not allowed to compete in the jumping team, we were asked to lend Finality for a man to ride in the training. Mother and I were honoured, although I did wonder what would happen to us while Finality could not win us the little prizes that kept us going.

There was no compensation for the loan of a horse. Final left for Aldershot on March 1st and was back at Gloucester station six weeks later, where I fetched my 'unsuitable' mare with relief. The team of three horses finished by having to be entirely provided by Harry Llewellyn. He lent Monty to Arthur Carr and Kilgeddin to Henry Nichol, while he rode Foxhunter.

The closing day of the Olympic Games at Wembley drew a huge crowd. There were thirteen teams to jump the course that had been built during the night, with the water jump and ditches dug and filled with water. The latter caused much grief and refusals during the competition, as few teams had much experience of international jumping. Our team won the bronze medal, with only three teams having their three riders finish.

Mexico won the team and individual Gold medal with Colonel Humberto Mariles on the one-eyed horse Arete, with Spain taking the team Silver. The ring craft of Mariles paid off that time, as he had observed that horses clearing the water jump were galloping too fast to clear the next and last fence, a big red wall. He had eight faults in hand as he approached the water to decide his own individual and his team's Gold medal. The crowd gasped as he slowly cantered splashing through the water and in complete control and balance cleared the wall, finishing with only the fault at the water and a couple of time faults; the Mexicans had the Gold in the bag.

Our Olympic friend's exploits were not always so praiseworthy. Ten years later, he showed me with pride his training paddock in Mexico City. One of the fences was built with parallel bars made of solid concrete pipes, with a cactus hedge in the middle. 'How does a horse get out of this fence if he falls?' I asked. 'The vultures do that' was his reply. I do not think that he was joking but I was feeling too sick to enquire. Before the 1968 Olympic Games held in Mexico City, he had been sent to prison for shooting the driver of a car that had collided with him at a road junction. Harry and a couple of riding friends who were at the Olympics telephoned him at the prison, as visitors were not allowed. This sentence did not tame him, for after his release he was caught in France handling drugs and finished his own life in a French prison.

Harry Llewellyn, who had showjumped and ridden steeplechasers before the war, with the great achievement of coming second in the 1936 Grand National on Ego, proved that he was still a top amateur steeplechase rider when he won, at the 1948 Cheltenham National Hunt Festival, the United Hunts Steeplechase on Bay Marble, a picture of a beautiful Thoroughbred, and the Foxhunter's Amateur Chase on State Control. This double was before Harry's showjumping team Olympic Bronze at Wembley. I watched both events, which increased my admiration for his ability to return from the war and then train, own and ride two top steeplechasers and three Olympic showjumping medal winners.

The greatest help for me from the age of eighteen into my twenties came from travelling in teams with the Llewellyns. Although we were rivals, Harry would discuss points of balance and ability of horses, that I could quickly pick up in order to experiment with my own jumpers, and see if I could benefit from his ideas. 'Teeny' his wife, had been brought up with the Broke collection of art, inherited by her Saumarez family. Through this upbringing with visits to Paris and Vienna, she had a thorough appreciation and knowledge of the arts. She would come with me to museums and historical places, where I could ask her about the beautiful and impressive things that we saw. 'Teeny' was also very pretty and chic, helping me to dress for the occasion. Her rule for the round of cocktail parties that one had to attend, if not in riding clothes, was the 'little black number', that could be dressed up simply with a coloured scarf or costume jewellery. With the friendship and company of the Llewellyns, I learnt much about showjumping and horses, and gained an insight into the culture of many nations. During the round of shows, there was a golden rule, that one never talked about the wonderful exploits of one's own horse! I had already absorbed the strict rule at school about never swanking, so the lesson of not being a bore sank in to stay.

In spite of Finality's 'unsuitability' for the Olympics, when being ridden by male riders, and my efforts not to sell her, the dreaded day dawned within sight of the elegant spire of Salisbury Cathedral. At the Royal Counties Show, she jumped brilliantly and on the last day she beat Seamus Hayes on Snowstorm in the Walwyn Challenge Cup under FEI Rules (International Rules). My heart was in my boots that night when Tommy Makin came with us to the Haunch of Venison for dinner, where he made the deal with Mother. The £1500 would be paid, half going to Johnnie Traill, but I could ride her at the White City two months later, because we had already paid for our stable and entry fees. On the way back to the show ground, Seamus gave me a very wet kiss, but the moisture was my tears.

I heard hurtful rumours that Final had stopped and turned a somersault with Seamus at one show before she came back to me for the White City week. She whinnied to me when we got her home, but my diary notes, 'very depressed when I jumped her. She won't take off and won't land. Head between knees'. Things must have improved rapidly, because her results at White City were not bad, especially as the Olympic teams were competing there after the Games at Wembley. She was second on the first day, and the only British clear round in our section of the qualifying competition for the King George V Cup. She had a touch of colic on the day of the final, but the men had a fright with two girls getting through to the final of the King's Cup. Lulu Rochford on Ladybird had qualified too, and we rode in the parade for the Cup on our 15 hh 'ponies', among the big German horses and the winner, Foxhunter, who stood at nearly 17 hh. The next year the Princess Elizabeth Cup for ladies was introduced, and the men were protected by their competition being exclusively for male riders.

Brian Butler and I were third with Tankard and Final in the International Relay before I said goodbye again to Final when we sent her off to Castleford by train to Yorkshire from Waterloo. My Final had gone, my boyfriend was engaged to someone else and we had left Crickley Lodge for ever. It was an unhappy drive back to Birdlip where we had a room, and the old stables of the Royal George.

During September I took two young horses to jump in the Welsh shows. 'Curley' Beard, elder brother of Don Beard who held the high jump record of 7ft 8in at Olympia on Swank in 1937, wanted me to jump and sell some horses for him, while I had nothing else to ride. I called in at Harry and Teeny's for dinner one night and saw David aged two and a half and Roddie for the first time, as he was only ten months old. I think it was then David began his long engagement to me, which made up for my disappointment of a couple of months before. I was easily caught on the rebound and my hopes were not dashed until he was nearly nine, when he told me apologetically that I was too old.

I decided to get a job in Ireland to see me through the long winter ahead, before I started point-to-pointing in the Spring. There was no house or special horse to keep me, so I answered an advertisement in *Horse and Hound*. The boat from Fishguard took me to Cork, and thence the train to Kilmallock. At Rathkeale in Co. Limerick I was shown the gate lodge where I was to look after the retired English couple and their horses for their winter sojourn hunting with the Limerick. At the police station I fetched my ration book and the kindly policeman told me where I could get black market soap.

I slept in the tower of the lodge, where the fleas lived too and did not sleep by night. In the day I looked after the horses, the peat fires, the cooking and shopping, and riding and leading the horses to the Meet. There I followed my employers in the car, while they hunted and I provided their sandwiches when they were hungry. There was a memorable occasion when I heard the dear old gentleman mumble into his sandwich 'Dxxx it they've found', as the Limerick hounds gave tongue and raced away over the famous banks of the lovely countryside around Croome. I kept giggling while I was hacking the horses the fifteen miles home that night.

The wireless, when I was allowed to use it, kept me in contact with the outside world. I was happy to hear that Princess Elizabeth had safely borne a Royal Prince. 'Cheers to herself, Prince Philip and the boy Charles at 7lb 6oz', I noted, before the entry a week later that I had a miserable twentieth birthday, not allowed out to tea, or to play classical music on the wireless. I escaped later to play the Rathkeale Church organ with permission from the Church, if not from the Lodge.

After six weeks working there, we parted by mutual consent. The fleas had the tower to themselves and a starvation diet again, while I had a few more clothes bought in sales with my £2 a week wages, for clothing was not rationed in Ireland. I'd also regularly sent a five-penny bar of Cadbury's unrationed chocolate to mother in my letters.

Sometimes out exercising I'd meet a young hunting doctor, who rode a wild chestnut Thoroughbred that he'd saved from the knackers yard and then had it tubed. It went cross-country, after that, like a racehorse and there had been the times when he'd had a fall in a brook, and had to get his finger in the tube in the horse's neck, until he found a cork to put in the hole, to stop the horse from drowning. Dr Paddy B was a difficult man to follow across country, even with his saddle bags packed with the instruments of his trade, flapping and flying about the horse's sides.

Once I was free, the hospitality of the Irish was terrific. I rode young race horses, schooling and hunting them with the former jockey and trainer Pat P. Hogan and his wife Morny. The Master of the Limerick Hounds, Lord Daresbury and his household became friends, with many others. Martin Maloney, the jockey I admired very much, lent me his pony cob to hunt. The old pony was brilliant, but I fell off at least once, and rode back happy and laughing with Martin's sister Kit, who sometimes had a muddy back too. The kind Limerick people from Mount Coote, Rathcannon and Ballysteen gave me a hectic and very happy Christmas.

Going to the races was always 'great gas' and everyone packed into the old car would cross themselves when a church appeared on the horizon on the way there. Coming back, no one bothered, whether the day had brought them luck or otherwise. In Limerick out hunting I met Stedo Johnson, who was the brother of 'Zulu' Blacker, and as I had no return fare, he offered me a lift across Ireland to Dublin. My cousins in Killiney, Eoghan O'Brien and his wife Frances lived at Mount Eagle, the house just above Court na farraga, that had belonged to Dick Smythe, where Coz Frances Lucy had been born and lived with her eight siblings and parents. They offered to put me up while I asked help from Dan Corry and Joe Dudgeon, the great show jumping Colonels, to find me a job. I looked after children's ponies and earned enough to get myself home in time to ride point-to-pointing.

'Only Just', belonging to Jimmy Cairns, out of his good mare 'Just Jane', was the little horse that I had to train and ride. He had only just survived at birth, being a wartime foal, but his heart was enormous. He was terribly sensitive and a worrier, so he needed to be treated with gentle tact, and loved his pint of beer after a gallop, to help calm him down. He gave me some good races over two seasons. My racing on several horses showed me how much scope a horse can have when standing off a fence. I also learnt not to ask for too big an effort on a tired horse.

I had made friends with a French girl, Michèle Cancre, who jumped successfully in shows abroad. She came to stay with me when we moved to Miserden, and she was the only rider that I allowed to hunt 'Only'. She loved him and her quiet and stylish way with him made a perfect partnership. Michèle and I had been the young lady riders competing with and sometimes beating the gentlemen in Switzerland, France and Belgium. We had a friendly rivalry then and have kept in touch over four decades.

Mother had been teaching children to ride while I was away in Ireland and now she had a request from the school for spastic children at Ebworth Park, near Birdlip, to give them riding lessons, just to see if it would help them in their limited life. I was there from the first lessons and saw the difficulties to be overcome. None of these children had had contact with ponies before, and they had a fear of the unknown. We began with them touching and fondling the ponies, and the children loved feeling the woolly winter coats and warm breath of the animals. We had sheepskins and surcingles instead of saddles, and neckstraps to hold on to. It was not easy to get some of the severely handicapped children up on top because they did not have the coordination for a leg up, which needs timing and spring.

The best way was to stand a child on a higher terrace of the yard, bring the pony along at the lower level, and then guide the child down onto the pony's back. The first time was the most difficult, because the child was stiff and nervous, and clung to anything like a drowning person, and the pony wasn't quite sure what was happening. Once in place on the snug sheepskin, the child would pet and stroke the pony and then move their legs and arms, while the pony stood. It was amazing how quickly the children started to relax, and all the ponies were as good as gold with their special cargoes to carry. Up to a certain point the children's progress was unbelievably rapid, and these sessions were eagerly looked forward to, while the teachers in the school were delighted to find the confidence and pride the contact and partnership that they felt for the ponies gave these children in every day life. That was in 1948, and now the benefit of Riding for the Disabled has spread like wildfire under the Patronage of the Princess Royal, and has given pleasure and a new horizon in the lives of so many handicapped people.

Among other children who came and rode with us were charming twins, David and Carol McLeod. Their granny, who had been the widow of Noel Wills, lived at Miserden Park. She had married again during the war, a Wing Commander Huntly Sinclair, who had come over from Canada and was stationed in Gloucester. The Pioneers, 32 Group, had been stationed in Miserden House, the Dower House to the Park, and now the house was empty. From our contact with the McLeods, Mrs Sinclair offered Mother the lease of the house and stables at a low rent, and we jumped at their welcome offer. Mother and I planned together to start a guest house again, as we had done in a small way at Crickley Lodge, and to take agricultural students from Cirencester College during the term time.

During my travels, while jumping on the Continent, I knew that several parents would like to send their children to us where they could ride and learn English during the school holidays. Our big house could be kept busy the year round with the students and the children, giving us the necessary financial backing for our life in Miserden.

We set to work with a will and repainted all the skirtings which had been left mud coloured, probably from a mixture of the paints that the Pioneers had left.

We went to sales for bargains in carpets and some furniture to add to our own that was in store. Using every nook and cranny, we made twelve bedrooms on the two upper floors.

We were back in a lovely house with space around us, a garden and the stables, which had not been used for horses since before the war and we could keep dogs again. We had worshipped at St Andrews Church in Miserden since we left Crickley and took the horses to be shod at the blacksmith, Mr Roseblade, with his boss Mr William Timms, and his son and daughter, Bert and Fanny. Fanny played the organ in Church and had inherited her family's country knowledge of how to make wine or liqueur out of anything that grew in the garden or wayside. I always thought that I had never tasted alcohol until I was given a bitter herb drink called Amer Picon in Belgium when I went with the team. On second thoughts, well before my eighteenth birthday, I remember Fanny giving me hot milk or tea that tasted different from any other hot drink and got me warm quickly, after my freezing winter rides from Birdlip. I had not then had the chance to ski in Switzerland and be offered Glühwein or Café Fertig, where the coffee is poured into a glass until the sugar lump at the bottom cannot be seen and then the glass is filled with Schnaps, either Cherry (*Kirsch*) or Plum (*Pflümli*) until the sugar lumps shows again. This is guaranteed to give you 'soft knees' for skiing and turning smoothly on the snow, the Schnaps working as *Kurvenoel*, oil for the corners.

The charming village of Miserden became a real home for us at last. The church with its Saxon arch in the porch and Norman tower, is full of history and the ancient tombs denote the village life through the ages. In the Doomsday Book the village was called Green Hampstead, but when William the Conqueror brought his Normans over, he ceded the land at Miserden to one of his knights, a baron called Hascoit Musard from where the village got its new name.

Edward the Black Prince had courted his Fair Maid of Kent, probably from the old castle standing on the knoll at the confluence of the streams forming an early tributary of the River Frome that flows into the Severn. We were back to the stamping ground of the Curt Hose family and Mother's ancestors.

The source of the Thames near Kemble, was also a source of fun for the children who were taken to see it, especially when it was suggested that if they sat on the spring London would run dry. Usually the challenge was accepted and we would return to Miserden where their clothes were hung in our airing cupboard before further use.

Mother and I had Miserden House ready for my twenty-first birthday party, by which time we had agricultural students staying with us. The day before, Mother had bought a length of stair carpet from a sale at a nearby country house. We had finally laid the carpet down the stone stairs leading to the hall by 3.00 a.m. After a short rest we had the food and drinks ready for the guests and a marvellous night of dancing and fun to celebrate our house warming in a home where I would be happy for the next twelve years.

My actual birthday was spent in Paris when I was returning from the round of International Shows with Harry and Teeny Llewellyn. We were driving back

(*above*) An historic moment for lady riders! The winning team for the Prince of Wales Nations Cup at White City, 1952. This was the first year that a lady could jump with the team. (*l to r*) My Tosca, Harry Llewellyn on Foxhunter, Wilf White on Nizefela and Peter Robeson on Craven A.

(*below*) Nice, 1953: Before and After. The bank was about eight feet high with only a narrow, hard and rounded top that gave the horse no foothold. No horse jumped this trick fence without floundering or falling. Tosca tried to clear the lot, but turned over as she landed, on top of me. Chevalier Paqui d'Orgeix was the first person to see if I was still alive. One man is pointing at the hole gashed in my right thigh by the studs in Tosca's shoe.

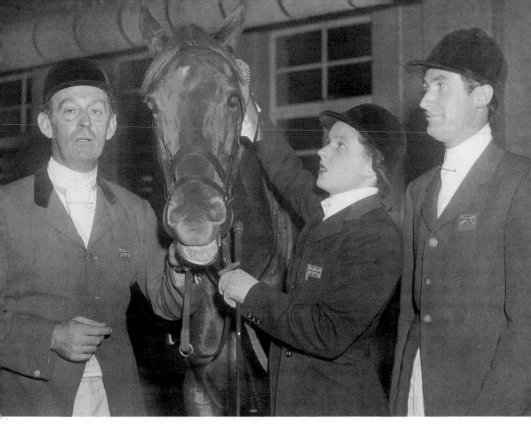

(*above*) Harrisburg, USA, 1953. Harry Llewellyn, Prince Hal, me and Bill Hanson. With Prince Hal, I had won all five international competitions at this event which gave rise to the headline 'One girl defeats the Americans'.

(*below*) Driving Authentic, from Mr & Mrs Frank Haydon's hackney stud, at White City, 1953.

from Geneva, the last of the indoor European shows, and met up with Comte Roland de Maillé and his wife. Roland was a great character in showjumping, and we all had a marvellous evening at the Folies Bergères, with that great artist Josephine Baker playing Mary Queen of Scots. I had 'come of age'.

It had been a showjumping year full of disappointments for me. I'd been asked to jump Finality at Badminton where we were second in the showjumping class. Again she'd whinnied to me before jumping superbly but after the competition we again parted. We had bought a bay mare Carmena to jump, but we had to sell an attractive chestnut pony, Irish Gold, a good jumper, for £275, the sum we needed to buy Leona, a grey mare. Mother was determined that I should have Leona and this little mare proved her ability with me for three seasons before having to be sold when Mother was suddenly killed. The bank had phoned immediately to tell me to repay Mother's overdraft of £1500, and my only asset was Leona.

The first Horse of the Year Show was held at Harringay in September 1949. Harry had taken Mike and Victoria Ansell, after the Wembley Olympics, to the indoor show at the Palais des Sports in Paris, where the enthusiastic public of the *Vel d'Hiv*, created a tremendous 'ambiance' for the horses and riders. As there were only about twenty international riders invited, the public soon knew everyone and made the most of their personalities, cheering on their favourites. I became *'L' Anglaise avec l'oeillet blanc'*, a custom that I always kept, wearing a white carnation on the left lapel of my jacket. Characters like Chevalier Paqui d'Orgeix and Comte Roland de Maillé played up to the audience and were immensely popular, while the public cheered their favourites, egging them on to do better than the last rider.

Colonel Mike deserves the credit for launching the success of showjumping in Britain after the war. He had been a top showjumper and horseman before the war; he was one of the youngest British Colonels in the army. After being blinded and captured in France, he spent his time in prisoner-of-war camps with Nat Kindersley and Bede Cameron where he occupied his time planning the organis- ation of international shows in Britain. He was the architect of our post-war shows, starting with the White City and, seeing the success of the Paris indoor show, dreamed up, with the support of Tony Collins and Colonel Vivian 'Pud- ding' Williams, the concept of an indoor show in London to provide a Horse of the Year Award with competitors in all types of horse events. My destiny led me to a reunion with Finality where the mare became the first Leading Show Jumper of the Year in 1949.

It had been a shock to me when I heard by letter that Finality had been sold to Scotland, without my getting the promised first refusal to buy her back from Tommy. In July I was asked to go and jump Finality in a couple of Scottish shows for her new owner, Jimmy Snodgrass. After this, when she still did not go well for him, they asked me to ride her at Harringay. She was delighted to see me again, pushing me hard in the tummy with her nose, a habit she had developed when being hand-reared on a bottle when her dam died of a surfeit of stolen lettuces. Our partnership clicked once more and we won the big event. The emotion and joy of her triumph as the first Show Jumper of the Year, was again followed by heartbreak.

The Snodgrasses agreed to let Finality come with me for the indoor autumn circuit of Paris, Brussels, Zurich and Geneva. My cup was overflowing, but the dream of a month with Finality was soon shattered by a phone call from Scotland. Jimmy had decided to ride her in a local hunter trial, so the mare could not come with me to Europe. She did not win at the hunter trial.

I was left with only my grey novice Leona, when Mary Whitehead, who had jumped abroad with her Nobbler, generously offered him to me for the first two shows. He had been turned out in the field, but we got him to the train and had his shoes put on, to arrive in time for the Paris '*Le Jumping*'. He was not fit, but Leona won the ladies class, her first international effort and Nobbler puffed his way to fitness. At Brussels he astounded everyone, winning the Grand Prix, while the top international riders were searching through the rule book to see if a lady could compete in and win a Grand Prix.

In 1988 I was invited to the fortieth Anniversary of that first Brussels 'Le Jumping' and our Grand Prix victory. A special competition for riders of those days had been arranged for 'Paqui' d'Orgeix and Pierre Jonquères d'Oriola of France, Raimondo d'Inzeo of Italy and Frank Lombard of Belgium. I sat back and watched my colleagues with admiration, and thanked my lucky stars that my two false hips and open heart operation prevented the possibility of this old girl beating them again, forty years on! I did wonder if 'Paco' Goyoaga and Roland de Maillé, were looking down on our celebration.

The National Hunt Meeting of March 1950, introduced me to Prince Hal, when I stood at the last fence, my usual place on the Cheltenham course, where one needed no ticket. One could go to the start and then run to a fence, getting a close-up of the action and hearing the jockeys' comments, often not meant for other ears. I'd been standing at the last fence in 1948 when Harry won his two races, now this was the Kim Muir Trophy for amateur riders. It was the lovely chestnut horse, well behind the leaders, that caught my attention. Obviously tired in the deep going, he still put in a big rounded jump at the last, not touching a twig, but losing a lot of time in the air. His name was Fourtowns.

The stroke of luck that gave me the chance to meet this horse's charming trainer Alec Kilpatrick was to change the fortunes of this chestnut horse and myself. The horse was for sale, as he was too slow and had a big tendon that had been treated, but the leg might not keep right for racing. Mother and I went to Collingbourne Ducis to try Fourtowns. I was legged up on the gallops and as soon as we set off he held his head to the right and had a very one-sided mouth. I already loved him, although he was so difficult to steer and balance, so after galloping over a couple of steeplechase fences, which he jumped very cleanly, I persuaded myself that I could remake his mouth in spite of his age of eight. We bought him for £150 and he came back to Miserden. I knew that I was in for some hard work with teaching the Thoroughbred his new job, and first we gave him his new name of Prince Hal. He had to make a success with his noble title, and my hopes were eventually justified. Lawrence Olivier had been my inspiration in the film of *Henry V*, with his unique performance as the Prince.

At the first show that I jumped Prince Hal, the fences were old-fashioned but the venue was next to Cheltenham Race Course with the same view of Cleeve Hill in the background. This was his first outing since the National Hunt meeting. He thought he was back on the racecourse as he fought me trying to restrain him over the flimsy fences, but at the sight of the water, his brakes failed; he galloped over it and out over the rope around the arena, while I wrestled with him, being lucky to pull up before we arrived in Tewkesbury.

Carmena, my bay mare, was my only entry qualified for White City that year, although I was given one ride on Nightbird, a nice brown horse from Wales, who finished second with me in the White City Stadium Cup. I wished that he were mine. For many years I longed to ride several of the horses that were competing, just to feel how difficult or good they were to jump.

Prince Hal came to White City too, with Carmena, but to be ridden in the Cavalcade of Horsemen from Early Britons to William the Norman Conqueror, the Black Prince and his Fair Maid of Kent, Queen Elizabeth and the Earl of Leicester, Dick Turpin, followed by Mother, riding Hal side-saddle as the Marchioness of Salisbury, ahead of Queen Victoria and Prince Albert, through other famous characters to the rising generation of the Garth Pony Club. We thought Hal's experience in the Parade, around the arena every day and under the evening floodlights, would help next year if he qualified to come and jump with me. Mother was courageous to ride him side-saddle for the first time with her long blue gown tickling his side, and her blue plumed hat waving in the breeze, while he cavorted and pranced, attractively playing his part like a trained parade horse.

The Horse of the Year Show gave me my last reunion with Finality. She was in the prizes every day culminating with a great duel in the Puissance to tie equal first with Foxhunter. The event, with its climax of the pony battling against the great horse, was televised, catching the attention and imagination of the viewers. Showjumping began to become a spectator sport and Finality and her courageous performance played a part. Finality couldn't be seen from the far side of the wall as she approached, then she put everything into her effort and appeared over the jump. Foxhunter, who had won the King's Cup at White City for the second time that year, was at the height of his career. So was his rider Harry Llewellyn who was the leading international rider for four seasons 1949–1952, by the L'Annee Hippique points for international show jumpers, a remarkable achievement when the army riders like Piero and Raimondo d'Inzeo had horses provided for them and were paid to do nothing else.

Harry with Foxhunter and Monty went to America with Wilf White and the team for the international 'Fall' circuit of Harrisburg, New York Madison Square Garden, and the Royal Winter Fair at Toronto. He very kindly lent me Kilgeddin to take to Paris with my Leona but he made one condition, that I would ride Kilgeddin in a light racing snaffle with no martingale. I knew that Harry could never hold 'Killy' with that bit, although he was nearly twice as heavy as me!

Still, Killy and I came to a compromise in the small arena of the *Vel d'Hiver*, and he was placed in every event, winning the High Jump for me, at that time a ladies' record. He and Leona won me the Coupe Carven, enabling Harry to say on his return, 'I told you so, that bit would work', while I showed him my biceps that had hardened considerably.

Although Prince Hal had not qualified to jump at International Shows that year, he won me one big competition, an Area International Trial with a £40 first prize. I was thrilled to tell Mother of his victory when I arrived home with the horses from Weston-super-Mare. It gave us a ray of hope for the future. Tom Brake, a Somerset friend, known as the 'Best in the West' had seen and liked Hal, although he had beaten Tom, who himself had jumped in the team at the first international show after the war.

While I was in Geneva in 1949, Mike Ansell had introduced me to his old Swiss friend Colonel Ernest Haccius. He had been a brilliant trainer of men and horses, having ridden with the jumping team since just after the turn of the century and becoming *Chêf d'equipe* of the Swiss team from 1921. He trained the Silver medal team for the 1924 Paris Olympics with the individual Gold medal winner, Lieutenant Gemuseus on Lucette, one of the Swiss remount horses bought in Ireland. As well as buying roughly 2000 remounts a year, Colonel Haccius was an excellent course builder, an important art that can make good horses jump fluently, making competitions more attractive. He became Vice-President of the FEI and his knowledge helped the post-war rebuilding of international shows. His educated and understanding approach in dealing with people and problems made him much admired and respected by everyone from his pupils to his contemporaries. I was naturally delighted to meet this perfect gentleman and complete horseman, who also had a great sense of humour.

At Miserden House the students from Cirencester Agricultural College returned in October for the new term. Colonel Haccius had also recommended our guesthouse to friends of his in Switzerland, among them, Sam Koechlin, who had jumped in the Swiss team, and had his own event horse. He was coming to England for a winter course at the London School of Economics in London and wanted to bring his horse 'Tambour' with him, to hunt and train for the Badminton three-day event in April 1951. Sam arranged with Mother for Tambour to stay with us; I would get the horse fit during the week, and he would come and stay for weekends to ride the horse. He was a very welcome guest, and he also gave us his ration card while he lived only on black coffee and grapefruit. The other students were grateful for Sam's extra rations, while he controlled his riding weight, being 6ft tall.

We had just bought Tosca from Phil Oliver for £150 and although she was only 15 hh she had no mouth and was as strong as an ox. She would fly buck when she saw a fence and either throw herself at it or stop at the last minute. I began schooling her in circles, so that she could not run away. She was inexhaustible and I asked Sam one day to try and calm and discipline her. With his height and long legs, he could hold her together, and with endless patience he persevered with her training. I learnt from him the basic principles of dressage which he had studied in Switzerland while training his horses. As Tosca progressed we went to the Cotswold Hunter Trials and jumped the course together on Tambour and Tosca. I hunted Tosca and usually rode her to the meet to try and quieten her. Even after a full day's hunting she would not relax or walk, but would trot high in a back breaking 'passage' all the way home.

Before Christmas I was sending out our Christmas cards to friends and Sam was there when I sent one to Colonel Haccius, so he signed it too. The Colonel wrote back a charming letter congratulating us on our engagement, but Sam had already become engaged to a childhood girlfriend in Basel.

I had to have the veins of my legs removed in an operation in January and could not ride for several weeks. Sam kindly took Tosca hunting for me, with my specific instructions to jump as many gates as possible. This sometimes caused some amusement in the hunting field, when he once gallantly opened a gate for a non-jumping lady rider, and then turned back himself and jumped the closed gate. Another time Tosca came back without Sam but luckily neither had hurt themselves. He had helped with her schooling immensely and she was ready for me to ride in novice jumping classes that spring.

I was ready too for point-to-pointing and had several rides on Charlie Cooper's 'Skate' from Farleaze in the Beaufort Country. He won the Beaufort, the Bathurst VWH for the second year with me, the Berkeley, and came second in the Belvoir open ladies race. 'Only Just' had won the Berkeley with me the year before. That was my last season in racing, because horse shows began to have events much earlier in the year, and my game was showjumping.

We had a fun house party for Badminton, with Sam's mother and father, Marguerite and Harty and sister Mimi, and Sam's fiancée Kiki. Mimi and I became great friends and while I was driving through our lanes to the Badminton Ball at the Hare and Hounds, Westonbirt, an unfortunate rabbit ran under the jeep in the dark. Mimi shouted 'stop', leapt out, gathered her long gown over her arm, retrieved the dead rabbit from the wet road, and threw it into the back of the Jeep. Meat was still rationed then.

Sam came second in the dressage on the first day, but had a fall in the cross-country, although they finished the event sound, with their Swiss team mate 'Hasy' Schwarzenbach winning on Vae Victus. Hasy and his family became good friends. His granddaughter Michelle is a friend of our daughter Lucy and they rode ponies together, bred from our mares and Palomino stallion at Sudgrove. Soon after Badminton, Sam packed up to leave England having finished his LSE course. He already had his doctorate in Swiss Law and had studied in Paris. He left Tambour with us, to find a buyer for him, as Sam was going to work in the United States after getting married. I was sad when I watched him drive up the village with his little $1^1/2$ hp sports car loaded to the hilt. We had had fun and laughed a lot together during those weekends, but now I had to get going with the showjumpers.

Tosca had to jump in novice classes until she had won enough to be upgraded, while Prince Hal was just in Grade A when I was picked for the Madrid team with him. The year before we had turned him out to grass a lot, to get him fatter and calmer, but we did not realise until the spring that warble flies had laid their eggs on him while he was out. Now just when I was starting to jump him, the warble lumps began to appear, where the worm was forming under the skin before popping out and hatching. The lumps came up on his back during the journey to Madrid, with one right under the saddle. I cut a hole in a thick felt pad to put under the saddle, but even then his back was very tender. This meant that I could hardly work him in Madrid before jumping, and he was a horse that needed endless work to settle him down. We did win a class there and were placed in the Grand Prix but his poor back made jumping nearly impossible for us both. When he returned to Miserden, Colonel 'Mouse' Townsend operated on his back to release the poison from the warble. He could not be ridden again until just before the White City in July.

My introduction to Spain enchanted me and I soon learnt Spanish and bought a guitar, picking up the basic chords to start playing. Several friends played and sang Spanish songs while I got records so that I could learn the words and music. We had marvellous nights of singing through until dawn. The Prado with its art treasures opened a new world for me and Spanish friends took me to Toledo to see El Greco's pictures in his home town and capital of old Spain. We watched the great procession of Corpus Christi, with the white-robed children walking to their first communion led by the Madonna carried high among the banners and bright colours of the crowds in Toledo's narrow streets, jammed with gipsy carts and festive people. The scene was a vivid contrast to our visit to El Escorial, the huge and sombre palace in the shadows of the Guadarrama Mountains where Philip II died of melancholia.

The Duke of Pinohermoso was an old friend of Ruby Holland Martin, so we were invited to his estate at Monasterio where he bred fighting bulls, the *toros bravos* of the arenas. He had beautifully schooled horses which he rode as a *rejoneador*, who fights the bull from horseback as opposed to a *matador* who fights on his feet. Although a horse is naturally afraid of the bull, these superbly trained horses would have such confidence in their riders, that they could perform difficult high school movements in front of the bull. As the bull charges, a quick movement of the horse and rider evades the pointed horns as the baffled bull finds no target.

I rode one or two of these strong and springy Andalusian horses, and enjoyed their suppleness and obedience, but I kept well away from the bulls. However I was 'roped in' to try caping a Vacita with the other *matadors*, including Dominguin and Ortega. The heifers are tested for bravery in the private ring, before they are selected for breeding. A bull is never tried before he is taken to a fight at his full strength, because he can learn too many tricks from previous experiences with the cape. My little 'Vaca' was very active and brave, luckily following the cape with my passes, and not knocking me for six, as happened with one of the Portuguese riders. Ortega was kind to show me how to handle the cape and we did one pass, *a mano a mano*, where the vaca passed between us. The challenge was exciting but I had no ambition to become a *matador*.

The drive back through the Château country in the valley of the Loire, this time with Ruby driving the old Bentley, introduced me to this lovely district. On the way down I had driven the Bentley from Nice to Madrid, accompanied by Harry and Teeny in their Land Rover. The potholes in the roads were still unrepaired from the Civil War, and I had been relieved to hand over the Bentley undamaged when Ruby flew in to Madrid, to join the team for the horse show.

Leona came to White City with Prince Hal, but he was fresh and green after his enforced rest following the warble trouble, and hurt himself on a fence in the first competition. The grey mare compensated by coming second in the Princess Elizabeth Cup, again won on time by Iris Kellet on Rusty, who had beaten me in 1949 when I rode Carmena, and Teeny Llewellyn had divided us in second place. A win in the International Relay, with Marie Delfosse, put us girls at the top of the international line up. The bruised leg of Prince Hal improved and he won the Country Life and Riding Cup, but was beaten by one-fifth of a second in the jump off for the Daily Mail Cup. It was the great Foxhunter who beat my 'broken down racehorse' for the International Victor Ludorum of the Show. I was astounded that Hal could do so well in only his second international show but I made it plain to Harry, being a friend, that I was furious about that one-fifth. Every time I visited Harry and Teeny in Wales, I used to look at that cup with a wink to Harry. Sadly the cup has been stolen from their home, but I was not the culprit. I was second by the same margin three times in this trophy with Tosca, who was beaten by Brian Butler and Tankard at White City the following year, and Flanagan was beaten in 1956 while stumbling in the timed jump off and losing a shoe and the vital part of a second. Prince Hal in 1955 and 1957 and Scorchin in 1960 and 1962 made up for these disappointments by winning the Daily Mail Cup, the only trophy that could be kept permanently.

All the 1952 season Tosca had gradually upgraded, and qualified for the Horse of the Year Show. I entered her there for the Prix Caprilli, that entailed a dressage test and a jumping round. I thought that I would use the knowledge that Tosca and I had learnt from Sam in the spring. We showjumpers were looked down on by the dressage people who thought, rightly sometimes, that our riding was rough and uneducated. Tosca was as tense as a jack-in-the-box before dressage in the outdoor arena, but I sat as still as a mouse, while I needed to be a very strong mouse to stop her exploding, although we did an adequate test. The jumping was no trouble as she enjoyed the indoor arena at Harringay. Our 'Caprilli' win was frowned on by the dressage experts and no doubt caused fears that the showjumpers might start to poach on the preserve of the elite dressage circle. For me it was only a discipline exercise that I used for Tosca's first international show. It worked too and she won the BSJA spurs for the most consistent national jumper, the prize that Finality had also won me in 1949.

Tosca was allowed to come with Prince Hal for the European indoor circuit of Zurich, Geneva, Paris and Brussels, and it was at Geneva that I saw Colonel Haccius again. We laughed and talked together of the Swiss team at Badminton in the spring and the exploits of Sam and Tambour. When we parted, he told me I would not see him again. I was shocked when I heard of his death a month or so later although he was not yet seventy and the news brought home to me the frailty of man.

Over Christmas we had several young visitors for the holidays and the guest house was going well, with more than enough people wanting to come or send their children, hearing by word of mouth about our venture started only eighteen months before. The international jumping season ahead looked full of promise with Hal, Tosca and Leona all coming into that class. A cloud appeared when we were told that Ruby Holland Martin had suffered a bad hunting fall. Mother and I took our old American Jeep over to see him at the Radcliffe Infirmary at Oxford. He was lying nearly flat in bed with a broken neck, but his spirit was anything but broken. He had arranged for a wine rack to be put against the wall opposite his bed, so that he could sample his best wines at his leisure, and was in no danger of falling over while in bed. He lived into his eighties and although his riding days were over with a partial paralysis, he then married Dagny and they had a daughter Penelope. I went to the joint party for his eightieth and his daughter Penelope's twenty-first birthdays. The celebration at Overbury Court was a great occasion and we talked of the early shows where we had been on the team together.

After Christmas, Mother and I had Ronald's visit to look forward to when he came home from the Theological College at Ely where he was nearing the end of his training. He had changed his opinions since his Oxford days and after working in the Department of Education he had decided that his vocation lay in ordination. Over a year later, Ronald's Principal, Canon Henry Balmforth happened to switch on the radio just as I was being interviewed by the BBC on my return from America, 'You have a brother, don't you, what does he do?' 'Oh, he is a composer' came my immediate reply. Ronald was then confronted with my statement and had to live it down.

The two Chinese boys from Hong Kong, who spent their holidays with us, had to return to school on 14 January. The day before, a Sunday, Ronald came with us to make our communion at our church. In the evening, Mother suddenly decided to have an impromptu party with a few good friends. Tony, who farmed nearby and kept his hunter with us, and Marjorie Frenkel who were parents of my godchild Jossie, came along with Tony Thorpe our Rector and George Arthurs, the Miserden Park Estate Agent and his wife Betty. Mother was in sparkling form and Ronald enjoyed the evening too.

I overslept the next morning, a rare occurrence as I was the early riser. I rushed down to see if the Chinese boys were ready to go, but Ronald had already woken Mother with a cup of tea and she had left for Stroud station in the jeep. Ronald was about to leave too for London, on his motor bike, a machine that we considered highly dangerous.

It was Ronald who heard first that Mother was dead, when George Arthurs received a call and came to the house. I had already felt a premonition of disaster before Ronald broke the tragic news to me. The Jeep had skidded on a sheet of ice by the War Memorial on the steep pitch of the road at Slad, slid over the side with no rail or curb to stop it and somersaulted down the rough bank. Mother had been killed instantly, but thank goodness the two Chinese boys were safe.

The numbing shock that blinded me on that bright day, had to be quickly conquered by practical action. First the boys were brought back and I made their beds and put them in to rest after their shock. Eric was miraculously unhurt but William had a cut and bruises on his leg that had been dressed at the hospital. Ronald had left with George to do the grisly job of identifying Mother's body. Without Ronald and his practical support and presence at that time I would have been really lost. He arranged the funeral with the Rector Tony Thorpe and coped with all the organisation needed to inform people.

In the evening, Harry and Teeny Llewellyn motored over from Wales to give us support on that awful day. It was wonderful to have them at home while I cooked us a meal, as we had no cook at that time. We felt too that Mother's happiness was still there and this was the house where we should stay. Uncle Gordon suggested that I should join the Army to have a steady job, an idea that was abruptly rejected from my agenda.

Bad news travels fast; that afternoon I was phoned by Mother's bank manager to say that he was sorry about the accident, but please could I repay her overdraft of £1500 as soon as possible because we had no securities to cover the sum. I couldn't believe my ears, as I was more geared to sympathetic phone calls. I vowed to myself that I would change my bank if and as soon as I had any money to help me. The opportunity came after writing my first book *Jump for Joy* two and a half years later, when a delegation came down from the Westminster Bank head office in London to see me in Cheltenham and try to stop me taking away my account, by then with no overdraft, elsewhere. Their request fell on deaf ears.

Ronald had visited the same bank with Mother after Dad's death. Mother needed an extra overdraft to move from Crickley to Bath and find accommodation for us and the horses and ponies, suitable for teaching riding. She arrived late for her appointment at the bank with Ronald, who was embarrassed by her complete lack of punctuality. She was ushered into the Manager's office, which was in a long and dark room. 'Mrs Smythe, do sit down,' he said as he closed the door. Mother had seen a chair and sat comfortably while he also found a chair and perched himself on the edge in a tense way. Mother, who had great charm, explained how she would use the money to concentrate on making a great success of a riding establishment now that she had no other income. 'Yes, Mrs Smythe, of course we can help you, Mrs Smythe. Certainly we will arrange that, Mrs Smythe,' agreed the Manager while he looked more and more uncomfortable. Ronald, who listened with astonishment at Mother's ease in getting an extra loan, suddenly realised the situation. Mother was sitting in the Bank Manager's chair.

Mimi, Sam's sister, solved my banking problem for me. She had said that a Swiss friend had liked Leona, when he had seen her jumping in Geneva, so I phoned to tell Mimi of Mother's death, I also asked if the friend would still like to buy Leona for £1500. She understood my problem as Leona was my only confirmed international horse. Almost immediately she phoned back a positive answer that her friend would like Leona and also a pony for his children. The first fence seemed to have been jumped.

A housekeeper was my next need, because I couldn't go away jumping horses while the guests needed looking after, and without guests I couldn't afford to keep the house and stables. That obstacle was cleared too before I left for Switzerland with Leona and 'Jumper' a little grey pony who lived up to his name. The boat crossing was very rough and uncomfortable for the horses sliding around in the soaked hold on slippery planks. The two greys were better off than the valuable brood mares, heavy in foal, but we all got to Boulogne, where a goods train was waiting that took us across France in a draughty wagon built for forty men or eight horses. I had food for the horses and some cheese, wine and water for me, but it was often difficult to find water for the horses in the sidings where we were shunted. The engine driver became a friend after I had unexpectedly turned up at his footplate to ask if he could tell me where I could find a tap to fill the bucket, also please could he shunt more smoothly so that the horses wouldn't fall on me, my sleeping bag didn't give me much protection. The wagons were freezing cold and very noisy. But after two days we arrived in Basel to be greeted by Leona's new owner. The luxury of the car to Biel was matched by the horse transport with the Swiss groom, and soon we were made warm and comfortable, myself having a hot bath and a good meal.

Mimi came to fetch me and I stayed for four wonderful days with her and her two children in Wengen. Skiing under the shadow of the Eiger, Monch and Jungfirau, landmarks of the Bernese Oberland Alps, made me fit for the tough time ahead running Miserden House alone, and getting the horse's programme organised for the coming season.

4

The Early Fifties:
Showjumper and Author

In my horse's favour was their guardian groom, Pauline Sykes, who had come to work for me before the start of the 1950 season. She was a couple of years younger than me, and she cared for the horses as children. 'Paul' or Paula (never Pauline), became as well-known at the international shows as she was in the English circuit. It was very tough for a girl at that time travelling with horses abroad, as no provision was made for girl grooms at the shows, apart from travelling alone on goods trains which could be quite dangerous. After one bad experience in Italy, she decided to carry a knife with her as self-protection. The horses had her attention continually and her efficiency was widely recognised. No doubt Paul's favourite horse was Prince Hal, as he was mine, if one can have a favourite among one's family of horses. He bit us all on occasions and once when Harry put a notice on Hal's stable 'The Vampire, feed this horse on fresh blood', Paul was furious. She was not pleased when Prince Hal was chosen for Olympic training in 1952 for Helsinki. I admit that I made a big mistake when I acquiesced to the committee's request. The result was even worse than it had been with Finality, when I was told I could fetch Hal from Badminton at the Event in April, because he was not required after two months training at Aldershot.

I went joyously to get him from the stables, but when I saw him I was shocked. Instead of the rounded happy horse that had left our stables in February, I found a thin and nervous wreck. I was allowed to jump him in the Badminton Grand Stakes, a jumping event that was held along with the three-day event. He was so nervous and upset that I walked him through the woods, talking to him. We happened to meet the Queen who was also having an early ride through the park. When I got back I started to quietly jump a two foot pole, working for about an hour until he began to relax and calm down. I was very depressed and exhausted from trying to hold him, but after one or two bigger practice fences, I thought I could compete. He was not easy to ride over the big course but we won, to the astonishment of everyone who had seen him during training. His confidence over ditches and water never fully returned, so he must have had a bad experience with other riders. He soon settled happily back in his Miserden stable, while our Olympic team that was picked for Helsinki brought back the team Gold, the only Gold medal that Great Britain won in the Helsinki Games.

Paul was at Miserden when Mother was killed and helped me through that tough time. She was discretion itself and only slightly more communicative with the press than Lester Piggott. She guarded my privacy and dealt with the

intrusive probings of the media with tact and firmness, especially when they
wanted to discover or invent some romantic attachment in my life.

I used to go regularly to the Kingston Agricultural Show, held on August Bank
Holiday Monday, when Lord Belper as President of the Show, would have a
house party in which I was included. The horses had the excellent stables of his
hunters, which were resting out at grass, and Paul would be well looked after, too.

One of the chief attractions of winning the open jumping at the show was that a
whole Stilton cheese was presented to the victor, from the exhibits at the cheese
competition. Everyone at Miserden insisted that I must go and win the cheese, for
good eating at least until after Christmas. My horses usually obliged, but one
unlucky day when I had already won the cheese, my young horse in a small speed
class hit the last fence, sending a pole up to hit me on the head and knock me out
cold. I am told that I was laid out on one of the four-poster beds, before being
taken to Nottingham Hospital. When I came to, the first thing I said was that I
had promised to jump at the Gower Show in Wales and must get there.

Lord Ronnie Belper brought Paul to the hospital to see me, with the Press,
hoping for a romantic attachment to be revealed, with his concern for his k.o.'ed
guest. Paul was surrounded by the media as she left the hospital and her only
quote in the papers was that, 'She looks rather battered and has a nasty bruise on
her face, but she is tough and is already feeling better. She has had worse falls
than this.'

I escaped from the hospital with the help of Ronnie's chauffeur, with just the
headline 'Cloak and Dagger escape with Lord . . .' I turned up and jumped one
horse at Gower, keeping my promise, but with a black eye, battered face and a
headache.

My horses behaved as good as gold, ensuring that we could win enough to stay
on at Miserden. At White City Tosca became the first horse ridden by a lady in
the British Team to win the Prince of Wales Nation's Cup. Ladies still had to wait
three more years before they could compete in the Olympics. She finished the
year with the BSJA spurs for the second time at Harringay and won the leading
horse in Great Britain in her first full year. She and Prince Hal made me leading
rider in Paris with Prince Hal as the best horse. My regret was that Mother had
not seen this great year, after all her courage and belief in the future.

Roy Plumley caught me with my 'Desert Island Discs' before I started the next
season, so it was appropriate that the opening international show should give me
my first introduction to Africa and the desert. Harry had lent me Monty and a
novice horse St Teilo to jump in Algiers, so that his horses would return fit for him
to ride at Nice and Rome shows, while my Tosca and Hal came to Marseille
before Nice and Rome where I was in the British team. Algiers Show was an
extravaganza run by André Mathiot, the show's President, who had an estate,
Lavaronde, established by his grandfather on the fringes of the desert, 100 miles
south over the mountains. Irrigation had transformed the dry land, and turned it
into a prosperous fruit and spring vegetable farm for the French market. André
with his middle name of Napoleon had collections of tin soldiers in the battle
array of the Napoleonic wars. A coach house with English and French coaches

together with glittering sets of harness and saddles formed part of the immaculate stable yard, with a jumping arena and permanent fences and banks just a part of the whole set up. The hospitality of a five hour luncheon eaten under the shady trees of his garden, with oranges ripening around us confirmed his standard of living. The hand-painted porcelain and crystal glasses constantly replenished with the appropriate and best wines, made it a feast to remember.

The highlight of this show for the riders were the gold buttons that went to the winner of the Grand Prix. Monty had fallen with me in an earlier class, but he tried his best in the Grand Prix. The first speed round was within his scope and he was the fastest clear. The second 'Puissance' round was too big for him and he touched the far pole of the huge oxer which put him third, really beyond my expectations for him in this class. Two years later Prince Hal would come with me and we would return with the last set of gold buttons, at the final show before the revolution.

Prince Hal, fresh from his winter's rest was a challenge for me to ride at Marseille, but indoors I could get better control within the confines of the arena, and he jumped faultlessly through the show. Tosca received a prize from Mme Giscard d'Estiang, who was the daughter of the President of the *Jumping de Marseille*. With both horses in form I hoped that we would contribute to the team at the official shows of Nice and Rome, but disaster loomed.

A narrow bank, over seven feet high was built in the arena at Nice, with a rounded sun-baked top that gave the horses no purchase or place to put their feet securely. The *Chêf d'Equipes* of the teams complained to the Jury about this fence, but the Jury was adamant that it must be jumped.

The first horse to try to jump the bank fell and so did the second. Prince Hal managed to scramble over it landing on his nose without actually falling like several other horses, then Tosca's turn came. She was clear to the bank, but as she saw the narrow top she tried to clear the lot, caught her foot on the far side and turned over, falling on me. Pinioned against the bank she couldn't avoid treading on me as she struggled to her feet, so the jumping studs in her shoes tore my thigh. By a miracle the fall was not worse. Paqui d'Orgeix was first at my side saying 'Pat, *Est ce que tu es encore vivant?*' Are you still alive? Not quite sure myself, but not wanting to make a fuss I dug myself out of the ashes, the surface of the arena which was made of cinders that embedded themselves under the skin. Thankfully I found that I could stand while I asked for a leg up, so I could jump a fence, to give Tosca back her confidence, before our team grabbed me in my dishevelled and torn clothes caked with black ash and blood, and dispatched me to the hospital.

My leg was operated on that evening, to take out the damaged muscle and the cinders in the wound. The next evening the team came to visit me with the cheering news that Bill Hanson had won that day. A bottle of champagne was produced while with glee they found the commode and filled it with ice to cool the champagne. I soon felt much better and decided I could ride the next day. The doctors thought otherwise and the stable news was more depressing. The show blacksmith had chipped Hal's pedal bone when he changed his shoes by cutting too deeply into the front of his thin Thoroughbred hoof, Tosca was lame too from her fall, having twisted her back as she turned over. Her mental injury went far deeper, as she never wanted to touch a jump and she could not understand why she had crashed while trying her best over the trick fence.

In Rome neither horse was right while I had to spend my nights in hospital to prevent gangrene in the deep wound. It was a disaster when I did try to jump Tosca and we both finished our effort much lamer than before. During the show it was a privilege for the teams to have an audience with the Pope, an event that I looked forward to, especially seeing inside the Vatican with the Swiss Guard on duty, but with my heavily bandaged leg, I could not genuflect. Pope Pius XII saved my embarrassment by taking my hand asking, 'How is your beloved country?' Also he enquired after Sir Winston Churchill's well-being and our impressions of the Rome Horse Show in the arena of the lovely Piazza di Siena surrounded by Umbrella Pines.

Once we had all recovered at home, the showjumping year went wonderfully with both horses, and Tosca's confidence seemed restored while she carried off trophies with rarely a fault. Our same team won the Prince of Wales Nation's Cup for the second year running at White City and Tosca carried off the Victor Ludorum and Harringay Spurs at the end of the British season. Again she was the leading Show Jumper in Great Britain. The sum in prizes she won for this yearly honour was totalled at £1542 in 1952 and £1350 in 1953. Today this sum would be the prize for one minor placing in one championship. In 1953 the Harringay Victor Ludorum won her £20 for first prize.

Funding our team for the American circuit in the autumn was again a problem, but through the efforts of Harry Llewellyn and Colonel Mike Ansell the journey was eventually arranged and financed. I was chosen for the team with Tosca, but my second horse, Prince Hal, was only included in the plane load when room was found for six horses. Our slow flight over with refuelling stops at Shannon and Gander, Newfoundland, was delayed by Bill Hanson's seemingly placid 'The Monarch' panicking in his small crate as the plane started to taxi out onto the runway at Heathrow. I was in charge of the morphia and tried to calm him with an injection, as were my instructions, but he became stimulated instead and even more crazy. Paula, my groom, was trying to hold Prince Hal's head clear of The Monarch's flaying hooves and we just stopped the pilot from taking off, although he had to come back from the cockpit to see the mayhem being created among the horses before he was convinced that we must unload The Monarch. The planes had very low doorways and a big horse had to bend its knees to get in and out. We were almost the first guinea pigs in the transport of big horses by air, and Foxhunter had hit his head when being loaded through the doorway.

My first sight of New York City sky line was from the plane as we arrived at Idlewild New York, now JFK airport. The Pennsylvania Horse show at Harrisburg was the setting for my American debut. While the horses got over their journey with rest and exercise, we were taken by Harry to his war-time friend Tommy Bullitt, at his Oxmore estate, Louisville. The famous breeding ground of Thoroughbreds was nearby in the Kentucky 'Blue Grass' country around

Lexington. Here we had the chance of seeing the cream of the celebrated sires with Nasrullah, Blenheim, and old Mahmoud while at Calumet Stud we saluted Citation and his sire Bull Lee.

After a couple of days spent touring the heart of the American Thoroughbred industry and seeing the efficient luxury of the top stables we were back at the show for the opening event. Tosca was my first ride before the American public and we certainly gave them an opening thrill. A wide double of parallel bars, with too long a stride for Tosca between them, caught us out. She tried to bank the far pole and we had a crashing fall. I bought my first bit of American ground in the arena and acquired several bruises. The consequence of this fall was to bring back to Tosca bad memories of the bank at Nice, also she had hurt the same hind leg, but her morale had suffered a deeper blow.

My champion mare became second string to Prince Hal, the 'reserve', who took over from her and won every competition through the show. The Individual Championship and the Team together with the four other big events made him the unbeaten horse of the show. As one journalist wrote 'At last we've seen a flying saucer!' He continued to be consistent at New York and Toronto, where he was in our Nation's Cup Team.

At the next show in Madison Square, Tosca came back into form for the President of Mexico Trophy which she and Prince Hal won in this two horse contest, a prize I had set my heart on, although it was a challenge trophy, so I only retained a photo of the sculpture in Mexican silver of a mounted cowboy throwing a bull by its tail. This method is a way of bringing down a bull in the wild, in order to give it medicine or treatment for an injury, before releasing it again to roam free. The most dangerous moment for the cowboy doing this work is when he leaves the prostrate bull, to leap onto his horse, hoping that the furious animal will not get up and charge before he has galloped away.

The trophies that the horses won had no prize money attached for the events in America, as an 'amateur' was expected to pay for the privilege of competing. At the end of the tour I had nothing but the friendship of people at the shows. I had gained an American friend, Carol Durand, jumping in the USA team and Shirley Thomas from Canada. All three of us had held our own with the gentlemen riders in competition and it was Shirley's father who invited me to their home in Ottowa after the shows and then to drive to Florida with Shirley, as he needed his car there in the New Year, so I could be a companion for Shirley on the trip, as she was younger than me.

We left Ottawa as it froze up and 'hunted' our way south to Florida. Friends at the shows had invited me to hunt with their packs, so we progressed from one Hunt to another as the cold travelled behind us freezing the land. We first sampled the timber fences of Pennsylvania and Maryland following hounds, then the 'Tiger Trap' country and south to Beaufort, South Carolina, where the marshes froze in the early morning when we went riding. It was time to get to Florida and leave the car in Fort Lauderdale. As we followed the sun to the citrus areas of Florida, we assuaged our thirst not where the sign read 'Grapefruit or Orange Juice 10c a drink' or the more generous 'second drink free', but '10 cents for all you can drink'. Full of vitamins we didn't need to stop for food, but only stopped if a State Speed Cop saw us pass, when we would dash for a large tree draped with Spanish moss and hide there until the traffic cop had given up the chase.

A Smythe cousin called Marjorie, descended from the family of twelve siblings of FBS and Tiger Smythe, whose father had settled in America, contacted me over Christmas when Shirley and I flew back to Ottowa. She told me that her husband, Ralph Beerman, would fetch me from Chicago so that we could spend New Year together in the Midwest. I had been suspicious at first when Ralph had turned up at the Waldorf Astoria, just as our team was leaving to jump one evening in Madison Square, and told me to my surprise that he was my cousin. My leg was pulled all the evening by Bill Hanson and Harry, before I could assure them that he was an authentic relation. Ralph met me at Chicago airport, landing in his Piper, following in the airliner that had flown me from Ottowa. After a turn around the great stock yards of Chicago, he set the plane for Illinois, giving me a flying lesson en route. I found more cousins there, two were about the same age as Ronald and myself and surprisingly called Meade, one of Ronald's names, and Patricia. New Year was celebrated with this unexpected family reunion on the northern reaches of the Mississippi. We flew on to South Sioux City where Ralph and his six brothers ran a grass drying business. From there, a long drive to Denver, Colorado took us over the vast corn plains of the Middle West, to the Rocky Mountains, where I met Tex Ritter in the 'Mile High Restaurant' named from the height of the hotel above sea level. We all went to the Rodeo where I found that the riders and the animals lived a travelling life going from one rodeo to the next, like the showjumping circus.

The wild rocky country in the mountains left a great impression on me, as natural habitat has an ageless fascination. We even met a cougar lion crossing the rough track, with its eyes shining like lamps in the evening winter darkness. My love for wild places and animals was realised again, down south in Texas on the King Ranch, at that time covering one million acres north of the Rio Grande River, that divides Mexico from the United States.

Cutting out cattle, the weaners having to be separated from their mothers, was the job for the beginning of the year. Bob Kleberg, and Helen his wife, gave me this chance to see how the work was done with the herds of thousands of Santa Gertrudis cattle, a breed that Bob had developed from a Shorthorn Brahma cross. He had picked the foundation bull as a calf, and this bull which he called 'Monkey' stamped its qualities on all his stock. The Brahma genes gave the cattle resistance to disease and flies in the southern climate, while the Shorthorn influence produced quality beef. He also set up ranches with the breed in Cuba, South America, North Africa and Australia, where the cattle flourished and upgraded the local indigenous stock. 'Monkey' left his mark in the many lands where Bob Kleberg introduced a legacy of Santa Gertrudis.

I had to shed my chaps, sombrero and cotton neck tie to return to England, house and horses. Arriving in London was a complete surprise, as I had not realised the impact that Prince Hal's American victories had made at home. It

(*right*) Tosca at the last fence, clear to win the Nations Cup with the British Team at White City, 1953.

(*left*) Prince Hal jumping with his typical ease.

(*left*) Signing copies of *Jump for Joy* in Exeter, 1954.

(*right*) The late Marquis and Marchioness of Exeter, when he presented me with the Sportswoman of the Year trophy in 1952; Len Hutton was Sportsman. The Marquis (as Lord David Burghley) won the hurdle Gold Medal for Great Britain in the 1928 Amsterdam Olympics. We both suffered from hip problems and had hip operations in the Sister Agnes hospital.

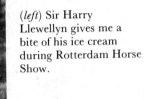

(*left*) Sir Harry Llewellyn gives me a bite of his ice cream during Rotterdam Horse Show.

was a time when America was at the top of most sports along with their high standard of living. An English girl riding a broken down racehorse stealing a little of the American thunder, had tickled the English press. Then I had disappeared, without means, money or programme for my unscheduled six week trip. I was hardly given time to wash the Texas dust out of my hair before Eamon Andrews had me on 'Sports Review' and Peter Duncan introduced me to Violette Elgin the ballet dancer and Jack Hawkins the actor on the programme 'In Town Tonight'. I had only landed that morning and mentally was thinking half in Spanish, the language of the Mexican cowboys on the King Ranch. My dogs gave me a great welcome when I was allowed back to Miserden the next day, where I was inundated with the waiting stacks of post that had accumulated while I was away.

In New York, I had seen Sam and his wife, as he had gone to work in America soon after leaving the LSE in England and his marriage in Switzerland. He asked if I knew of a horse that might make an eventer for him when he returned to Switzerland in the New Year. I had a nice chestnut mare, that I said was brave and good across country, but she was too impetuous in showjumping and would need patient ground work. He came to see 'Goya' in the spring and after jumping her, he decided to take her back to Switzerland for cross-country and three-day events. His success in training her gained them a place in the Swiss Olympic three-day event team at Stockholm in 1956, where they finished the event. The cross-country course there wrought havoc with the teams, when a thunderstorm and deluge made the ground so slippery and difficult that one or two fences caused pile-ups like a motorway disaster in the fog.

The publishing firm of Cassell had approached me to write a book on my reasonably short life, while an agent, George Greenfield, suggested that he could take over the business side of contracts and promotion if I came to an agreement with Cassell. He also persuaded me that the remuneration from a book might give me a little more security in my life at Miserden. I pondered on the thought of my bank manager, who had forced me to sell Leona, and the possibility of another bank in the future, if I had a regular income.

The result was a *fait accompli* and I succumbed to the new world of publishers, agents and deadlines, the dreaded moment which sometimes forces one to work around the clock. I enjoyed writing and had written stories from an early age progressing to essays at school where I worked hard. Various articles that I had written for magazines had brought in some pocket money but now time would be at a premium as I was launching into the new season of horse shows.

On top of this was the 'Sportsman of the Year' presentation at the Savoy, the Sporting Record Award and Madame Tussauds who needed me to be measured for a waxwork. My first priority was to get the horses to Stroud Station to travel to Ireland for the Cork Horse Show, while I followed on through Punchestown to see the racing over banks and the stone wall which must have bruised a lot of 'chasers as the stones went flying.

My friends from Limerick were there, but I tore myself away and continued to Cork where Tosca won the International event and the An Tostal Trophy.

Inevitably this led me to nearby Blarney Castle and the famous stone that required a back bend from my much battered vertebrae in order to land a smacking kiss on the unpalatable and hard surface.

Dorothy Paget, the wealthy and eccentric daughter of Lord Queenborough, owned a string of National Hunt jumpers, among them the most famous and incredible Golden Miller, perhaps the best and bravest steeplechaser of the century. He won the Cheltenham Gold Cup five times running from 1932–36, the blue riband of the National Hunt season, and in 1934 he won the Grand National as well, a unique achievement. He was wise as well as a brilliant horse, and after his 'National' triumph, decided that he had proved his ability at Aintree and when asked to race twice more over the huge fences he declined to oblige. He did not get his due desserts on retirement, finishing his days on a distant farm with a donkey and insufficient food.

Golden Miller's jockey in two Gold Cup wins (1934 and 1935) and his 'National' victory of 1934 was Gerry Wilson, who trained at Andoversford and was a good friend during and after the war. I met Evan Williams, Miller's last Gold Cup rider, when I was working and hunting in Co. Limerick. Out hunting one only saw Evan's flying coat tails as he was always away in front with hounds, sensing the way that the fox had gone, or one saw his boots sticking out of an earth, where he was burrowing faster than the hunt terriers. He enjoyed his sport and I could imagine how well he would get on with a character like the 'Miller'.

I was at Cheltenham in 1989 for the Gold Cup to witness the unveiling of the superb bronze of Golden Miller which stands above the paddock, where at either end, Arkle and Dawn Run are also commemorated in bronze. The Gold Cup that followed was won suitably by another hero, the grey Desert Orchid, who in atrocious conditions of wet and snow, battled up the hill to regain his lead just before the post.

'D.P.' as she was known, decided to get some showjumpers in 1950 and keep them with Mrs 'Pug' Whitehead, an experienced showjumper herself. Pug's granddaughter Gee Armytage has now made her name as a top steeplechase jockey, carrying on the family tradition while Marcus, Sue's son has won the Grand National and the Whitbread Gold Cup in 1990 on Mr Frisk. One of D.P.'s first jumpers was bought from 'Curley' Beard, an Irish quality horse called Eforegiot, the Irish dialect for 'I for Idiot', with classy looks and a fun character that I admired. Once at the Richmond Royal Horse Show D.P. had suddenly told me that I would ride two of her horses in the ladies jumping: Eforegiot and Tommy. I already had my little French stallion 'Djort', an elegant *petit alezan* that I was riding and eventually selling for Michèle Cancre. One didn't say 'no' to Miss Paget as she confronted you, enveloped in an enormous shabby sacklike tweed coat, that had seen every racing and show venue for the past decade. So I jumped the three horses and including two jump offs had three clear rounds on each, eventually tieing first with all three horses. I did insist that my Djort should be nominated for the Cup; Miss Paget was displeased and I was only requested to ride Eforegiot in the team three years later, competing at Lisbon, Madrid and Vichy with my own Prince Hal. 'Egiot' won a class at Lisbon with me but Prince

Hal had a bigger triumph before I was introduced to Generalissimo Franco at the Spanish Embassy in Lisbon. Ten days later Hal also won the *Gran Premio de Madrid* in the *Caudillo's* own capital. The superb cup with handles of the Lions of Castille and the stem supported by the Bear of Madrid, made a little compensation for the last minute news, that ladies could not compete in the World Championship at the Madrid Show. I had come to the show with my two good horses especially for that event, but it was to be over thirty years before lady riders could compete in the World Championship on equal terms with the men. At Aachen in 1986 that chance was seized by the Canadian lady rider Gail Greenough, who with Conrad Homfeld, Nick Skelton and Pierre Durand qualified for the best four riders, to ride each other's horses in the final championship. Gail rode her own horse Mr T. and the other three horses without a fence down, beating the three men who all had faults. She had found a sympathetic way that suited each horse's temperament.

The World Title at Madrid, too, was decided between the best four riders from the championship events, riding their own and each of the other three riders' horses. I was then glad that Prince Hal was not one of these four horses to be ridden by different men. He had already shown how upset he became with other riders during the Olympic training at Aldershot. I guessed that Hans Gunther Winkler was not happy to see his mare Halla in other hands although he was the eventual winner, and this partnership would be Olympic Champions two years later.

Just before the presentation of the Championship by the *Caudillo*, where I would also receive the *Gran Premio* Cup, I fainted and was carried off. It was not only the discrimination shown against women in the World Cup, that made me sick, I explained later, but also the effects of an attack of the 'Madrid tummy'. The next day I dragged myself out of bed for the Nation's Cup which only started at 11.00 p.m. that night. Prince Hal jumped well although I felt so weak, but our other two team mates fell, one breaking his collar bone, leaving us out of it. The host country triumphed over the solid big fences while the Spanish public went wild cheering their team, with the band playing their National Anthem with gusto for the parade of the cup winners at 3.30 a.m. The band had been perplexed when Hal had won the *Gran Premio*, rendering 'God Save the Queen' in a minor key.

Vichy was in a minor key for me as Prince Hal was again lamed by a continental blacksmith used to shoeing horses with big feet and not a Thoroughbred's thin hooves, shades of Nice the year before. Eforegiot won the Vichy Grand Prix for me so that D.P. could gain her revenge for my claim on the Richmond Cup three years earlier, by firmly keeping the silver salver trophy. Although she didn't take it with her on her death in 1960 her executors told me that I could only have the trophy as a souvenir of Eforegiot on payment of £25, an offer I had to decline. The Egiot had already been sold to Japan before the Stockholm Olympics where I fear his end was no happier than that of the great 'Miller'.

One happy souvenir of that trip is a guitar that was given to me by a Spanish friend, after he had placed a bet on me to win the *Gran Premio* in Madrid at very long odds. The only other place where I knew that there was betting on the jumping was in South Wales. When I first ventured into the valleys and mountains of the coal miners, they did not expect me to beat their local hero but on occasions my young horses did win. It was then that I would hear whispered, 'Put the money on the girl from over the river'. The Severn Bridge had not been built so the river was a barrier.

My brindle lurcher bitch 'Windy' got their approval too. She used to catch me a hare every Sunday, when I went coursing on a young horse, with the terrier Fina La Ina searching the hedgerows while the poodle 'Bliss' sent any game out into the open, where Windy would course and retrieve the hare for our next Sunday lunch. The Welsh are great sportsmen and experts with working dogs.

We were lacking one good companion on our team that year, when Bill Hanson fell ill after his 1953 success at Nice, the Grand Prix in Rome and on the North American trip. His older brother James, now Lord Hanson, was not interested in showjumping, but Bill was a popular team member with a quiet and successful style and a great friend to us with his sense of fun and humour. There was a moment that had shocked me in Toronto when we went one morning to Bill and his wife Patricia's bedroom to laugh together and discuss the day's competitions. Patricia told us about a bad dream about him that had upset her and although we laughed it off then, I recalled that incident later.

Bill's father Bob Hanson, who had made a success from his transport business, bought a horse from Brigadier Lyndon Bolton for Bill to showjump that year. Lyndon, who has since made his ninetieth birthday in active health, had bought Flanagan in Ireland. He had seen the young chestnut grazing in a field with some Thoroughbred youngsters. Flanagan used to visit this good field of grazing when he was hungry, by jumping the banks and joining his friends. His breeding had not been arranged, a forward young colt having covered the mare, his mother, one dark night. The crofter who owned the mare wanted £40 for the love child but the Brigadier offered £35 and eventually split a fiver for £37.50. Training the spunky youngster around Alnwick, Lyndon's home, showed him that the horse was brave enough to tackle cross-country events. He had already completed the famous Badminton three-day event before he was bought by Bob Hanson, who had a good eye for a horse.

Bob asked me if I would jump him when Bill's illness stopped him from riding. I saw Bill in September at the Harewood Trials, where I jumped Flanagan for him. He was glad to see him go well and know that I loved Flanagan. The added contact with Bill and Patricia through Flanagan made Bill's death soon after, all the harder to bear. The show had to go on while Flanagan stayed at Miserden for the winter.

Prince Hal confirmed his Madrid form with the Harringay Victor Ludorum, followed by the first 'Million' or £1000 in French francs then, in Paris for the Grand Prix.

He finished the season with three wins, gaining the High Jump record for ladies of 2m 24cm, making me the leading rider and Hal the best horse in Brussels. The Million sounds a lot of French francs but the franc was soon devalued by several noughts. Another custom amongst the English riders was to split any prize money, so that with three riders, my share of Hal's win was only just over £300. Paula, my groom did not approve of this practice, any more than she had approved of Prince Hal being borrowed for the Helsinki Olympic training. My identity with the Paris *Vel d'Hiv* public as *L'anglaise avec l'oeiller blanc* was at least not shared. A year later when I was jumping Janet Kidd's little grey mare Finesta in Geneva on my birthday, a surprise birthday cake was carried into the arena during the prize giving, and presented to me with the band playing the appropriate melody. The snow white cake was made of carnations which matched both my buttonhole and the mare.

The horse world mourned three other great horsemen in 1954. One was Federico Tesio, the famous rider, Thoroughbred breeder and trainer, a very respected Italian gentlemen whose racing stock has influenced the best blood lines in racing. A great loss to the British equestrian scene happened when Tony Collins was killed in the Comet air crash, on his way to judge in South Africa. He had won the Badminton Olympic Horse Trials in 1950 and was manager of the British three-day event team at the 1952 Helsinki Olympics. After serving through the war he rebuilt his Porlock Vale Riding School into the largest riding academy in the world and he was among the planners for the first Horse of the Year Show in London. He was in his early forties when we all lost his talent and influence for the good of equestrians. Michael Tubridy was the brilliant Irish rider in their showjumping team who died in an accident with a young horse when he was only thirty-one. The loss to Ireland and to us his friends, finished a depleted year in the ranks of horsemen.

Algiers was the first international show for Flanagan, where he could learn over good courses in the Spring sunshine of Africa, while Prince Hal could work harder in the big competitions. Our first appearance in the ring together, was a painful one for me. Flanagan was most interested in his surroundings and the jumps in the Hippodrome arena. He was clear until we were galloping over the water, when he suddenly thought that this must be a cross-country natural obstacle and put a front foot down into the water, making a great splash as he turned over. He trod on my leg and foot as he got up; he was fine and I only had a swollen black leg and a grazed face but I could still ride.

On Easter Day, Prince Hal fulfilled my ambition to win the coveted gold buttons engraved with the crest of Algiers, the prize for the Grand Prix. Hal with the only double clear round had beaten Pierre Jonquères d'Oriola and Paco Goyoaga, the winner of the famous buttons two years before when I had been third on Monty and again Hans Winkler was fourth. These were the final buttons at the Algiers Show, a fact unknown to us at the time.

In *L'Année Hippique*, Jean Bridel's report on Algiers show says that in the Puissance while I won on Hal and was 3rd on Flanagan, 'the remarkable seven-year-old of Mr Hanson *donc on reparlera*'! Indeed he spoke of Flanagan again for the next twelve years. Dear Jean and his co-editor and founder Oscar Cornaz started their remarkable yearly record of the shows in 1943 and continued over three decades. It is the most complete and unique record of the start and growth of post war showjumping, added to by their knowledge, comments and expertise. In Switzerland I could keep in touch with them both and Jean's records and photos helped me immensely with my books on showjumping, while I could visit Oscar with his library collection, and his father's *Badminton* magazines from the turn of the century. Marceline, Jean's widow, and 'Miura', a nickname that Oscar gave his wife after seeing the famous breed of Toros Bravos, the best fighting bulls of Spain, are mutual friends with the happy memories of our special Swiss husbands.

On the strength of the gold buttons of Algiers, with the same four riders from four different countries being at the top of the line on the two occasions in 1953 and 1955, the genial President of the Show, André Mathiot, invited us four to a private jumping competition at his superb estate at Lavarande the following January. We would jump his own horses over a course in his arena, stay in his house and be entertained exquisitely, plus the bonus of visiting the oasis of El Golea to ride camels and see and experience the desert and its environment.

On 1 January I turned up at Algiers airport to find conditions evoking memories of the blackout and war. Anxiously I looked around and felt a foreboding of vulnerable isolation and ignorance of the situation. I had not noted or been warned that a potential revolution was brewing in Algeria; I could not know that not only had I won the last of the gold buttons, but our friends of the concours with their origins in France, the *pieds noire*, would soon be thrown out of Africa losing everything. Lavarande was destined to be returned to the desert from whence it had been created by André's grandfather. But dispelling any fears for the future, André turned up to meet me.

'Where are the others, what happened?' I asked anxiously. He told me that the others had not risked coming because of the 'unrest', but that I would jump all his horses and go into the desert. I had a feeling of 'unrest' too as we travelled the mountains to Lavarande, with a loaded pistol in the glove drawer, which André showed me and explained how it worked in case of an emergency. I felt isolated without the others to enjoy the fun in their company.

A freak rain storm had flooded the desert around Lavarande, and André's arena was under water. Undeterred, he rallied his Algerian staff to build two big fences on the circular sandy drive in front of the house. I reluctantly climbed aboard his four horses, one after the other, and the fences were gradually raised to six foot, while I dodged under the weeping willow, my toe knocking an orange bush as I approached the jumps. To my relief I soon found that all his horses could have become top international material in the right hands.

The leisurely morning's work in this Gazira of the desert, a green and fertile island among the sandy waste that stretched to the south, was noisily interrupted, as a helicopter arrived from nowhere and proceeded to land. The pilot, a wiry, fit Frenchman, came across the lawn and introduced himself as Jacques Castaing.

He was working for the troops who were fighting the bandits in the mountains, and had spotted André's prosperous estate from the air and would be delighted to join us for lunch.

Another place was laid at the table and Jacques enjoyed to the full the Lavarande spread of food and wine, a complete five-star treatment and a welcome change from Army rations in the Atlas mountains. After his second balloon glass of Napoleon brandy with the coffee, he offered to take me up in his helicopter. I suspected that this was not the first time that he had drunk, driven and survived so my fears were overcome by my curiosity to learn how the machine worked. Perhaps if the battle came suddenly closer we might have to be evacuated by this means, as there was another mountain range to be crossed en route for Algiers, where the uprising could erupt at any time, as I had learnt when André showed me the pistol in his car.

The gusty wind blowing desert dust and sand splattered the glass bowl of our helicopter with stinging rain as we rose and hovered dangerously close to haystacks and other obstacles. To my relief Jacques suddenly shot the helicopter up in the sky and showed me the controls. I was never sure if he had left the machine in my charge or if he was in control, but he caught me by surprise, when he said that he found me *sympathique* and what about getting together with him for an exciting and dangerous life together. If I'd said *Non*, would he have dashed the helicopter to the ground, or if I said *Oui* would he drop everything and embrace me? To avoid these possible disasters I suggested that he showed me how to land. André was relieved when we returned safely and Jacques thanked him for the excellent lunch and flew off into the blue, as the storm had passed.

True to his promise André did take me to El Golea, then a remote oasis on the route to Timbuctoo, which only recently had acquired an air service. The oil companies were beginning to prospect around the oasis, so the calm and unspoilt village would soon change. We made our way by van in the cold dry desert wind, rattling across the rutted sand and through the empty market square, past the sand walls of the houses to a yard where a circle of Arabs were sitting in the sun. They pointed at an archway with a passage beyond which we were happy to find M. Grosjean, mine host, in front of a welcome open fire. He was surprised to see us too, saying that he had watched me jump at Vichy, when Eforegiot won the championship. This was only the first of the coincidences concerning myself, Jacques and M. Grosjean.

Our host had a list of 698 stories, from which he took a selection to recount to us that evening over supper. He had an ear for music, having been a director of the Opera in Algiers, and as a *conteur* in various dialects, he kept us in stitches until the desert dawn broke. I then donned my baggy black camel trousers and leaving my shoes behind, I mounted the *rehalla* strapped on my pure white Mehara camel's hump. It was one of the fast and pure-bred mounts of the desert patrol of the Meharistes, which are ridden with one's bare feet crossed in front of the hump. With only a rope in one hand and no command of Arab camel words, I did not feel any more in control of my destiny than I had in the helicopter with Jacques. My luck held and I returned safely to England where I had been invited to go to Ascot with Flanagan, to join the other riders on the short list for Olympic training.

M. Grosjean came into my life once more, after the French had to leave Algeria and return to France. The upheaval in Africa hit the *pieds noire* hard and André lost more than Lavarande and the business accumulated over three generations. I saw him once more in France, a sad shadow of his hero Napoleon. I was jumping at the *Vel d'Hiv* in Paris, for the autumn *Le Jumping* after Michèle Cancre and Paqui D'Orgeix had been married and were living over the Theatre Danoux where Paqui was acting. They had invited me to lunch and I arrived at the theatre in the middle of Paris and climbed up three flights of steep stone steps to their apartment. When I rang the bell I heard scuffling, growling and swear words, but no one came to the door. I rang again and the noise of chaos increased. 'Stay there Pat, I must catch the leopard, she doesn't like women' shouted a French voice from the other side of the door.

As I waited, I figured out that having been living recently in Cambodia, just before the collapse at Dien Bien Phu, they had brought back an animal from the jungle which they were now keeping in a Paris apartment! My anticipation was correct; I was let in when the leopard had been shut in their bedroom, where she slept on their big bed, and the mess that she had left in the living room had been cleaned up.

During lunch, we talked of their adventures in the Far East and my travels to shows and the Olympics. The phone rang, Paqui went to answer it in the bedroom. '*C'est pour toi Pat, viens!*' I took the phone perplexed that anyone would know where to find me, and a man's voice said in French 'Ah, Pat, we met in El Golea you won't remember me!' I recognised the voice, 'Of course M. Grosjean, I remember, and I've a couple more stories I can tell you for your collection!' He had seen in *Paris Soir* that I was jumping at the *Vel d'Hiv* and had rung Paqui to find out where I was staying. At that moment I saw the leopard stretch herself on the bed and slide down to the carpet where I was standing with the phone. Suddenly she bit my knee joint and I gasped '*Paqui, vite*', I didn't dare move or hit her head, in case she came for my throat, meanwhile, could I say to M. Grosjean, 'Excuse me a little moment, I'm being bitten by a leopard'? Paqui ran in, telling me that I was bleeding on the carpet when I pointed to my leg and the leopard under my skirt. He removed his leopard while I still held the phone and said that I hoped to meet M. Grosjean at the show. Tissues were quickly produced and then Michele bandaged my knee where luckily the leopard's eye tooth had hit the bone on the outside of my knee, so I was able to ride that night in spite of being sore, with a souvenir lump and fang scar to prove my story to this day.

My second encounter with Jacques was even more extraordinary. I had been invited to join in the Inter-Continental Championships in Chile, representing Europe with General 'Monkey' Blacker, Piero d'Inzeo, Pierre Jonquères d'O-riola, Paco Goyoaga, Hans Winkler and one or two others. I had broken my nose badly ten days before when hunting a super horse of John King's with the Belvoir, while in the evening we were invited to go to the Hunt Ball. During a great hunt, I saw a short cut over a gate and asked my horse to jump the black and solid gate post. We had been galloping and leaping over hedges and ditches dividing the big grass fields; alas the change of obstacle confused the horse and he galloped straight through the post which broke near the ground, both of our faces hitting the stones in the gateway at the same time. When I got my head out of the mud and stones, I found that my nose was in my left eye. Freddie Welch kindly stopped to put me back on the horse, and pointed the way back. There was no Hunt Ball for me that night, only an operation at 7.00 a.m. the next morning. On the way to London airport, a doctor had removed the plaster from my nose and I had boarded the Chile-bound plane after being told that I must not sneeze for a fortnight.

In Santiago de Chile the riders were booked into the Hotel O'Higgins, the porter took my case up with me to my room and as I entered, the phone rang. '*Bueno*', I took the phone and in Spanish a man asked me if I was Senorita Patte Smithe. I thought I was, so he proceeded to tell me that I would not remember him but we'd met in the desert at Lavarande. 'Jacques Castaing? It is not possible,' I exclaimed in Spanish, yes it was, we changed from Spanish to French; he was in the foyer and had borrowed a car so would I like to go to the beach with him. That was the quick answer, I decided, for me to swim after the long journey crossing the Atlantic and the Andes, as I had arrived with very swollen legs. It was two years since I had seen Jacques in Algeria.

There was no one for miles on the lovely sands with the roaring rolling Pacific ocean breaking on the beach. The sand was hot and I had come from mid-winter in Europe, but plunging into the sea was a shock to the system, as it was freezing cold from the Humbolt current that flows from Antarctica. I dived through a roller and swam in the sea beyond, but when I got cold and wanted to return, the *resaca*, the undertow, kept me back. Determined not to be intimidated by this experience, I found some surf that rolled me into the beach and then drew me back as the next huge wave smashed down. I just got to the beach battered and panting, with my nose still in the middle and I hadn't sneezed.

Jacques told me that he was employed with a helicopter on a dam-building project in the Andes. He had happened to see in a newspaper, left in a cafe, that I would be riding in the Football arena that weekend. As we talked, I saw a sturdy man approach us, as we lay on the sand chatting. 'Are you Pat Smythe?' he asked. I wondered who could have known that I had gone to the beach within an hour of arrival? When I nodded, he told me that he was a friend of Uncle Hugo, who often came to Chile from Buenos Aires for Reyrolles work. 'I thought it must be you, only a person fresh from Europe, who doesn't know the dangers of those big seas, would try to swim here.'

Confused by jet lag and the unexpected events of the past hour, I introduced Jacques, 'This is a friend I met in Algeria, M. Jacques Soustelle.' I hesitated as Jacques looked at me grimly and then shook Doug Mackenzie's hand, 'Castaing' he said firmly. Doug didn't notice and invited us for a beer at a beach hut, telling me that if I stayed in the sun any longer, I wouldn't be able to wear a shirt for the show. Jacques mumbled to me, 'I could strangle you for less than that.' It dawned on me that I had introduced him with the name of the Governor General of

Algiers, who had been a guest at the Algiers show, but later, political difficulties which I had read about but not absorbed, had put him in many people's bad books. It can be dangerous to speak foreign languages less than fluently, as I also found out with the different meanings and usage of Spanish words in Spain and the South American countries. There can be trouble enough when using the same English words that have developed different meanings around the world.

I had to return to the reception for the riders, so Doug took me back to meet his family and then to the O'Higgins Hotel. Jacques was going back to work with his helicopter, so we said, '*Adios, y hasta la vista*', a figure of speech when our paths were not likely to cross again.

One summer's day, when I was writing at my desk, having a rare free day in which to finish one of my books, before going to another show, I heard a helicopter fly over Miserden House. At that time helicopters did not often fly around the Cotswolds, although now it is commonplace. A thought of Jacques might have crossed my mind with a smile, but I got on with my work. Twenty minutes later I was disturbed by a knock on my door. One of the French boys, who were spending their summer holidays with us, came in excitedly telling me that he had seen the helicopter and had borrowed a bike to follow it. He saw it land near my jumping paddock at Lypiatt beyond the top of the village. 'The pilot, he wanted to see me', he said. It couldn't be, but it was, Jacques and it was lunch time.

Our third meeting had happened through Jacques' employers buying a helicopter from near Bristol. He looked for Miserden on his map and saw that it was only a short hop onto the Cotswolds. Navigation was easy for him after his experience with bandits and snipers in the Atlas mountains and the inhospitable heights of the Andes. He had met no resistance from the ancient British camps or the Roman strongholds along our Cotswold escarpment, but after a good lunch he regretfully had to leave and get his new steed back over the channel. We said *Au Revoir* for the third time and left it, as on the other occasions, like that.

Miserden House was always a hive of activity, but as I met many more friends one would never know exactly who would drop in. A year before the 1956 Olympic Games a school friend Jacquie Huxley, who had been my secretary and right hand for fourteen months, left to get married to Angus Moon. We had received a letter from a Miss Paddy Bury, just after Jacquie arrived at Miserden, asking if I had a job for her, as she was interested to come and work for me, after reading extracts from my book *Jump for Joy* that had been published in the *Liverpool Post*. We had written back to her, saying that her letter would be put in 'pending', as at the moment Jacquie had just taken over the secretarial side. When Jacquie became engaged before getting married, we asked Paddy if she still wanted to come and see me. Paddy came and decided to stay, now living in our Sudgrove Cottage, after her work over three and a half decades; even now keeping the filing system up-to-date, together with plenty of unwritten anecdotes along the way.

The Farriers' Company were the first Guild to offer me the Honorary Freedom of their Company, a year before the 1956 Olympic Games, the year of their 600th anniversary. The Guild holds fifty-fifth place in the order of precedence, over the eighty historic Guilds, which dates from the time when the Guilds took allotted places on State occasions. I was told that I was the first woman to be honoured in this way by the City Farriers and the Duke of Beaufort, 'Master of the Horse', was the only other honourary Freeman. I made my speech at the dinner held in the Mansion House, when I could truthfully say that I had shod a horse myself. The village blacksmith was being replaced by travelling teams with forges, and our blacksmith, Mr Roseblade had just died in Miserden. The village forge was then closed.

My brother Ronald accompanied me to the Apothecaries Hall for another Farriers dinner where I had my next City function to receive the Honourary Freedom of the City of London. I then learnt that my perk from this honour was the permission to drive a flock of sheep over London Bridge, although living in the Cotswolds it would be more appropriate to drive them over the Severn Bridge at Gloucester, near the market. I was told too, that if I had to go to prison, I need not go in the Black Maria, but could take a taxi, although not at Her Majesty's expense.

I drove myself to Buckingham Palace when Her Majesty invited me to a dinner party. Prince Tungi of Tonga, the Prime Minister of Tonga and son of Queen Salote, sat next to me at dinner. He was already twenty-three stone, which must have been a strain on his heart. I had admired his mother who had driven in her carriage with the hood open during the coronation of the Queen in 1953, when the rain had been relentless. She cheerfully disregarded the weather, waving to all, while getting as wet as the waiting public who warmly cheered her colourful contribution to the great occasion.

My later invitations to become a Loriner, the makers of bits and stirrup irons and then a Saddler, have brought me many new friends. The Saddlers Hall, that was badly damaged during the wartime blitz, was rebuilt together with St Vedast's Church that stands next to it in the City. The British Showjumping Association has been well supported by the Saddler's Guild and we have held our annual AGM in its hall. The twice Master of the Saddlers, the late Chappie Snowden, with his wife Viv, had been skiing friends at Wengen over many years, while all their family had long connections with the Saddlers Guild.

Malcolm Sargent, who often came to the White City for the Horse Show when his concert tours permitted also visited us during the summer holidays. Ronald had rightly removed Mother's baby grand piano once he had a vicarage with a room large enough to take it, so I went about finding a replacement for Miserden House. A lovely grand piano of full dimensions, caught my eye in Cheltenham Chicken Market and the huge instrument was obtained for £5.00. The horse box carried it back and our friendly piano tuner did his best, once we had removed the worst of the chicken manure, and polished the wood to restore a little of its old glory. A young Frenchman was staying as a guest during the school holidays at the time; he was a piano student with the ambition to go to the top. Sir Malcolm, who was very kind to young people, sat with Bernard, the boy, encouraging him and playing himself on the bargain piano in the drawing room. A heavy piece of the ceiling did fall on the piano one day, but luckily not on the keyboard or on any of our residents.

We were decorating another room, next to the kitchen, where a Pioneer, with artistic tendencies had, during the war, covered the nice oak panels with a painted frieze of Snow White and the Seven Dwarfs. While we scrubbed off the offending paint to return the room to the original oak, we found a naked lady painted under one of the dwarfs. She too had to be washed away, after our friends had been invited to make her acquaintance.

Another privilege of success in sport was meeting other sporting characters at some of the Sportsman and Sportswomen presentation evenings. In 1954 I shared this honour with Roger Bannister, and also met his team mates Chris Brasher and Chris Chataway who had helped him run the first sub four minute mile, and both won the award another time for their track records.

Gordon Pirie was Sportsman twice when I was the Sportswoman, in the *Sporting Record* and *Daily Express* awards. Lord Brabazon of Tara presented the cups one time and Mr Iain MacLeod, the Minister of Health, another time with many interesting people present. In the junior *Mirror* Sports Hero of 1954, Roger won, I came second and Stan Matthews third, followed by Len Hutton, Denis Compton, Stirling Moss and Don Cockell the boxer. It became a real party when one got all these sportsmen together.

In the Martini Award for the leading gentleman and leading lady rider, I was lucky enough to be voted winner from the first year of 1957 until 1961 when they gave me the trophy to keep, saying it would be cheaper to make another trophy than having to run to Miserden every year to fetch and take the present trophy each time. Lord Knutsford was involved in the presentation of this trophy and was very friendly to us riders. After Sam and I had married, I was surprised to receive a very disapproving letter from his Lordship, to the effect that I should not have married a foreigner. It was written on the House of Lords writing paper and signed Knutsford. I was so angry that I did not reply and tore up his neatly handwritten letter, which I now wish that I had kept. Bob Dean used to laugh a lot over this story and never missed a chance of pulling my leg about it.

Peter Scott had been a friend from our early days at Miserden. His daughter Nicola was very keen on ponies and we had plenty at home for friends and guests to ride. Peter, with his great knowledge of natural history, was a wonderful friend, and I showed him my films of the King Ranch after I had been there. I had been fascinated by the thousands of resting geese crowded along the brackish waters of the Laguna Madre inside Padre Island that lies along the coast of the Gulf of Mexico; even Bob Klegberg had not seen so many geese on migration before. The wildlife on the great ranch was specifically left undisturbed with the javeline, wild pigs, armadillos, deer and the great variety of birds, living alongside the cattle.

When Peter with the group of Founders started the World Wildlife Fund with its International Centre in Switzerland, a cousin of Sam's, Luc Hoffmann, was one of the Group. Later, we were able to spend one Easter weekend with Luc and

Daria, his wife, and their four children, at Tour du Valat, their home and research station in the Camargue, just at the time of the spring migration, while the flamingoes were breeding on the lagoons.

My first introduction to David Attenborough was a coincidence when we had both been invited to a charity event in Hull. I had been told to get to King's Cross Station for the train, and having found the station, where I had never been before, could not find any parking. In those days one could park nearly anywhere in London, and I had my first ever new car, a Standard Sportsman. Departure time was looming, and in desperation, I left the car on the ramp to the station and dashed to the ticket office to explain what had happened. Was it possible to leave the car keys at the station office, if the car had to be moved? The ticket clerk looked blank, but a tap on my shoulder made me turn round. 'I do know who you are, Miss Smythe, and I have a firm that makes gloves for riders. Would you like me to park your car for you, and I will leave the keys at the Railway Office with a map of the place where I can find parking. I know how difficult it is around here, this is my card, if you want to contact me.' The clock ticked, what could I do but say thank you very much, give Mr Millar, the name on the card, my new car keys, and race to catch the train by the skin of my teeth. David was sitting placidly in the carriage when I breathlessly introduced myself. He was not sure that I had acted wisely with my car keys, but the train was on its way. Other people that evening increased my doubts, but I have faith in mankind. On my return to the station in London, my keys were there, with an accurate map of the parking and a pair of riding gloves had been left on the driver's seat with the compliments of Mr Millar.

Our meetings since then have revolved around our interests in the conservation of nature. David has never let problems of parking his car get in his way, because he holds no driving licence, with his wife Jane doing the taxi work for him, although he holds a pilot's licence.

The guests who came to stay at Miserden enjoyed the highlight of a visit to Stratford on Avon for the Shakespeare productions. As I got to know some of the artists, they would come over to spend a relaxing rest day with us. The Redgrave family and Dame Edith Evans became very welcome visitors. A happy afternoon was had when Lynn Redgrave aged fourteen won a prize in a competition run with my Three Jays series of children's books, when she came to a demonstration of training that I gave at Miserden for the busload of the prizewinners.

One time when John Geilgud had given an outstanding rendering of King Lear with George Devine as Gloucester, that had left us emotionally drained, Sam and I were asked to go backstage. We crept to the dressing rooms expecting the actors to be as exhausted as we were, but John Geilgud with his paint mostly washed off and a towel around his neck was humming a happy tune and welcomed us in. He had been able to switch off from his part very much quicker than his audience were able to do.

When General Lord Ismay was elected Secretary General of NATO in 1952, I was invited to visit 'Pug' and Kathleen Ismay at Villa Säid while I was jumping in Paris. We had first met with my uncle, Colonel Gordon Smythe at Swindon

Manor; Pug, who was three years younger than Gordon had served in India while Gordon served with the Burma Rifles. He was a great and charming man and when he retired from his five years with NATO, he returned home thankfully to his herd of Jersey cows and we used to meet at the Evesham Show, where he was President.

Other valued friends were Lord Exeter, David and Diana Burghley. David, an Olympic Gold medallist himself, took a great interest in the Olympic Games, and started the three-day event championships over the superb Burghley Estate, following 'Master's' popular and successful Event at Badminton. David like myself had severe hip problems and came with Diana to the Sister Agnes Hospital when I was operated on for my replacement hips. He was a very welcome visitor with all the Sisters and staff who had looked after him as well.

Working for the *Daily Express*, writing occasional articles on the horse shows and skiing events, gave me an opportunity to meet some of the people involved and a chance to be on the side of the media. It was an interesting exercise of the theory, 'if you can't beat them, join them'. Carl Giles, the superb cartoonist, is always involved in charity work, and we met when we were invited to the same evening event. I stayed with Carl and Joan, his wife, and I was most impressed by his workshop, where he carried out work on heavy agricultural machinery as a surprising hobby. He came with me to the Suffolk County Show where I was competing in the jumping events, and within no time had summed up the activities of the horsey crowd with a series of brilliantly funny drawings.

Janet Kidd had become a great friend and her house was always full of people enjoying her hospitality. Together with her children Johnnie and Jane, her home was a secure base for other people's children like the daughters of Deborah Kerr and Tony Bartley, Melanie and Francesca, called Frankie. I was with Janet on her eightieth birthday in 1988, before she died later in the year. She had invited me in the spring when she had bravely made her last long journey to 'Holders', her home in Barbados, which she loved and had created over three decades on the Island. Sam and I had visited her briefly years before, when she started to bring horses over from England. Now I found a thriving Polo Club with visiting teams to play in tournaments and enjoy the relaxing hospitality of the charming Bajan people.

Janet's brother Max Aitken, two years her junior, took over the reins of the *Daily Express* when their father Lord Beaverbrook retired. Max had been a brilliant fighter pilot during the war and was a good skier. He had many Swiss ski friends in Wengen in the Bernese Oberland, where he had often skied before and after the war, occasionally with Karl and Antoinette Molitor who were Swiss Olympic ski medallists in 1948. Max's birthday party in February was sometimes celebrated at the Eiger Restaurant by Wengen station with people arriving on sledges, or *Schlitten* in Swiss dialect, as there is no road up to Wengen, only the mountain railway. He was a great sailor too and with his yacht *Drumbeat*, practically won the Fastnet Race. Uffa Fox was a close friend of Max in their sailing days and was a 'marvellous' man, one of Uffa's favourite words in his Isle of Wight dialect.

Uffa took me to his place at Puckaston to show me his chestnut mare 'Frantic'. He also showed me photos of him riding, while we laughed about his 'sailor style' on a horse, with the rider's feet, knees and elbows stuck out, while his heels were telling the mare to go faster. That evening we sang songs with friends around the supper table, after Uffa had showed us his boat and demonstrated how he comfortably steered his yacht, sitting on a well-placed horse's saddle that kept him steady when his boat was bucking in rough seas.

One of the most generous people to be with, Uffa gave any money he had to other people. The taxi driver would be given double the tip he expected, and the waiters in 'Rules', a favourite eating place of his in Covent Garden, always were well rewarded. 'Pear-shaped', said Uffa as he patted his belly, 'that's what I am.' When he married his French wife Yvonne, she put an end to his indulgencies and Uffa became slim again. It was always a mystery to us how Uffa and his wife communicated, neither with a word of the other's language. I can recall his voice every time that I listen to his record of 'Song of the Sea', sung in his inimitable way. He had been encouraged by Max Aitken to make a recording of these old sea songs that he had learnt from his father and other old sailors, which had never been written down. On a wild night sailing Max's stay sail schooner *Lumberjack* back from France they kept watch together. As the two of them took turns at steering all night through the gale, Uffa had sung during the exhilarating sail through the stormy sea.

Uffa's Commodore's House next to Sir Max Aitken's Prospect of Cowes was always full of activity and interest. He was a brilliant boat designer and builder of world reknown in small yacht racing. One of his most popular designs was the famous 'Flying Fifteen'. Prince Philip used to enjoy racing in this class with his *Coweslip*, a boat that Prince Charles learnt to sail too.

I was given a chance to dine with Lord Beaverbrook at his Somerset farm when I was jumping at the Yeovil Show. I was driving the lorry with the horses and the West Country weather had rained its worst all day. My horses were soaked and cold by the end of the competition; I felt that they needed to get home to warm food and stables as soon as possible, so I phoned to say that in the circumstances I was unable to come for dinner that night. I was never asked again, an opportunity I regret having missed with the invitation to meet this great character, but my horses were fine the next morning, and recovered from their soaking.

The telephone exchange at the Post Office in Miserden had been controlled by Doris since the 1930s. It was most convenient when one asked her for a number and she'd tell you 'No good ringing her on a Wednesday, that's her day in town', or 'I've just seen him go down the village, so try him later'. However it could be inconvenient when one heard heavy breathing down the phone, during a private conversation. Once, Mr Hamilton Mills who lived at Sudgrove before the war, had contacted his number and was heard to say 'You there Doris?' 'Yes Sir,' came the prompt reply. 'Well put the dxxx phone down'!

I was telephoning Paqui d'Orgeix in Paris one evening, when the Gloucester-shire dialect of Doris broke into our conversation, 'How do I know what they're talking about, I don't understand a bloody wurrd!' When the automatic exchange was installed and Doris's Telephonic Services were no longer required, she got married and started a new life at fifty with Bert our nice roadman.

Wilf was our source of village gossip; he had come to us when he had no where else to go, and although he wouldn't have been top of the class if he had gone to school, he was not stupid. He was born just after the turn of the century like his friend Millie, one of the six children of Jesse the Miserden baker who used to deliver the bread in his pony and trap. Wilf's favourite occupation was standing at the sink doing the washing up while he observed the people passing by the window. We could not invest in a washing-up machine until he eventually took his place in our churchyard. He had enjoyed some good holidays by the sea, when he and Millie went off together. 'Hallo Wilf,' we'd say on his return, 'You look fine, did you have a good holiday with Millie?' 'Oh lovely it were,' he'd tell us. 'We jumped into bed and was asleep in a jiffy.' Then he'd shuffle off with his small bent body shaking as he chuckled at the memory.

When jumping at the Suffolk County Show I stayed with my friends Carl and Joan Giles and he accompanied me to the Show. The result of his observations appeared in two cartoons for the Daily Express: *the top one of 'We can't all be Pat Smythe, Miss Ringbone', and Giles himself being the little child with my autograph in the right hand corner of the other.*

(*above*) Prince Hal beat the best in the world for the gold buttons with the Championship of Algiers, 1955. Second was Pierre Jonquères d'Oriola, Olympic Gold Medallist. Then came Paco Goyoaga, the only other winner of the famous gold buttons two years earlier, when I had been third, and fourth was Hans Winkler, who would become a treble Olympic Gold Medal winner.

(*left*) Sam Koechlin jumping the final cross-country fence on Goya, for the Swiss team in the Olympic Three-Day Event, Stockholm 1956.

(*left*) Stockholm, 1956: the first time a lady received an Olympic medal for show-jumping. Our Bronze Medal team winners, Wilf White on Nizefela, Flanagan and myself and Peter Robeson on Scorchin'.

(*below*) Flanagan clears the parallel bars at the Stockholm Olympics.

5

Olympic Medals and other Honours:
The Late Fifties

My Olympic training in 1956 was, up until then, I might admit, one of the best times of my life. We were stabled at Ascot in lovely boxes where I could keep Flanagan, Prince Hal and a young horse Brigadoon, and we usually started riding the horses at 6.00 a.m. which meant that the rest of the day was free. Paula Sykes looked after my Ascot horses while Pam, another energetic girl, with a sense of fun, had joined our team and kept the horses and ponies at Miserden. I would drive down to Miserden for an afternoon's work, but the evenings and nights were free to explore London life. I seized the chance to see as much theatre and opera as possible together with a social round that I had not experienced before, going dancing at the '400', the Allegro and some of the other night clubs and getting back to the stables in time to blow away the cobwebs with a good workout.

Sue Whitehead, Pug's daughter, was also in the Olympic training with Scorchin. It was Sue who had the distinction of having her photo taken with the Royal family in the box at Aintree, during the terrible moment when the Queen Mum's horse Devon Loch with Dick Francis, suddenly collapsed spreadeagled on the ground while approaching the winning post a way ahead of the Grand National field. All in the Royal box looked stunned with shock and grief, except for Sue, leaping up behind the sad and frozen figures, with joy written all over her face. We realised quickly that she had seen her friend Dave Dick plodding along on E.S.B. to overtake the fallen royal horse and win the Grand National. Dave who said to one of his fellow jockeys during the canter down to the start, 'See that there?' The other jockey looked and saw some religious group carrying a banner, 'Your sins will find you out' Dave quipped. 'If that's the case, I'll fall on the flat before the first fence.'

Another string was added to my bow when poor Sue broke her collar bone falling from another horse, so I was asked to ride Scorchin' for her; the horse belonged to Dorothy Paget who by then had sold Eforegiot to the Japanese. Flanagan and Scorchin' together hardly touched a fence with me on the run up to the Games, with our final International show at Lucerne a month before the Olympic event. Prince Hal, who was not wanted by our trainer for the Olympics, had already won the Grand Prix and four other events in Brussels that spring, where he was leading horse having not touched a fence throughout the show, making me the leading rider without the help of Flanagan. He was allowed to come to Lucerne where he won two classes. As both Flanagan and Scorchin' were going so well, Colonel Talbot Ponsonby, our trainer, decided to try Peter Robeson on Flanagan, as his mare Craven A was getting old. Flanagan did not go well, so I got Flanagan back and Peter took over Scorchin', who he kept to ride in the Games. I then won the *Grand Prix Militaire* on Flanagan, with another lady in second place. But the Cup was presented to the French officer, who was only third; the cup was then inscribed with his name. At the end of the show I was the leading rider on points, but the prize went to a man several points behind me, while I was designated the leading lady rider. The Military had to start preparing themselves for winning rounds to be jumped, on their sacred ground, by ladies. It was reported that my three horses had hit only two fences in 23 rounds over 275 obstacles at Lucerne. Another winner in the Combined Training event at the show was Sam Koechlin on Madelon, an exceptional Swiss Army mare, but Goya would be his eventing horse in the Olympics.

While away at these shows, I would arrange with Paddy to get my important post to the first place where I could look through it and phone her about urgent matters. I had flown in to London, where I picked up my packet of post and took it with me as I was driving to a charity event, with Sir John Smyth and Lady Frances. I opened some letters, as I was in the back of the car with 'Jackie' Smyth driving. One official letter puzzled me, so I passed it forward and asked Frances to tell me what this was about.

She looked at the letter and then shrieked 'My dear, you've got the OBE!' Jackie seemed as pleased and excited as when he got his VC! I was glad to have such friends to share my thrill in this Birthday Honour, wondering too if the Olympic Games ahead would decide whether I was worth the award.

On the same day that the Honour's List was published, our final team had its last work out at the White City. The *Daily Mirror* had sponsored a Cavalcade of Sport where the evening included the top sportsmen in soccer, rugby, cricket, athletics, polo, showjumping, greyhounds and speedway, finishing with fireworks. It was a very happy entertainment and provided enough noise and activity to prepare any horse for an Olympic crowd. My friend Noel Whitcomb wrote up the events of the evening for his newspaper. The headlines were in large print, 'IT WAS A GAY NIGHT FOR THE SPORTING DUKE'.

'It was a gay Duke of Edinburgh who took a night off from the Palace last night. He was doing what comes naturally, looking at sport.' In 1956 we could use that formerly happy word that is without an exact substitute and so now our language is left the poorer.

Noel Whitcombe had introduced me to Danny Kaye, a year before, at a Variety Club of Great Britain luncheon, after his 40,000 mile tour around the world for UNICEF, working for the same cause as Save the Children Fund. I admired him both as an unique artist and for his unflagging work with children for charity.

Stockholm provided us with all the facilities needed for the Equestrian Games, the stadium had been built especially for the 1912 Olympic Games. In June the sun hardly set and the horses had to be worked very early before it was too hot. The heat of the sun also encouraged swarms of flies and especially the large and fierce mosquitoes that devoured us night and day. Our horses joined the rest of the competitors from twenty-nine nations at the Military School with an enormous indoor *manège*. There was a crisis one night when the beautiful wooden building caught fire, probably caused by a cigarette carelessly thrown into straw. The old timbers flared up, while the horses were quickly evacuated from the stables nearby and walked around away from the fire. The burning roof collapsed and the whole *manège* was destroyed before the last sparks were extinguished by the firemen. It was a tragedy for the building but no animal or person was hurt although the grooms and horses had a long and disturbed night.

The Queen and Prince Philip arrived in the Royal Yacht *Britannia* for their State Visit during the Games. The yacht had to be navigated through the archipelago of little rocky islands, where I saw an untidy giant nest of the rare white-tailed eagle. The sea mist covered the coast, hiding the huge brown birds with the distinguishing white tail, but my Swedish host had often observed the eagles.

The opening of the Games presented a spectacle of horses, with the King and Queen of Sweden and our Queen and Prince Philip driving into the arena in open carriages with the colourful Swedish Royal Guard dressed in spectacular blue uniforms with white helmets, mounted on chestnut horses, the sun breaking through the storm clouds to light the scene of riders and horses representing their many nations. The Olympic flame had been carried by a relay of 100 horsemen from Malmo to Stockholm, where the last riders lit the Olympic fire in the bowl at the entrance to the arena. Two Swedish athletes, both former Gold medallists then lit their torches from the rider's flame to run around the arena and up the steep steps to light the flame on top of the tower. The lovely blonde girl caused a breaking of the ranks in the Spanish team next to us, as she floated by with her torch, while Flanagan was distracted by his chestnut girl friend Goya who was in the Swiss team next to us, as he had not seen the mare since she had left Miserden with Sam. Great Britain in Swedish is *Stor-Britannien* which accounted for our place between Spain and Switzerland.

The Parade and the long wait, whilst being devoured by the biggest fiercest Swedish mosquitoes, took its toll on Flanagan, who caught a chill on his kidneys. Only Paula's nursing and care of him over the few days before our final competition and the closing ceremony, had him ready to jump for his life. I was depressed to see him suffer the pain in his back, a discomfort that I knew so well myself.

The Three-Day Event took my mind off Flanagan's problem when we went to help the team with their troubles on the cross-country course. We were there to rescue horse or rider if they had a disaster at the difficult obstacles. A downpour during a thunderstorm had made the ground very slippery and there were many falls. I saw Goya near the end of the course and was relieved to see Sam and the mare still going strong. I did not know then that they had already had two falls and she had cut her knee, but she finished and was able to complete the jumping and final phase the next day.

In the jumping competition too, there were only three horses and riders allowed in each team, so that every score counted for the Nation, and one elimination would put the whole team out of the event. Our Three-Day team excelled themselves to win the Gold medals. There had been a worrying night after the cross-country endurance day because the Queen's horse Countryman had slipped badly during the cross-country and pulled muscles in his back. Paula joined his Event groom to treat Countryman all night, so that he was sound and comfortable for the jumping the next day. The Olympic spirit was shared by grooms and riders alike.

On Sunday 17 June we walked the Nation's Cup Course at 7.00 a.m. It proved to be a severe Olympic test with related distances between the fences. As I measured the distances, I thought that the course would have been ideal for Prince Hal, but that Flanagan would be pushed beyond his limit with his stocky build and short stride, apart from having had only one year's experience in international jumping.

Scorchin' with Peter Robeson was first to go for our team and finished with sixteen faults. The rain poured down while I was working Flanagan to go next in the team, and the ground in the arena was becoming very holding. Thirteen horses had already been eliminated and the best round had been for eight faults with Piero d'Inzeo on Uruguay. Flanagan cantered into the ring perkily, to face the biggest test of his life. He stretched his utmost over the huge spreads in the heavy ground, which held him each time he landed. He tried his best but could not reach the second part of a rustic double of parallel bars, which he hit hard to break yet another pole of the wide double that had caused the downfall of so many horses, shattering the rustic poles, already known as the Swedish matchstick double. He bravely recovered to clear the open water ditch and poles, and only one more pole fell in the very big treble, to finish on eight faults.

Wilf White with his great horse Nizefela, who had nearly won the Individual Gold medal in Helsinki, where they had been in our team winning the Gold, had eight faults as well. Halla, Hans Winkler's great mare, had the best round for four faults, but in hitting the last but one fence, she tried so hard that Winkler pulled his riding muscle as he gripped her with his legs. He had finished in agony and was taken away for medication.

Great Britain with 32 faults was lying second to Germany with 28 faults at the end of the first round with Italy on 39 faults. The Queen came to watch the vital second round. Our Scorchin' had five fences down for 20 faults while Germany and Italy had good rounds. If only Flanagan could go clear. He tried his best again clearing the lethal 'matchsticks' double. He was clear to the treble, third fence from home; jumping in over big parallels he stuck in the mud on landing and could not reach the next fence, a gate with a pole over it. His next effort got him over the first two parts but he just caught the far pole on the third wide parallel bars. He jumped the last two fences clear, but the one treble had cost us 13 faults. Winkler went clear for Germany, his wonder mare taking him around with pricked ears, while he shouted with pain from his muscle. This was the only clear round of the event, to give him the Individual and Team Gold, with the brothers d'Inzeo individual second and third for Italy with the Team Silver and ourselves three faults behind with Team Bronze, which we were relieved to bring home as a proof of our exertions. Harry Llewellyn summed up Flanagan's effort accurately when he wrote in *Horse and Hound*, 'The short-striding Flanagan is very co-operative and obedient but lacks scope for the huge Olympic spreads.'

The official International Show followed the games in the same arena. The courses were back to a size within Flanagan's scope, so he showed the others what he could do by winning the opening class, beating other Olympic horses that had been above him in his tenth individual Olympic placing. Our team also won the Nation's Cup after a jump off with Italy over raised fences. Flanagan went clear to clinch the King of Sweden's Cup in the last round giving us a great finale to our first Olympic experience. I found flowers left for me by a Swedish fan at the hotel that night, they were addressed to Miss Pok Sunnytte, such is fame.

I did not have my original medal for long because it was stolen from the car of Major David Satow, when he was organising a display for the Royal International Horse Show at the White City, a month after the Games. David was one of Mike Ansell's right hand men in the BSJA and had parachuted into Yugoslavia during the war to work with the Partisans. His post-war hobby was change ringing, with the bell ringers of St Martin in the Fields. He soon organised a substitute medal for me, but we doubted if the thief would have gained much kudos from a stolen Olympic medal valued at £2.

The last shows of that year started with an historic moment, when I was passing through Rome en route to meet the horses in Sicily. I met a friend, Natalie, a French showjumper who had married Sandro Perrone, the editor of *Il Messagero* and we decided to go to her husband's office at midnight. There was Sandro with telephones in both hands and others ringing around him. It was the night of the Suez crisis when the Russians took advantage of the media's eyes fastened on Egypt while they marched into Budapest, to crush the Hungarians.

To emphasise the memory of that night, Sandro whipped all the framed sketches of Rome from his official walls and pressed the heavy load into my unready arms. *Par hazard* as the French say so aptly, I safely made the journey to Sicily and back; the pictures still hang at Sudgrove, without one crack in the protecting glass.

Palermo and Catania Shows finished on a happier note with Prince Hal becoming the Leading Horse and making me the Leading Rider, in front of the d'Inzeo brothers, the Italian Olympic Medallists.

The winter's rest put the two chestnuts Prince Hal and Flanagan in top form for Paris, in spring-time. Prince Hal was jumping at his best after seven years with us at Miserden. During that time he had learnt to have confidence in my judgement, and he had become more manageable and obedient. Therefore it was a shock to me during the first Ladies European Championship in 1957 at Spa in Belgium, when the show committee told the Italian rider, Giulia Serventi and me, that we must jump our second horses, to decide the tie, as we had finished our four rounds on the final four horses with equal faults. I had specifically nominated Flanagan for the Championship as he was forgiving with other rider's mistakes. The last horse that I wanted anyone else to ride was Prince Hal. Giulia had rough horses, which needed to be ridden in a rough way. Over the first fence, Prince Hal did not understand why his new rider was hurting his mouth and holding the reins so short as he jumped her clean off over his head in his big leap, but unfortunately she held on to the reins as she fell and cut his mouth badly with the bit. I bitterly hated that win for me, which left Prince Hal with his undeserved wound, and I blamed the committee for their sudden decision to bring in the second horses, which had not been written into the schedule.

After winning this championship Hal beat the Italians in the Victor Ludorum *Daily Mail* Cup, winning it for the second time at White City. He won two more championships at Blackpool the next week but suddenly fell ill a fortnight later. He never jumped again, in spite of the expert care that he got at the Newmarket Research Centre. A post mortem showed that he had an irreversible heart condition, but he died suddenly at Newmarket while I was jumping in New York during the American fall. I was second that night on Flanagan, after reading the tragic telegram from Newmarket; some people thought that I was crying because I had been beaten. Pauline Sykes was as shattered as myself with the awful news, as she had loved that horse more than any other, putting up patiently with all his naughty and playful habits. Hal's death had been announced on the late news programme of the BBC.

Inevitably Toronto was an anticlimax with the shadow of Hal's death hanging over my horse activities. Flanagan and Private Enterprise, a horse I had been lent for the American circuit did win the two horse event for me, but Flanagan, in great form for the Individual Championship, was ten seconds ahead of Ted Williams on Pegasus, over the last fence of the final jump off, only to duck the wrong side of the time finish, thinking he had to cut the corner to go round again. This cost three faults and second place. Ted and I can still laugh about this British Victory. Avery Brundage also disturbed one of my short nights of necessary sleep. When the English press phoned at 3.00 a.m. to enquire about my reaction to Mr Brundage declaring that I was a professional, after winning a Rolex watch in Geneva two years before. The Brundage accusation I laughed off, but I gave them my reaction to be awoken an hour after getting to bed at the end of an exhausting late evening show.

Toronto finished the season and I did not feel like returning to Hal's empty stable. Scraping enough together for a cheap return flight from New York to Buenos Aires with the $225 that Flanagan had won in the only competition of the three shows with prize money, I decided to spend Christmas with Uncle Hugo and Evelyne in Buenos Aires. I had made many friends in South America during the Stockholm Games, and hoped to see some of them again. The Chilean team were on the American tour and insisted that I came to jump at a Santiago show in the New Year.

After a lift back from Toronto to New York, I flew to Miami, then Caracas for the allowed twenty-four hours without a visa. There I happened to meet my old Spanish friend Angel Peralta, the *rejoneador*, who was performing that afternoon. Conversing with my Venezuelan military team friends, I noticed a lack of response when I enquired out of interest as to how their country was run.

Knowing that my Spanish was limited, I changed the subject to horses which I could talk about fluently and everyone else became enthusiastic too. At my next stop, Rio de Janeiro, I read in the morning paper that there had been a coup in Venezuela during the night, and I had just escaped in time. Perez-Jimenez, the last dictator of Venezuela had been tumbled, possibly just on the eve of invading British Guiana.

I was asked to ride two horses in the Prova Prince Hal Stakes, held in his memory, at a night show held under floodlights. Not only was I entertained by the Brazilian team, but Sir Geoffrey and Lady Harrison asked me to lunch at the lovely Embassy with a marvellous view over the bay. They were not looking forward to their impending move to Brazilia where all the Embassies would be centred in future. I was also initiated into the sport of water skiing with a boatful of beautiful Brazilian girls and sporting young men. On my first attempt I was towed around the bay sitting on my skis and blinded by spray without being able to get up. No-one wore life jackets in those days and the falls were hard. I bought half the Pacific Ocean in mastering mono ski as I returned along the western seaboard on that trip.

Christmas Day was passed in the campo north of Buenos Aires in Guarani country, with Hugo and Evelyne and their friends. We played the guitar until 3.00 a.m. on Boxing Day and I increased my repertoire of Guarani and Spanish folk songs with the Southern Cross shining down in a starry sky. It was the season for mosquitoes and pamperos, the tropical thunderstorms that came suddenly and violently in the New Year.

I was invited to the Military School at the Campo de Mayo to see their horses in training. An officer took me to their Mess where he gave me a picture from the wall, of a gaucho backing a bucking *criollo*, the wild Argentinian horse of the Pampa; it was *La primera ensillada*, the first saddling and has joined my other gaucho pictures at home.

Carlos Delia, now General, a top rider in the Argentine Olympic and International team, has been a good friend for the past thirty-five years while his quiet and effective jumping style has brought him success with many horses. He was appointed as UN Ambassador in Brussels where he could use his tact and fair diplomacy.

Hugo flew with me to my next stop in Chile, where he had Reyrolles Company work to do. I had been invited by the *Carabineros* to the *Escuela de Caballeria* to see the Cavalry school where Colonel Pelayo Izurieta entertained me at Quillote, after an exciting drive in a police car with sirens. At the horse show 'Huaso' was paraded, the great Thoroughbred, then twenty-five years old, who still held the High Jump record of 2m 47cm that he had achieved in 1949. He was ridden by Captain Alberto Larraguibel, who came to Europe with the Chilean team in the '50s. I was asked to give a demonstration of jumping on a four-year-old mare called after a Chilean melody, Tonada. This liver chestnut, Alezán Tostada, or toasted chestnut in Spanish, gave me such a nice ride that although she was young and inexperienced, I later bought her and brought her to England where Bernard, the Duke of Norfolk, took a share in her.

At Viña del Mar I learnt to dance the *Cueca* to the Chilean songs that I had already learnt on the guitar, before going to Concepción for a visit to the Schwager mines, where coal is mined from 7 km under the sea. Hugo had been down the mines, but ladies were banned from the shafts, as females were supposed to bring bad luck underground. That night, there was a little earthquake and everything in the room rattled with a frightening noise, while our hostess, the charming Inez Carhill, dropped to her knees in the doorway, the strongest place in the shaking house. She had survived the big Santiago earthquake some years before and experienced the death and destruction that followed. I felt relieved that ladies were not allowed down the mine shafts, with this additional hazard.

My departure for Lima was delayed by spending a day with a good friend, Isabel Aguirre, at her Santa Isabel Fundo, for a *Paseo al Campo con corrida en vacas*. Enjoying the *Huasos*, working the cows in a *Media luna*, the cowboys galloping to catch the young cows in the arena, we were sitting under trees that had runners of litre or poison ivy creeping over the trunks and branches. Soon after I began to feel a rash spreading up my veins while my eyes began to close with swollen eyelids and my throat felt that it was becoming constricted. A friend saw my plight and rushed me to the Carabineros Hospital. The first doctor to examine me shouted with joy, 'Get the others to come and see, this is the best case of litre allergy that we've had for years.' I had suffered from nettlerash desperately when I was a child, there had been times when I had written in my diary, 'Terrible nettlerash, I wish I could die.' I thought I had grown out of this unpleasant allergy but *litre* triggered it off again; however antihistamines had been refined and the allergy was calmed in a couple of days with injections, so that the raised red patches on my skin itched less and I could breathe comfortably again and fly on for a fascinating few days with Peruvian friends.

An ancient vase or *huaco* that was given to me in Peru, gave me a contact with the Pan Agra pilot who took me on to Mexico. He was intrigued by ancient South American civilizations so on seeing my *huaco* with the snake god, he took me down at dawn during the flight to fly around ancient pyramids in the jungle near Huehuetenango, after passing the volcanoes of Fuego and Agua in Guatemala. The other passengers were luckily sleeping so they did not note our descent to jungle level in order to inspect the site of an ancient Mayan civilisation. Mexico City was our destination, marked by the volcano pyramid of Popocatepetl and the sleeping lady Iztaccihuatl, where I arrived in time to be taken to the races and present the winner's trophy, by chance won by an English-bred filly.

A visit to Acapulco gave me my first experience of skin diving, an exhilarating experience once I had discovered that one had to swallow, to alleviate the pain and pressure from one's ears, while descending to the reefs so full of beautiful fish. The Mexican boy who accompanied me, suddenly reminded me that it was time to surface as the oxygen was running out after an hour of enchantment down below. We came up from deep down on the ocean floor too quickly for comfort but I dare not let him out of my sight, because there were big breakers on the surface. A month later, poor Pablo, the boy, came up too fast from a similar dive and got the bends, and had to be flown to the United States in a paralysed condition. Now people have better preparation and instruction, but I had been lucky to escape lightly in my ignorance.

A flight from Mexico to New York with another to London got me to Heathrow where I hoped to find my van, repaired after breaking down on my way to the airport several weeks before. To my relief some kind person had left it there, so I could fill it with my various acquisitions, like the rawhide *bosals* for horses, which are unbreakable head collars from Argentina, and the *huaco* vase from Peru, before driving home alone. On the way back I wisely pulled in to a layby for a half-hour snooze. No allowance was made for jet lag in those days!

The horses were ready for work and came with me to Davos where we got fit for the season ahead. I spent most of my spare time skiing, changing my boots and trousers directly each competition finished, to dash up the mountains to the ski runs, while the light still lasted. The next show, in Torino, also had ski slopes not too far away and I had a couple of days experiencing the Italian Alps, and seeing mountains that I had read about in the annals of the mountaineers. The horses benefited too from their Davos work in the pure mountain air, the resort that had cured my grandfather of TB and where Gordon and Eric, my father, had grown up. Horses and riders alike stored up energy from the mountains for the year of tough international shows ahead.

Two new horses came for me to jump in June 1958. Janet Kidd's 'Grand Manan', a strong horse to ride, was a novice, but 'Mr Pollard', belonging to John King, a friend of Bob Hanson's, who I had met with his wife Lorna and family, came to me too. Mr Pollard, a sensitive chestnut horse, that had been refusing with another rider, seemed to enjoy our partnership. We won the *Daily Telegraph* Championship at the Richmond Royal Horse Show, which surprisingly was worth only £10 in 1958, while Flanagan was 3rd for £5! He won the Ladies Championship at Aachen followed by the Queen's Cup at White City for £50. I had always had to save my horse for the Nation's Cup which followed the ladies competition, and had not been able to risk a galloping jump off in the Queen's Cup before the big Team event. This was my only win in the Queen's Cup for the ladies while in the Victor Ludorum after the Team event, one could risk all to win. Mr Pollard was not in the Nation's Cup, which meant that I could take risks in a timed jump off that would be inadvisable with a team horse. I was grateful to 'Mr P' for my one Queen's Cup victory, after a string of seconds in this competition, although my horses had done me proud in the *Daily Mail* Victor Ludorum which was the goal for the cream of the International Championships.

John King's Mr Pollard also gave me a last win at Harringay. Finality had won the first 'Leading Show Jumper of the Year' in 1949, and 'Mr P' won the last one in 1958, before the show was moved to Wembley, where Flanagan won this same class in 1962. In 1989, forty years on, I was able to congratulate Steven Smith, Harvey's younger son, for his victory in this prestigious competition. Steven had helped the British Team to win a Silver Olympic medal in the Los Angeles Games as a young amateur, when his brother Robert, a very polished rider and Harvey, were both professionals, therefore ineligible for the Olympics.

Horse Box Lane at Harringay and Wembley could have told many stories. Paula, my girl groom and I used to muck out our horse box, when the horses were unloaded and put in their clean stables, while we turned the horse box into our living quarters. In wet weather, nothing got dry and the floor of the box had a damp horsey perfume of its own. Kind cousins in town then offered to put me up for the show, giving me a key, in the days when one had little trouble in parking around Kensington High Street. It was a luxury to have a bath, washing the cinders of the collecting ring out of one's skin, hair, nose and throat. Now the warm-up arenas are covered with friendly tan bark and sand. If one had a fall on the cinders, the black clinker would get into wounds and could scar for a lifetime. We always coughed for a week after these shows with one's lungs coated with the horrible black dust.

This did not deter the night life of various sportsmen and women. I was lucky enough to have special friends Frank and Cynthia Haydon, who were the great breeders and drivers of the hackney horse. They also were involved in the show management and expert in organising displays and showmanship for the public.

One evening, Frank mentioned that he had found an excellent restaurant that stayed open late, so would I like to come and dine. During the show I was jumping in qualifying rounds from 8 a.m. until the championship classes finished at 11 p.m., so one never had time to sit down for a meal. I gratefully accepted and went out for a superb late dinner. Meanwhile at the show, some bottles had been drunk, probably on empty stomachs, like mine had been before my welcome luxury meal. The move to Wembley had provided a new toy or torture, to the night life. There was a pond between the caravans and horseboxes of the inhabitants of the show and the cinder collecting ring, which was immediately sized up with mischievous joy or foreboding from the knowledge of past experience. That night, a gathering of friends and riders drifted up to Cynthia's caravan. 'She's gone off with your man has she? Let's hang the witch!' was the general consensus and Cynthia was a ring leader where fun and games were going on.

The shops in the passage around the arena were closed for the night, but that did not deter the guys who went to find a model with a lady's black riding jacket on it. They chose Wetherills, obviously sensing that a touch of class was needed, and another got hold of a white carnation to put in the buttonhole. The noose was fixed and the rope thrown over the branch of the tree by the pond. My effigy was then hauled up amidst cries of 'Burn the witch!', together with other descriptive shouts.

I had a wonderful meal and went back for a good sleep at my cousins, while Frank returned to the revellers at Wembley. History does not relate if Bernard Wetherill, since our 154th Rt Hon. Speaker of the Commons got to hear of the escapade, but at the height of the revelry, Harvey Smith came running back from the Arena building and shouted, 'Hey Cynth, the coppers after you, get that bxxxxx dummy back into Wetherills, quick,' so a hurried return of the rather battered dummy and classical black jacket, saved Cynthia from getting copped and left the Bobby probably laughing under his helmet. Bernard Wetherill has also remained a good friend who I meet at functions of our mutual Guild of the Worshipful Company of Farriers.

The following night, the highlight of the evening was the Hackney Horse of the Year Championship. Sir Michael Ansell, the Show Director, who had been given a report on the previous evening's escapade, and chose to ignore it, asked me to present the Championship Cup to the winning hackney. Sir Mike had a great sense of humour which maybe tempted him to give me the honour of making the presentation. He knew that Cynthia, the outstanding lady whip, or driver, was competing with their great horse Finality, a top showman in the ring.

My eye glinted as Finality took the honours. Amongst the championship rosettes I had placed a cord, made into a noose. I came to Cynthia to shake hands, then while giving her the rosettes I said, 'Many congratulations, Mrs Haydon, for your great victory with Finality – and you know what you can do with the other,' I added *sotto voce* while keeping a straight face.

No one was exempted from the 'treatment'. One time Douggie Bunn drove his new Rolls Royce to the show with his caravan attached. This was too much for Johnnie Kidd, who proceeded to remove the wheels of the Rolls while Douggie was dining at the restaurant overlooking the arena. When he came to drive home, he did not notice in the dark that the wheels had gone, but tried to get his caravan up to the exit. Later that night the wheels were found where they had rolled down to the hollow which used to contain the pond.

Another night Frank Haydon awoke with a start, to find a monkey in his bed. It had escaped, perhaps with help, from Eric Ixer's caravan, a gentleman who always travelled with his monkey, and it had climbed through the Haydon's open window.

The Wembley pond has long been drained and Frank and Cynthia are still my best friends who I have turned to in any time of trouble since my first heartbreak over Finality.

My horses went home to rest after Wembley and Paris, but I went on to Sicily without them, where a storm flooded out the first day's jumping, but I could enjoy the island and its history. The sons of the Principe Vincenzo di San Vincenzo had stayed at Miserden to learn English and agriculture, and their parents were friends from Palermo, when I had first competed there. The riders already knew Taormina well, where we used to go to eat pizzas and dance at night during the Catania Show. Pietro and Guiseppe took me to Enna, Monreale with the Cathedral mosaics, to the Roman town of Salunto, where we lunched with their uncle at Solunto castle and bathed in the sea off the rocks below, getting stung by Medusas, the little jelly fish pest of the seas, before going on to Cefalu with its superb *Duomo*, although the boys were more fascinated by the French nudist camp!

Montelepre had been the home of Giuliano who lost his young life with Mafioso affairs, a contrast to the less violent lives of the Capuccini monks, whose tiny bodies were preserved in the dry air of the catacombs. A Sunday mass in the beauty and peace of the Capella Palatina with Dr Carlo Cheli, the expert who cared for this chapel gem, gave me a moment to digest the turbulent times that

Sicily had suffered through the centuries. There had been a British Bishop of Palermo about the time of the murder of St Thomas à Becket, who figures in some of the Sicilian mosaics of the saints.

Two days later while returning, I was present at St Peter's Rome for the white smoke that signified the choice of the Pope Giovanni 23rd, after which he appeared on the balcony to give his blessing. My ten days impromptu culture tour was rounded off by hearing Boris Christoff singing *Boris Godunov* at Covent Garden.

South America called again with the Inter-Continental Championships of 1958 being held in Viña del Mar, Chile. The Equestrian Federation had invited myself and 'Monkey' Blacker, from the UK with two riders each from France, Germany, Spain and Italy to compete against riders from Chile, Argentina and Colombia. We had to draw for horses that had been lent for us to ride and mine turned out to be an old Thoroughbred with a foot problem, but luckily 'Monkey' rode a good horse superbly to gain second from the French Olympic medallist Pierre Jonquères d'Oriola.

My last round in the arena had caused great participation and sympathy from the crowd, when my horse had lost his nerve and stopped, falling in the second fence on top of me. Although my back had been hurt on the poles of the fence, I remounted and finished the rest of the course clear. The faults for this fall with time faults added were 29$^{1}/_{2}$ faults. The crowd were furious, 'Put on the tax!' or VAT, 'How much for dying?'. Whistles and boos for the score had to be quietened before the next horse could compete.

Paco Goyoaga of Spain and d'Oriola were invited with me to Lima and Mexico where we again drew horses to ride at the Colegio Militar and made many friends. Our hosts rewarded us with surfing at Waikiki near Lima and water skiing, skin diving and ocean fishing at Acapulco, where we watched with trepidation the young *clavidistas* diving 135 feet from the top of the Quebrada into the narrow and shallow gully of swelling waves below, lit at night only by the flame of burning newspapers on the other side of the rocks. We riders agreed together to keep to our own sport.

Bob Hanson being a Yorkshireman and holding an important place in the Great Yorkshire Show Committee, including a stretch as President, liked me to bring Flanagan to his show, where Flanagan rose to the occasion and usually did very well. One of the great pleasures of being in Yorkshire, was being invited to stay with Major and Mrs Horton Fawkes at Farnley Hall.

In this rambling sixteenth-century house, Walter Ramsden Fawkes had entertained the artist Turner. He was keen on agriculture and bred exotic breeds of animals; politically he was a Whig representing the County of York in Parliament. He had bought Turner watercolours from 1803 and acquired the series of Rhine drawings and views of Farnley and its neighbourhood in 1817. Turner became his best friend and was a regular visitor from 1810 until the death of Fawkes in 1825. There were superb watercolours of birds and plumage that Turner had painted for the book that Fawkes' brother had written on ornithology. The *Frosty Morning* hanging in the Tate Gallery was painted on his way to

Farnley in 1813, and *The Slavers* was painted to depict Fawkes' goal in Parliament: the abolition of slavery.

They would fish and shoot on the grouse moors together but after Walter Fawkes died, Turner never visited Farnley again. My room there had a great Turner painting on the wall, which would gradually light up with the sunrise, letting me absorb all the details as the light increased and rays of sun touched the colours.

Flanagan seemed happy to come jumping again in the spring when I took him to Lisbon, where he won the Grand Prix and was the best individual with the only two clear rounds in the Nation's Cup, and again the best individual in the Madrid Nation's Cup and in the winning team at Rotterdam.

The Olympic year of 1960 started for me in Cape Town, where three horses lent to me won the four competitions at the show, before Flanagan started his Olympic training. I was also given the chance to ride Sunsalve, a fantastic horse, but as he got fitter he became too strong for me and David Broome then jumped the horse in the ring, while only his father Fred rode him outside the ring. This excellent teamwork between father and son worked well as the horse was quiet with Fred, knowing that he would not be jumped, although he could get excited beyond reasonable control when jumping. I had won the Cardiff championship on him and had clear rounds in the Olympic training display at Newark, Windsor and Devon Country, but at Wiesbaden he was jumping recklessly and I was happy to keep to my obedient Flanagan, who cheerfully won the Grand Prix at the following show in Lucerne.

Sam's mother and father Marguerite and Harty Koechlin had a lovely holiday house, called the Eichstutz, built into the lake on the opposite side from the Halde where the show used to be held. They always entertained the riders there, and I saw Sam briefly, when he told me sadly that Goya had hurt her leg in an Olympic trial event and she would not be sound for him to ride in the Swiss three-day event team in Rome. I agreed to take her to England to breed from, as I already had bred four foals from Tosca and Goya could run out in the field and go to the stud together with Tosca.

The Eichstutz party for the teams was luckily on one of the fine evenings in Lucerne that year and some of us were brave enough to swim in the freezing lake. When I climbed onto the moored raft to warm up before the sun went down, the vet from the Romanian team came to join me. He spoke to us all in fluent French, which the Russian commissar, to his chagrin, could not understand. We had been talking about folk music and I wanted to learn the words of a Russian song for the guitar. He taught me the words and melody as the sky changed colour with the rays of the setting sun shining on the raft, while the commissar watched from the balcony of the Eichstutz, frustrated because he could neither swim nor speak French. At the Rome Olympics two months later, the Romanian team vet had been replaced by one that only spoke and understood Russian.

The Russian team too, had this awful fear of being watched all the time, feeling guilty of being seen with any foreigners. I talked several times with Sergei Filatov, the dressage Gold Medallist at Rome, but sometimes his expression would change and his voice trail off as he saw another Russian approach to monitor our conversation, which held no security risk, but often laughter, as I tried to find a brighter side to the lives of these civil servants.

The Russian dressage riders at Rome seemed to possess only one hunting stock tie between them. A special and unusual knot finishes the stock to perfection but the stock is only used once as it needs to be crisp and starched with a tie pin to fix its appearance. My stock pin was made from the floating false collarbone found in a lion's shoulder, a small bone with native mythical luck attached, and given to me by a close friend who had been born and raised in African lion country.

In Rome the weather was hot and riding a dressage test needs hard work for the ten minutes that the competitor is in the arena, so the Russians' stock got soggy and wet as it was passed on to the next Russian rider. The last one had to ride with a limp wet rag tied around his throat, a far cry from the elegant image of an immaculately-dressed showman on a proud dressage horse. Filatov's lovely little horse Absent stood only 15 hh, making up in showmanship for what he lacked in size to merit the Gold.

I remembered the time at the previous Olympics in Stockholm, where the Russian team had first competed after the war. Their technical delegate Colonel Abel, had suggested to me, at a party for the riders given by the Russians, that I should marry a Russian. I would then be given the best horses and facilities for training and my life would be happy ever after. Our team had been warned not to drink anything at the party, but no one had cautioned me of the possibility that I might be tempted to Russia for a future of breeding little Russian riders, who would be taught to show jump by their mother. I was still damp from dancing with a Russian team official, an imposing and large man, from whose clutches I had escaped to recover from my low tolerance to BO.

Scorchin', my old friend from before the Stockholm Olympics came back into my life, when he was given to me to ride as reserve horse for the Rome Olympics. We soon renewed our partnership and he won the Victor Ludorum *Daily Mail* Cup at White City, while Flanagan won his old partner's event, the Prince Hal Stakes and also the *Country Life* Cup. Dorothy Paget died at this time and later in the year I was able to buy Scorchin' from the executors, so that he could spend the rest of his life with me, his last years hunting happily with the Cotswold Hounds where he was much admired.

At Dublin, Judge Wylie was the kingpin of the show and a character of that era, and we became friends. He had once dared me to smoke one of his cigars before a big competition. I could not let down the name of our team and smoked the cigar, although I do not smoke, to the bitter butt, and then won the competition.

Olympic Teams were competing in Dublin before the 1960 Games in Rome. The Judge congratulated me with a wink when I was presented with a silver cigar box by the Royal Dublin Society with the Ball's Bridge Trophy for the Leading Rider of the Show.

The Rome Olympics were magnificent, but lacked for me that camaraderie that had joined all the riders together in one big family at Stockholm in 1956. We were segregated in nations in the Olympic village and as I was the only lady rider I had to sleep with the ladies' team of fencers who finished their event at 2.00 a.m.

while I got up at 3.40 a.m. to carry my boots silently down the concrete stairs. My showjumping friends were finding the same problem as they had not met their national athletes or swimmers before, but at least they had the companionship of their own male team mates.

The team event was still held with only three riders, each score counting for the final result as at Stockholm. Our team trainer, Colonel Jack Talbot Ponsonby decided to use the Individual Jumping competition to decide whether myself or Dawn Wofford would be in the team. Dawn was riding her husband Warren's grand old horse Hollandia which had jumped in the American Olympic team eight years before.

Flanagan had proved he could be trusted for the team event even if he was not athletic enough to get in the individual medals over a huge course. David Broome on the brilliant but unpredictable Sunsalve was in both events, but Jack was so sure of David Barker and Franco, who had been consistent in training but lacked big competition experience, that he kept him for the team and did not test him in the individual event.

The course in the Piazza di Siena was of maximum difficulty, with the treble altered by the technical delegate to an almost unjumpable distance. Good horses fell there and Flanagan as well was caught out by the one-and-a-half strides to the last element, but we extracted ourselves from the shattered poles without falling and we were balanced before clearing the following fence. In the second round he just managed to clear the treble with a huge effort, pulling us up to individual tenth place, the same as at Stockholm, to put us in the team. Sunsalve, superbly ridden by David Broome, was undeterred by some wild jumps and a stop and won the Bronze medal behind Raimondo and Piero d'Inzeo. The only clear showjumping round of the games was jumped that morning at 7.30 a.m. by Raimondo on Posillipo, witnessed by most of the riders but few of the public.

One of the casualties of the terrible treble had been our German friend Fritz Thiedemann who fell there with his great international showjumper Meteor. During an exercising session before the competition began, we had heard one of the dressage riders saying he had watched Fritz doing flying changes at the canter and thought that his own horse was better at one time changes. Fritz was a unique rider who was competing in both Olympic dressage and show jumping on two specialist horses trained for the different disciplines. When the dressage rider saw Fritz ride, we were laughing because he had been amusing himself doing flying changes on Meteor.

Our medal chances looked possible when we walked the Nation's Cup course early on the closing day of the games. A fair Olympic course had been built with a very big water jump. Our first horse in was Franco, eighth to go, but already Turkey and Brazil were eliminated with their first horses and the Russian had finished with 50.75 faults. David Barker entered quietly on Franco, perhaps underestimating the daunting effect that entering down a steep ramp into the huge bowl of an arena, can have on an inexperienced horse. Approaching the treble he got slower and Franco lost his impetus and stopped at the second element of a wall. No one had seen Franco stop before, he again refused a second time, and with both of them flustered they got going until the last fence, a parallel over a water ditch. Again he slowed down and ran out to the left of the fence. Our team was eliminated before 8.00 a.m., the culmination of the years of preparation for us all.

I did not expect to jump now that the team was eliminated, so I left the stadium to go to the collecting arena for the horses. I found the grooms with long faces having heard the shattering news over the loudspeaker, but I jumped onto Flanagan to give him some work before the sun was too hot. Colonel Jack appeared, to tell me that we would jump, as already four nations had been eliminated and the committee were afraid that there would be no entertainment for the public in the sold-out arena that afternoon. Flanagan and I got to work seriously and were soon heading down the ramp feeling like early Christians being fed to the lions in the arena. I knew we were only jumping for the public and not competing in the Olympic Games. However we concentrated on doing our best and Flanagan finished well, with just three fences down. Sunsalve and David Broome also had the same score, but in the afternoon for the second round in the packed and stifling arena with the sun beating down, Sunsalve was duly impressed with the atmosphere and heat, listened to David's accurate riding commands and jumped a round that everyone thought to be the only clear of the day, but a late decision to call a fault at the water changed the electric score board from 0 to 4.

That afternoon's ordeal had been intensified for me through an unnecessary mistake. The vets had given me a lift to the stadium where one of them had seized my small cap bag, with my riding hat, spurs, gloves and clean stock in it, saying that he wanted to carry it for me. I hung onto my engraved whip, one that Prince Philip had presented to Wilf, Peter and myself after our Bronze medal in the Stockholm Olympics. The vet then disappeared. As the time drew nearer to my entering the arena, my cap bag had still not been given back to me. I sent messages over every microphone that I could get hold of, but in the tight security I could not go to the officials' stand. At the last moment I started to borrow a hat, I could not find a spare stock or gloves to fit me and I was in a furious panic when my cap bag was brought to me.

Trying to tie my stock while I was on the ramp leading down to the arena, put me in a fighting mood to give Flanagan the best ride I could to help him jump this huge course in the hot and stuffy weather that he detested. He responded with all his heart and gave his all over his sixth Olympic round in two Games. He was the bravest of them all, and even cheekily stuck his tongue out, over the bit, which did not help my steering problems. I have a photo to prove his defiance and show-manship to the packed crowd on all sides of the arena.

I left the bright lights of Rome for the muted lighting in Budapest, where a friend, David Ascoli, a Director of Cassell who published my books, invited me to see Budapest with him, a city he had known before the time of the Iron Curtain. The streets were now empty and the houses were still pockmarked with bullets from the 1956 uprising. I had heard the live reports coming into Rome, four years earlier, when the Russian tanks had rolled into the city. The loss of an Olympic

(*above left*) Serenading Flanagan with the guitar. (*above right*) A different sort of mount: a white racing camel at El Golea in Algeria, 1956.

(*below*) With Colonel Gordon Smythe, Uncle Gordon (Dad's older brother), at Buckingham Palace 1956. I had just received the OBE from the Queen.

(*above*) A sporting encounter with Danny Kaye.

(*above*) Tosca with her second foal, La Favorita, 1958.

(*right*) Mr Pollard, belonging to John King, now Lord King of Wartnaby, who won me my only Queen's Cup at White City, 1958.

medal was quickly put into perspective when one witnessed a nation's loss of freedom. The older generation who had learnt German, as part of the Austro–Hungarian empire, would whisper *Freiheit* to us, when they sensed our sympathy. I hear that life in Budapest has greatly changed since then and the lights are bright again, with traffic busy on the roads. In Vienna and Munich, where David Ascoli had been educated after the Great War, we heard wonderful opera performed by top singers. We were given a special performance of the Spanish Riding School with Colonel Alois Podhajsky who entertained us with several of the Olympic riders from Rome and General Stoychev of Bulgaria, friend and representative of the FEI at the Olympics.

When I got home, full of my new impressions of Austria and Hungary, I found that the horses had also benefited from their fortnight's break after the Olympics, and were full of energy and mischievous ideas. My attempts to give them enough work, the first time I rode them, finished with my being so exhausted and stiff that I had to go up the stairs on all fours. Two weeks away from riding had affected my muscles but the horses did not show any relaxation in their Olympic muscle power although their holiday had given them an increased sense of humour.

6

Round the World:
1961

The interest that I had always had in wildlife in our countryside was stimulated by Peter Scott's far seeing plans for conservation. Together with his naturalist friends and fellow scientists, he had discussed the urgent need for a world wide plan to conserve nature, as species of animals were becoming endangered and disappearing along with the natural habitat on which their lifestyle depended. The whole project would need to be financed by forming a world wildlife fund. This would also aim to increase public awareness of the international problems with the environment and the immediate importance and urgency of the work involved.

Already the IUCN, the International Union for Conservation of Nature and Natural Resources, had been formed in 1948, when Sir Julian Huxley was Director General of UNESCO. The scientists and specialists working in the IUCN, hoped to influence Governments and other organisations to cooperate in stemming the destruction of the forest, flora and fauna, with the resulting danger of the extinction of species.

Sir Julian had written alarming articles in the *Observer* in 1960, warning that the unique wildlife of East Africa could be extinct within twenty years, if nothing was done to avert the dramatic decline in many species. Prince Bernard of the Netherlands, who was involved with other conservation movements, then became the first President of the WWF; the Duke of Edinburgh also gave it his strong support and was to become the President twenty years later.

The World Wildlife Fund formed in 1961 became a focus of public attention with the first public realisation of the effects of man's exploitation of the wild, and the consequences to the ecology of the countryside. The essential funds being raised by the WWF were then used for financing the IUCN's projects to protect endangered species and habitat in the world, with well-known and successful people encouraged to join the organisation to give their advice and expertise in finance, advertising and management, to see that all donated money was put to the best use. Some incredibly generous Trustees gave their free time and often their staff and business facilities to help the cause.

Peter Scott had been a friend since the 1940s when he came to Slimbridge to create his sanctuary for wildfowl on the River Severn below our house on the Cotswolds. I was fascinated with his knowledge as a naturalist, and his expertise in any activity in which he became involved increased my esteem. His complete modesty camouflaged a constant interest and quest to gain further experience and information from the world around us. In 1945 he had spotted the two lesser white-fronted geese among the resident flock of white fronts on the Dumbles, the tidal marshes of the Severn at Slimbridge. This was only the second recorded sighting of these geese in Britain. His plan to set up a centre there, now called the Wildfowl and Wetlands Trust, has been fully justified. It represents the world's most complete collection of wildfowl.

At the first meeting of the British National Appeal of the World Wildlife Fund in 1961 Peter was surprised to be elected Chairman. When he died just before his eightieth birthday in 1989 he was still Hon. Chairman of the International Council of the World Wide Fund for Nature as the WWF had become. He had seen his original plan grow into the biggest single conservation organisation in the world, which today has branches in twenty-eight countries and exercises a powerful influence on all governments.

Setting up the WWF in 1961 to work in collaboration with the IUCN, was the first step in recognising the critical situation arising from the increasing world population. More land was being exploited world-wide for subsistence by refugees or squatters, while profit-seekers too were moving into virgin forest and habitat with the aid of modern machinery. There had been no overall control of indiscriminate killing of wildlife for meat, ivory, horn or other commercial aspects. In India the tiger population had decreased drastically by being killed for trophies and as an enemy of man and his livestock. The human population explosion was taking over increasing areas of the natural habitat of the wild animals, which were becoming confined to smaller areas with an insufficient supply and variety of their normal food. Man was encroaching on the historical range of wildlife causing an incompatible situation for coexistence.

The WWF 'Project Tiger' was launched in 1972 when the census of the Bengal Tiger showed numbers had sunk to under 2,000 from an estimated 40,000 in 1900. Guy Mountford played an important part in this project, which resulted in the creation of fifteen wildlife reserves and National Parks in India. He was one of the original group of conservationists to have founded the WWF in 1961, in 1976 being awarded the Gold Medal of the WWF. He was a leader in the Tiger Project that has indeed saved the tiger, which now has a population of about 4,500, and has restored a superb part of India's natural heritage.

Guy, an internationally famous ornithologist has written many books on conservation and ornithology. He also leads expeditions to Coto Doñana in Spain, through central Europe, the Middle East, Africa and the Indian continent to the Himalayas, creating many wildlife reserves through his influence and contacts in these varied and valuable habitats for the local flora and fauna.

The plight of the world today, still suffering from the rapid destruction of the environment, would be far worse but for the conservation movement aroused by the action of these dedicated people over the past three decades. My contribution during this time was to encourage the people I met in the world of sport and influential positions, to become aware of the need for concerted action for the protection of our precious resources and the life that they sustained.

I had the chance to learn more about wildlife and different habitats while visiting Africa and South and North America, staying with friends who shared my interest and who knew the local flora and fauna of their region. In 1953 I found that the King Ranch had a carefully planned wildlife policy for conservation, even forming breeding stock units of endangered species to breed in the safety of monitored areas of the huge ranch. One of the less popular species that Bob had given sanctuary to during the war were the white and wild Park cattle, an ancient British breed that were so aggressive, that the cowboys treated them with the greatest of respect and dared not go near them.

I was to meet Bob Kleberg's friend and business partner in Australia at the Royal Richmond Show in 1958. Sam Hordern and his delightful wife wanted to invite me to Australia to the Easter Show at Sydney. I already had invitations to South America and Africa on my agenda before the Olympic Games, so he cheerfully asked me for Easter 1961 which I gratefully accepted, as I was longing to see the flora and fauna of the Antipodes, and to meet the people.

Sam was a most kind and humorous friend and I admired his efficient and broad-minded approach to life. It came as a terrible shock to hear that he had been killed in an accident while returning from the races in a chauffeur-driven car. His loss left a void in the lives of his many friends and in the activities that he had sponsored and encouraged.

After this tragedy, I thought no further about the invitation, but later I heard from the Sydney Royal Easter Show Committee that they would still like me to ride there in March 1961. The air ticket that accompanied this invitation provided an opportunity for me to stop on my route around the world to see new countries and people and to learn from them about their wildlife and ideas for conservation needs. Friends helped me with contacts who knew the background of each country where they lived and worked. I had let my New Zealand friends know that I would visit them on my way to Sydney, and they immediately organised a three week tour of both islands, with me giving lectures and demonstrations in a different place every day. I was surprised to receive their tough itinerary and had to shorten my brief visit to Hawaii and cut out my planned stop in Fiji.

Peter Scott had started a breeding programme at Slimbridge for the rare Hawaiian geese, néné, a word like their soft vocal calls. The first pair of geese that were sent to Gloucestershire from a ranch under the Mauna Loa volcano, had both laid eggs. The two sexes are so similar that they can only be distinguished apart while courting. Peter then returned for a gander in order to start one of his very successful projects to breed an endangered species. When the numbers increased some of his Slimbridge-bred birds were reintroduced to their native home in Hawaii. The research programme carried on at Slimbridge with breeding rare and unstudied species of waterfowl, has added a wealth of knowledge for conservationists.

Storms over the Hawaiian islands disrupted my plan to visit other friends of Bob Kleberg's, Haku and Richard Baldwin who lived on the edge of the caldera of Maui, a smaller island than Hawaii. The bird life was not too visible during the rain that pelted the islands, but I hoped that I could return in better conditions and with time to give to the very active Pony Club, and to see some of the rich and varied nature of the islands.

New Zealand was ahead of me with the daunting three week programme. I was to see some of the beautiful parts of these lovely islands, but had little time to explore the wilder and most fascinating places.

The limestone pastures make the country ideal for breeding horses, with good bones and strong limbs. Some of the young Thoroughbreds were most impressive and trainers in England have since become buyers of their horses, especially for National Hunt racing, where the horse needs more time to mature. Between my engagements of jumping demonstrations and judging at shows, and the lectures and Pony Club talks that had been arranged, I visited a few of the excellent studs where some English Thoroughbreds were standing and saw the good young stock that was being produced. I had bought a part-bred New Zealand show-jumper after the Rome Olympics and was impressed by his ability.

The changing countryside with volcanoes responsible for so much of the differing habitat was an education for me. Lake Taupo with its cold clear water and yet with boiling hot springs around parts of the shore, provided a hazard for water skiers, who had to get out of the lake through the very hot water. The thriving fish showed that they flourished in those waters, and were unaffected by the hot sulphur and radium springs with geysers spouting to tremendous heights, steaming and gushing up from the silica rocks. A cold trout stream ran through without the temperatures being affected, even after flowing over a bed of hot pumice sand. Guide Rangi was the famous Maori who showed us the Maori village at Rotorua, while telling us the history of her people and her pride when she had conducted the Queen and Prince Philip around her village, with the big geyser cooperating and spouting while they watched. Trees grew quickly in the thermal belt and the natural resource of steam is harnessed for energy. The scenery around the blue expanse of Lake Taupo and the beautiful Waikato River, especially where it leaves the lake and cascades over the Huka Falls foaming into a deep blue pool, made my short visit there a unique memory, before getting back to Taihape in time to give enthusiastic Pony Club people, who had travelled as far as eighty miles, an evening talk and films of the Rome Olympics.

Several New Zealanders had stayed at our guest house and had become good friends like my hosts there, Will and Joyce Duncan, who by chance had stayed with us at Miserden in the early 1950s. Just before they arrived, Mother had been killed, leaving me alone to entertain and cook for them. This experience made us close friends. Another New Zealander, Dudley Chambers had come hunting with us, sometimes riding Mother's chestnut hunter Rolling Home. Dudley was doing a parachute course at the time and once as I drove him to Cheltenham station down the steep and rough Leckhampton Hill, the passenger door on our utility van flew open, a habit that I had not warned him about. 'Head in, feet together, left shoulder roll' I heard him mutter his parachute drill, as I grabbed him just in time.

He and his wife Pauline invited me up to their back country station, Mangao-hane, where from the dirt tracks along the mountainside there were beautiful views across the flat topped Aorangi, the Maori reserve of the mountain of the long white cloud. From another high point the distant top of the 3,000 metre Ruapehu was hidden in cloud. The sheep, cattle and horses on the station shared their range with wild pig, stags with herds of deer, possum that also had to be controlled and the wild life of the mountain sides. Every shepherd had his sheep dogs that were always near at hand.

During my round of shows I heard of the brown weka bird with a short square tail, that runs but cannot fly; so I asked to see one, as the young men at the show had told me that they were easy to catch. A full night's search was required before the weka was secured and showed to me by an exhausted rider. After the bird's photo had been taken, it walked back happily into the scrub and disappeared.

In South Island, my furthest stop to the south was Dunedin with its Scottish background that shines through in place names and speech. The great mountains on the west coast beckoned me to further visits after one day's tantalising visit to Lake Wakatipu, the lake that breathes, with its rise and fall of three inches every five minutes. The lake is famed for its fishing while the surrounding jagged peaks top 2,600 m with a constant change of colour that gives them the name of 'The Remarkables'.

Between shows I was taken back country to the lakes to see Merino and Corriedale sheep living precarious lives on the sides of the gorges leading down to rocky tumbling streams; the local bird life that abounded would need weeks of study, although the black swans on the lakes I could identify from Peter Scott's breeding pair at Slimbridge.

During the lunch break at the Christchurch Show I'd arranged to hear Maori songs at the Maori girls school. The harmonious and musical singing remains as a highlight of my New Zealand visit. Water skiing on the Pacific swell of the Gisburn rollers and swimming in the fast-flowing Ngaruroro River at Tukituki, riding bareback on Rajah, a grey showjumper, followed by his friend a tame deer, were other brief but unforgettable impressions from this varied and lovely country.

In Australia I met many friends and acquaintances who had emigrated from Europe. There was Franz Mairinger who had spent many years in the Spanish Riding School at Vienna, and had since trained the Australian team for dressage. Carl Jurinack was building the jumping course at the Camden Show where I first tried out the two horses that I had been lent to jump. He had been at the Stockholm and Rome Olympics and we could discuss the courses for those events. My hosts were Clive and June Ogilvy. Clive, several years later, joined the board of Ciba Geigy Australia, when Sam was Chairman of the International Board at Basel. I also made a new friend in Jim Barnes' wife, Anya, who had been dancing with the Russian ballet before she married and we could talk a little of the artistic world that she had left. This country gave me a feeling of being more international and less isolated than I had expected.

Sydney Royal Easter Show proved to be a grand spectacle with the valuable livestock being displayed as well as all the horse classes and jumping; the final night providing floodlit hazards of the rodeo with buck jumpers and wild bulls carrying big horns, reminiscent of my North American rodeo souvenirs from 1953. My two horses, Colin Kelly's Polar Bay and Ted Dwyer's Ocean Foam carried me well and Ted's big grey won for me and eventually was ridden in the following 1964 Olympics by Kevin Bacon for Australia.

Early on Easter morning there was a Sung Eucharist at St Mark's Church, Darling Point, where the vicar told me that he knew my brother Ronald. In New Zealand too, I had found little churches in country places, which gave one a better insight and feeling for the life in the locality, with friendly and welcoming people.

The comparative sophistication of Sydney was quickly put in perspective on the drive north following the show, to Camboon in Queensland. The miles of road, sometimes bitumen and sometimes dirt, took us through forests of white gum trees which survive with little nourishment on the rocky mountains, swept by wind, rain and lightning. In the fertile river valleys the farms carried milking herds; one breed, the Irrawarra shorthorn had originated from an Ayrshire cross with Shorthorns.

Arriving off the plateau onto the dark and rich soil of the Darling Downs, the shimmering reflection off the black earth caused by the temperatures of earth and air, caused amazing mirages that I found more sensational than any desert mirages that I had seen. After another 400 miles of gravel roads north, we turned into the bush, where road casualties included a wombat, a kangaroo rat and a big wallaby. The wombat is a primitive and nocturnal animal, a vegetarian that lives in burrows and is descended from the wolves of Asia having arrived in Australia with migrating Aborigines. About the size of a small pig and as strong as badgers they can damage fences, making them unpopular with farmers.

We were not the only ones to make the trek to Camboon for the Picnic Races the next day. People had brought their swag, a bundle with a sleeping bag in it, and bedded down on the veranda, while young children slept in the back of their parent's shooting brakes. They were perhaps among the few to sleep that night, while a continuous party raged through Bill Bell's homestead, finishing with a barbecued breakfast of sausages and steaks done on an open fire.

The course for the races was a natural clearing in the bush which had been chain harrowed in parts. Bookies were already raising their radio aerials so that they could take bets for the races at Brisbane, Sydney and Melbourne. These picnic races were for 'grassfed' horses, that had just been caught up off the station for the event. Some started bucking when they saw the saddle, and most had no experience of being groomed. One hopeful guy holding a dandy brush near his nervous horse said 'If he's not the fastest, he'll be the prettiest horse!' His jockey was bucked clean off when they mounted for the race, but we didn't wait to hear if the horse was still thought to be pretty.

After the races local horses were loosed into the bush, while a barbecue was cooked for everyone. As the food, wine and goodwill flowed, the Abos started to dance a *Corroboree*, a saga sung to movements depicting the story, like the Maori action songs.

Returning along the more fertile, but developed coastal road, it was a hurried drive to Gunnedah, on the road before dawn each day, to be in time for me to open the show. I was asked to jump two nice horses and then presented the champion ribbons to the best Merino and also the Hereford bull; this was followed by more bronco riding. After meeting many Pony Club children, I had a new sport lined up for me; a trotting match against Bert Jacobs. Bert had ridden in the Stockholm Olympics, but was also an experienced driver of trotters, and had won his heat during the afternoon. I put on my silks and settled behind my little mare. Bert was off quickly and I felt my way behind him, getting the dirt back in my face. On the final circuit I had the feel of the mare and she was flying, so I pulled her outside Bert, with my very tired arms. We just passed him before the post, winning by a head. That was the good news, that the shouts of the crowd affirmed. Some of them had risked their money on me, the rank outsider, although officially there was no betting. The bad news for me was that my arms had given out, with the terrific pull that the mare had enforced during the race. I couldn't stop and my next lap, taken by the crowd as a victory *tour d'honneur*, was really a runaway round. At last I edged her onto the grass in the centre and she slowed down and stopped when she left the running track. My hands and arms were trembling from the exertion when I received the Championship red, white and blue rosette. Written in gold letters on this prize was 'Champion Male'.

To ease my stiff shoulders the next morning, I water-skied on a new dam, that was full of barely submerged stumps and fences, while slaloming around any trees that were still standing. I felt better when we left for the drive to Haddon Rig over part of the oldest mountain range in the world, the Warrumbungles, with odd-shaped rocky peaks that are difficult to climb.

The 95,000-acre station looked brown and dry from the drought. At the gate we crossed a creek, smothered in blue water hyacinths. A nurse had introduced the 'pretty plant' only eighteen months before and already the menace had spread down the creek to the lake. I had heard of the problems that this plant had caused, blocking waterways, in other continents. Introduced species have caused ecological upsets all over the world; once the balance of nature is affected in a locality, causing possible side effects, it is very difficult to put things back to normal without starting a chain reaction of other problems.

George Falkiner was a great authority on merino sheep, and his breeding stock commanded the best prices world wide. Pauline his wife was a judge of horses and a good rider who had also taken up driving hackney ponies. I had met her at the Royal International Horse Show at White City, when she was over to buy some ponies with Mr and Mrs Frank Haydon.

As well as the superb sheep, the station was overrun with kangaroos. The drought was serious and as one roo eats as much grass as five sheep each day, the kangaroos were having to be culled. I went out with the manager of a 25,000-acre division and saw the amazing sight of hundreds of kangaroos hopping everywhere. Up until then I had hardly seen any, and although Sam and I were to visit Australia several times in the following years, we were never to see a district where kangaroos thrived in such numbers.

It was tragic to see them culled but the alternative would have been starvation for the sheep. The red kangaroos were bigger and more beautiful than the grey ones, but they all had charming deer-like faces with big eyes and rabbity noses. There were so many kangaroos that the culling seemed hardly to affect their numbers. It was a relief that the emus were spared, although they eat grass too, but their large tough-shelled eggs make good eating. They are delightful to watch, running with long fast strides, then reaching a wire fence they put one foot on the top and hop over in a hilarious way. The flocks of galahs add colour to the scene and these parrot-like birds can become very tame.

When the kangaroo gives birth, the tiny blind naked joey clambers through the mother's belly hair to the pouch, where it fastens to the teat inside. It looks at first like an embryo before growing for weeks on the teat. Joeys only hop out of the pouch when they've grown a coat; leaping back into the pouch head first with their tail sticking out while their mothers hop along, they have to turn themselves the right way up. A koala cub is born the same way; only 2 cm long at birth, it stays on the mother's teat until it emerges at six months when it rides on the mother's front or back, being weaned before it is a year old.

Driving up the East Coast to Queensland, the short rivers from the coastal mountains to the sea are always prominently named as one crosses them, although signposts to where you want to go were noticeably absent. Water was a priority in a land of expanses of dry desert, where the other side of the coastal range was dry and barren. South of Canberra while staying with Ross and Anne Field, fellow conservationists, on their lovely Lanyon station, we went to see the Snowy Mountains scheme. The engineering project was designed to stop the waters of the Snowy River wasting their potential flowing into the Tasman Sea, by turning them back through the Great Dividing Range to irrigate the dry western plains. Hydro-electric stations were planned to create power while harnessing the water re-routed on its new course west, instead of east.

Canberra was turning an autumnal colour with its many British species of trees, a change from the gums and indigenous evergreens of much of the country-side. On the hillside grew kurrajong trees, and poplars lined the river which ran through deep fish pools and over rapids. Flocks of ibis, cockatoos, galahs, cuckoo shrikes and many species of honey eaters showed flashes of colour as we drove through the sheep stations. I left for Melbourne on the way to Victoria to look at farming conditions around Caramut where I stayed with Colin Kelly and his family, and had a cross-country ride over the rolling grassland on young horses, finishing up with schooling over a showjumping course.

I had to return to my own horses at the start of the season, but my route home took me first over a desert of red furrows, running from north to south, with no visible habitation. I heard a theory that Antarctica extended over Australia a long time ago, which might have caused the furrows to have been cut by the ice formation. It looked very barren after the fertile coastal plains where I had been.

Singapore in the Northern Hemisphere, had been prominent in our minds during the war, while Hugo was in Changi Prison Camp. He had been working on the power station there for Reyrolles, when the Japs came through the 'backdoor' by land from Malaysia rather than the sea. The same tactics had succeeded in the Philippines when they captured Corrigador, the unassailable island fortress, with all its guns facing out to sea, while the enemy took the island from the mainland.

My warm welcome in Singapore came from Lady Hull and General Sir Richard, who was our Commander-in-Chief in the Far East during a time of crisis in Laos and Vietnam. It was he who kindly advised me against attempting a visit to Angkor Wat, as Thailand and Cambodia had broken off diplomatic relations. I had read about the history of the Khmer people, their art and the architectural triumph of the great temple which I longed to see, but there were other wonders to visit in safer circumstances.

The little tropical islands near Singapore had a wealth of marine life around the coral reefs where we could snorkel. At sunset the dark outlines of palm trees and the distant volcanic mountains of Indonesia contrasted with the colours that the setting sun reflected on dark clouds, with occasional flashes of lightning and large white clouds of cumuli. The humidity of the tropics and stillness of the evening warmth made me thrive, although Lady Hull told me with a smile, that she had threatened to avoid all official receptions unless her husband obtained an air-conditioner in the car. She said she refused to arrive in smart dresses that had collapsed in damp wrinkles, covered in dust after driving in a hot car with the window open in self-defence against the heat.

The sight of Changi, still used as a prison, with the turrets manned by armed guards and sentries marching along the top of the vast walls, was daunting. We passed it before crossing the causeway to the luxury of the palace of His Highness the Sultan of Johore, where we were invited for lunch. In his air-conditioned stables which prevent a horse from suffering the fatal condition of an inability to sweat, each horse had his own groom. In India horses can be taken to the hills when the climate threatens to cause this trouble. All the facilities for playing polo were laid out in the superb grounds.

In the palace we were shown game hunting trophies, like the male and female tigers that the Sultan had shot with a right and left barrel. I appreciated more the fabulous jewels of the state crown and sword. My brief tour and first experience of the Far East continued in Bangkok, the capital of Thailand. Siam was the country's old name, but Thailand means Freeland, which is appropriate for a country where the charming people have never been dominated or colonized by a foreign power. I had met many Muslims in Africa but Far Eastern religions were new to me, so I learnt a little from friends who could explain the history of Buddhism; the ancient spirits worship of Animism is also tolerated by the Buddhists, as toleration is a doctrine of their religion. Every Buddhist boy has a compulsory apprenticeship to serve as a novice monk in one of the temples. At the age of twenty, he must stay for a hundred days under the robe, as a Buddhist monk.

In the temple of the Emerald Buddha, Wat Phra Keow, young monks with shaven heads and orange robes were being read the laws from the *Phra Tripitaka*, the Buddhist scriptures. The sacred image of the Buddha had been carved in India from a block of green jade in the fifth century, but during a journey it had been captured by King Rama I and brought to Thailand. The stories of Prince Rama and the monkey men was derived from the older Sanskrit epic poem in India, the *Ramayana*. Scenes from this poem were acted in a masked drama, the *Khon*; the episode that I saw ended in a hand-to-hand fight with the monkey king killing his cousin Virunchambang, the villain. The battle with double swords was really exciting, with the performers combating with lightning strokes and parries, leaping over each other's swords with brilliant timing and skill.

My introduction to exotic fruits was an experience in the floating market down the Chao Phya River and in the open market in town. The colours of the people's clothes, the bright hues of the fruits and, in the country, the endless variety of bright and beautiful flowers and birds, with brilliance added by the sunshine, seemed to be an unfair advantage for the warm countries to have over our often drab shades in the shadows of cold rain clouds in the North. My thoughts were suddenly brought back to the West Country; as I descended the high central tower of Phras Prang at Wat Arun, the Temple of Dawn a voice behind me said 'It's a long way from Devonshire, isn't it?' I turned and was astonished to see the President of the Bideford Horse Show, where I had competed at the invitation of Colonel Sir Mike Ansell who lived there. We stopped a moment to exchange impressions of Bangkok and Devon memories of Sir Mike catching trout at dusk, in spite of being blind, in a stream near Bideford.

The formal *wai* greeting among Thais on meeting or leaving, bowing with the palms of the hands together, was ubiquitous at the airport, as I left for brief stops in Hong Kong, Nepal and Delhi, to make the best use of my air ticket. The faith I had placed in kind people who I had never met before proved to be fully justified. I never ceased to be thankful for my journeys and contacts working out so well, from very little back-up or organisation – I had the luck of a successful hitchhiker, meeting wonderful people and seeing as much as I could in my limited time.

In Hong Kong the rain was sheeting down, making the tricky approach to the airport between mountains and sea even more hazardous. To my relief on landing I found a car waiting to take me to the races at Happy Valley, to meet my hostess Miss Elma Kelly. She was involved with the Cathay empire and had lived in Hong Kong for most of her life. The last time that I saw this kind and formidable lady, was at the christening of my younger daughter Lucy in Miserden Church. She arrived unexpectedly in a large car, to join the family gathering. My uncle Hugo, the survivor from Changi and an experienced old hand of Shanghai life was there on holiday from America, and Elma Kelly felt an affinity to him. While tea was being served in the living room, Hugo escaped up the front stairs and down the back stairs to seek sanctuary in my study. As he opened the study door, he found Elma sitting in my chair in the empty room, she greeted him with the pronouncement, 'I knew you'd come in here!'

Before leaving England I had asked a Chinese man, standing on a moving staircase in Holborn tube station, if he happened to know William Kwan in Hong Kong. The surprised man said he did, 'He's a good friend of mine and I have the telephone numbers of his London office.' William and his friend Eric Ko were the two boys who had been in the Jeep when Mother was killed, but luckily they were unhurt. By coincidence they were both in Hong Kong and we were given a Swiss meal at the Saddle Club by William's father; a Chinese meal was no treat for them.

The flagship HMS *Belfast* was an impressive sight in the bay. The unexpected privilege of attending the Ceremony of Sunset and then dining on board in the Captain's cabin with the Admiral and the Governor General was another highlight.

The lure of the highest mountains of the world enticed me to make the complicated journey to Nepal. There was no road to Kathmandu from India at that time, but I found that if I stayed part of the night in the airport of Calcutta, I could catch a little plane in the small hours to fly me into the Nepalese capital. I met Colonel Proud who had lived for many years in Nepal and had entertained most of the climbers on Himalayan expeditions. He had arranged my twenty-four hour visa and invited me to stay at home with his wife and daughter.

The monsoon was building up its rain clouds against the mountains, but for an unforgettable ten minutes they rolled back and I saw the breathtaking sight of the great range in the evening light. We were at Bhaktapur, sometimes known as Bhadgaon. This fascinating city with all its Buddhist and Hindu temples, once a capital city of great rulers of the Newars, who were defeated by the Gurkhas in 1768, was then the end of the road to Everest, where the climbers had to start their trek to the foot of the Himalayas.

Flying to Delhi in a little Dakota and looking down at the mountains below, a cloud above me suddenly revealed the peak of Dhaulagiri. Gazing in awe at the 26,795 ft summit soaring over the plane, gave me a respect and admiration only repeated when flying through the Andes to Cuzco and again over Aconcagua to Santiago de Chile.

Delhi was hot and humid in the grip of the monsoon but I made friends that evening with an Indian who took me sailing at dawn to see the birdlife of grebe, duck, heron and storks on the old dam of Ohkle, constructed by the Moguls, and on the surrounding marshes. Another Sikh friend arranged for his car to take me to Agra with a Hindi girl I had met, to visit the Taj Mahal, a dazzling sight in the heat and brilliant sunlight. We were grateful to the brigadier of the regiment in Agra and his wife for letting us have cold baths later in darkened rooms, to rest our eyes from the glare of the pure white marble mausoleum that Shah Jehan had built in memory of his wife Mumtaz Mahal in the seventeenth century. A superb Indian meal with the family then allowed me time to learn more of the traditions and history of this great country.

Back in Delhi I was taken to inspect the bodyguard of the cavalry regiment where some of the horses were brought out to jump a course of fences. It was already time to leave my kind new friends and take the Comet back to London, to get into the saddle and start the showjumping season with my own horses.

7

A New Home and a New Life: The Sixties

The ground was dry and hard in the spring of 1961 in England and my horses had benefited by quiet work to get them fit while I was away rather than jarring their legs by jumping on the rock hard surface. They rewarded me by having a first class season starting by winning the Danish Grand Prix at Copenhagen, and the Ladies European Championships at Deauville in appalling weather.

My brother married in the spring and it had been a very happy day, his wife Jill having stayed with me at Miserden House several times. On the morning of the new John Player Trophy at White City in July, I learnt that she was ill, with the fear of cancer at the age of thirty.

Feelings of shock, and the thought of the pain that Jill would have to suffer with the part that Ronald would have to bear, too, dominated my thoughts through the day's competitions. The biggest competition that had ever been held at the Royal International Horse Show, with a first prize of £500, was the finale of the floodlit evening session in the presence of the Queen.

Scorchin' was my ride; although he could jump big courses, his speed in a timed jump off was not renowned. He came through the two rounds over a big course without a fault, but now faced the pick of the top class and well-bred jumpers for the final round against the clock. We had nothing to lose and everyone was jumping as fast as they dare to get that prize. I laughed as I saluted, comparing my chances to sitting on a friendly lorry that was racing against sports cars. We went as fast as we could to each fence but cut the corners so much that he had to jump the fences sideways on, which seemed to suit him and he revelled in his power to go up like a lift over the gleaming obstacles. Finishing clear, he gave a buck of delight to amuse the applauding public. Paula rushed to me, 'He's just the fastest!' There was still the Olympic Gold medal pair from Rome, Raimondo d'Inzeo on Posillipo to go, but they hit the last fence in trying to beat Scorchin's time. The National Anthem was played for his win in the floodlights before the Marine Band performed the Ceremony of Sunset. The Queen presenting the trophy seemed as happy and amused as I felt with Scorchin's keeping the Trophy at home that first year. Frank Weldon, the three-Day Event Olympic Gold medallist, wrote about the Championship in the *Telegraph*, aptly summing up the winner as: 'Scorchin', built more for comfort than speed . . .'.

The St Gallen Show in Switzerland had invited me to jump in a big Ladies Championship as their special event. The lure of this show for me was to meet the President, Colonel Hausamann, who had played such an important role in

Switzerland during the war. The key part that this gentleman had played was brought to light in the book *Spying for Peace*. Telebrae, my New Zealand horse, brought home a length of the lovely St Gallen lace, that went with the Championship, which although I did not know it then, was to be made up two years later as my wedding dress.

At that time my top priority was the exciting fact that during the year my good friends Gerald and Audrey Godwin wanted to sell Sudgrove House with their 150 acres and pig farm, while now I had a little money that my books had earned. My first book was published in 1954 and I already had eleven books on the market, including the children's adventure stories in the 'Three Jays' series, and two more were to be published in the spring. Since our family had left London at the outbreak of war, we had not had any land or house of our own.

In 1950 when we were settled in Miserden House, Harry and Teeny Llewellyn came to visit us. They mentioned that they were looking for a place and that they were attracted by this area of Gloucestershire. Mother and I knew that Sudgrove was then empty and was coming on the market. We had often ridden that way and loved the house and its situation, looking south over the unspoilt wooded Cotswolds. Mr and Mrs Yarnton Mills and their forbears had owned the house for 250 years, but they had left two years before as their health failed – the final straw had been when their elder son Daniel had been killed in a fall from a horse in New Zealand in 1947 when he was only thirty-three; their younger son Hamilton was not interested in Sudgrove.

One hundred years before, William Yarnton Mills, the Rector of Miserden, had added a new half to the old house, with the proportions blending well, increasing the size and length of all the old leaded windows. It is said that he had twelve children to fill the larger house.

We got into the house through an open window, as no-one seemed to have the keys. In the Master Bedroom there was an old-fashioned bath in the corner, a luxury then with the water pumped up from the stream running into the Holy Brook, and a little engine in the yard to generate electricity. Uncle Gordon at Swindon Manor had also had water pumped from the river Chelt, at the bottom of the garden and an engine which sometimes did not start, so we would have to revert to candles rather than electricity. Harry Llewellyn decided that there was too much work to be done on the place, while his interests were mainly in South Wales. Mother and I had already fallen in love with Sudgrove, but alas, she was never to know that it would eventually become my home.

Gerald and Audrey Godwin had bought it in 1952 and divided the house so that his sister and family could live in one part. He also sold off the farm and part of the land to the sitting tenant, just keeping 150 acres to farm himself. Unfortunately he did not keep the field with an avenue of old chestnut trees planted a century ago as a drive for Sudgrove House. They put in a lot of work in the garden, but gradually found that it was too big for them. We were good friends and they told me first when they decided to sell, so I could have a chance to buy Sudgrove and achieve my ambition. The income from my books had just made this possible; even a top rider could make no profit from amateur sport at that time.

Sudgrove was recreated for me as one house by the local craftsmen who love and know how to work with Cotswold stone. Originally, centuries ago, the house had been built with stone from the quarry in one of our fields. When Martin Partridge and his sons started work on the house, old beams were found, under the roof in the attic of the original building, fastened by wooden pegs; above those ancient ones were beams attached with hand made nails. Martin, being locally born and bred, was fascinated with the history of the district and was delighted when we found a Norman gargoyle under the hedge, which he fixed above the porch where we christened him George. He also gave me an ancient Saxon stone gutter, now planted with flowers. More history was added when we found a Roman drain in the field; the Romans had lived in the area, leaving the famous Chedworth Villa and other proof of their lives in the surrounding countryside especially in their city of Corinium, Cirencester, a crossing place of the Roman roads of Fosseway and Ermin Street.

In the spring when I went jumping in Davos, to get myself and the horses fit, I took Martin for a holiday, as he had never been abroad. We met my friend Milton Asquith, who was still skiing at the age of seventy-five. Martin and Milton enjoyed each other's company, announcing to everyone, '150 together we are'.

The horses liked their Sudgrove stable yard, looking out of the boxes at each other, having come from the indoor boxes at Miserden, which although very convenient in bad weather meant they could not see their friends. The move from Miserden House after twelve years, kept the horse box and ourselves very busy, but the shows had to go on and I left the organisation of Sudgrove to my friend and faithful secretary Paddy Bury, who had been with me since 1955, through two Olympic Games, often shielding me from the press when I was suffering from bad falls.

Scorchin' was in the British Team when we won the Nation's Cup at Lucerne and Barcelona. I was riding with a broken nose at Lucerne because an inexperienced horse had fallen with me before the show. My poor nose was broken on four occasions, because when a horse falls with you, the horse's head and the rider's face are the first thing to hit the ground, unless it throws you clear. On this occasion as soon as my face hit the floor, I started to check up while seeing stars and lying in a heap. Neck OK? Yes; my fingers move; back OK? Hope so, it was bad enough before; nose broken? Feels like it; teeth? Good heavens, I've lost the lot, I thought as I ran my tongue around my mouth. How can I go to Lucerne this week with no teeth?

By then the ambulance men had run to us as I got shakily to my feet. Paula had already caught the horse as she was well used to these occasions. I turned to an ambulance man asking furtively out of the less sore side of my mouth, 'Have I any teeth?' He looked at my bleeding mouth with a frown and nodded positively. I could not believe it and thought he was just being kind. Later when I dared myself to look in a mirror, I saw with astonishment that my teeth were still there, in spite of my rapidly bruising face. My trouble had been caused by biting off the tip of my tongue which had luckily protected my teeth from the impact of the ground. My tongue took about six months before it regenerated so that I could feel around my mouth again, to my relief. Knowing that I was not toothless, I continued with jumping the other horses that day because they needed top competitive work before they left for Lucerne.

My black eyes did not deter Flanagan from winning a competition in Lucerne or Scorchin' in helping our team to win the Cup. Again he was in our winning team at Barcelona while Flanagan won three other competitions.

Soon after we returned Flanagan achieved our ambition of winning the Hickstead Derby. He had shared second place in the first Derby the year before, but now had to jump two clear rounds to win on a jump off. He is still one of only three horses to have jumped a double clear. Our first prize in that year was £200, presented to a very happy horse and rider, Flanagan eating his laurel wreath during the prize giving. In 1991 the winner had £33,000 with an extra £5,000 offered if a double clear was achieved. Jumping the Derby course on a happy horse is the experience of a lifetime, and Scorchin' won me the Colonel Mike Ansell tankard for the best performance by a horse owned by its rider. In the first Derby he had given me a heavy fall banking the thick privet hedge growing in the oxer, thinking that it was solid, a mistake that other horses made too.

The following White City week Scorchin' won the Victor Ludorum *Daily Mail* Cup for the second time to go with Prince Hal's two wins, and a second place by one-fifth of a second on three occasions with Prince Hal, Tosca and Flanagan. This gave me the Loriners Cup for the leading rider with two horses and the Saddle of Honour with Flanagan as the best horse. I was already a Freeman of the Worshipful Company of Farriers, the Loriners and of the City of London. The next year I became a Yeoman of the Saddlers Guild with Sir Mike Ansell, Colonel Frank Weldon, Lord Oaksey and Freddie Winter, all close friends. Flanagan rounded off the year by taking the Leading Show Jumper Event at Wembley to join Finality and Mr Pollard in winning this championship. At Madrid the next week, in spite of cutting his hind leg on the journey, he came from behind to secure me my third European Ladies Championship with a brilliant final round. Madrid was Prince Hal's favourite stamping ground for his triumphs and Flanagan must have got inspiration from thoughts of his old friend. The Caudillo presented me with a championship in Madrid for the third time.

The snow came that winter and piled up to fifteen foot in the lanes. We cut a way through our hedges, where the snow on the fields had partly blown away, so the provisions for our hamlet could be fetched by our pony and sledge, the same as I had done when snowed up in Lansdown near Bath in 1946. To get to London for business meetings I hiked across the fields with my bag on my back to the place where a lane had been dug out enough for a Land Rover to get me to the station. In London no-one could believe our conditions in the Cotswolds, which lasted for weeks before the lane was cleared. While we were cut off with no telephone, I had time to organise my writing and put the house in order.

The respite that the snow and lack of communications gave me was a welcome short break from the constant life of travel that I was used to, but my happiness

(*above*) Scorchin' winning his first *Daily Mail* Cup with me at White City, 1960.

(*right*) White City, 1961. The Queen presents me with the first John Player Trophy that Scorchin' won; we beat the Gold Medallists of the Rome Olympics 1960, Posillipo and Raimondo d'Inzeo. 'Master', The Duke of Beaufort, is with the Queen.

(*above left*) General Franco presenting the European Showjumping Trophy, Madrid 1962.
(*above right*) Laurie Lee with his daughter Jesse came to open our Miserden Church Fete in 1965. He arrived in our Ralli trap with me driving Scorchin'.

(*below*) Flanagan eating his laurels after winning the Hickstead Derby, 1962, jumping two clear rounds with a jump off.

and sense of achievement with Sudgrove as my own was not to last. As the year continued I became deeply worried as I fell in love. Never before had I been overwhelmed by someone who would be more important to me than my career and to love someone so much that I wanted to have his children. Never had I considered marrying a man who was already married, but Sam Koechlin and I were suddenly finding ourselves not only with a very close affinity but also he was making it clear that he really wanted and needed me.

Since I had been a teenager on the international show jumping scene, I had been very careful not to get romantically involved with the showjumping men. They all eventually accepted my stance and I could become a good friend without being compromised. Many of the Agricultural students from Cirencester who stayed at Miserden House during the term time were older than me, but I was busy with my life and they had their own friends. After mother died I had to engage a housekeeper, a lovely lady, but one of my students shocked me with a warning as he left at the end of his course, that the lady offered them more pleasure than just her cooking. It was most inconvenient at that moment to replace her, but regretfully she had to leave, before I travelled abroad to the next show. When Sam came to Miserden while Mother ran the guest house, he was already engaged to marry a distant cousin, who had grown up within his circle of Basel families. While he took his London School of Economics course, we had kept his horse Tambour in training for Badminton Three-Day event in the spring of 1951 and he came down from town to train Tambour at weekends. We kept our respect for each other and had great times riding together, training, hunting and competing in Hunter Trials. We had danced at local parties and the Hunt Ball, also learning the Charleston together with Jeryl Gurdon, now Lady Smith-Ryland, who was a friend and who had learnt expertly to Charleston with an Irish aunt during the war; then Jeryl lived nearby in Cotswold Park.

The Koechlin family stayed at Miserden for the Badminton event when Sam had been second on Tambour in the Dressage phase, although he had a fall on the cross-country, to put him out of the prizes. I already knew his sister Mimi, whose husband Mario Mylius was a top show jumper, an army officer and stylish rider in the Swiss team. Mimi and I had become great friends and their parents Harty and Marguerite Koechlin and Sam's fiancée Kiki Sarasin were welcome guests at Miserden House.

I put thoughts of Sam out of my mind when he left. He did return a few years later to look at young horses, then he bought Goya, his Olympic mount at Stockholm, from me, although I hardly registered his visits except for a note in my diaries.

Sam and I had met by chance again at a show abroad; he offered to take me out to dinner. I had no official invitation that night so we went to a restaurant that he knew in the country. I became a little scared that evening when we found ourselves so compatible, but I explained that in my way of life I had friends, with one special friend that he knew too, while the work, travel and contacts that I made through the shows and publishing, suited me well. Sam was not to be put off by my statement. The following months, my feelings for him that had been put into cold storage for all those years, were gradually melted with his persistence and became more intense. Instead of the joy of love there was the agony of torn feelings, as he had three small children and lived in Switzerland; the future hung in an unhappy balance.

During the very emotional time before we were married, my circus of shows went on. At Hickstead in 1963, the European Ladies Championship was being held during the Derby meeting. Flanagan was lying ahead after the first two legs of the Championship, and everything depended on the results of the third leg. Unfortunately the Derby was held on the day before the final of the Championship, so I could not risk Flanagan tiring himself over the strenuous Derby course, to defend his title of the previous year. He was jumping against some excellent horses that were younger than him, in the last day's final.

Over the Championship course, he gave his best, making the Ladies European Championship a hat trick for him and four times in all, as he and Prince Hal had won the first title at Spa in Belgium in 1957. As I received my prize, I knew that this would be the last time that I rode under my maiden name. Abrupt changes were due to take place in my life, as I was about to get married, and leave my dream home of Sudgrove to live in Switzerland with Sam and become a *Hausfrau* in a tiny flat in the suburbs of Basel. No-one at the show knew of these thoughts passing through my head.

It was no time to sit and meditate on the future. The house and farm had to be organised for my long absences, although Sam wanted us to come back for the holidays with the children. The agricultural students would still be there in termtime. There were the horses to be looked after, as Paula would leave, to run her own school, now that I would do little international jumping. Flanagan and Scorchin' would stay at Sudgrove keeping fit but only jumping when I could ride them and prepare them for an occasional show. A young horse would come with me to join Sam's two in Switzerland, who were looked after by an English girl called Jill. I had the youngsters that Tosca had bred every year, so there was a lot of responsibility for the people at Sudgrove. It was fortunate that the Heathrow to Basel flight only took an hour and a quarter so that I could return quickly in an emergency.

I knew that I would not be popular when I arrived as Sam's wife in Basel, where nobody knew me except for the showjumping riders. Mimi had always been my friend and ally for over a decade but the rest of the family would not take so kindly to a stranger in their midst.

The loss of Sam's father and the divorce of Mimi had already rocked their mother Marguerite, and Sam's failure in his first marriage was to intensify the situation. Sam and I had been to visit the Archdeacon of Cheltenham, Canon Ronald Sutch, a highly respected friend who had prepared me for confirmation when he was Vicar of Cirencester. After his good and helpful advice we went to see the Bishop of Gloucester, Basil Guy, whose enthronement service I had attended by invitation. We discussed all our problems together and I was advised that I would be excommunicated after marriage with a divorced man, but later my position might be reviewed.

The Swiss Evangelical Church, in which Sam was confirmed, allowed us to have our wedding blessed in London by Pfarrer Wyss, who we had met for several discussions in the previous weeks. At that time the Church of England did not bless weddings when a divorced party was involved, especially as I would be officially excommunicated.

The day arrived for our legal wedding in Stroud Registry Office, with our friend and solicitor since my father's time, Eric Watterson being a witness along with Paddy Bury, who had also helped me through my private life during the past years. The office opened for us fifteen minutes early. Paddy had said to Sam, 'D'you have the rings?' 'Of course not, I'm keeping them for the Church tomorrow.' Paddy advised him to take them along to Stroud, and the rings were an essential part of the civil wedding. We returned to Sudgrove to pick up our overnight and Church clothes, quickly removing a cork for a glass of champagne. The half empty bottle we corked again and put into Paddy's hands in the back of the car, while Sam drove us to Swindon station. On the way, a huge explosion nearly put us in the ditch, and Paddy, soaked in champagne, was saying, 'Sooner blood was spilt!' We pulled in and finished the dregs, just catching the London train in time and leaving Paddy with the car, all sprayed with champagne, to return to Sudgrove.

Once settled in the train at a table, Sam fished another bottle of champagne out of the poaching pocket in his jacket and some glasses. An old lady came and sat with us, and was surprised to be offered some champagne just after 10 a.m.

As I had worked for the *Daily Express* at that time, writing on showjumping and skiing, I had promised the *Express* exclusive photos of our wedding reception the next day at Sudgrove after the Swiss Church blessing in London. Up until now none of the rest of the press had an inkling about this great event in my life, and we wanted to keep this special time to ourselves and our friends. Max Aitken was letting us use the *Express* flat in town as no-one would find us there before the Church blessing and our return to Sudgrove. Janet Kidd, Lord Beaverbrook's daughter, had been a friend for years, while Sam had met her too when he bought a young horse from her called Drumbeat, named after her brother Max's racing yacht.

Sam and I arrived at Paddington, to have a relaxed family lunch in the hotel with my uncle Nicco and Mary who were over from South Africa during his farming holiday. We also met up with Babbyns and Robert, now Lord and Lady Borwick with their three little girls who would be my bridesmaids, the middle one Mary-Anne being my goddaughter. This had been a Miserden House romance, when Robert stayed with us as a student at the Agricultural College, while Babbyns had brought her horse to ride and train at Miserden. I had just had time between two international shows to get to their wedding in Bala, mid Wales, a beautiful part of the country.

We arrived at the flat, ready for a quiet evening together; we had both been working continuously to get everything arranged, myself to leave Sudgrove running smoothly while I went to live in Switzerland taking enough essentials to start married life in a two-roomed apartment. We found Max there looking anxious. 'The cat's out of the bag, it's in the evening paper!' As no-one knew our plans for the next day, we assured him that the *Express* photos of the reception at Sudgrove would be exclusive; our confidence proved to be justified.

Apparently a young Stroud reporter had happened to go through the records at the registry office and had seen our marriage signatures. He had phoned the house to get more news on his 'coup' of a lifetime, but Paddy, the most truthful person, confirmed that we had got married but had left the house at 9.30 a.m. and she did not know where we had gone. Well not exactly, she explained later, while the house was being polished for the next day's reception for sixty people. The Press had been alerted and had sped to Heathrow, checking all the flights out that evening.

The next morning, the daily arrived at the flat and was let into our secret. She was delighted to help me dress in my white gown made from the lace that I had appropriately won in the Ladies Championship at St Gallen in Switzerland, after the Rome Olympic Games.

The lady who was Sir Malcolm Sargent's right hand for so long, Sylvia Darley, had arranged for a choir of a few ladies with superb voices. There had been a lot to arrange and check up on without the press knowing the facts. My uncle Gordon had come up to London from Swindon Manor, to give me away, and Mimi's husband Verduno would be Sam's best man, before they had a short holiday at Sudgrove.

The Church service was simple with an intimate charm, with only the few special friends. Gordon carried his seventy-eight years well, looking distinguished in his morning suit as he gave away his younger brother's daughter to become a Swiss wife in the land where he and his brother had been raised and educated.

Outside the Church our car waited, but a photographer from the *Evening Standard*, who must have had a pal in the *Express*, took one photo of us while I just stopped Sam from boxing him on the jaw. 'Please not now, it's our wedding day' and the man was spared while we drove down to Gloucestershire.

The Sudgrove phone stared ringing again. 'Oh yes,' answered Paddy, 'I expect they waited for the Church service and have now gone on their honeymoon.' The press after a sleepless and fruitless night at Heathrow rushed back there again.

We were back at Sudgrove in good time for the reception that afternoon. I had written a personal note to about sixty people inviting them to celebrate our wedding, with a request to keep our marriage private until afterwards. These trusted friends did not let us down.

Paula and Pam, the other girl who looked after the horses for me, had Flanagan and Scorchin' suitably dressed for the occasion in grey top hats with carnations in their headcollars. Champagne was offered to people on the lawn while the guests arrived, with the Duke and Duchess of Beaufort coming in time to see Fred Hillman, dressed as a bridegroom, too, showing the young stock with pride, the offspring of Tosca that had already been bred at his Stockwood Stud, and were now here in the yard. Tosca had already bred seven foals and had two grand-children from Lucia, her eldest filly.

Late at night after our party, one of our Cirencester Agricultural students ran us to Heathrow, for the trip to Switzerland for our honeymoon. We still evaded the tenacious press, right to our destination in a remote valley of the Tessin, the Swiss–Italian part of Switzerland, where the old fashioned village of Coglio lies on the river hidden between the mountains in the Valle Maggia.

Sam had left his little white beetle VW at Kloten, but Verduno had told him that he had parked his smart Italian car next to the beetle and that we could use it for our honeymoon and the long drive over the Alps to Verduno's family home at Coglio, where he had been born and raised. There was no-one living there now, as the family used it as a holiday home, but the village was still very primitive, although he had installed water and inside sanitation into the old house. It was after midnight at Kloten when we found the cars, but unfortunately the smart one was not built to take luggage, so we took the beetle, leaving Verduno's car for his return, and chugged off to the Lake of Lucerne.

The holiday chalet was built by Sam's parents on the lake in the early '30s, with the boat house under the living room. We camped there that night and woke to the lapping of the lake when the small waves broke on the shore from the wake of a passing boat. After coffee and sharing a loaf with a family of ducks, a pair of swans and the wagtails, we left the 'Eichstutz' to its winter's hibernation.

Our route took us winding over the St Gotthard Pass and down following the Ticino river to Locarno on Lago Maggiore. It was too late to buy food for the house at Coglio so we decided to go to a place up the road for breakfast the next morning, that Verduno had told us about, after getting some sleep.

We were rudely awakened the next morning by a deafening helicopter flying practically into our open window. It was 6.00 a.m. so we turned over and tried to sleep again. The rest of the village had been awoken too and gradually an increasing babble of voices came from below, as the local black-clad women gathered around the horse trough outside to do their weekly washing. The crescendo of gossip made further sleep impossible, for the sharp tones of Arabic, Spanish or Italian women, all vying to make themselves heard, is the same typical accompaniment to gatherings all around the Mediterranean and southern Europe like here in the Swiss Tessin.

The thought of coffee and croissants seemed a good idea as we dressed and wandered out into the cool sunny autumn morning. Greeting the curious washer-women with *Buon giorno*, we wandered in the direction of the small garage a little way out of the village, where one could find a bar, coffee and snacks served by the Signora herself. She was very friendly when we arrived and showed us to one of the small tables. The room was empty, so she came to chat when she brought us the coffee and croissants. It was the quiet season now, but she told us that she kept busy during the summer with tourists that found their way up to the valley. Her mainstay was feeding the workmen who came to work on the dam, but didn't live locally.

She told us that she had one regular, a foreigner who took loads up to the building site with a helicopter. Then she left us to go the kitchen for a moment. I told Sam while we were alone, about the extraordinary coincidences of my three meetings with Jacques over the past eight years. I laughingly said that it could only be Jacques who could disturb us on our honeymoon.

When we'd finished and bade the Signora farewell, we heard the helicopter coming down from the mountain and land a little way from the garage. Sam said, 'Come on, we'll go and see.' We followed the engine noise and came to the helicopter with its gyrators still turning, while a lithe man was chaining a big stack of timbers together and fastening them under his machine. As he straightened I shouted 'Jacques' several times. At last he heard and saw us and with a bound he rushed over with open arms just missing the turning blades. *'Pat, c'est toi, ce n'est pas possible!'* *'Non ce n'est pas possible maintenant,'* said Sam as he stepped forward. She's mine now, he added. The reunion called for a coffee break as the three of us returned to the Signora's bar where she was delighted by our company again, although perplexed by the rapid French conversation. That really was the last time that I saw Jacques.

In the afternoon we wound up the mountain valley on a narrow road with a sheer drop on one side and only a few passing places. Sam showed me the signs depicting a French horn, which meant that the post bus had right of way over other vehicles. I was glad that the road did not have any other tourist traffic on it as we approached the end of the valley at Bosco Gurin. The Swiss–Italian frontier runs along the top of the mountains above the village, where in the middle ages a group of refugees crossed the mountains to form this colony, and they still speak a medieval Swiss–German dialect, rather than the Italian patois spoken by all the other people of the Tessin.

The old houses were immaculate in this picturesque and isolated village, but the steep grass slopes made work very hard. Old women were leaning against the turf as they cut the short grass above them with a hand sickle, then holding on with one hand and wielding the heavy rake with the other, to pull the cut grass down to the bottom of the slope. An extraordinary sight met us along the path, a big pile of hay, like a hay cock, was approaching with two black feet walking under the load which had the hay rake and scythe stuck on top as well. Sam turned to me, 'That's the Frau!'. Behind came a man riding comfortably on a donkey, peacefully puffing on a curly pipe, and carrying nothing, 'and that's her husband! So you know now why we came here for our honeymoon, to learn the ways of Swiss wedded bliss!'

I do not deny that it was a shock to change from the freedom of the countryside, to a small two-roomed flat on the ninth and top floor of an unfurnished apartment tower on the outskirts of Basel. Our bathroom window was only put in several weeks after our arrival and the lift often did not work during the day which meant a long haul to get the food and drink up all those concrete stairs. The nicest part was the address of 2 Paradis Strasse. We could keep two horses at a stable we rented on the hill above us; the country was open then and riding was a pleasure in the woods that stretched into France. We were practically on the border, so we had to carry the horses' passports and our identity cards with us at all times.

We also had a farm just below us, in an old building that had been in the country but now was surrounded by the built up suburb. The friendly clink of milk pails rattling and the cows mooing was more to my liking than the grinding squeal of the 5 a.m. tram. The cows stayed in all the winter, while in the summer they would be driven through the streets to a strip of grass enclosed by one single electric wire, up on the hill near to our stables. Swiss cows are very well behaved and seemed to respect that nearly invisible wire, while I am sure that English cows would have had wild initiative, quickly wrecking the flimsy fence and running amok in the city of Basel, or escaping to the lush pastures of the Alsace in the rich farming lands of France. Sheep too had a different way of life, lambing in the autumn and being sheared as winter approached. They were housed all the winter, never having to fend for themselves against the elements. The whole of the open country beyond our stables is now covered with housing as far as the French frontier, the old villages of that time having since merged into continuous buildings. Basel has a three-cornered frontier with Germany and France, leaving only one direction for expansion in Switzerland.

A break from office routine came with a business trip to Lebanon, when life was prosperous for the people of many races and religions in 1963, at a time when Lebanon was known as the Switzerland of the Middle East. We had business friends of all creeds and we observed the rules of their lifestyle when entertained in their houses. At one old pillared house in the city we were given a great dinner with many courses. Sam disappeared towards the middle of this feast and did not reappear, so I excused myself from the table to see where he was. I found him fainted on the stone floor of the bathroom having succumbed to a tummy bug. He recovered soon and we could laugh then of our first experience of marriage 'in sickness and in health'. Our Lebanese friends managed to get us through Baalbek over the frontier to Damascus for a day, where we visited the Great Mosque, and I haggled for some dress lengths of Damascus silk in the Souk. Returning to Switzerland Sam was anxious that I might forget to declare the lengths of silk, remembering my poaching days when he was a student and the occasional hare, rabbit or pheasant that supplemented our meat ration. However, our luggage continued to London when we changed planes at Athens for Zurich. The next day our cases together with a camel footstool with the camel's wooden head looking cheekily out of a cardboard box, a humpty, and the silk were delivered to us, but no declaration of goods had been requested!

I had been shown in Lebanon the remaining couple of the Cedars of Lebanon, on the bare mountains, a sight as sad as the bare plateaux of Castille in Spain that have been deforested for centuries.

I was writing one of my books at the time and nearly all the young couples in the twenty-seven apartments had babies. One could hear every sound while the constant vibrating noise of electric drills being used to complete the building drove me to distraction. The trams starting at 5 a.m. with a screech as they turned on the icy rails at the end stop below our window, made sure one didn't oversleep. The Swiss are early risers, with school and offices starting at 7.30 a.m.

One evening in November Sam took me out for a birthday dinner to an old mill deep in the Alsace countryside. At the Moulin de Kaegy there were not many guests that dark night and we had a snug little candle-lit table in the corner. Our dinner was probably from the 'Wild' menu, the specialities of the autumn season taken from the culling of local deer, wild boar and partridge of the forest land.

I only remember that the shadowy figures in the dark timbered room became quiet when a radio was tuned. Suddenly subdued exclamations were heard as the atmosphere became tense. The shock announcement on the French programme was that President John Kennedy had just been assassinated.

A happier souvenir of my birthday is that I shared St Cecilia's Day, the patron saint of Music, with Benjamin Britten and we would sometimes exchange notes on the occasion. Peter Pears kindly wrote when Ben was very weak before he died. I have been privileged to hear them working together with perfection and have heard Ben's operas in many countries. The last time was in the Basel Opera with Paul Frey as Peter Grimes with his own son Ben acting as the boy. It made a great impression with the brilliant performance, especially as the Frey family became our neighbours along with Rupert and Elizabeth Forbes, also working in the opera, when we moved to Burg in 1965.

We returned to Sudgrove for our first Christmas as a married couple, and Uncle Gordon and Dorothy joined us for Christmas dinner. Dorothy seemed to be very fragile with Parkinson's disease, but Gordon hardly seemed to change through the years. We discussed our plan to buy some farm land on the Alsace frontier, on a mountain that rose to 1,000 metres in the chain of the Jura, not far from Basel. The village was called Burg-im-Leimental, with less than 180 inhabitants, and was below the imposing Schloss Burg, which stood on a sheer-sided rock. The castle had been built by a nephew of Charlemagne and the four main families who had been established in the commune for centuries, may have had forebears who were footsore soldiers from Charlemagne's army, who could go no further. Below Burg over the frontier was our next village, Biedertal, that had the winter castle, or château, built for use when Burg was snowed up. In both villages the people spoke the same dialect at home, but in Burg school, the children were taught High German as their first foreign language, while the Biedertal children learnt French.

Gordon was delighted to hear our plans, especially as he and Eric, my father, had been brought up with Swiss dialect, German and French as their languages, together with their English mother tongue. He was looking forward to visiting us there, but was worried over Dorothy's health. Only ten days after we returned to Switzerland, Paddy phoned us with the unexpected news that Gordon had died on the eve of his eightieth birthday. Sam had to continue working but I took the next plane back to hold Dorothy's hand.

Dorothy in her frail state was completely shattered; but she was able to tell me how Gordon had driven to Cheltenham to buy a large capon for his birthday dinner. He was looking forward to entertaining his friends the next day, he told her over lunch; then he left the table and went upstairs. Surprisingly he went to an unused room with a double bed that they had shared before the war. In later life they had separate rooms. Florrie, their daily and 'treasure' who kept the house in order, heard something and went to that room to find Gordon dead on the bed.

It was pathetic to see Dorothy's immediate decline and death within three months. The nurse, who her old cousins had hired to look after her, departed at the same time as her jewellery that Dorothy had unaccountably taken out of the bank when Gordon died. The cousins who were unmarried and in their seventies, inherited everything from her pre-war will, but luckily they did not want the larger furniture. I asked Paddy to go the manor for the probate sale within the family, before the public sale of properly and contents. Paddy managed to buy for me enough of my favourite pieces, the dining room table and sideboard, the sofa and some easy chairs, a few smaller cupboards and heavy teak Burmese tables, so that I had some useful things of sentimental value to put in our future house at Burg. Paddy had spared me the ordeal of competing in the drawing of lots for Gordon and Dorothy's possessions that I too, had lived with over my thirty years visiting and staying with them at Swindon Manor. In Switzerland I was fully occupied with Sam's programme, the horses and writing, also the important planning ahead for Burg.

Sam's children Catherine, Sibylle and Dominik came to Sudgrove for the holiday time and were learning to ride the ponies. Once we had the Steinacker fields fenced at Burg we could take ponies over to Switzerland, for them to ride there. Kiki, their mother, had married Michael Gelzer, who was a Swiss Diplomat with a post in Washington; the children would be in an American school while they lived there. The Gelzer family were friends of Sam from Basel and Michael had two older boys from his first marriage.

Our neighbours at Burg would be Conrad and Margrit Diem, who first told us about the land on the Swiss side of the border. They had spent some years camping and picnicking around the hills where the land was cheap and unspoilt, looking for a site to build their house, within reach of Basel. For us it was ideal, the surrounding forest was full of wildlife, especially birds and the great raptors that are now rare in England. The forests stretched along the hills deep into France while the view ahead of us was the Ballon d'Alsace, the two rounded peaks of the Vosges and beyond Basel the Black Forest dominated the skyline, often showing us the snow-covered heights of the Feldberg in winter. If we rode up the 1,000 metre Remel behind us, one could see on clear days the high Alps of the Bernese Oberland, the Eiger, Mönch and Jungfrau being the familiar landmarks of that region.

Sam needed the greatest degree of tact to negotiate the buying of the strips of land in the agricultural clearing in the forest where we wanted to live. Napoleonic law, with each child inheriting an equal part of his father's land, had meant that the local farmers owned a small strip here and another there, with yet another one or two strips over the border in France. Slowly Sam won the confidence of the local people, except for one farmer, who was very suspicious and shy of strangers. His strip of land was in the centre of the field that we needed. At last Sam tracked him down in a haystack, where he climbed up to join the farmer and offered him some tobacco while they smoked their pipes. Luckily they did not set the hay rick on fire while negotiating the deal before descending as the best of friends.

The centre piece of the land was ours and the farmer became a new Burg colleague who would help us sometimes with our hay making and cherry picking. One talent of Herr Ackermann that I appreciated more than Sam, was his brilliance at finding wild mushrooms of many hues in the forest. He would suddenly appear from around a bush, while I was out riding, and offer me a cap full of mushrooms. I would fill my pockets, after thanking him gratefully, then I had to smuggle them into the house as Sam had a great fear of *pilz*. He gave me once a double volume of the complete guide to mushrooms and fungi, but still would not trust the judgement of myself, the book or Herr Ackermann. Another delicacy around us were truffles, and the wild boar who have the keenest snout for this luxury would plough up large strips of land during a night rooting for them. We would see men with trained dogs looking furtively for this expensive tuber fungus that each owner of the land guarded zealously.

Planning the building of the house and stables with a garden to plant on the hillside, took time to do. I could spend most of my days with the workmen so that any decision could be made on the spot. We had a contract that the house would be finished by the beginning of July, so to the consternation of the foreman, we moved into the only room that had a door to close, on the last day of June. Sam did not mind the semi-camping when he returned from the office at night, and I was there from the time the workmen came at 7 a.m. until they left at 5 p.m. There were four Catalan stonemasons building the living rooms walls with our local stone. They handled the big honey-coloured blocks with an artist's care, chipping rough pieces off to fit in an uneven pattern like it was quarried in its natural state. It was very similar to the Cotswold stone which had been used to build Sudgrove and taken from our quarry field centuries before. I had repaired Cotswold dry stone walls when I was working on farms as a child, and I appreciated the Catalans in their work while I could chat to them in Spanish. The natural stone buttresses and the wood that formed the walls camouflaged the house nestling into the mountainside.

French was no problem to me, but at that time I found the Swiss dialects difficult, because they are not written and have to be learned by ear, so constant practice is essential and also one needs exposure to the dialects that change considerably from town to town, or mountain valley to valley. We had two sides of the Swiss frontier stones on our land, making a corner of Switzerland and our covered riding school we built on French land just below our house. The local dialect of Alsation was similar to our Swiss–German dialect. The local people in the Alsace were all orientated towards Basel for work, and they spoke of Paris in the third person, the difference between 'them' and 'us'. Neither French-speaking people could understand the Alsation dialect, nor the Germans who only spoke High German. On the other hand, with Swiss people speaking other languages, their dialect would shine through their accent in French, German and English. Sam could usually tell which part of the country a Swiss came from when they spoke in another tongue.

Before the house was completely finished we had a party for all the workmen and the village. The patio was still not paved but there was room for the long trestle tables. A notice was pinned to the village tree saying that everyone was welcome to come and join us for dinner with about forty of the builders and workers from the house. Out of 180 village people about 178 turned up, only a couple being too immobile to climb or be pushed up the steep hill through the village.

Everyone came through the front door, the hall and into the unfinished living room and out of the large sliding glass door onto the patio with the tables and chairs. The flickering flames on the grills for chicken on the spit helped light the surrounds of the house, along with lanterns hung around the walls. When everyone had found a place and the children's excited chattering was quietened, the Parson rose to say grace. He said the equivalent to 'For what we are about to receive, may the Lord make us truly thankful and I give you a special dispensation to eat chicken on this Friday night, so enjoy yourselves.' '*E'Guete!*' The 'good appetite' in dialect was roundly applauded as everyone tucked into half a capon each. Young Thomas the village President's son rounded off his meal with at least five of the large creamy desserts that other people could not manage. Not only appetites were satisfied but the villagers had all been invited to the house and so their curiosity was satisfied too.

The village was mainly Roman Catholic and the Priest had the use of the private chapel of the Schloss for the village. The Schloss and chapel were built like a boat sitting on a precarious rock that guarded the pass through our ridge of the Jura. We did not know our Pfarrar's personal history, but it seemed that he had been banished to Burg for some peccadillo in the past. He was amusing and eccentric, enjoying the good things in life, as we learnt when we were invited with our neighbours and friends Conrad and Margrit Diem, to dine at his house. There was constant laughter during the excellent meal that he had prepared, and I learnt some new Swiss expressions as the wine flowed. Sam explained to me later the place and circumstances where some of these phrases could be used. As my first child Monica, was due to arrive about two weeks later, I was a little puzzled and not very comfortable when I thought he was telling us about various sauces one could use with cats. Margrit told me the next day that my interpretation of the dialect had not been mistaken.

The Swiss Protestant Parson from Laufen, an old walled market town on the other side of the mountain, would come to the village school for a Protestant communion service. In the Munster, Basel Cathedral, the Church of England Parson took services in the St Nicholas chapel, in the oldest part of the Munster, looking out over the Rhine. To my relief, I had been given dispensation by then and could make my communion again, while Sam had also been confirmed into the Church of England, a choice that he made, although the Ecumenical service embraces the Swiss Church. The Bishop of Gibraltar in Europe came to the Munster every year for the confirmation service, and there were many regular worshippers including Swiss families, with a Sunday school for children. We met young people and couples from many countries working and studying in Basel and passing visitors who all enjoyed the active church community. Some of our English girl grooms during those years made friends with Canon Tom Roberts' circle of helpers. Tom Roberts had worked as a missionary on the Congo river for ten years, so he took a great interest in our travels in Africa especially around Zaïre, formerly the Congo.

Sir Winston Churchill had died in January 1965 and I recalled the occasion of meeting Sir Winston and had the privilege of shaking hands, when he laid the foundation stone of the new Cassel building in Red Lion Square, Holborn. It was on St George's day in 1956, and as Sir Newman Flower pointed out, Sir Winston had some practice as a builder at laying stones. On the day of his death I had a miscarriage after walking across town and back from my Berlitz school German lesson. Apart from my disappointment, I did not learn much German, as the Hungarian lady who taught me discovered that I spoke and enjoyed Spanish, a language in which she wanted to improve herself.

After moving into 'Im Steinacker', the stoney acre that produced the stone of our house, we had a short summer holiday back at Sudgrove, while our Swiss home was progressing. The workers only moved out in late autumn, and I doubt if they would have finished by Christmas if we had not already moved in.

At home in the established comforts of Sudgrove, our fortnight included the Miserden Church fête. Laurie Lee our friend and neighbour at Slad, came with Cathie his wife and their daughter Jesse, to open the fête. We had dear Scorchin' in the Rallye trap and drove in style to the front of the house, Scorchin' playing up proudly to what he must have thought was a Nation's Cup crowd. Laurie had a basket of carrier pigeons, which he loosed to the skies with the words, 'Take the glad tidings to all corners telling that the Sudgrove fête is open now and all are welcome here.' The story of Jesse's birth nearly started at our wedding; 'Jesse' was arriving after fourteen years of their marriage and that was going to be his or her name. The champagne and laughter during our wedding reception had inspired Jesse to soon make her appearance. Now I was expecting our first child to be born the following Spring.

Sam and I did a riding display in the field; I grabbed Sam's horse when we finished, while he sprinted down to the lawn where the bowling for the pig was nearly finished. He was the last to go and equalled the best score of the afternoon. He and the expert local bowler had a 'bowl off' like a jump off which Sam won, to the disappointment of the other bowler, who was already 'counting his pigs'. 'Belle of Sudgrove' stayed in our yard while our horses disapproved of her addition to the stables until they got used to her.

Sam had increased his responsibilities since the board of Geigy had voted him as Chairman of Geigy's Executive Committee, to take over from his father's brother Carl who was well into his seventies. The generation gap had created problems caused by lack of modernisation, and the new creative thinking that was essential at the helm of an international public company. Sam was taking on a world wide business, and the management needed tightening up, so he got in the McInsey firm of management consultants to advise the firm.

At Geigy's AGM in March 1966 he was going to set out his plans to the shareholders; it would be a challenging morning, followed by a luncheon for all the top people involved.

Our baby was already a week overdue by my calculations, but my gynaecologist said that it would not come for at least three more weeks. I had explained that I was a rider, and an old one at that, because girls in Switzerland did not ride to the extent of the British or share my full-time occupation with the sport. The doctor was reluctant for me to have an x-ray, but he arranged it and I searched Basel, just fitting behind the steering wheel, for a parking place and the premises of the x-ray doctor. My back was bad and exhausted I returned to the car, to find a traffic warden putting a ticket on my windscreen. I had been well under the time allowed for parking, but in my panic I had forgotten to put the time card in the window. To my shame, I burst into tears, in frustration that I was completely within the law, except for that card. The warden looked with consternation at my bulge and distressed state trying to state my case in broken Swiss. He tore up the ticket and smiled. I could smile with relief too at this unique and friendly warden.

Only a couple of days before, I had been driving to Basel in the early and dark morning, I had taken the shorter and flatter route from Basel that took one through four frontier posts. The hilly route through Switzerland often had icy patches on the steep slopes, but this time I had hit an icy patch on a corner and gone into a skid, but played with the steering wheel until I was again in control. My heart was beating with the shock of the skid when I got to a customs post. There was a young and unfriendly man there who demanded that I opened all the laundry to see if I was smuggling anything. On a cold, dark and icy road I had to heave the laundry out and open all the sheets, when I could hardly bend with the baby in the middle. The young guy did not even help me load the laundry back into the car while I imagined the unlucky wife he might marry, having to live with this pompous and ill-mannered youth. I arrived late for my work that started at 7 a.m. in a home for babies, whose mothers, mostly of Italian and Turkish nationality, worked in Basel. It was a very good training for me to handle babies of all ages and to learn the correct routine. When Sam came back that night he said that he had skidded on the way to work that morning, the same patch of French ice having caught us both.

A snow storm at midday swirled down on our Burg home while Sam was at his important AGM in Basel. The telephone disturbed my worries that Sam might not be able to get home, as the authorities had already ordered people with the spiked tyres that we needed for our hill in winter, to change to summer tyres. The gynaecologist was telling me on the phone that I must come straight to hospital as he must do a Caesarean operation immediately; he had only just seen the x-rays from yesterday.

I phoned Sam during the Board lunch after the AGM, to say that we could meet at the hospital in an hour. He stopped me from driving there and came straight away to fetch me in the snow storm. A year or two later, one of the older members of the Board admonished Sam for leaving the luncheon as a lack of etiquette. His reply, stating he had his priorities and his wife was having a baby, shocked the other gentleman into silence bringing home the generation gap between their Chairman who was over a decade plus a quarter of a century younger than his predecessor.

I had awful nightmare dreams during the operation, and when I came to, I felt so weak that I could not speak. I longed to tell them that I needed blood while I wanted to know why my shoulder hurt so much. Sam was there and showed me Monica who had big wide open eyes. I was thrilled, but only later was I strong enough to speak to Sam as I could not understand the Swiss nurses, so he could explain why I was so weak. It turned out that I had had to have a serious operation for a varicosed condition inside after Monica had been fished out. I had lost a lot of blood and had been given blood transfusions, but I was treated as an imbecile who was unable to understand the crisis. When I could speak, I asked if my collar bone had been broken, perhaps falling from the operating table, to account for my agonizing and paralysed shoulder, but I was told that this was caused by the anaesthetic. Nineteen years later when I had an embolus on the lung after my open heart operation, the same agonizing pain recalled memories of that occasion.

Monica made me very happy, in spite of biting my breasts with her strong gums while drinking, a habit that she lost to my relief. The pleasure of having a baby made me determined to have more as soon as possible, although the specialist told me that I would only be able to have them by Caesarean section in future. Monica had been saved with oxygen and we were both lucky to pull through on that Lady Day.

I was surprised that the operation affected me so much, far more than the 'knock out' falls that had put me unconscious in hospital before. I decided to work out my training programme, starting with getting from my bed to the windowsill so I could crumble my breakfast rolls to attract the many birds from the old trees in the hospital garden. As soon as a nurse was allowed to take me out, I wandered among the blossoming magnolias, where suddenly it was spring. I still was not strong when I left for home, but once there Monica and I improved although I had no help with her at that time.

Arriving back at Burg, I gently took Monica up the steps to the hall; Kimmy, my little Lucas terrier who was devoted to me, was sitting there smiling. The smile turned to a snarl and his hackles went up, as he showed his disgust at the small bundle I was carrying. He turned his back and his jealousy was so obvious that I took care that he and Monica were kept separated in future. He confirmed this dislike when Uncle Hugo's wife Evelyne, came from Africa to see us. She took Monica in her arms, while sitting in an easy chair. Her expression of motherly delight changed to horror, as Kimmy, who had sneaked into the drawing room, furious to find Evelyne holding Monica, lifted his leg against her foot and filled her shoe.

The three older children Catherine, Sibylle and Dominik came to Sudgrove for Monica's christening in June. Catherine was already eleven; she had recovered completely from an awful fall from a bannister onto a stone floor over two years before, when she had fractured her skull. She had not been allowed to ride for six months, but now they were all riding in Pony Club and around the farm.

Catherine was very good with Monica, helping with bathing and changing her. Now Catherine has to care for three little girls of her own but life has been simplified with disposable nappies.

Ronald came to stay for his birthday and Monica's christening, sharing the service with our Rector and becoming one of Monica's godfathers with Mike Roberts. Paddy Bury took on the responsibility of a godmother with Sam's sister Mimi. Sam and I had become the godparents of Mimi and Verduno's two sons, Patrick, who was two years old and Guy who had been born three weeks before Monica. Mimi's children by her first marriage were nearly grown up and Mariette, younger than her brother Robert, had lived at Sudgrove for several months, helping to look after and ride our horses. She was a sweet girl and full of fun, who could think up even more pranks than our girls who worked in the house and stables. Mimi bought Favorita, Tosca's second filly, for Mariette to ride when she was back in Switzerland as she had ridden and liked her at Sudgrove. Favorita, by Blue Duster, was a pretty chestnut and very comfortable ride with talent for jumping.

Lucy our second daughter had just started when I was asked to be *Chéf d'Equipe* to the British Team at Aachen. This is a tough and long show for horses, riders and their helpers, but our team was rewarded by their first win in the German Nation's Cup and I think that I was the first winning lady *Chef*, while Andrew Fielding won the Grand Prix on Vibart, the horse with a great kick back like Wilf White's Nizefela. The competition was marred by Graciano Mancinelli's black horse Turvey, dying of a heart attack during his round and the authorities prolonging his removal through mismanagement.

The emotion of the show and a bad journey back on the train alone, where I could get no help with my case at Köln station after parking my hired car in the station yard and giving the keys to a friendly stranger, because the firm failed to turn up to meet me, was not an auspicious start for Lucy, but she held on until the appointed time to be born in the following February. Sam was relieved to meet me at Basel station and delighted to hear that I thought we had started another baby, which was confirmed later that week.

A more serious health anxiety started while we had a short summer break at Sudgrove. Sam was obviously ill spending terrible restless nights sweating and shivering cold, but the doctor found nothing wrong. On return to Basel our great friend and doctor, Gilgi Ryhiner, Sam's cousin and nephew of Marguerite, Sam's mother, diagnosed the cause as hepatitis. Rest was required, but Sam was frustrated by not being able to tackle all the business activities that were his immediate priority. Gilgi firmly sent us off to the beautiful Engadine in September, to a hotel with a swimming pool that was heated and half outside, so one could swim in the crisp autumn days, with steam rising from the pool. We walked and took a pony and trap up the valleys, seeing and hearing the marmots whistling the news of our appearance to warn their families, and watching the bird life of the mountains and valleys.

This enforced rest restored Sam's health and Lucy must have profited too from my holiday in this lovely part of Switzerland at a time when there were no tourists crowding around. Sam had already had jaundice as a young man in the army, so the complete cure was essential for his future health.

While I was expecting Monica, my arthritic hips had given me no pain, so I hoped that I would get the same respite with my second pregnancy, but it was not to be. I was very lame with back and hip trouble before the birth. The Caesarean for Lucy went smoothly with my gynaecologist having a good team in case he ran into the problems he had met the first time, but Lucy had an easy birth. One bonus of this operation is that babies do not have their heads squashed during birth, so they look perfect on arrival.

Monica was not so sure of Lucy's charming looks when she came with the older children to see me in hospital. When I got home this time, Monica and Kimmy were both at the top of the steps in the hall. They both had one look at the bundle I was carrying and turned away together, becoming the best of friends. I mentally noted that perhaps neither Monica nor Kimmy should be left alone with Lucy for the moment.

At Lucerne three months later I was *Chéf d'Equipe* for the British team, and Sam's mother let me open the Eichstutz on the lake, so that I could set up house for a week with baby Lucy and two-year-old Monica, as I had Christianne, a teenage girl from the next Alsace village of Wolschwiller, to look after the girls while I was at the show. It was ideal for Monica who could come out in the boat with me early before I left, but my hips were crippling me badly and I was in pain night and day. After the show, Sam persuaded me to go to see Bill Tucker in London as my painful immobility was making me despair.

I came back in a state of shock, as Bill had told me that I must be operated with an osteotomy on my left hip, and worse that I would be six months on crutches before I could put that foot to the ground. Bill had proudly shown me x-rays of Kay Stammers, the great tennis player, on whom he had operated successfully and she had recovered well. He told me that I was too young to have the hip replacement operation, as I was just under forty and they only did this operation on people over sixty, because they were not sure of the life of the replaced hip with metal fitted into a plastic cap.

The night before going into the Nuffield, Sam took me to the film 'Star' which we enjoyed, but coming out into sheets of rain, there was not a taxi in sight. We had promised ourselves an evening dancing at the Edmundo Ros Club, an old friend of ours and our favourite dancing place. I was afraid that maybe my dancing days were numbered. The long walk across London to Regent Street with soaking shoes did not improve my trouble, but once in the Club we danced the night away although I was a weight in Sam's arms, with my bad hip, as Sam told me long after, when I was dancing lightly and sound again with my two replaced hips.

The operation in October at least coincided with the Mexico Olympics, which I watched night and day, able to give the latest news to anyone interested in sport. Monica came to see me with Paddy and first the kind taxi driver took them around by Buckingham Palace and let them feed pigeons in Trafalgar Square while he drove around, and then brought them to the Nuffield Hospital. Monica

(*right*) Paul helped Flanagan to dress for our wedding reception at Sudgrove in September 1963.

(*below*) Monica's christening at Miserden Church in 1966. With Sam, Sibylle, Dominik and Catherine.

(*left*) I am mounted on Bayridge, with Lucy in front of me; Monica is on Dimple.

(*below*) Lucy, on Dimple, giving Gordon Richardson, now Lord Richardson of Duntisbourne, some useful banking tips.

(*below*) Sam and I watching Monica and Lucy playing ball with Tiggy, the cairn.

climbed gladly into bed with me to show photos of pigeons on her head and sitting feeding out of both her hands.

Shortly after I arrived home I was trying to hop up the stairs on my crutches to go to our bathroom. As I hopped off my right leg, it gave way, and my foot hit the stair toppling me backwards onto my back and head. Like the falls with horses, I gave myself a mental check, but other than a shock and a big bump on the back of my head, I seemed all right. Poor Monica, aged two, had rushed to help, when she heard the crash. That right hip deteriorated during the six months I was on crutches, and by the following October I had to have a replacement operation as it had gone too far for an osteotomy. The replacement was done in Sister Agnes Nursing home, where I qualified to go as a daughter of an officer. David and Diana Burghley came to see me, as he had been in Sister Agnes, when he had hip problems. He was fondly greeted by the staff there, and having been such a great sportsman himself with the Olympic Gold in the 400 m hurdles in 1924, the Exeters were a good moral booster for me.

This time I was soon walking without sticks and climbed onto my lovely little Thoroughbred Bayridge before Christmas. I felt so good that I jumped a couple of small fences with him and even rode him to the meet of the Cotswold at Miserden Park, where Monica sat on the front of the saddle with me. She happily ate a sausage roll, as the reins were in my hand, while I had a smile like the Cheshire cat, feeling so proud to be on a horse again, with my daughter enjoying the occasion too.

The strain of looking after a baby and a two-year-old while I was on crutches had been horrific. If Monica fell over, which adventurous two-year-olds are bound to do while Lucy needed to be carried, I had no hand to spare with my crutches. Now I could behave more like a normal mother.

Sam had turned our cellar in Burg into a swimming pool, that helped me to get fit. It was a great investment, because not only did I profit from the weightless exercise but also Sam could swim when he came back tired from the office, in the dark winter evenings. The girls could swim too, without armbands, by the time they were three years old. Before that they did not have breath control to stop getting big tummies full of air, but they never had a fear of water. Other little children from the village came and learnt to swim in the pool without getting cold.

In the summer the water was used for the outside pool. One evening I was swimming outside at midnight, because Sam was away. As I lazily swam on my back looking at the stars and full moon, I was surprised by the beginning of an eclipse of the moon and fascinated, stayed watching the whole eclipse that night.

I have been lucky to live on the hills most of my life, where one feels close to the elements, when surrounded by forest and country. In the mountains the elements could vent their passion with terrible storms, hail and torrential rain. Looking out over the Alsace to the Vosges mountains and the German Schwarzwald, we could sometimes see three raging thunderstorms over the three mountain ranges in different countries, often converging with spectacular lightning and sheets of rain or hail. Complete crops of cherries could be wiped out by a hail storm, but we were lucky that our guardian mountain of the Remel, protected us by parting the storms that came in from the west while the next village, Metzerlen, was not so lucky and often took the full force of the storm that had passed us by.

Our home bred ponies were becoming an important part of the children's lives. It is usually little girls, rather than their brothers, who want the responsibility of looking after an animal, perhaps to satisfy their maternal instinct. Often children develop an immediate empathy and mutual trust with their animals. Man Friday, who would be Monica's pony until she was grown up, was born at Sudgrove on Good Friday where Monica, just two years old, and the older children saw the birth. Springtime, his dam, was usually ridden by Sibylle in the summer. The mare had been covered by our palomino Welsh pony stallion Ginko, that we had bought from Dick Richards off the Welsh mountains as a yearling. He was a wonderful pony, who not only covered many mares for twenty years, having some lovely foals with many palomino-coloured ones, but also competed in showjumping, gymkhana, cross-country and hunter trials with all the children. Monica won a walking race on him when she was three. Springtime obligingly foaled at breakfast time so Monica could tell other people who had not seen the birth, that Springtime had licked Man Friday dry and she had helped by rubbing him with straw.

Man Friday was a smart chestnut with socks behind and became a miracle youngster when he recovered from tetanus at eighteen months. Mary Hales was looking after my horses then and noticed that Friday was not picking up the hay normally in the field. The vet was called and recognised the dread disease, luckily diagnosed early so that with careful nursing he could be restored to health, joining us at Burg a month before his fourth birthday. Monica started to ride him then and their partnership flourished.

Both my girls had learnt to ride on Biscuit, a Welsh pony, that had also been Dominik's favourite ride in Steinacker. The pony and child would follow me riding through the forest and jump any little logs or fallen trees that I went over, so jumping was all part of riding and not a special skill in itself. Lucy had Twinkle, a palomino mare out of Sparkie and by Ginko, who was a year younger than Man Friday. They matched each other too, with Twinkle's palomino mane and tail flowing and Lucy's long blonde hair flying from under her riding cap as they leapt the logs in the field full of yellow buttercups.

Monica still did not approve of Lucy, but they had an understanding between them. The older one had always spoken good English and not baby talk, so Lucy did not bother with our languages but spoke her own. She was a small child and at Sunday lunch one day, Sam said, 'Lucy, when are you going to be a big girl?' She looked at us with round serious three-year-old eyes and replied, 'When the horses go away'. We were astounded at this first sentence in English that she produced, but the meaning perplexed us. Monica said, 'Silly girl, she means "when the cows come home"!' The movement with her favourite animal was Lucy's interpretation. She had a way with birds too, catching a lost bird that had flown into the house, in her little calming hands, and releasing it quietly outside.

Sam and I had friends from the circus world for many years. I knew the

Bertram Mills family and Bernard was a special friend, also Jimmy Chipperfield and Mary his daughter. We had taken the children to Longleat when Mary and her husband Roger, with their two children had an orphanage of animals at their house. Ours rode the baby hippo and had tea with Charles the chimpanzee who seemed to live in the house.

In Switzerland Sam had known the Knie family who ran the Swiss National Circus and they often exchanged horses and acts with my friends in the English circus families. As the Knies travelled around Switzerland, their Basel stand was for two weeks. Our house and swimming pool was always available to them for any of the little spare time they had to relax while in Basel. As often as possible I made time to go and watch their early morning training in the circus ring where the horses had to be exercised every day. The patience used in this training was a lesson while discipline had to be learnt as well. The horses soon knew and were pleased when they were clever, or when they were being naughty they showed their guilty conscience. Like good showjumpers, horses know and are proud to be stars and good at their job.

James Fillis in the nineteenth century had arrived in St Petersburg with an English circus, when he was spotted by the Tsar for his sympathetic riding and brilliant presentation of his horses. The Tsar then engaged him for the post in charge of the Russian Equestrian centre, where he became the founder of the world famous Russian School of Dressage. Many riders have improved their horses for world class dressage competition with the help from top trainers in the circus families who have been brought up in the tradition of the equestrian arts.

The work and patience needed for training animals and understanding their psychology is absorbing, together with the stable management necessary to keep animals mentally and physically healthy and fit during a season of constant travel. An apprenticeship with a successful and dedicated animal trainer would be invaluable to learn the sympathy and capacity for consistent behaviour needed to keep the attention and interest of the animal. Working with children and animals always entails inconsistent hours, as you cannot switch them off when you want to leave them; or end the lesson with a bad experience. The happy note of progress with the pupil must be achieved before the end of the training time, finishing with a reward and praise.

Monica aged four was given a great chance during a circus performance when Fredy Knie invited her into the ring during his act with eight stallions, four grey and four black. He left her in the ring with his long lunging whip held upright in her hands. From outside the ring he signalled to the stallions to sit on their haunches and then lie down. He then went into the ring and gave Monica a handful of horse nuts, which she fed to all the stallions as they lay waiting with anticipation for their reward.

8

Travels with Sam:
The Seventies

My right hip replacement let me be mobile again and, nearly without pain, I felt free from the fetters of being crippled. My legs were not the same length but that definite disadvantage was put right six years later when the left hip had the osteotomy replaced. As soon as one is evenly balanced, the strain is taken off the spinal column which reduces the risks of back problems with pinched nerves and slipped discs.

I still felt that I had been given a new lease of life and could participate in most activities with the family. Sam took me with him on a business trip to Japan via Moscow, where we spent two days. This was 1970 and the people looked unsmiling and grey, even the children coming out of school were not laughing and joking. It was depressing to see the queues everywhere, with very little to buy in the shops. I bought some stamps in the Post Office and was nearly arrested because I refused to pay twice. I had the number of the rouble note that I had given the lady, because I had new notes changed in Switzerland, but the girl had made a mistake, but would not look in the till to see the number of my note. An overseer was brought and I explained politely again with my phrase book. Just then Sam came quickly to pay again and take me away, but my bank note was there in the till and my original payment was acknowledged. I realised later that Sam was right to try to extricate me at any cost, as he forsaw a bleak future with his wife in a Moscow prison, but as I had proof, I was too stubborn and maybe unwise to be cheated. Sam wiped his forehead as we left the Post Office with my stamps and without a police escort and handcuffs.

We returned to change for dinner at our expensive hotel with no hot water to fill the bath with, no plug and one bedroom window broken with no glass to keep out the freezing Moscow wind. The inefficiency at the Moscow airport delighted Sam, just as the time wasted by Russians in endless queues for any commodity could not produce an organisation that could hope to rule the world at that time. Eventually we left on our plane and after the long flight over Siberia and the Amur river dividing the Soviet Union from China, flying too high to see the massed troops in this very sensitive area, we landed at Tokyo with the cone of Fujiyama on the horizon. The airport was bustling with passengers but we passed quickly through customs and immigration with the mixed feeling that this nation was leaving no stone unturned in getting ahead with efficiency as its priority. The road systems had been more crowded and dangerous than any other capital city but the Olympic Games in Japan gave the incentive to produce new highways to help with their traffic problems.

A business trip to Australia gave us the chance to go to the Northern Territory, to Gove in Arnhem Land. We were invited by Alu Suisse to their bauxite operation in the Aborigine Reserve and as well as learning about the processing of aluminium, we learnt something of the Abos living on the Reserve and the dangerous wild buffalo that roam the outback. The main stretch of bauxite deposit had included the runway for an American air base during the war, for air strikes in the Far East. Although the runway consisted of the red metallic coloured bauxite, no-one who was working there had realised its potential worth, until after the war, one of the pilots now in civilian work, remembered Gove and returned to inspect and analyse the soil to make his profitable find.

Africa had intrigued me on my showjumping visits, especially seeing the wildlife in the vast expanses of beautiful scenery. Sam and I had a great chance to join with the Strage family when they went to Tanzania in 1972 where Henry, who worked for McInsey, was an adviser to the Tanzanian Government. The Strages with their four children stayed in Dar es Salaam for the summer holidays, while Henry was working there. We travelled with them in two safari VW mini buses from Nairobi to Dar, taking Sam's older three children Catherine, Sibylle and Dominik with us to see a developing African country and the wildlife, which gave me an insight for my work with the WWF.

Our two weeks were filled to capacity with a 2,000 km safari through game reserves mostly on rough stone roads, a flight to the Mission and Hospital at Ifakara, 320 km into the Selous from Dar and meeting several of the Tanzanian Government officials.

The Ifakara hospital had some sponsorship from the Tropical Institute in Basel with Professor Ruedi Geigy, a distant cousin, travelling and working there over many years. In the Mission we met the Swiss doctor in charge and we were taken around the hospital. The children were fascinated by the snake pits holding many species of venomous snakes, kept for the education of students. The wards were spotlessly clean, with each patient cared and cooked for by their relatives so that they had the food that they were used to eating. Only special cases were fed by the hospital. Some of the patients had trekked or been carried for days to get to the hospital which catered for all the surrounding tribes.

The equipment was modern with an excellent operating room and x-ray machine. In the maternity ward the mothers looked after the babies and learned hygiene and correct feeding methods. We learnt that there are three times the European rate of twins born to Africans, although the reason was not known. The lack of proper nourishment for babies born in the bush, especially with twins, means that the mortality rate is high.

We had left Dar at dawn and flown up the railway being built by the Chinese from Dar to Kapiri Mposhi, 1,859 km away in Zambia. The project to open up the country had been inaugurated by President Nyerere and Mr Fang Yi in 1970, and the Chinese workers, who were completely self-contained, built their own villages along the line, which had just reached Ifakara, with the first 500 km completed in eighteen months.

Sam made sure that our family of five travelled in the two-engined Piper Aztec with a young Englishman who was an excellent pilot. The other plane carrying six was piloted by an experienced and handsome American war veteran, who took his single-engined Piper down to see the elephant and other game drinking from the river Kilombero. Two months later he was killed with all his passengers while returning from a bush flight. The news of that tragedy shook us to the core.

We all arrived safely at Ifakara landing strip where nine lions had taken over the strip only a week before while another lion had been shot in the village during the night. We were taken for an evening boat ride on the Kilombero to see the wonderful bird life and game along the river, and saw the fishermen catching kitoga, a delicious river fish that we had eaten for lunch. Leaving the river with elephants bathing and hippos submerging while water buck and buffalo gathered to drink, we flew back to the city lights of Dar. My thoughts were still with the blue and pied kingfishers, long tailed cormorants, African darters and skimmers sharing the river with waders, egrets, spoonbills, hammerheads and purple heron, flanked by palm trees laden with pelicans in silhouette against the African sunset.

Our mini bus safari had taken us first to Tsavo West National Park where we went directly to Mzima Springs to see hippo and the barbel fish before dark. Approaching the springs on foot with black-faced vervet monkeys playing around the warning notices of 'caution wild animals', the roar of a hippo echoed up from the pool. The threatening sound surprised the children, but we reached the pool in time to watch a hippo seeing off a crocodile, both just below the surface of the water. The crocodile's length of jaw and quantity of teeth showed that the enemy of Captain Hook was no fable.

Returning to Kilaguni Lodge, we were unloading the luggage, when Sam came back from the reception desk saying mysteriously, 'Just come and look at this!' I walked through the door and across the terrace ahead, where within one or two hundred yards were at least sixty elephants of all sizes, bathing, drinking, paddling or just relaxing around the three pools. The sight took one's breath away. Sitting on the terrace during supper we saw buffalo and rhino join the elephants, with tiny dik-dik browsing within a few feet of us along with impala, the larger antelopes that had delighted me so with their fantastic leaps in the Kruger Park on my first invitation to South Africa. I stayed up watching the floodlit pools until early morning, with the changing population of elephant, rhino, buffalo, giraffe, antelope and zebra.

After midnight, when the three boys had turned in and Sibylle was just going in from our bedroom terrace two rooms away, a buffalo approached in the darkness grazing towards the wall of our terrace, only a metre above the great black beast. It peered over the wall at the boys' closed door making it impossible for me to step along the wall to wake them or warn Sibylle. Three minutes later the buffalo moved away and Sibylle came floating along the wall in her hot pants pyjamas like a spirit in ecstasy after a successful brush with the devil. The buffalo saw the apparition and fled. When she did turn in, a rhino was approaching through the bushes. Her buffalo adventure was supplemented in the Serengeti when she was in the other mini bus that just escaped a charging buffalo.

The spell-binding night in Tsavo with the wealth of game at that time was followed by a night in Naivasha where evening and dawn boat trips on the lake gave us an initiation in the varied and colourful African bird life. The trees with lilac-breasted roller birds and the African starlings, superb in name and colour, made one wonder why their European cousins were so drab and untidy in the grey north where one craved for colour.

A pair of fish eagles cruised around us as we drove to the higher ground of the Masai Mara which joins the Serengeti National Park on the Kenya–Tanzania frontier.

We came across four ostriches having a dust bath and saw many herds of cattle guarded by a Masai herdsman who always carried a spear, and sometimes a bow and arrows. These tall and proud cattlemen live on milk and blood drawn from their cattle. Their villages consist of round flat-topped huts made of mud and wattle, looking like an outcrop of smooth rocks, until you see the growing cactus or thorn fence around the village and the cattle corrals.

Once in the Masai Mara reserve on the way to Keekorak, we came on the tail end of the migration. If this was not the full flood, one wondered how many thousand animals must have already passed this way. As far as one could see, on both sides, there were groups of zebra dotted about the bush. One aspect that I was interested in was a piece of land called the Lamai Wedge, adjoining the Kenya frontier of the Serengeti Park, through which the migration passes. The animals migrate at a certain time of year to follow vegetation that contains certain minerals and vitamins, so it is essential to their health, and therefore their existence, that their routes are left undisturbed.

The children saw their first lions lying on a rock before the Lobo Lodge in the Serengeti and the next morning we saw a pride of ten, the subject of a lion research project. Our first leopard made her appearance for us near Seronera tented camp on Swiss National Day, the first of August. The leopardess was watching her two cubs tearing at a Thompson's gazelle that she had caught for dinner. The camouflage of these elegant spotted cats has to be seen to be believed. We were within a few feet of them, and yet when they were still, only a flick of the ear or tail would give away their position in the grass. Leaving the cubs to scrap and eat in peace we returned to the camp seeing the sun setting over the great plains, lighting with its last rays several hyenas and two couples of bat-eared foxes.

Sitting near the huge bonfire fed with dead trees in the tented camp, reminiscent of the bonfires lit throughout Switzerland on the first of August, we met the research director Dr Tumaini Mcharo, who had spent many years in America.

Hearing hyena whoops and lions roaring in the night, with a background of weird moans from the hyraxes living in the rocks close to the tents, gave us all the thrill of an African night, although protected by the luxury of safari tents!

A ranger came with us before breakfast and our reward was immense. Before sunrise, the African pointed at a dark tree, 'African barn owl', and our eyes took a minute to focus on the dark shape in the depth of the branches. Light was coming onto the plains where three lion cubs were waiting for their mother to return with their breakfast. The ranger borrowed my binoculars, 'now we'll go over to the four rhino a mile or so away'. The three adults with superb horns and the young one were a picture lit by the first rays of the sun.

A Land Rover by a stream gave us a cause for investigation and there lying in the grass was another leopardess. If the first car had not seen her walking to her lair, no one could never have picked her out as she lay in the grass only a few feet away. We waited and our patience was rewarded. The beautiful creature came out of the grass, gave us a scornful glance and glided over a log across the stream, to disappear immediately in the undergrowth.

After this spoiling with the sight of so much big game, I was hardly allowed to stop and look at the rarest of birds. Before we returned to camp, there was another treat in store with two lionesses, that we were watching, suddenly flushing a serval cat from the bushes and seeing it off in no uncertain terms!

We drove out of the park over the dusty plain on a corrugated track which made everything in the bus rattle noisily. On the way to Ngorongoro reserve, our first stop was at the Olduvai Gorge where Dr Leakey had discovered the remains of the 'Nutcracker Man' and we found his wife was working there at this time. The name Olduvai comes from the Masai word for the bowstring hemp, or *Mkongi*, the wild sisal used for making bow strings, which grows throughout the gorge. The skull of Zinjanthropus was only found in 1959, thirty years after Leakey's first discovery of the gorge. The skull's enormous back teeth gave it the nickname of the 'Nutcracker Man'. Since then earlier skulls have been discovered, so probably the ancestors of man took their first steps in Africa more than two million years ago.

The first view into the caldera of Ngorongoro was breathtaking. As we descended down the precipitous sides of the crater in a Land Rover the mass of dots below soon identified themselves as various animals, antelopes, zebras and elephant in the tall swamp rushes. There were still 250,000 flamingos on the lakes, but 1½ million had left last week we were told. A moment later there was one less, as a young jackal carried one triumphantly out of the lake, only to be set on by a big male, probably his father, who took it aggressively and then himself was chased by a wildebeest and was considerably hampered by the long legs and neck of his stolen prey. When he did stop to feed at a safe distance, the young jackal was still not allowed a mouthful although he tried every trick with the older one.

We saw a pack of hyena sunbathing, maybe some of the characters studied by Jane and Hugo Lawick Goodall for their book on hyena, jackal and wild dog behaviour. A sleeping lion and lioness did not stir when we came within a foot or two of them. They were like an old married couple on a Sunday afternoon. No wonder they were tired, the ranger told us, as they had just started their ten days of mating, a tiring time before the cubs arrive four months later. The male then stays with the female until she has her litter. Five black rhino allowed us to get close and a beautiful big eland, usually a very shy antelope let us take his picture. A tiny Thompson's gazelle got to its feet for the first time and ran wobbling after its mother, showing the miracle of independent movement that these babies have so soon after their birth. As the shadows lengthened in the crater, we had to get into four wheel drive and struggle up the rough track out of the crater. We left the rim just as the sun was disappearing below the far edge of the crater.

A hyena trotted towards us in the dusk, as we came to the memorial stone to Michael Grzimek, killed when a griffon vulture hit his little plane, when he and his father, the famous zoologist were making a survey of the Serengeti in 1959. It was dark as we drove down to the rain forest below, on the way to Lake Manyara. The bright starlit night with the moon shining on the lake gave us promise of the superb view from the side of the rift valley looking across the sweep of the lake to the distant mountains. In the morning we were not disappointed and from the lawn of the hotel one could look down at the National Park below and see rhino, elephant, giraffe and other game, grazing and browsing.

It interested me to see that elephant and giraffe move in the sequence of near hind, near fore, off hind, off fore like a 'pacing' horse. The unwieldy-looking gnu or wildebeest were always balanced and never cantered disunited, for however much they dodged and played, they always changed leg in the same stride fore and aft and occasionally with a one time change of legs, like a Grand Prix dressage horse.

Arusha was our next stop below Mount Meru with Mount Kilimanjaro standing majestically at 6,500 metres beyond where we were invited to stay the night at a farm on its slopes. A brief visit to the Ngurdoto Arusha National Park was nearly prolonged by our VW bus stalling on a steep slope; as its battery was flat, we got out and pushed while a hippo browsed by the lakeside and a great elephant stood like a statue on the hill beyond. Above this superb scene, the snowy cone of Kilimanjaro hung like a cloud over the Ngurdoto crater rim. The sunset turned the cone to rose-tinted gold, as we found our farm in the fertile wheatlands just below the Kilimanjaro Game Reserve. Later that night the Southern Cross was very clear.

We rode out early the next morning through the ripening wheat and barley, before we caught the midday plane to Dar from Kilimanjaro airport, watched by a crowned hawk eagle as we departed. The Europeans who had opened the farm land in 1950, were getting ready to have to leave this fertile farm at Independence.

The children were encouraged to keep a diary on these special holidays and Dominik summed up his account of his first experience of Africa with the words (maybe inspired by some other writing), 'Never has so much been seen and learnt by one small person in so little time,' which expressed the feelings of us all. I was already hooked by my earlier visits to Africa and yet I have still so much to see and learn in this great continent.

Two years later, in 1974, Sam and I went to Africa again in spring. We first stayed in Lagos where Ciba-Geigy had a Nigerian office, and we could meet Chiefs who came from as far as Kano, where we went on another visit, 700 km to the north east. Chief Edu of Lagos was also an important member of the WWF and a personal friend.

We flew on to Zaïre and Goma in the Rift Valley where we could drive to the Rwindi Park. The route showed us more of glorious Africa, passing by the smoking volcano of Nyiragongo and over the watershed of the Indian Ocean to the south-east and the Mediterranean to the north. We were shown around the Domaine de Katale coffee plantations before we stopped at the picturesque Rutshuru falls near the source of the White Nile, called the Rutshuru Nile until it enters Lake Edward. Crops grow in abundance on the fertile lava land but since independence there have been problems with transporting the goods to the distant cities like Kinshasa.

The Rwindi Park was superb, the rift valley scenery being amongst the most beautiful that we had seen, with the backcloth of mountains on either side, topped by volcanoes. The green sea of grass watered by the Rutshuru Nile and the Rwindi river, both feeding into Lake Edward, made it a paradise for the well-fed wildlife. President Mobutu was a great supporter of the reserves and he had visited the Park two weeks previously. Most of the mini buses had African clients but there were two or three other parties of French-speaking white people in the camp.

We saw huge herds of elephant and many of the 25,000 hippo and 4–500 lion in the reserve at that time. Buffalo, topi, bush buck and Thomas's Kob antelope, water buck and a bongo all showed off for us and the bird life was abundant, with long crested hawk eagles, African fish eagles, flappet larks clapping their wings; then the wealth of wader birds on the shore and inlets of Lake Edward. We visited the fishing village of Vitshumbi and saw tilapia and catfish laid out in the sun to dry on the racks, while we ate grilled tilapia in our fingers from a charcoal fire in a hut. This was provided free but one could also buy beer and orangina.

Along the river our guide, called Matimano, suddenly told us to look closely at an euphorbia tree as there was a leopard in it. We thought the shape was too immobile and inspected what proved to be a formation of wood. Disappointed, he told us that he had fobbed off other tourists before us, sending home happy clients! On the river bank a mother hippo appeared with its new born baby, and colobus monkeys climbed through the trees.

During the night buffalo grazed around the hut while hippos roared and grunted in the Rwindi river below the camp. A large elephant stood nearby at dawn while we watched the flag raising ceremony at 6 a.m. with the guides parading and singing their national anthem. The ceremony of sunset was at 6 p.m., when the guides dismissed and went home. It was not by floodlight, nor did the Marine Band play the 'sunset', but it touched me with memories of the close of each evening at the White City, yet we were in the heart of Africa, speaking French with the *citoyens*.

Before we left we saw a family of six lions showing like a streak of light with the sun shining on their golden coats while they snoozed on a ridge. Approaching a mud pool seething with hippos, there were more old male hippos converging on the pool from every direction. In spite of their age they looked very happy in their communal mud bath, the Rutshuru river providing a haven for hippos of all sizes.

My cousin Philip Ridsdale, who was Bishop of Boga–Zaïre from 1972–1980, was not at his mission in Bunia just then, nor did we have time for the difficult drive through the Pygmy forests which we would like to explore. Philip (who had been a pageboy at mother's wedding in Cromhall) and his wife Lucy, had frequent safaris in the bush to meet the widely dispersed population of their diocese. To emphasize the hazards of the route, a French party arrived at the Rwindi camp, completely exhausted after their drive from Bunia around huge potholes and tracks washed away. They told us that the pygmies had been dispersed by Government policy, to absorb them into the life of the *citoyens*. Their village had been abandoned and no dancing for tourists was allowed any more, while some pygmies were in the army.

We had seen the elegant dancing of the tall Tutsi tribe, in the lava dust on Mount Goma, and toured the lava fields where the Mission had been destroyed in 1938 and the Lac Vert formed in a crater. In the rain we took off from Goma and flew over Lake Tanganyika, with thoughts of the gorilla study project starting in Rwanda and then below us at Ujiji, the historic meeting place of Stanley and Livingstone. Back in Kinshasa, Stanley was just being removed from his stand, gazing up the river and shielding his eyes with his hand. The locals said that he was saying '*Nom de Dieu, il n'y a pas de femmes!*' or 'Good Lord, not a woman in sight!' Stanley's statue was dropped down by a tractor, leaving his boots behind, but then it was said later that he was reunited with his boots and he would stand fully dressed in the museum.

I had visited the Leper colony on arrival at Kinshasa with the medical staff. There was family life in the huts, with little children having school. I was shown how breasts on men and ulcerated ears were a pointer to the disease while dressings were changed and ulcers washed with care. Then I saw the rehabilitation of patients doing weaving, chair-caning, basket-making, sandal-making and book-binding, also being given things to carry to make them walk and use their limbs. The patient helpers were giving these unfortunate people a new meaning to life.

A flight in a small plane took us to Muanda to visit the Sozir refinery, flying back over Matadi port and the rapids to the new Inga dam and hydro-electric scheme, designed to become the biggest in the world. The Swiss firm of Brown and Boveri constructing the project had been founded by two Englishmen at Baden near Zurich. I was sitting with the pilot when we landed back at Kinshasa where we encountered the Cassius Clay and George Foreman entourage arriving from Brussels before the big fight. Mohamed Ali was not among them, but would arrive later when the ground had been prepared for the boxing match.

We flew back from Goma via Lubumbashi where we had been invited to tour the Gecomine complex of mining copper, cobalt and zinc. At dawn we loaded into a small plane to Kolwezi, very close to the source of the river Zaire. At Kamoto, a resumé told us of the set-up for the 29,000 employees. First we toured the above ground and surface mining, where the huge grabs and lorries engaged in non-stop loading struck me with their size as forcefully as the size of a real elephant had astounded Monica my elder daughter, when she was two. Before that she had confidently chatted about her friends the 'Emilys' that she'd seen as pictures in her books, but the first time she stood beside a real elephant at the circus, she was speechless.

The copper seam first exploited in 1892 at Kolwezi, ran through to Zambia. The tracks were very slippery in the rain. At the old mine entrance, we were fitted out with gumboots, overalls, a belt with a battery and the light on a helmet. The truck took us down 350 metres, where we stopped to peer down further at the mining and collection of rock and rubble by conveyor belt and claws, which loaded onto trailers towed by caterpillar tractors. The stone crushers were fit for a James Bond setting, where 'goodies' or 'baddies' could be equally efficiently disposed of, leaving no trace! The noise was deafening while walking was hazardous with water filled potholes of various depths. I hoped that my replaced hips would stand the strain, and they did.

It was in this border area between Zaïre and Zambia that the aeroplane had crashed killing Dag Hammerskol, the Secretary General of the UN, who had interests in mining.

Another visit to Africa that year, gave us our first contact with Morocco and the Ivory Coast. In Casablanca one of the interesting people we met had his family origins in the Tessin, the Ticinese part of Switzerland where we had spent our honeymoon. M. Jean Soldini was a businessman deeply involved in Morocco and a supporter of King Hassan II. I discovered that he had met Bob Kleberg from the King Ranch, Texas and John Cypher, his business manager, both of whom I knew from 1953 and my stay on the ranch. He had been with Bob while he was finding land to reseed the grazing and establish Santa Gertrude's cattle, which would help to upgrade the local breed. I mentioned that Bob had died just three weeks before, a coincidence that saddened Soldini.

Soldini himself had already had three of his nine lives, but remained remarkably untouched by these terrifying experiences. He had been in the earthquake of Agadir and was one of the few lucky survivors, and he had witnessed the young Prince (now King), sent by his father to organise the rescue and clearance after the disaster, make the agonising decision to spread lime over the whole area to prevent the ravages of epidemic diseases, in spite of the possibility of further victims under the rubble that just might still have been breathing.

His second miraculous escape was from the crash of a Caravelle coming into land in Casablanca in fog. It hit the ground before the airport, breaking in two, and throwing Soldini attached to his seat into the field. He had ribs cracked and an arm shattered, but only remembered telling the rescuers who were cutting him free to get him away from the burning plane, not to damage his new suit. He was one of eleven survivors out of eighty people. He could even ring his wife the next day from hospital.

The third escape was in the coup at the Palace on the King's birthday. During the lunchtime celebrations, the rebel soldiers arrived and shot at random, throwing a grenade down a chimney and killing all the cooks and caterers in the kitchen below. Soldini was in the courtyard where everyone had to put their hands up. The Belgian Ambassador tried to tell the rebels that he was special with a diplomatic passport but as he put his hand to his breast pocket to show the passport, he was shot dead and fell beside Soldini. In spite of Soldini's crippled arm from the plane crash he forced himself to keep his hands up for two and a half hours, helped by the certain knowledge that he would be shot if he let the arm drop by his side. The King had evaded being captured by hiding under the sofa.

We had a tour of the phosphate mines in the complex of the Gisement Khourigba where the phosphate is surface mined, a little reminiscent of the Kolwezi copper mines, which we had seen in April, with the huge grabs and gigantic machinery. The Chief Engineer, who sat next to me at lunch, had been trained and qualified in Moscow where he married a Russian wife, and they and their children go to Russia every year. Several Moroccans had been trained in Moscow, starting with an intensive Russian language course for six months, and then six years study of engineering.

On the high plain towards the Atlas mountains we visited one of the King's Domaines, Tazeroualt, where we saw sheep and well-irrigated and fertile land. It was dark by the time we arrived at the Hotel Mamounia, Marrakesh, the famous hotel where Sir Winston Churchill had taken many holidays. We went to the show at the Casino, with acrobats, a snake charmer whose snake kept its fangs open while he put his nose in its mouth, then an excellent belly dancer. We did not try to emulate this lady's style, but Sam and I danced two delightful old-fashioned tangos.

I hoped to swim at daybreak and see the sun rise over the Atlas mountains, but dawn broke on a thick fog, before a dust and sand storm blew in and obliterated everything. Driving back away from the storm, there were pairs of a camel and a donkey pulling a plough and one tall camel had a very small pony as its partner, a most uneven couple.

We met a gentleman in the plane for Abidjan, a great character whose father had been assassinated in Togo. We were told later in French, with a big wink, that our new friend was 'a baker, who made very good bread' – a description that I had not heard before.

The deputy Governor Coulibaly met us for dinner in Abidjan; he was chief of the Senoufo tribe and had arranged for our visit to Korhogo, capital of the north, the next day. First we flew to Ferkéssédougou in a Piper Aztec twin-engined plane to be shown around the Sodesucre cane plantations and irrigation scheme with an enormous factory to process the sugar. Most of the 'sugar men' had been trained in Madagascar and were old pals together. Our Algerian French pilot, a *pied noire*, had brought a crate of wine for the Lonrho group there and was busy drinking it at lunch in the canteen when we came in. Sam stopped him quickly from finishing the bottle, before he flew us on to Korhogo.

Safely landing there with big thunderheads threatening, we went straight to Koni, where the villagers had been waiting all day to dance for us. By then unseasonal rain had started and a thunderstorm was gathering. The ground was a bit slippery already but we were taken to see the iron mines where the miners climb down a narrow round hole and carry a bag of ore back up the sheer sides. Back at the village of round thatched huts, the dancers were warming up and the music with drums and xylophones was beating out. The white cloaked elders and chief of the village were seated ready to receive us and start the dances. The little children were already swaying to the music. There were two lots of musicians who alternated their playing, marching on and then off when the others were signalled to come.

There were dances of masked men doing gymnastics and flip flaps, then men with head-dresses and girls who danced with great movement bending forward from the waist with straight swinging arms. As it got darker from the storm and the evening, we had a backcloth of vivid lightning, but luckily the heavy rain waited until the end. The spectators and dancers got very worked up, with one small child falling flat under the feet of the dancers in a trance. The father, who first kicked her aside eventually picked her up and carried her off still out for the count. After the dances we were shown the smelting of the iron ore on the roofs of certain huts that had a central furnace. A man stood on the roof organising the ore while below the formed ingot was removed from the furnace. Some little scamps were watching Sam and he blew a few smoke rings with his pipe which thrilled them.

We drove back in the storm with terrific flashes of lightning. There was no water in the hotel but we brushed up and had dinner. We got up in good time the next morning to go to the market and see a little local life in Korhogo, as there were no tourists. We enjoyed the astute people before we were taken to a nearby village where the carvings are done. Bargaining with the elders was a long and patient process, while I took photos of the village life and a little girl pounding the corn. Unfortunately it had been too dark to record the dances of the Senoufo panther-man the night before.

Sam was determined to get a carved ebony hunter, a little man carved in the last century, who soon came home to Switzerland, to stand guard in our hall and now is on duty at Sudgrove.

At the Nestlé Foundation we were shown the green mamba snakes and other lethal serpents that were coming back to Basle for Professor Rahm, Director of the Natural History Museum. I had met some WWF contacts especially Dr Lauginie who could tell me about the Tai forest, that I had no time to see. The problems accompanying the infiltration of prospecting miners have increased in the past two decades.

We stopped in Abidjan for two days on the way back from Zaïre in 1980, where I could talk to Dr Lauginie again, the vet and ecologist, who was *Chêf* of the Project on Fauna in the Ministry of Water and Forests. At that time there were still some bongo in the Tai forest with other rare species, but they needed immediate protection. Even in the Azagny Park, only two hours drive west of Abidjan, a pilot had just reported seeing poachers and dead elephants. I talked to one of the ministers that we met about these problems, while more positively some wives who were trained teachers, became involved with producing an education programme on the conservation of nature with their children's classes.

On our first trip to Zaïre, our curiosity had been aroused in Goma when we heard of the gorilla project in Rwanda, within easy driving distance, but we had neither the time nor the visas to visit the Virunga Reserve. Six years later on another business visit to Kinshasa, Sam made sure we would not miss this experience.

Our introduction to these wonderful apes was beyond all our expectations. We had arranged the two-day trip to Rwanda, after meeting Dr Sandy Harcourt who had worked at Karisoke on the gorilla project in the Parc des Volcans on the Rwanda side of the frontier. It joined the Parc des Virungas on the Zaïre side of the mountains and the Kigezi Gorilla Sanctuary in Uganda, the three countries making up the Park reserve, touching at the summit of Mount Sabinio. We had slept the night, well-equipped with provisions and sleeping bags at Jean-Pierre von der Becke's place up the mountain, having picked up *Un Zamu*, a sentinel, to lead us the three quarter of an hour's drive up the rough and slippery track from Ruhengeri up the base of Mount Muhabura to Gisiza at 2,400 metres.

We had been met with mixed feelings, as there were no guest facilities, but as we unpacked the stores, faith was restored in our camping abilities! Jean-Pierre had returned from a wet day's abortive search for Group 2 gorilla family and had been charged several times by the lone silverback, Brutus, a mature and aggressive male. Sam settled on a mattress by the living room fire, but I was given a bed nearby behind a bead screen and slept between two blankets, in a sweater and socks to try to keep warm while annoyingly my heart played up, probably because of the height on the mountain.

We woke early to a lovely morning after the soaking day before. Outside it was perfect light to take photos of the panorama of volcanoes, and the flocks of pretty little dark red birds, the red-billed firefinch, that I'd identified in Goma the day before. Driving to Visoke camp we heard tales of the gorilla families that were within the boundaries of the park. Dian Fossey's Group 5 were only observed by herself and some scientists, but Sam and I were invited to join this mornings observations with Jean-Pierre and Rosalind Aveling; Conrad, Rosalind's husband had been in charge of the Orang-Utan Rehabilitation station at Bohorok in Sumatra, when we had tramped through the rainforest to join them for a night in 1977. Now they were studying gorillas in Rwanda and by chance our paths crossed again. They came out of their tiny Rondaval, a round native hut, where they had to sleep in a curve, and as I presented Ros with a jar of marmite, she grabbed it saying 'I was nearly suffering from withdrawl symptoms and you've saved me!' Three years before we had finished the last of the marmite at Bohorok.

Conrad left to look for Group 11; he too had been threatened by Brutus the day before. Sam and I went with Ros and Jean-Pierre, led by Rolocana, a first-class tracker who had worked for years with Dian Fossey, straight up the mountain on a steep and slippery track, often only a foot wide. We regretted our gymshoes with no profile.

Rolocana slashed our way with his mupanga blade through giant stinging nettles and elephant nettles with huge leaves, wild celery, which the gorillas find delicious, and gallium or ladies' bed straw, a favourite food of the gorillas who love to eat it, pulling a handful and rolling it in a ball before popping it in their mouths. They eat the bamboo shoots, thistles and the nettles, but only once had Rosalind seen a gorilla eat a bit of the root of elephant nettle. Galium is their delicacy and a filling food. An adult needs twenty-five kilos of food a day to be satisfied.

We felt very privileged to be allowed to look for Dian Fossey's scientific study Group 5 which consisted of thirteen gorillas at that time. It was the original group that Dian started studying thirteen years before after being advised by Dr Louis Leakey, the famous anthropologist. Dian had left for America a few months before but the two Americans, Peter Veit, qualified in conservation zoology and doing a two year study of Group 5, and John Fowler, studying to be a vet, were living at Karisoke, Dian Fossey's research station of seven huts built on the ridge between the extinct volcanoes of Karisimbi, 4,481 metres and Visoke 3,784 metres.

Rolocana gave me a hand up some of the steep and high steps up the mountain and I used my bamboo cane to steady me too. He heard the two Americans talking and before we appeared up the track he tapped his blown cheeks to make a gorilla noise, the Americans started to 'chest beat' and so we were introduced. They had been waiting for an hour and had nearly given us up for good, as we'd been delayed by the tourist office where we got our permits to see the gorillas, and the very rough route.

Icarus, the younger silverback of Group 5, had attacked Rolocana, our tracker, once when he came unexpectedly on the group while they were resting, and Peter had been far back and could not warn them of Rolocana's approach by making his usual 'belch vocalisation'. They had rolled down the slope in a bear hug, but Rolocana had dropped his mupanga and relaxed, so they just separated and looked at each other as Peter approached and Icarus realised that they were all friends.

As we fought our way up, Peter started to make his 'belch vocalisation' like a clearing your throat noise as we got close to the group, to show the gorillas that friends were approaching. The going was tough with no track through the forest undergrowth, then Rolocana stepped aside to let Peter take over, and he waited behind, while we made our observations. In the groups that the tourists can see, the guide uses a 'pig grunt' to keep the gorillas from approaching too close. We didn't hear the gorillas singing like people which they sometimes do while feeding contentedly. Before Rolocana had located the group, we had seen and had the smell of fresh gorilla dung. We quietly continued and as we got closer Peter made more throat clearing noises to tell the group that we were coming and not to worry. Peter had told us to hang on to our things but not to move suddenly if they took something. We should sit quietly and let them investigate us, as they are curious and will approach us. We must move very slowly and drop our eyes submissively if they look aggressive.

I was puffing and panting as well as trying to make friendly gorilla belch sounds while my heart pounded from the height and steep climb but I was determined not to weaken in the quest. Suddenly there was a real gorilla looking at me from a bush. I couldn't believe the proximity of this big black gorilla, who was Pablo. I stopped in my tracks, but Ros beckoned me on. Around the bush was a clearing with the whole family of gorillas resting. A huge silverback, the senior adult male Beethoven, caught my entire attention. I got a shock as I looked down and saw a large gorilla at my feet touching our friend Rosalind's face with its lips and feeling her long auburn hair. I slowly sat beside her with one leg out, clutching my camera only a foot or so from the gorilla – its attention was immediately drawn to my white gym shoes that I'd borrowed from my daughter Monica, for the trip. Ros told me later that perhaps Tuck had mistaken her identity because Dian Fossey had the same length hair as Ros, who was a stranger to this Group, although she was used to being with primates, after their work in Indonesia.

People working in the Rain Forest around Karisoke at 3,000 metres on the Virunga volcanoes sensibly wore brown climbing boots, so the sight of white laces on my gymshoes fascinated Tuck and she fiddled with them. Luckily I'd tied a double knot as I would have been in trouble getting down the mountain without a shoe. Friends who had lived in Zaïre for ten years also in gorilla country, but lower down, had told us that gymshoes would be best for tracking gorillas, but in the Rwanda rain forest, we regretted the decision to leave our heavier boots behind in Switzerland.

The two silverbacks were resting quietly while Tuck was getting more and more friendly and put her face close to Rosalind, played with my gymshoe laces and felt my socks and then lumbered round to Sam and whipped off his little mauve round hat by the pom pom and scampered away. The fun and games with that hat were hilarious, and the fighting for ownership was marvellous to watch. The somersaults with it in hand or foot and the chase to get it, finished with a climb up a small tree and the holder looked like 'I'm the king of the castle', then another started creeping up the thin stem to try and grab the hat. The Americans were busy scribbling notes on this new behaviour pattern, with Sam's cap for a plaything! Our children who had knitted the cap were tickled pink when they saw our film of the 'Cap Game!'

Meanwhile Tuck had got a bit out of the picture and Rosalind had unwisely, as it turned out, taken her bag containing her hat and films, having just changed a film, off her shoulder. Jean-Pierre had put my Laufen market fishing hat in his rucksack so it would not be pinched too!

Tuck approached Rosalind and me as quick as lightning, grabbed the bag that was lying unattached between us and leapt away. Rosalind said 'shit' then 'sorry', but the gorillas didn't need an apology as they had got their new plaything. The super unique film was in the bag with other useful things. No-one made a move while the mischievous family played and tried to open the canvas bag without success.

Both Sam and I had a run out of film by then, which did not please us, as we'd left, by mistake, some more film in the rucksack 300 metres below at Rosalind's hut. Rosalind lent me a black and white film, but not before the moment when Puck put her little two-year-old Cantsbee on her shoulders, sitting in front of us to show him the human beings from close up.

Icarus, the younger silverback, had moved past us once or twice, before the canvas bag was dropped by Tuck. Peter approached quietly and firmly, while Tuck submitted to his authority as he took the bag and returned it to Rosalind. She was most relieved to find everything intact. Tuck was not pleased at losing her toy, so she came back to see if there was anything else to pinch, but we all enfolded our belongings.

Apart from the games with the cap and fighting over the possession of the canvas bag, there had been great wrestling tussles between the gorillas with holds like in a rugger scrum. They were showing off because they were only used to the Americans or Dian observing them and now they had us as an additional audience. Rosalind's hair fascinated Tuck, as she sat face to face touching her, maybe because Dian Fossey also had shoulder-length hair.

Effie, the mother of Puck and Tuck came to look at us and put her new infant of five months old, Maggie, on her head. The baby sat looking at us with a sweet face and round eyes. Peter said she had only started being carried dorsally for a couple of weeks, before that she had been carried under the belly. Later while Effie fed she lay astride along her mother's neck. As far as they know Effie had only produced females, Puck, Tuck, Poppy and Maggie, but Puck had her son Cantsbee.

Both the silverbacks rolled on their backs to get attention and grooming, stretching one leg at a time straight up in the air, looking ridiculously helpless. Ziz suddenly decided to climb the slender tree that the two small gorillas had climbed while playing and disputing about Sam's cap. The tree bent under his hefty weight and he lost his balance and swung around the branch just holding on by one hand. He looked immense as one could see his length from hand to dangling feet forming a superb silhouette. He still had about four years before he put on more weight and became a Silverback.

Beethoven then rose on his four limbs and came slowly towards us, passing between Sam and me without giving us a glance. This was the signal to the group to move and feed – they did not go far but dispersed among the bamboo, feeding leisurely. Like children, the young gorillas had got tired of playing with Sam's cap and just left it on the ground when they moved off. Peter retrieved it and gave it to Sam. He sniffed at it and said 'It's funny, I can't smell gorilla on it!' Peter replied, 'No, but they could smell you!'

We had been watching the group and sitting among them for nearly two hours and we now stood up and discussed our fantastic experience. Peter wrote out a family tree of the group, that Rosalind copied, because even she was not allowed normally to see this group. Jean-Pierre brought out a welcome thermos with sweet tea left over from the day before. It was like a delicious nectar although normally I don't take milk or sugar!

While we waited for Rolocana to appear to lead us back down the mountain Rosalind told us the news from Indonesia, where Lucu, the young orang-utan that I photographed in 1977 for our Bohorok Christmas card, had become rehabilitated successfully. The people who took over from them at Bohorok had let Riang free too soon and he had died of pneumonia. Gorillas are very prone to pneumonia too and it is a major cause of death.

At first the Americans were going to stay in the forest and then return to Karisoke, but one decided to come down with us, and then, hearing that we had brought wine and beer, both of them decided to come back for the night.

We had seen an antelope on the way up on the agricultural side of the fence and now we climbed through the fence and clambered part of the way down outside the forest. Before we descended the last steep bit in the forest, we sat on the water tank looking out at the fabulous view across the valley with the two lakes showing hazily in the distance.

Rosalind went ahead to put the kettle on for tea and John chatted with us. He asked Rolocana what the Rwandans thought of the Zairoise. 'Bad,' he replied without hesitation. Back at the hut we drank our tea and waited for the mini bus driven by Kamada. As they didn't turn up, we started off in Jean-Pierre's Toyota, leaving the Americans to pick up their van and Rosalind to wait for Conrad. They were all coming to Jean-Pierre's for supper and to camp for the night. The Americans sent a porter up the mountain to Karisoke to fetch their sleeping bags. I was glad that I did not have to climb back through the forest to 3,000 metres.

We had heard thunder and now Muhavura looked very black but we got back safely up the track and put a big pan of water on the fire for a hot wash. The others turned up only as darkness fell. Conrad had had a long day and seen several gorillas but had not recognised any of Group 11. He thought he had met Brutus too, but was not sure, as he had not stopped to see if he would attack!

The evening turned out to be real fun and there was much banter between the English and Yanks. Jean-Pierre enjoyed it all and produced the *pièce de résistance* – tiny banana flambées, accompanied by some ribald humour from his male guests.

Eventually everyone bedded down, Sam brought his mattress to my part of the room behind the strips and the three men and Rosalind lined their sleeping bags towards the fire. Kamada slept in the house that night, having frozen in the mini bus the night before, although he was invited in. I, too, was frozen but this night I felt no pain because the success and experience of today had astounded me – I slept well and deeply until I felt a wet tongue working its way under the blanket that I'd put over my head to keep out the light – Mutti then gave Sam the same treatment although no one wanted her love at 6.00 a.m. The big talk from the Americans about getting up a 6.00 a.m., resulted in total silence until after 7.00 a.m. in spite of Mutti's repeated efforts. Mutti was Jean-Pierre's charming fluffy chestnut bitch, only eight months old; she had tried to persuade me to take her for a walk the morning before, when we had to leave early for our gorilla adventure.

The time spent among the gorillas had been a dream come true, because I am in my element in the field observing any animals, but that day had been a very special privilege. It is important to see the conditions for people in the field working for nature conservation and the protection of endangered species. So often this is very dangerous and thankless work, especially when involved with criminal poachers, as was tragically proved when Dian Fossey was murdered in her hut at Karisoke during the Christmas of 1985. The heartbreak that she and her team had when finding murdered gorillas that had been observed as family since they were born, was brought home with that final evil murder of Dian, the unique researcher of these wonderful primates. These sad events were ahead, together with the disappearance of Beethoven and deaths of other gorillas in the Park.

My thoughts included a deep appreciation for the love and efficiency that Sam had put into planning his crowded business trip to include this two-day excursion into Rwanda. My three hip operations had also carried me safely on the two replaced hips through the rough and difficult terrain of the rain forest. It was Sam who had encouraged and supported me through these operations, when I was crippled with osteoarthritis just after our second baby was born in 1968, while our first daughter was nearly two. The trauma of having a toddler and a baby, while trying to cope with crutches for six months, had proved to be worth the patience needed by the family, with my disability. My heart too had responded to the frequent physical stress that I demanded of it. Only five years later, the doctors found that I'd lived a life on borrowed time and only open heart surgery might carry me further. There would not be many more lovely places than Karisoke for a permanent resting place, but it would have been very inconvenient for Sam and the others if my heart had given up in the forest.

After a healthy breakfast with wild honey, we packed up. The black and yellow weaver birds and the red-billed fire finches around us, did not make the parting any easier. We said our thank you very sincerely, in Kinyarwanda, '*Murakoze*', while we were used to '*Asante Sana*' in Swahili.

We had learnt from Kamada, our driver from Goma in Zaïre to Ruhengeri and the Park, that Rwanda used to be one country as far as Masisi until the 1914–18 war. When we first met Kamada and climbed into the mini bus, we had asked him if he knew what had happened in the United States. He told us that he had heard on the German radio, in Swahili, that the 'other one' had been elected President. When we got to Goma, our friend Popol confirmed that the new President was Reagan!

Popol had entertained us and others on the cargo plane that had brought us from Kinshasa with gorilla stories. He was in charge of transport for the Kitale Coffee Plantation and they have two old Britannias from the RAF, with all the mechanics, who are ex-RAF and live in Goma. I was told that ours was once the Queen's Flagship, which did not prevent it from returning with a plane full of game carcasses for the butchers of Kinshasa. Flying back with that smell and getting liberally smattered with blood, was enough to turn one vegetarian. My clothes continued in a perpetually damp state, after washing them during our half night stop-offs!

Popol had once been bitten by a gorilla on his back side. He was on his way to pay a social visit to an English Doctor on a tea plantation. The Doctor saw the wound and exclaimed 'The bugger bit your bottom? The bloody bastard!' and gave Popol a tea cup full of brandy. English can be a concise and descriptive language.

We met Popol's wife and little daughter at their house looking out over Lake Kivu; his gorilla photos were really impressive. He kindly lent us some sleeping bags and a camping fridge box and thermos for our trip and told us of the three types of monkey in the Virunga Parks, the blue monkey, the diademed guenon and the colobus monkey.

We drove through the market at Sake, weaving our way through piles of vegetables and colourful peppers, with the road full of women carrying huge loads and staggering under enormous bags of charcoal attached to a band around their forehead. Colourful goats and groups of Watutsi cattle with widespread horns, also filled the way to the market. Beyond, we felt our way through the fertile valley to inspect a very derelict plantation, with a view to setting up research projects, for Sam's firm. There were possibilities for the future with labour from a small village nearby, that we saw as we walked through the fertile but abandoned terrain.

At the frontier there was a garage and, petrol being like gold in Goma, a *citoyen* was filling his car, although holding the nozzle in the same hand as a lighted cigarette. It was Guy Fawkes Day! In Rwanda the intense agricultural cultivation in terraces up the mountain sides, contrasted with the wastage of land in Zaïre. There were impressive villas built along the lake, left from the prosperous Belgian times. Red kites were flying over the lake, reminding me of the kites at our Burg home in Switzerland. A cormorant, on a rocky promontory, spread its wings to dry.

I had an introduction to meet M. Dario Merlaut, who had taken the name of Kasuku, when the *citoyen* of Zaïre were asked to take native names. Kasuku is the word for parrot. He farmed large areas of land, and had tracts of native forest and growth where there were chimpanzees and gorilla families along with other wildlife, that he wanted to conserve. He needed help to guard against poachers for these areas where the WWF is involved in financing viable conservation projects, with donated vehicles and material to set up patrol units. He told of the daily killings of gorilla around Pinga and although he estimated the numbers in the gorilla families were over 200 then, they would rapidly drop at that rate of poaching. He was President of a Cooperative, organising education in country districts. He bred cattle and farmed at Masisi and his hobby was breeding horses from an English Thoroughbred that he had bought after it had raced in Kenya. He was delighted to discuss pedigrees until late in the evening after our dinner of tilapia fish. He invited us to call at his lakeside house the next morning to see the monkeys and birds that lived around there.

That night I sat outside our hut wrapped in a blanket, watching the southern sky and three thunderstorms with great flashes of lightning reflecting in the lake. A large planet twinkled to the south, but the bank of thunder clouds on the horizon must have hidden the Southern Cross. Bats flew around in a friendly way frightening the mosquitoes that, for once, spared me. When Sam finished reading we both slept deeply until 'boom' at 5.00 a.m. when an almighty thunderstorm hit us with crashing thunder and rain and the hut was illuminated by lightning. Our flight that should have left at 6.00 a.m. was put back to 4.00 p.m., so we could visit Kasuku's lava stone house built above a bay in the lake, with a black lava sand beach. The lake was in a collapsed crater or caldera and the steep hills down to the rocky shore are forested habitat for monkeys and many birds that are protected there. A monkey appeared behind the house, my book showing it to be L'Hoest's monkey or *Cercopithèque de L'Hoest*, with a white collar. They have a very limited range and must be rare, but there were blue monkeys too – I saw some pairs of Ross turaco and would have liked to observe the bird life for hours. An African hawk eagle was sitting on a little tree on the cliff, but we had to leave, while the boat from Bukavu approached over the lake.

I took a last look at the lovely volcanoes of Karisimbi, Mikeno and Nyiragongo that I had last seen in 1974 when we visited the Rwindi Park. Now there was a new little volcano, Muraha, that had appeared in 1977. One of the baby gorillas at Karisoke, born that year, had been named Muraha.

We had first met the Avelings in 1977, when they were in charge of the orang-utan rehabilitation centre at Bohorok. We landed at Medan, Sumatra at the beginning of our Indonesian trip. Driving in the WWF Land Rover to the Gunung Leuser Reserve, we passed enormous clove trees and endless rubber plantations, lurching over potholes and puddles in the rock road. The land was very fertile and beautifully farmed with healthy paddy fields while little kids waved to us and shouted 'Bye, bye'!

Many of the Batak race, originally from Burma, had settled around there; we were told that they were good workers and said what they meant! The Malays live mostly along the rivers and on the coast, as they are fishermen.

We left the Land Rover at the last group of houses, and carried our luggage for the next fifteen minutes, climbing through a rock tunnel and then following the river through the forest. The water was cascading down over the rocks until we came to a canoe attached to a cable, where we could get across the river. When the water was higher it was impossible to cross, but we only got splashed as we swung across the torrent.

At the hut we met Ros and Conrad Aveling, also two baby orang-utans, Riang aged seven months and Lucu at ten months, who were too young to look after themselves in the forest, but two bigger orang-utans were in large cages outside. They are very prone to human diseases and had to be kept in quarantine after being rescued from captivity. One had lost the use of its hind legs from polio, but was swinging around and there was a chance that it might improve.

We settled into the bungalow, quickly shutting the netted door to keep out the mosquitoes. I gratefully grabbed a *spirale* and kept it near me, burning night and day, to discourage the mosquitoes. In Buenos Aires, one Christmas, I had learnt the value of a smoking *spirale* to prevent me from being eaten alive. The bathroom had a shower, cleverly powered directly from the waterfall. The rainwater tank was handy to scoop out water for heating or flushing the loo.

We heard tales that night of some of the rescue operations of the orang-utans and some of the terrible conditions that they were found in. One was so neurotic from its treatment that it had to have constant individual attention, and although it was released in the forest, it kept near the feeding place and didn't try to build a nest. Usually the first instinct of an orang, when it is old enough, is to make a nest to sleep in a tree. Even if a baby has been taken before it could observe or learn from its mother, the natural instinct is there. The orangs are very solitary apes in the forest, whereas gibbons and monkeys live in social units. When young gibbons are taken into captivity, they have to be taught the ways of survival that otherwise they would have learnt from their social upbringing. An orang is therefore a better subject for rehabilitation to the forest, after the quarantine, once it becomes confident in its freedom and old enough to cope for itself.

The Avelings had also inherited a baby sun bear when they came to the centre. They suffered from its fierceness and use of lethal claws as it grew, and were relieved when it was old enough to be left in the forest after having it for seven months as an unruly and destructive guest.

The rain poured down in sheets and we wondered if the river would rise too high for our return tomorrow. During the night the sound of waterfall, river and rain merged into one soothing lullaby. Early in the morning we were woken by noisy gibbons calling to each other, while staking out their territory.

We left early for the feeding ground up the mountain. The red clay was wet and slippery and steep and high steps cut in the clay made tough going. Conrad had lent me a stick which helped while I hauled myself up with the other hand on the lianas and branches. It was very humid but one was glad of the forest shade, as the sun was hot in the few gaps between trees. On the ascent we saw the strips down the mountain opposite where the trees had been removed quite lately and the first monsoon rains had already scoured the mountain side making the river run red with the eroded top soil.

The conservation of nature in the Reserve was unfortunately in the hands of a sub department of the Forestry commission, where the interest lay in logging. This was done indiscriminately rather than selectively, leaving bare strips down the mountains. The monsoon rains washed the soil straight down to the river below and once the land was eroded nothing could grow again. Selective logging would have allowed secondary growth to hold the shallow soil and allow the balance of growth in the forest.

The ruthless loggers also came across the slow moving and trusting orang-utans, shooting the mothers in order to steal their babies and sell them for pets. Most often these babies would die and as a female only breeds every four years, the breeding stock was horribly depleted by the poaching.

We passed the old feeding ground, seeing how several orang-utans converging there could damage an area of trees, by their constant nest-making as the same nest is rarely used again, bending and breaking the branches. I looked at the steep, slippery track ahead with a sigh, and continued up to the new feeding site. The wardens and one of the Avelings fed the released orangs up the mountain twice a day.

Just before we arrived at the site, we saw a family of siamangs, black gibbons, sitting in two trees. On our way back we were to see how graceful and athletic they were as they passed over our heads. First the father, the mother with a baby and a juvenile following, and then a young male that kept at a distance and displayed himself spreading like a big octopus across branches of a great forest tree. He was probably about ready to leave his family group and make his own way in the forest.

Only five orang-utans had come to get the bananas, a good sign meaning that the others had found their own ripe fruit in the forest. Bananas are a staple but dull diet, so encouraging the apes to find more interesting food on their own. We were fascinated by their behaviour and three of them made superb nests in no time with expertly woven branches before settling down after their fill of bananas.

All was at peace in the forest when the leaf monkeys (langur) started their cries and then the white-handed gibbons called with different whooping noises from male and female. We watched the siamangs swinging gracefully over the tree-tops; they put the slow and clumsier orang-utans in the shade.

After the climb we took the two young orangs to the river while we swam. The rapids and eddies in the white water were hard work to combat but we got cool and clean. The orangs protested when we left them in the bushes by the river, obviously feeling insecure when left to their own devices. The most beautiful sight against the background of the torrent were the enormous butterflies. They were as big as birds and of superb colours, coming to alight on our discarded clothes while we swam and sat in the sun, always choosing their own colours to match that of our clothes!

We wandered back to the house for lunch, finding the long-tailed macaques, naughty little monkeys, stealing the bananas from the two orangs in the outside cages. One of the quarantined but otherwise fit and nearly adult orang-utan, put a banana through the bars and onto the roof of its house. Later, it put its hand through to get the banana, but couldn't feel it. Frustrated, it looked around the ground to find a stick, which it then grasped and pulled inside. Then it climbed up and got the stick through the bars and turned it back to feel the roof. The banana was found and pushed off the roof and caught by its other hand as it fell in front of the bars. It had invented a diverting and rewarding game, as the banana must have tasted much better after the thought entailed in its recovery.

While listening to the calls of the white-handed gibbons in the forest, the two young orangs started climbing over us to attract attention. They loved to hold onto Rosalind's hair and Lucu would give a playful bite to make you notice him. They invented a great game with a chair that had tipped up; they would rock it until it fell over and imprisoned them and then they would tip it back, showing off to us with great delight.

Before we left Rosalind told us of a shooting safari operator who had boasted that he could show her tiger, rhino and elephant in the park. He did not know that she worked with the WWF, but one's heart sank to hear of the illegal safaris and logging encroaching on the 786,000 hectares of the Genung Leuser Reserve.

An orang suddenly appeared at the window; she was the female of a pair that had grown up together in the centre and then had been successfully released in the forest. The male must have left his companion to look for a wife, while she being lonely came back to look for him. She was returned to the feeding place up the mountain by the rangers carrying the bananas. We too had to leave through the forest to load into the Land Rover.

The rain poured down as it got dark. None of the bicycles had lights and most had wide sidecars. Dark people walked in the road while lorries honked their way through the chaos without care. One heavy lorry overtook a bus coming towards us and filling the road ahead. If the bank of the stream had been one foot closer to the road, we would have toppled in but this nerve-wracking drive ended safely in Medan, before we continued by plane to Java.

Our helicopter flight from Djakarta to the Ujung Kulon Reserve was just as interesting. While loading our limited camping baggage and some fresh vegetables into the chopper, the pilot appeared and we stopped in our tracks. The small, grey haired man, surely well over three score years, came to greet us with his one hand.

The pilot's left hand was missing and he had an arm stump below the elbow with a stocking over it, which he fitted into a padded ring on the elevator stick. We were slightly shaken but loaded up into the three places behind the pilot in the nose. We started up and everybody cheered as we rose from the ground while we waved goodbye, only to descend back to earth. 'Too heavy,' our pilot reassured us, only to rev up and take off at speed over the paddy fields horizontally and not vertically. We held our breath as the trees approached, but just in time elevated over them. Our Ciba-Geigy friend on earth got such a shock with our take off, that he forgot to film it! There followed an absolutely fascinating flight.

We scared the life out of some of the rural oxen supposed to work in the water and mud of the paddy fields, and nearly all the agricultural workers looked up from under their big conical straw hats to watch and wave. We had both sides open and so could wave back, if one's hand didn't get blown off. The palm tree lined rivers showed the wealth of Javan water, with the intricate and well-organised irrigation schemes for the paddy fields.

Our captain took us right over the roof of the Sultan's Palace at Bogor and the famous botanical gardens filled with wonderful trees. We were told on the way back, that our captain had piloted the Sultan in the old days and had landed on the vast lawns, but then in the war the palace was used for American and British prisoners-of-war by the Japanese. Now no-one dare sleep there because of the haunting by the ghosts of the tortured and murdered prisoners. He enlarged on the experience of a couple of friends who had slept there, not believing the ghost rumours. After a frightening and sleepless night, they vowed that they would not repeat the experience and were from henceforth firm believers in ghosts.

We continued to climb over the central ridge of mountains that run along Java. At 600 metres, the highest point necessary on our flight by following the passes, we saw the Indian Ocean ahead. Descending rapidly towards the fishing port of Pelabuan Ratu, we landed near the beach to refuel from a helicopter pad and little runway where we became objects of interest to a large group including many children. Taking off again, we followed the coast and beautiful beaches washed by the surf from the ocean rollers. Beyond the harbour full of fishing boats, we flew over President Soehato's summer residence on the beach of Samudera. On along the coast we saw fishing boats and most of the people manning the rigging waved with enthusiasm.

There were pretty villages among the palm trees, but on the very few roads we saw, the one or two vehicles were crawling along, showing that the surface must be atrocious. We were amazed at the friendliness of these people living in remote areas, who ran out and waved shirts or anything that they could lay hands on.

After the fertile paddy fields, carefully farmed and irrigated, we came to the depressing area where scrub and trees had been burnt and smoke was still rising around the horizon. A great deal of the ground had marks of erosion already, and the little top soil left only needed the monsoon which was already due, to wash it away, leaving the land barren. A vivid contrast was the ancient rain forest which had been protected by the wardens of the Game Reserve. Some of this had been encroached by the nomadic people of that part of the coast, who graze their animals, plant one crop and move on, leaving desolation behind them.

The real rain forest of the Ujung Kulon peninsula looked green but dry, before the monsoon arrived to refresh the land. We were flying at about 60 metres, very near the tops of the forest giants. Coloured flashes of hornbills flying amongst the trees, were nearly the only sign of life except for an occasional rusa, the local deer. Of course we were all trying to see our first Javan rhino, unique to this Reserve and reduced to only about 20–25 before the work of people like Professor Rudi and Dr Lotte Schenkel at Ujung Kulon. The numbers have increased since then, but only with constant care and policing by the team of wardens.

I saw the new volcano replacing Krakatoa on the horizon, 50 km north in the Sundra Straits.

Aided by maps personally drawn by Rudi Schenkel, we found the island of Pulau Peucang among high trees on the coast. Our captain made a safe landing, although the boat was waiting on the mainland beach where there was a safer clearing to land. The head of the Reserve, who was the *Kepala Sexi*, Mr Widodo, was based in Labuan, a rough boat journey from Peucang. He came across in the boat when he saw us land on the island and we all had lunch of fresh fish on the open verandah.

A three hour walk across the island took us to the cliff at the point where the two currents meet, the point of Tamjung Karang Copong. We had listened to the birds and observed crab-eating monkeys, wood doves and a sea eagle, wild pig and rusa, a stag scratching its wide antlers in the bushes before leaping away. Sitting on the cliff we looked down on huge barracuda cruising around the rocks and a sand shark with its fin cutting the water. The butterfly fish shone yellow against the coral, and when we came back to fish around this point we got a big horse mackerel with blue and orange stripes; then a nice barracuda with needle teeth and a salmon that made our delicious dinner, and which alone proved almost too much for seven hungry people.

A couple of rusa fawns were by the camp when we got back, but we took the boat to Cidaun to see if the banteng were in the clearing, but the wild cattle had been frightened away by workmen building a jetty on the mainland opposite the island. At that time, we landed on the beach and waded the last few feet, which was fine on sand but agony on coral. A colony of blue throated bee-eaters were silhouetted on a tree but hurrying before dark I took a photo of a monitor lizard and rusa in the camp.

I swam in the dark rather than douche myself with the dibber, not heeding the dangers of the deep, and felt much better after our journey and island walk.

Coming back in the boat at dusk, the sky above us was full of flying foxes, great bats with wings like crows, clumsily flapping their way from the island to the mainland. In the morning they all flapped back again. They can fly for some distance in spite of their awkwardness, as they island hop right to Australia. In the Ivory Coast we had seen the Abidjan fruit bats hanging in the trees along the main boulevards.

At supper, under the stars of the Southern night we got some good Indonesian stories. There was first the one about the best quality coffee beans. The mongoose has very good taste when it comes to coffee beans, so he only selects the top quality. These beans go straight through him, so that the wise people who collect the beans from his droppings get the best. This was topped by the durian story. The durian fruit has a terrible smell when it is opened, but people who get over their revulsion the first time can progressively like them more and more until it becomes their favourite fruit. However, the most sought after durian, exceeding all deliciousness, is the one that had been through an elephant.

Then there was the reason why the cock crows at 4.00 a.m. before dawn. Sanguriang, an important man, wanted to marry a Princess and she was delighted, until suddenly she realised that he was her son. She had been blessed with eternal youth but she could not divulge her secret. So she made it a condition of the marriage that a new dam must become full overnight before the cock crowed at dawn, which was his habit. As she anxiously watched the dam being filled rapidly by Sanguriang she inveigled the cock to crow at 4.00 a.m. just before the dam was filled, and so saving her from committing incest. Ever since then people have been roused by the pre-dawn cock crow.

We sat chatting by the light of a hurricane lamp and candles, but suddenly one of the camp boys came to tell us excitedly that there was a python in the well. We got there quickly and saw it under the side of the well in the water. Stones dropped in did not dislodge it, but later we saw part of its tail across the bottom of the wall. Our invitation to one of the boys to climb down and get it out was turned down immediately.

Next day, after breakfast, we left by boat at 7.00 a.m. in spite of a tummy upset which was not ideal for a rough boat ride and long jungle walk. We let out the fishing line with a water lily on it as a lure, and let it troll. The boat was going much too fast for serious fishing but suddenly we saw a flash of silver and a huge tuna was leaping at the end of the line. Everyone yelled to slow down but the boy hauling in the line did it so quickly in his excitement that we lost the fish.

As we rounded the point of the mainland we hit the rough ocean rollers, and a new steersman took over who had more experience of these seas. We made it to Tanjung Alang Alang but had to land on very sharp coral, carrying our walking boots and socks. It was agony getting through the waves on the coral barefoot but then we sat on the sand and gratefully put our boots on. The whole coast is full of coral and walking through jungle was very rough, with pieces of coral washed up in tidal waves and bits of dead wood from the coastal scrub.

The great explosion of Krakatoa, on 27 August 1883, had not only made the loudest noise that the world had ever known, but it caused 30 metre waves to sweep over the whole peninsula of Ujung Kulon, drowning the population and wiping out villages, leaving jagged pieces of coral and lava high on the coastal hills. Indirectly, in leaving the area depopulated a natural reserve was created with no access by road and a difficult approach by sea and Javan rhinos moved in undisturbed in this ideal habitat for the rare and shy animal, that was already hunted and poached to near extinction.

We followed Widodo to a clearing where the grass was very bare from the drought. It was already hot, so the banteng had moved to the shade of the forest, although there were plenty of fresh droppings. Peacocks and jungle fowl were abundant and I collected peacock tail feathers while a wild pig sauntered across to the bushes, then in the trees as we made our way cutting through the undergrowth, we saw the great black head and horns of a big male banteng. He was in a deep thicket protected from the flies but crashed away when he sensed us there. It was difficult to be quiet as the two men cut the way with their *goloks*, the local name for the machete forest knife, which is carried as their only defence. Another Indonesian name for the knife is *parang*.

As we approached another clearing the big male and a younger male banteng galloped by in a flash, too quickly to photograph. We continued hacking our way across the point to the calmer side of the island where we could follow a track that had already been cleared parallel to the shore. It was not very comfortable walking, with the sharp little sapling stumps, that had been cut to make the path, covered by leaves and twigs of wood.

The path was also used by animals marking their boundary areas with urine. A leopard left scratch marks where he had kicked away the leaves after urinating, and the wet patch could be seen by gently stirring the leaves. Some enormous termite hanging houses, like big round footballs, were fastened to the trees; Widodo made a grinning face on one, hacking with his *golok* the eyes and mouth, but Sam wouldn't spare his pipe to complete the picture. One still had termites in it, but most had been abandoned.

A tiny mouse deer ran across a small clearing where the ground was very dry, although it is under water in the wet season, and the tidal swamps and beach forest are not accessible for part of the year. Widodo knew the Latin names of nearly every plant and tree and had a wealth of information on the whole ecology of this region.

When we reached the beach where the boat was meeting us, we saw a lot of leopard tracks in the sand. One of the rangers went to look at a clearing to see if it had game there, but at mid-day everything had moved into the shade and we climbed into the boat to return to camp, still trolling a line but 'in the heat of the day when the fish don't bite'.

Our quest was to see the Javan rhino, and even Widodo with seven years of work on the Reserve had only had twenty-nine sightings. A jungle fowl rooster woke us before dawn so we took the boat early to the most western part of Java. From there we walked to a rhino wallow, which one could smell from afar, but the beast had only left its large imprints. Following a rough track through the forest, Widodo showed us where the rhino had browsed while it bulldozed its way through the jungle leaving the long thin palm leaves broken off half-way up. Where it had passed under half-fallen trees or branches, rhino hair was still sticking to them and in places it had pulled down a young tree to browse off the top growth. Where it had urinated to establish its territory, the urine had splashed high up the foliage. We were making our way to a favourite wallow up the mountain, and although we followed the tracks, when we came into the clearing where the spring came through the ground, the wallow was dry. The rhino dung, which smells like sweet hay when dry, is supposed to cure a cough when smoked in a pipe but Sam rejected my suggestion that he should collect a bundle.

We did discover an eleven centimetre spoor of leopard on the way and I photographed a lovely red jungle flower growing out of nothing. At last we came across a water liana as we were very thirsty, so the rangers quickly cut the liana as high up as they could reach and even more quickly lower down, so the water would not be drawn away by the capillary system and osmosis. We all drank plenty of the delicious water dripping out of the stem, but when handed a thicker section, the water tasted bitter. It was like drinking from a Spanish *bota*.

An impressive sight in the rain forest were the great tree buttresses formed to support the base of the shallow-rooting 45 metre trees. Another great wigwam of tree roots had been formed by the wild fig, at least 45 metres high, which, having strangled and killed its host tree, kept a few lumps of wood in its clutches as proof of its past support. The roots of the kacembang, joining in a high apex at the trunk 9 metres from the ground, made a perfect place to build a hide, way above the path of the rhino and yet not in too dense a foliage for photos.

Cool, clear coconut milk assuaged our thirst when we later reached the hot shimmering beach. Widodo sent his chief ranger up a 30 metre palm trunk to reach the clusters of young coconut fruits far above him. This intrepid man had to pause a few times when the force of the wind bent the high trunk. As the fruits were not ripe, it took a lot of hacking to break them away from the tree. The rangers below shouted with annoyance as the individual coconuts split after the 30 metre fall. At last with patience he got a whole cluster and as they fell, the coconuts underneath cushioned the top of the cluster as they clouted the ground. When we had found enough uncracked ones for all of us, Saridan was allowed to climb down and only then enjoy the fruits of his labour. Cutting spoons from the green fibrous covering of the fruit, we could scoop out the delicious soft green fibre inside and drink the colourless liquid. No mature coconut could ever compare with this delicacy.

We snorkelled along the coast among the coral reefs of the Marine Reserve, with every shade of sea anemone and fish of many colours. Young and transparent barracuda cruised through the water with the parrot and butterfly fish. Brightly painted little blue striped 'cleaning fish' gathered around the mouths of the larger fish, but Widodo signalled to me to swim back as I was watching a lobster sticking out of some sea cucumber growing on a coral crevice, because he had spotted a sand shark. Sam had swum around a rock and come face to face with an enormous grouper, which looked him in the eye and opened its large mouth. More dangerous was the highly poisonous leopard fish, a grey form lying in a murky hole. I kept well clear as I am allergic to many things, but invisible little jelly fish did sting us, especially on the top lip between the mask and the snorkel.

Returning to the camp, a big banteng bull appeared in a clearing; he watched us, looking menacing like a black Spanish *toro brava*. His attention was diverted by a little chestnut calf that trotted out of the bushes and went to touch noses with its father. The bull, with his young charge, gave us a last look and bucked around showing his white bottom and smart white legs as they galloped off into the bushes. The calves are all born chestnut and then only the males turn black.

Our last day then dawned as we left by boat at 5.30 a.m. to reach Cidaun to meet the helicopter in an open safer landing place. There was not much time left to canoe up the Cigentar river to see the dazzling kingfishers and wildlife in the thick green foliage along the banks; we were expected in Djakarta that evening, so we had to leave the Reserve by 9 a.m.

We had seen a fresh rhino track coming down the bank of the river, which over our three days exploring showed us that there were several about. Banteng, pig and rusa slots also showed that they were customers of the sweet river water, while the archer fish spat water up to catch insects, which tumbled down into their open mouths. Still no python had been spotted in the trees, when we all stiffened to the magic word '*Badak!*' There ahead of us was a dark head with its single horn breaking the surface of the water. A Javan rhino was wading up the river towards us and had no chance of getting up the bank before we had drifted close by. We slowly converged in silence, holding our breath, hardly believing our incredible luck; then as we drew close to the rhino it hauled itself out of the mud and heaved itself up the river bank. At the top of the bank it halted and turned to face us. It looked enormous, crowning the territory above us as it snorted its challenge with a frightening noise.

I prayed that it would not charge down the bank and overturn the canoe, as my legs were jammed under wooden slats across the middle of the dugout canoe. We breathed again as it decided on discretion and turned away crashing through the undergrowth. The rangers were as thrilled as us with the encounter of a *badak*, releasing their tension in a chatter of dialects. Sam had taken the scene on our 8 mm cine camera, the first colour film of a Javan rhino.

Ten minutes later we were in the helicopter, taking off to join the bright coloured hornbills flying over the giant trees of the rain forest before the shock of the desolate land beyond the reserve where the birds and trees had gone leaving some smoking brush, burning anything that was left, on the silent bare slopes that already showed signs of erosion.

I was interested in the flying of the machine but anxiously noted the fuel gauge as it dropped to E, while we were far from the refuelling station. A village near the beach appeared in the nick of time to provide a landing place on a dry corner of a paddy field, as we spluttered down on the last drop of gas. The whole village quickly gathered to see us while children poured out of the school and crowded onto the bank by the helicopter.

Our captain had been inscrutable through the crisis, but after questioning he conceded that fuel for our machine could be brought to us from a depot about 10 km away. We were relieved to hear that it was not further as the terrible road surfaces slowed traffic down to 5 km per hour. We were cheerfully led to the Police Station, where the wives and children came to greet us, while the grandmother made us tea. Chairs were found and we sat together in the immaculately clean office, exchanging photos of our children and the farm at home. Their children fetched us fresh mangos from the gardens while we passed a delightful time with these kind and hospitable villagers. They were fascinated to hear that we had seen a *badak* that morning, to them a mystic animal from the tales of long ago.

No-one had told them before about the unique wildlife in the Ujung Kulon reserve, or how irreversibly their heritage of unique flora and fauna was being destroyed daily. These intelligent people were thirsting for information and knowledge about the ecology of their lovely country and this emphasised the importance of spreading conservation education at a grass root level so that could be made available for everyone. Our emergency landing had not been wasted time with our new friends.

I had read some books that John MacKinnon had written on his conservation research so I was fortunate that our paths crossed at Bogor, at the Indonesian equivalent to WWF offices. He and his four-year-old son were recovering from an attack by a wild pig in Sulawesi. The boy had been savaged and bitten, breaking his arm, as John dashed to save him but the pig bit off John's little finger as he rescued his son. His wife, with their younger boy, had to take them by boat to the main port where they could fly to Singapore for treatment and unpleasant anti-rabies injections in the stomach.

The conversation had also covered the grisly facts that a Frenchman had just disappeared on Commodo Island leaving only a crushed camera, suffering the same fate as a boastful Swiss who was eaten by a Commodo dragon, having disregarded the safety instructions to stay with the tourist group. Liberties cannot be taken with wild animals, even domestic animals can bite and kick, but I envied and admired people who had worked in the field with often inhospitable conditions and difficult situations. The compensation for their tough life must be from the reward of discoveries in their research and the knowledge gained in wild and beautiful places.

9

Sudgrove and Sitatunga:
Holidays with the Children

At Sudgrove I had started to breed ponies when I got married, having bought our palomino stallion as a yearling colt in Wales from Dick Richards. Palo was born on the Welsh mountains and he grew to 14.2hh. His official name became Criban Ginkgo of Sudgrove, because we have a ginkgo tree by his paddock, the maidenhair tree which is a conifer with fan-shaped leaves, sole survivor of a family of trees which flourished 200 million years ago. Palo never had a bad foal and his stock are spread through England and Switzerland. He was also a perfect child's pony, winning a walking race in a gymkhana with Monica when she was three, competing in cross-country events, showjumping and dressage. When he was used for other gymkhana events with the children, they sometimes let go of his reins by mistake while in obstacle races or musical sacks, but he never took advantage of them. He only showed off as a prancing stallion when his stallion bridle was put on before taking him to the covered school to serve a mare. He has retired to live in our house paddock with the ginkgo tree, hearing all that is going on, having been part of the family for nearly thirty years.

The children had plenty to do with their homebred ponies in the holidays. After my wedding and move to Switzerland, Paula Sykes left to start her own riding school in Norfolk. I then had girls who could help the children with the ponies. Mary Hales had been at Talbot Heath, where her elder sister Jean had been my contemporary at school, and she was excellent in her care of the ponies and children. There were also the two 'Anns' that stayed. Ann Sherring worked in Switzerland for us with Sam's eventers and the ponies before returning to work at Sudgrove. Anne Fitzpatrick came to live in the house while she became a schoolteacher and taught at Miserden Primary School. In the term time the agricultural students boarded in the house and we returned during the holidays.

Miserden House had been the romantic meeting place of some of our girl grooms with students from the Cirencester Agricultural College. A happy marriage had also grown out of the meeting of Robert Borwick, now Lord Borwick, who was studying at Cirencester, and Babbyns Johnstone a riding friend who came to stay with me several times. Their second daughter became my godchild.

Romances continued at Sudgrove when Mary was the first to marry, after meeting Roy Sandy who lived locally. Ann married Robert Cook who had been tiling the roof of our Sudgrove House Cottages when he saw this nice girl riding past below him every day, so my Aunt Lini decided to introduce them at ground level. One of our students studying at Cirencester Agricultural College stole our

(*above*) Family jump! Lucy
on Twinkle, Monica on
Man Friday, Pat on Legend
and Sam on Springtime
(hidden) at Steinacker,
August 1975. The house
can be seen in the
background.

(*right*) Our one-handed
helicopter pilot who took us
to Ujung Kulon in 1977,
and on the way back ran
out of fuel. The school
turned out to greet us as we
made a forced landing in a
paddy field, and the police
and their families looked
after us until the fuel
arrived.

(*above*) Orang-utan at Bohorok
Rehabilitation Centre 1977. Lucu
was our Christmas card in 1978.

(*right*) My mountain gorilla photo
of Pablo feasting on bamboo at
Dian Fossey's study Group 5,
Rwanda National Park,
November 1980.

other Anne to make her Mrs Tim Clarke. These are some of the many romances that have sprung between our guests at both Miserden and Sudgrove mostly with happy endings, our children becoming godparents to Anne Clarke's first two children.

While Monica and Lucy were small and occupied with Pony Club Camps and events with local gymkhanas, we took the older children on summer trips. We went to Scotland, Ireland and Cornwall, seeing friends and exploring the countryside and shore. Three years after their first African safari they came with us in 1975 to South Africa where Sam had business appointments during which we were shown parts of the Boputhatswana homeland where the Chief invited us to his house to visit his family for tea.

Leaving for Botswana, where my Aunt Mary had been born and raised, the flight took us over the Limpopo river on the border, then the great salt pans of the Makgadikgadi and on to the huge green delta of the Okavango river, where the water at the base of the delta triangle disappears into the ground at Maun. We landed at Shakawe at the neck of the delta to get our first sight of the Okavango river at Shakawe tented camp and then continued to the Victoria Falls and Chobe Game Lodge, a new experience for us all.

Botswana with its contrast of Kalahari desert, salt pans and lush delta habitat with fertile land along the rivers, fascinated me. At the Shakawe tented camp, I heard that a couple were running a houseboat on the Okavango, where trips of several days could be organised for a party of not more than three couples, to go into the uninhabited delta and see the wildlife. Tim and June Liversedge had started this enterprise, so I wanted to meet them. By chance a small boat was just coming down the river with two people, avoiding the family of otters that I was watching. The otters dived as the boat passed them and then a lady stood up with the painter rope in her hand, looked at me and exclaimed, 'It can't be Pat Smythe on the banks of the Okavango!'. The people in the boat were Tim Liversedge and his wife June, who had been a showjumper from Scotch Corner in Yorkshire before she had married. We had a lot in common to talk about with wildlife in Botswana and her interest in the present showjumping scene in Europe.

We compared notes on our lives since we had married and ceased to compete in our chosen sport. She had always loved Africa, when one day she was sitting in the shade of a bush in the Chobe reserve, Tim happened to pass by and picked her up.

Sam joined us as we drank beer by the river while the sun turned red and set, with its reflection highlighted in colour on the water with the otters splashing around again. We decided to take a week on the boat in October of the following year, but it seemed a long way ahead as the little boat took them back to their present clients on the *Sitatunga*, the name of the houseboat and the aquatic antelope of that name, with its special elongated hooves for moving around in the reed beeds, where their favourite food is the papyrus grass. Our route then took us to the Zambezi.

The wonders of the Victoria Falls were mixed with the horrifying fact that a visiting American girl had been shot dead by a Zambian guard on the other side of the Zambezi, when climbing down the rocks below the hotel. Chobe Camp provided another wildlife thrill for Sibylle, when she found the trunk of an elephant waving at her open window while a big warthog boar was rooting in the lawn by the path to the dining room, although he stayed on his knees grubbing for his dinner as we passed close by on the way to get our meal.

Back at Sudgrove Monica and Lucy had been involved in Mike Roberts' preparations for the Sudgrove Roman Fair which we were holding for the church funds. This was on a grander scale than a fête, with the gladiators performing and battling on a pole over a burning pool, the losing combatant being knocked off the pole and into the flames below. They just avoided disaster towards the end of their display when the pool started to leak with the impact of armoured bodies crashing down. Our small children had not made such demands on the prefabricated material before. The day's events were a great success that benefited the church as well as giving entertainment on a grander scale than usual, finally ending with my two girls asleep that night almost before they had removed their Roman dresses.

Earlier that year I had my left hip replaced, as the osteotomy operation that had been done after Lucy's birth, was now causing me pain and discomfort. After the hip replacement I was walking comfortably a fortnight later, and now after fifteen years I am still very active and comfortable. When I was allowed to ride again, I felt so happy to be riding without pain that I gave Bayridge a few jumps which we both enjoyed together. I could now walk correctly with both legs the same length, thanks to Nobby Clarke the wonderful surgeon and keen fisherman from Northern Ireland.

Our return to the *Sitatunga* was preceded by a business tour of Kenya to farms on Mount Elgon and Mount Kenya, both mountains standing over 4,000 metres. I learnt a lot about seed being produced for the Kenya Seed Corporation with maize, grass seeds, bearded wheat to protect the grain from birds and various strains of barley. The low percentage of moisture in the harvested grain would be the envy of Gloucestershire farmers. The cattle were crosses of Charolais, Angus and Galloway crossed with Boran, the local breed with a hump on the withers. There were Hereford crossed with Bomana, another local breed with resistance against some of the problems of the region. Throughout the world many of the settlers who started to farm and raise livestock and crops have put in so much work and patience through generations, to find the best animal or crop for different climate, soil and altitude. There have been many sad occasions when the science and expertise that produces the ideal has been lost in war or revolution.

We spent the night at Samburu during our tour, on the Uaso Nyiro river. Three years later we would camp with Monica, Lucy and Dominik, with camels on the upper reach of this river where it tumbles off the escarpment of the Rift Valley through the rocks at Crocodile Jaws. We had our first sight of Gerenuk antelope with their elegant giraffe-like necks which help them to browse leaves off higher branches, standing upright on their thin hind legs balancing with a foreleg lightly touching a twig. Reticulated giraffe, impressively marked with dark chestnut-patterned rectangles parted like crazy paving with narrow cream lines, were browsing the higher branches. We studied the markings of the Grevy's zebra with narrow stripes, bigger and heavier than the common Burchell's zebra, with very rounded big ears. The oryx with long and elegant horns were playing and fighting among themselves. It was sad to leave them and a cheetah loped beside us before disappearing into the bush, while a family of elephant crossed the river as we returned, the large male tusker seeing that the river was clear of crocodile for the safe passage of a baby elephant that followed him across with the others in single file behind him.

Samburu is probably derived from the Masai word for butterfly. They are a beautiful race of semi-nomadic people with the fine, classic and aristocratic features of the Masai groupings of the Nilo-Hamites. We were to leave them for the Bushmen living in the Okavango delta, the little people of ancient origins.

First, I could visit Sandy Price in Nairobi; she had helped to set up the Wildlife Clubs of Kenya. The programme incorporated Wildlife Clubs in every Kenyan school that wanted it, with the pupils running their own clubs with the help of a teacher to co-ordinate their efforts. I was involved with conservation education and it was impressive to find the enthusiasm about the projects in progress, in spite of the clubs being run on a shoestring from a wooden hut by the museum. Already after seven years, one of the early school members had become a game ranger with others following in the same line. The museum provided an education too, under Richard Leakey the director, where Kenyans could see and learn the ancient roots of man found in their country.

Cornwall had provided us with two holidays during Sam's short July break, one with the older children; the younger girls then came with us to a little house near the cliffs belonging to Mrs Peggy James the former owner of Warneford. The special bonus of this week was that dear Betty Morgan came with us. She had worked at Sudgrove for Mrs Mills since she was fourteen years old, and also had spent many holidays in their neighbour's Cornish house with her husband Leslie. The first thrill for the girls was our overnight journey by train from London to Penzance in sleepers. Lucy had sickness problems in boats, cars and planes but the train provided a comfortable and happy start to the holiday.

Betty was an experienced hand to advise us about the best village shop, the coves and beaches, with best of all the Minack Theatre, a stage on the cliffs below rocky benches forming the amphitheatre, with the sea as a backcloth to the stage and the sound of the waves breaking at the base of the cliffs. This perfect setting for *The Tempest* gave the children an impressive introduction to Shakespeare, as we sat with our feet on the stage while an athletic young Ariel leapt onto the rocks above us, with the part suddenly taken by another spirit Ariel on the cliff above the opposite side. Since then, the girls have been able to keep in touch with productions of the Bard's works at Stratford-upon-Avon, an easy drive for a superb evening.

Sam had generously invited my family to join us on the houseboat *Sitatunga* on the Okavango in Botswana. Nicco, mother's youngest brother, with Mary his wife, and also Evalyne, the widow of Hugo, joined us flying to Botswana when Sam had finished his business commitments at C. G. Sparten.

We flew over the Limpopo river into Botswana, over Maun and the Delta to Shakawe where Tim Liversedge met us by boat. He had been up all night writing a paper on Pels fishing owl, while June had typed it. I sympathised, having often done the same while poor Paddy typed doggedly, to catch my deadlines. Our plane was to return with Tim's script, so Johnnie the pilot had to be held hostage until the manuscript was ready.

Gliding downstream into the Delta, the boat took us past white-faced ducks, spoonbills, skimmers, blacksmith plovers, marsh harriers, cormorants and darters and a black collared barbet nesting in a tree near the houseboat. These would be our companions along with the herons, African fish eagles, Pels fishing owls, bee eaters and other feathered friends, for our five days of idyllic life on the delta.

Before the big *Sitatunga* left its mooring with us to penetrate the papyrus of the delta, we took the small motor boat up the river to the controversial Caprivi strip, the no-man's-land, at that time inhabited by terrorists, between Angola, Zambia and Botswana, giving access to Namibia and the Atlantic for Zambia and Zimbabwe. Villagers living near the river had big triangular baskets for fishing. We stopped to look at two colonies of carmine bee-eaters with hundreds of birds nesting in sandy holes in the river bank. A wet meadow on the other bank was inhabited by a fantastic variety of birds including the sacred, wood and glossy ibis, open-billed stork, black-winged stilt, yellow-billed and red-billed teal, ruff, Ethiopia snipe, grey heron, white pelican and white-winged plover.

On the way back we saw a very big crocodile and heard that recently a dangerous crocodile had taken a village woman who was getting a bucket of water from the lagoon. Tim and Daphne Truthe (Daphne is the daughter of Bobby Willmot the crocodile hunter, who himself was killed by a mamba) were asked to get this crocodile. They eventually lured it with a goat, but the crocodile was keener to get them, having acquired a taste for humans.

Setting off in early morning sunshine, the best viewing place was on the flat top of the boat. Occasionally the head of a sitatunga ram showed in the papyrus reeds as they looked up curiously and then splashed away melting into their camouflaged habitat. The crocodiles slipped off the sand bank as we left and flocks of birds rose into the air and then settled back again. My favourites were the skimmers that nested on the sand, leaving their eggs and young unprotected while they went fishing, but the camouflage of the young was so complete, that with each step, there was a danger of treading on a chick or a nest. The adults performed swift aerobatic displays and then landed to sit in their typical flat crouching silhouette that is never shown in bird book illustrations.

Taking the little boat ahead of the *Sitatunga* we watched a huge colony of carmine bee-eaters nesting in the Red Cliffs. The lovely birds soared on the wind with their two long tail feathers showing well; while they gathered insects, the leguans moved to the nests to steal eggs, profiting from the birds' absence.

We startled a Bushman as he paddled his dugout canoe, with all his possessions on board, as he made his way to cut papyrus stems, to use keeping his fishing nets in place. Tim enticed him to our boat with three cigarettes and a stump for a light, while whispering, 'Be ready'. I took the photo as the Bushman turned his head to us for one second and the print showed an ageless face with good teeth. We continued up the red tinted Namasere that drains an area of the delta where spurwing geese and white-headed duck congregate in their thousands. Passing through a fish dam made by our lonely Bushman, Tim made for the island where the Bushman sometimes lived, as well as a Pels fishing owl that had safely nested there and was raising a chick.

The evening sky turned from yellow, pink and gold to fade into the dark, as we caught some tiger fish at the confluence of the Okavango and Namasere. The next morning we went out in good time to catch tilapia for lunch. There is only a small part of the tiger fish that is good to eat, but its fighting qualities and boney jaws that are difficult to hook, make it a sporting catch for the fisherman. Tim used a small tiger to hold above his head while he whistled for a fish eagle to come and take it from his hand. The eagle rose into the air to approach with a great swoop, he passed suspiciously a couple of times, suddenly getting courage, then like lightning, took the fish and returned to a distant tree, leaving me with a photo only of Tim's empty hand.

Nicco came with us to fish in the evening; having beginner's luck I caught two tilapia, which Nicco netted into the boat and gaffed, becoming renamed 'The Gaffer' instead of 'The Commander' to his delight. At night we went bird-watching in the boat with a searchlight, so I could get close-up pictures of malachite and pied kingfishers, herons, darters and cormorants. A little tiger fish hopped into the boat and Tim put his hand over the side of the boat to pull a small crocodile out of the water, about as long as his forearm. We watched while he offered it the tiger fish: with one snap the fish was chopped in two. It was a relief that those tiny jaws hadn't removed our fingers or hand.

Fishing for the next meal in the morning, we spotted a fish eagle flying with storks and white backed vultures at about 600 metres above us. Tim injected a tiger fish that had been caught the day before with air; he threw it out of the boat while whistling to the eagle. It closed its wings and came plummeting down to the floating fish, but the terrific descent had disorientated it and only after a few passes, did it come in with feet forward to grab the fish in its talons. The hippos ganged up against us in one waterway back to the big boat, so rather than having our boat capsized and damaged, leaving us floundering in the water while an angry hippo chopped off a head or a limb, we discreetly left their roaring and retreated to find another way.

Reaching the big river, a huge crocodile sitting atop an ant heap saw us coming and slid down the bank into the water. 'Do you want a crocodile egg to take back?' Tim asked. I thought it would be instructive for the children and could join at home my large ostrich egg, an African one that had been infertile. We nipped up the bank and dug our fingers into the fine tilth of the ant heap, quickly unearthing an egg from the huge clutch the crocodile had laid. The lady did not return before we beetled off in the boat. Another crocodile nest had the mother staying put so we left her and went to catch a barbel as we'd seen them leaping out of the water.

Walking at dusk on Motswabe or Python Island we found a mamba skin that had been cast off, but we did not come across any live snakes. A big untidy hammerkop's nest revealed an African barn owl, which flew out when Sam threw up a stick to see what was there. A young fish eagle crouched in a nest high in an old baobab tree with healthy and shining bark in spite of its age of perhaps 2,000 years.

The big boat had an elegant head of a sitatunga ram in the office, that had been acquired by a friend on the river who came across a crocodile with a sitatunga it had just killed. The crocodile left, so the friend took the head and had it mounted for Tim in repayment for a kindness.

We left the delights of the Okavango regretfully, after seeing a hooded vulture flying high over a colony of open-beaked storks. The fishing owl was asleep in a tree at Shakawe. Flying back to winter, Zürich was fogbound but we landed at Geneva which was freezing. As Sam tried to put his scarf on, we found a bream spinner stuck in it just before he got the barbed hook in his neck.

10

A Glimpse of a Faded Epoch:
The Mid Seventies

Sam concentrated on business visits abroad, covering different parts of the world. As I love Africa and South America, I was delighted when these continents came onto the agenda. However, in 1975 and 1978 it was his turn to visit the Arabic speaking countries of Iran and Iraq. I had learnt a few Arabic words when I was showjumping in Algiers, but I had conjured up my own picture of life in ancient Persia and Mesopotamia, the cradle of civilisation, based on books I had to read during war-time lessons at school. Our visits proved to be unforgettable experiences in those more peaceful times, although the Middle East has suffered from a perpetually turbulent history.

On the first morning after arriving in Tehran at midnight, we were taken to the Imperial Stables where I met Gail Rose. Her father was President of the Equestrian Federation in Toronto while her husband was marketing manager of the Iranian Aluminium Co. She had taught herself Farsi so that she could talk to the grooms and see that the stables were run efficiently and hygienically, especially on the stud side.

A display of the different breeds of the Royal horses in a well-kept arena, showed us Arab, Turkoman and little black Kurdish stallions before we were taken to see their young stock. No-one imagined that the future for these Royal horses on ceremonial occasions would be finished three years later by Khomeini's revolution.

Turkomans are the race horses of Iran, of which there are various strains: Yamout – Iranian, Akhltekeh – Russian and Cheneran. They are crossed about every three generations by an Arab sire to produce this type. I was told that the Arabs come mostly from the south of Kohelan and Saglavi and are bred at the RHS Arab stud farm, Kursestan. They migrate from south to north in May and vice-versa in October.

The Darashuri is an Arab that has been kept pure by the Darashuri tribe. They are recognised by the World Arab Association but there are not many available because the tribesmen keep them to ride and very seldom sell a horse. They live in the mountains outside Shiraz and the horses stand about 15.2 hh. Kurds, 'the work horse of Iran' are used by Kurdish Sheiks in the mountains of Kursestan – they are very hardy but the Sheik usually prefers to ride an Arab.

The Shah's parade horse Azar proudly trotted out for us and a son of Azar, another lovely chestnut was being prepared to take his sire's place. The Shah was to ride Azar in his fifty-sixth birthday parade a few days later; perhaps the son of

Azar never was able to take his turn in the spectacular parade of horses and carriages. The collection of Royal Coaches had beautiful harness made in London in peacock blue, but the coronation coach had been turned over in practice and needed expensive repairs to restore the damage.

We were away at 5 a.m. the next morning to fly to Isfahan – the 5,700-metre volcano Damavand showed clearly on the skyline while we flew over desert on the way to Isfahan where an astonishing number of American helicopters, at least 300, were assembled at the airport. Isfahan means 'the collection of troops' and was always a military centre from times long before the Arab invasion in AD 700.

There was tight security at the airport and we learnt that the red carpet was out for the state visit of President Bongo of Gabon, which overshadowed our stay with half of the Hotel Shah Abbas closed for him and his entourage, including the restaurant. The hotel is built around the courtyard of the old caravanserai that had been the original building, and rest place for the travellers meeting after long camel treks often over inhospitable terrain of mountain and desert. Sitting in the garden peacefully under the date palms, one could still imagine the hustle and bustle of the travellers through ancient Persia.

Our Persian guide had met Roger Stevens, the British Ambassador to Iran, who had written *The Land of the Great Sophy*. It was Friday, the Islamic holy day, so we saw the immense Friday Mosque. The Square of the Maidan-i-Shah measuring 560 × 280 metres was used as a polo ground, with the balcony of the Palace Ali-Kapu making a grandstand. In the middle of the Shah Abbas bridge was a Royal Pavilion; the river could be dammed above the bridge so that, in the early 1600s, the Shah Abbas could watch water polo; he must have been a keen sportsman. He also conceived the Shah Mosque, Masjid-i-Shah, in 1601 but it was not finished when he died twenty-seven years later. After his death the mosaic used for the outside became too expensive to complete the inside, so tiles were substituted for the vast interior, giving an impressive blue effect. Entering by the front arch and minarets the inside is reorientated to the right, facing Mecca, while under the huge dome a sound echoes seven times.

There was a lot to be learnt in the art field, with the flower design in Islamic mosaic while Arabesque mosaic has a round geometric stem pattern. Pictures in the garden of the forty columns were of the seventeenth-century battle at Tabriz between the Turks and the Persians, showing their various breeds of horses. A century later in a battle in India, the Indian elephants were routed by Persian camels with flaming packs on their humps which made me wonder how the camels fared.

Flying to Shiraz again coincided with President Bongo and his entourage taking a lengthy precedence at the airport; his large Air Gabon plane had to take to the air before anyone else could fly. We left Shiraz through the arch of the Qoran gate and up to the pass called Allah-o-Akhbar or God is Great, which is what the thirsty travellers say as they see the city ahead, after the dry 500 km journey from Isfahan. Although the Bongo entourage had lost us half a day we had a late snack near the tomb of Darius. The rock tombs of Naqsh-i-Rustah, a site chosen by Darius the Great contained his tomb and that of Darius II, Artaxerxes I and Xerxes.

A large herd of black goats enhanced the scene while we inspected the reliefs, and the inscription of Sassanian craftsmen in the third century AD, of Shapur and his High Priest Kartir. The horses in the relief were of a heavy war-horse type rather than the warm-blooded Persian breeds. I questioned this and the explanation was that the craftsmen had been brought in from Greece and Rome at a later date, so they carved the type of horse they knew in Europe.

Persepolis was close by, showing its columns against the clear blue sky, making us anticipate the treasures that it held in store as the reward for our trip. We arrived and found the whole site closed, for the sole viewing of President Bongo. We had not been warned at the airport and some other mini buses of tourists were equally frustrated. In order to take photos from above we climbed the hill behind the site, overshadowed by soldiers fully armed, hiding behind rocks and pillars. Eventually at 5 p.m. with the sunset, we charmed our way in to see some of the friezes for under fifteen minutes, which was better than nothing, although we had no chance of seeing the museum. Bongo did not arrive that night.

Persepolis was built by Darius I and finished by his son Xerxes, for court functions in spring and autumn, so that they never had to suffer the heat of summer. The great stairways have low steps so that horses could trot up and down, but certainly the stairs were made for Arab-type animals and not for a heavy horse.

It was dark by the time we returned to Shiraz and festivities were being prepared for the Shah's birthday, the next day. We had to go to the airport and flew back to Isfahan, over Persepolis illuminated for the *son et lumière* for Bongo.

We had seen the Agricultural College, the Veterinary College and a large fertilizer plant on the plain near Shiraz but the ancient bridges were very picturesque, especially the Shahrestan in Isfahan with Sassanian piers and pointed Seljuk arches. The women were doing their washing in the river and carpets were being cleaned by beating and washing before being left to dry on the dusty river bank.

The carpet factory in town gave us an idea of the exhausting work done by very small young girls, sitting seven or eight on a plank slung along the frame of a big carpet, tying the knots for the complicated patterns that were called out by the woman overseer. Only tiny fingers could make these fine knots which is why the children were so young, while the carpet grew by about one centimetre per day and large carpets could take two years to finish. The rigid discipline instilled into these young girls would continue through their life as Muslim women. It was difficult to understand when one had lived a free life.

In the bazaar, crammed with thousands of people and miles of passages between the open stands, craftsmen were hammering and chiselling silver and copper while their young sons sat doing school homework writing from right to left. Free education had only just been introduced, so even policemen could not read. When our driver substituted another document for the one he should have produced, the policeman just looked at the photo and let us through with a nod. I had seen no girls doing homework in the bazaar. Vegetable dyes with pomegranate for black, were used by the craftsmen printing cloth; I got some material with Persian polo ponies printed on it, to make skirts for myself and the children.

The Armenian Church, built in 1606, had an interior of tiles with Islamic flowers and Arabesque rounded stems but with the addition of angels and dragons from Armenia. A 1330 illustrated Bible in the museum had good paintings of Persians on fiery Persian horses of light bone and warm blood.

Caspian ponies were bred at Nowruzabad, an estate given to the horse society. They were small, active and naughty; they should not be larger than 12 hh, so like Shetlands are too small to be trained and disciplined by a grown-up, but I guessed that they were fed on corn, which goes straight to any pony's head, making them very hot and disobedient. Pony breeds have evolved for a tough life on mountain or moorland without being spoilt or cossetted.

We left for the Caspian on the northern frontier, to visit the area around Bandar Pahlevi, the port on the Caspian Sea and since then scene of the 1990 devastating earthquake. The winding road along a river with insecure but picturesque hanging bridges, took us up the mountain road past a half-empty reservoir and dam, climbing up to 3,000 metres to the Kandovan tunnel built in 1934, through the Alborz range. The zigzag road and the height required a strong stomach for the passengers in the back of the car. The highest point of this range is the volcano cone of the Damavand at 5,700 metres, that we had seen from the air.

In one of the long tunnels with two-way traffic, we met a caravan of donkeys being hurried along with no lights to show their dark forms to the motorists, leaving the beasts and their riders in dire peril. The traffic lights were against us through the one-way tunnel at the top of the pass. The light stayed red for one hour while a vehicle that had broken down in the tunnel had to be removed.

The northern side of the range was already damper and greener than the arid slopes on the side towards Tehran. As we descended towards Chalus on the coast of the Caspian Sea, green scrub bushes were being browsed by goats and there were a few sheep which formed a contrast to the bare mountains above. The air became more humid as mists rose from the trees and the pastures and cultivated fields lower down, where a terrific rain storm had been raging along the coast. We could see the breakers rolling in from the dark grey sea when we stopped for a cup of tea. The drive became more hazardous as we approached Rasht in the dark, as bikes had no lights and the women in black chadors, the cloth worn from head to foot, merged completely into the darkness.

After a night at Bandar Pahlevi we arranged for a boat to go birdwatching on the river Kalin. At 6.30 a.m. the morning looked bright and the storm clouds had cleared away leaving the Talish mountains snow-capped to the north west. Towards Russia the Caucasus were not visible, but there were two Russian trawlers far out to sea.

It was fortunate that our Iranian friend, who worked for Ciba-Geigy, was able to argue in his quiet Persian way to prevent our being ripped off over the price of the boat; at one point I was ready to cancel the trip. Our friend was adamant that he would only pay the boatmen on our safe return. He stated, 'How do I know these men, they may tip us out of the boat after demanding our money or our lives.' While this was going on in Farsi, I was learning from someone who spoke English that the nearby 'Game Reserve' only gave permission for people to enter who wanted to shoot the animals, the special attraction being the leopard, although I doubt if more than a few existed there. Certainly the Caspian tiger seemed to be more myth than reality.

We climbed into the boat and the boatman took off up the Kalin river, leaving the port with the Russian ships, passing the women doing their washing in the river, until the water opened into a large estuary looking not unlike the Camargue, although it was backed by mountains. The habitat was ideal for duck and geese, but every boat we saw was manned by people with guns.

Turning into one of two rivers flowing into the estuary, a notice in Farsi and English stated, 'No fishing or hunting (shooting) beyond this point'. As we progressed up the smaller river, we saw at least twelve rods and several people with guns. Conservation was not included in the vocabulary or the intentions of these people.

Bright little kingfishers, egrets, herons and smaller waders soothed my anger and marsh harriers swooped over the reeds before soaring overhead. In the shallows of the river the boat ground to a halt with the propeller stuck and twisted. While the boatman repaired the propeller we squelched our way through the marsh to join some little boys who came from the river village which had no road yet.

One young man rode by on a 13 hh pony with just a rope noseband as a bridle and the boys chatted to us as we asked about the tiny cows for milk, the humped cattle for meat and the fat tail Persian sheep, with their wide flat tails that serves them in time of drought when their bodies can draw from it like a camel with its hump. Some of the humps on the cattle were shaped like an oblong balloon, quite unlike Zebu or Brahma cattle.

In an open area were several stork feeding near grazing ponies that appeared to be sturdy beasts of burden with big heads. Our small guide had four brothers and four sisters and when asked how his father supported them all, he replied cheerfully, 'He doesn't, he's too old. Mother has to!'

The boat was workable when we got back so we returned down the river past the fishermen and hunters out into the estuary where a motor boat scattered a flock of duck with a man firing recklessly at the birds as they rose. Other boats had reed hides built in the prow which the men ran against an island and enticed the ducks towards the hide so they could net them. It was Friday, the Holy Day, and all the sportsmen were making the most of their holiday.

In Rasht at midday we thawed out with a vodka before our long drive to Tehran followed by a 5 a.m. start to the airport. We took off at dawn and the visibility gradually became fantastic; Mount Ararat appeared as we came over lake Urmia, south of Tabriz; Mount Ararat is in Turkey on the Armenian–Iranian three-cornered frontier. The 5,165 metre mountain, where the ark is supposed to lie, was visible for about 600 km of that flight to Ankara, before cloud over the Bosphorus and Istanbul, back to fog in Zurich but at home the glorious autumn colours of the forests around Burg greeted us with the children, who were fit and full of beans.

In March 1978 we arrived in Baghdad and slept in a room overlooking the impressive width of the river Tigris. At a street corner we had bought teka from a barrowman with a charcoal burner where he cooked the delicious pieces of lamb on a skewer with slabs of Arab bread; on another corner we got little glasses of sweet tea which warmed us against the cold wind. The hotel facilities had closed long before but we were refreshed and ready for a short night's sleep.

Sam had a meeting with ministers first thing in the morning and I was seeing the Director General of Preventive Diseases at the Ministry of Health. It was a great bonus for me to travel with Sam, because I could meet the people responsible for the environment and listen to their problems, which I could then relay back to the WWF & IUCN Head Office in Switzerland with any necessary information. There are often worries and suspicions in developing countries when dealing with an association without an obvious UN affiliation. These troubles can often be ironed out on the spot by listening and advising on the right person to contact back at the office who has the knowledge and understanding for solving the problem. In my case the list of names I had for contacts in Iraq was completely out of date, but Dr Al Bassam, from Ciba-Geigy, could put me in touch with the Director of the National History Research Centre and Museum at the University. The Director was delighted to have a contact with the IUCN and said he would certainly send them any surveys done through the University.

I joined a team of students working on tick research under an Indian Professor, learning how ticks compensate in semi-desert conditions by using grasshoppers as hosts for the egg development stage of their life-cycle. I learnt too that the Museum at Basra had collapsed, which I had hoped to visit.

Wilfred Thesiger's books had always intrigued me, and I had asked Sam, when he mentioned that Iraq was on his programme, if we could go and visit the Marsh Arabs who live in the wetlands of the south between the Tigris and Euphrates before the confluence of the rivers at Qurnah above Basra where they form the Shatt-al-Arab waterway into the Persian Gulf. Dr Al Bassam had been delighted when he had heard my request, for he had never been to the marshes and he arranged the trip with enthusiasm.

Meanwhile we had to tear ourselves away from the laboratory ticks, grasshoppers and interesting people because we were to join Sam and his office colleagues at a place on the Tigris where they had a special way of doing fish called kettan. This feast of fish is called Maskoof, and it is said that one has not visited Baghdad unless one has had Maskoof. One problem was that fishing is forbidden from 1 March for two months, but our fish had been kept on a line in the river, and we were assured that it had only died at midnight! The enormous kettan was opened from the backbone to the belly with the inside facing the fire and sticks holding it up, threaded through the skin. The front is baked for about forty minutes, then for the last few minutes the fish is put skin side down on the fire.

Once the fish arrived on the table in the garden by the river, we attacked it with our right hands. The left hand is considered unclean and must not touch food or the face. It is difficult to remember not to remove fish bones from one's mouth with the left hand, while holding a lump of hot fish in the right. We got burnt fingers too, but it was a real feast.

After lunch Dr Bassam took us to Babylon, which gave us our first impression of the complete flatness of Mesopotamia. We talked of the problems of salination, and the need for double irrigation, the first to wash out the salt and the next to water the crop. My imagined vision of Eden, with the land between the rivers as a 'bread basket', became depressingly tarnished with the sight of this desolate land.

I had not realised the extent of human activity back in Biblical times could have caused so much damage to the environment. The land of milk and honey looked more like an ecological disaster area, caused by exploitation over 6,000 years ago. The natural forests had been used up as the Sumerian civilisation began to farm the land intensively, using irrigation from the great Tigris and Euphrates rivers. The irrigation and raising of the water table gradually brought to the surface the minerals and salt, impoverishing the soil which caused the collapse of agriculture in the region. The civilisation declined with the failure of the crops and the land was left white with salt and robbed of natural resources, as has happened to many civilisations all over the world.

Lessons have still not been learned from the farming exploitation of the land in 3000 BC, with productive soil still being harmed by salination, caused by the misuse of irrigation schemes. A more recent example is the ancient walled city of Great Zimbabwe, now being rescued from collapse. At the height of its civilisation it would have supported a population of about 20,000, roughly the same as medieval London, actively trading with China and the Arabian merchants. As the wealth was based primarily on cattle ownership, the land may have become overgrazed and unable to support the herds. The city, with its chief's palace and temple, was suddenly abandoned in the sixteenth century.

Babylon lies 90 km south of Baghdad, the name meaning 'The Gate of the Gods'. It flourished as a centre of culture and government for fifteen centuries, from the arrival of the Amorites in 1850 BC to the death of Alexander the Great there in 322 BC. Unfortunately the bricks of the city were of such quality that they have been stolen over the past 2,000 years, leaving practically nothing but the foundations. A copy of the great gate with its glazed tiles stands at the entrance to the site, faced with the Mushhushu dragon, the Lion and the Bull.

No tower of Babel remains, to Sam's disappointment, but the Lion of Babylon is still there on his woman, though his head was cut in half in 1915 by the Germans, who thought he was filled with gold. We saw the animal symbols still on the remains of the Ishtar Gate and walked in the marriage temple.

Dr Al Bassam gave an informal buffet supper that night, prepared by his wife and daughters where I met more interesting people involved with conservation programmes, plant physiology and biology, some having studied in the United States and Europe.

We left for the long drive through the arid land to the marshes the next day. I had been warned that there was no tree or toilet for 500 km, so I would have to cope with less ease than the three men including the driver, during the journey.

Hardly out of our route was the Tessyphon, a Persian Victory Hall built 1,700 years ago. The great Taq Kesra, an unsupported huge arch, was where the Persian King received his guests. It was now a picnic place where people could get free government coffee in a big Bedouin tent. Nearby was the mosque of the happy friend of Mohammed, called Salman al Faresi, the only mosque in the world where one was welcome to go and drink and dance, with special celebrations in springtime.

The local alcohol is arak, distilled from dates and 95% proof. Dr Bassam remembered a day while he was a boy, when the grocer arrived carrying in his arms all the vegetables, so they asked where was his donkey. The grocer showed them the donkey flat on its back having drunk arak from a barrel, when it couldn't find any water.

Another nice true story comes from Qatar. The Bedouins are the nucleus of the original Arabian race and speak the most pure Arabic. A new hotel, the Gulf, had just been built there, and the lift had a capacity for fifty people. On arrival, someone was posted at the lift to put in the baggage for their room. The lift passed time and time again; when eventually it stopped and the door opened. There was a party of Bedouins having a picnic on the floor of the lift. They immediately invited everyone in to join their picnic, while they continued up and down in the lift.

One time Dr Bassam had to see the Minister of Commerce and Trade in Qatar, but he was unavailable. In the end he got desperate and so a secretary in the office agreed that he would take him to the Minister. They drove for hours deep into the desert and found the Minister, who was waiting for his favourite camel to calve, and would not leave her until the great event was successfully accomplished.

We stopped at Amara after 400 km, just in time for me, while we had a drink of tea at the resthouse. We still had another 100 km to do in the dark as our resthouse was at Qurnah, supposedly the site of the Garden of Eden with a large Adam and Eve tree growing there. We never made it to Eden, because a big burly fellow came in while we were sitting there and was greeted by Dr Al Bassam. The friend said that he was working on a large construction job nearby, which had to function twenty-four hours a day and he organised two teams of two shifts that were paid two days for each twelve hour shift. We asked if there was a hope of staying there that night to save the 100 km in the dark and another 70 km back in the morning to the marshes, especially as we had no confirmation of a bed in the Garden of Eden. As our construction friend was working that night, he offered his bed to Sam and me, while Dr Bassam shared another room with some engineers. That was over half the capacity of the resthouse, so it was a relief that the Marsh Arabs had not become a tourist attraction.

After dinner we had a quiet night's sleep, a change from Baghdad where every dog barks and howls the whole night through. We were up at 6.30 a.m. and took the Basra road south to the marshes. Luck was with us, as the enormous paper mill, contracted by the Swiss firm Sulzer was on our way before the turn off to Al

Majar Al Kabir. There we passed the big sugar cane factory, where Ciba-Geigy do business, and Sam was on the Sulzer board. I was asked to conceal the fact that I was taking photos.

We found our way along the track, with enquiries, to the place where a couple of boats were moored by the bank of the Tigris. However we were returned to the small and new village to give our names to the Police Officer, who did not even require identification papers. Back at the boats we met twenty-five-year-old Mohamed who was taking us. We were on the river by 9 a.m. and the wind was cold but the morning was bright and sunny.

Many storks and a few large pelicans were the first big birds to take one's attention. Black kites were busy everywhere too. Soon the marshes stretched in every direction. I did not see as many waders as I had expected, but the water may have been too deep and the season a little early.

The first of the villages of the Marsh Arabs appeared on the flat horizon, and that was where our boatman lived. When we got to the village made of island reed houses built on mats with their few sheep and cattle and water buffalo living along with the family, we stopped to bargain for fish. The fishing season had ended a week previously, so we could only buy smaller fish that the locals could catch for their own existence. These were bunni fish and we paid one dinar for about eight fish. Mohamed arranged that his mother and wife would cook lunch for us and we would be invited by his father into their house for the meal.

We continued past the other island houses and out again into the marshes, seeing little kids and fishermen in dugout canoes. There were herons but not the Goliath, egrets and some lovely pairs of marsh harriers. In the distance we suddenly saw a whirling mass of big white birds and I wondered whether they were flamingos, as there was such a quantity, but Mohamed shook his head when I showed him the picture of a flamingo, and said there were very few. He didn't have much interest and he was reluctant to go as far as the large colony of pelicans, as it turned out to be. He said he had never been so far into the marshes before – the wild land!

At another small marsh village we picked up a boat with four cattle that had been sold to Mohamed's own village and they asked for a tow from our anti-quated motor, instead of having to paddle and punt all the way! Against the river current it would be hard work. We saw blue kingfishers and many pied ones. Women paddling canoes loaded with cut reeds looked enviously at the boat with the cattle that we were towing. Before we got to the village they asked to be untied, perhaps in order to get a price for their work punting!

The Tuhain village is one hour's motor boat ride from the shore at Grimly village. At the *mudhif*, Mohamed's 73-year-old father, the patriarch invited us in.

The big reed-built house, shaped like a huge nissan hut, with its own island of reeds, the animals around the hut and a place where the water buffalo could climb out of the water, surmounted the other smaller *mudhifs* on adjoining islands. We removed our shoes and entered into the cool dark interior, blinking at first after the glare of the sun on the water outside. The hut had a reed partition across the middle and the women were doing the cooking and chattering on the far side.

We sat in a semi-circle on the floor of the *mudhif*, with myself trying not to show the soles of my feet which is impolite, and having difficulty as my replaced hips prevented me from sitting cross-legged.

The father was well respected and he was interested to exchange news from the outside world. His name was Obeid Nasir and Mohamed Obeid was his youngest son, who had married a year earlier aged twenty-four, which is quite late for his tribe. His wife, who now had a daughter with a little brooch in her hair, was his first cousin and the marriage was arranged by their parents. The wife was not too content with life in the marshes, as she was brought up in Baghdad and missed TV and other city delights. It must be hard to be suddenly taken back to life in Biblical times.

The family and the whole tribe are Fartousi with a sub-tribe Benni Amer. They came to the marshes about 150 years ago from the Al-Ghraf area, because the landlord of that area of Mesopotamia kicked them out and they had nowhere to go but the marshes, which have been inhabited by other tribes for at least 3,000 years.

They would be starving if it wasn't for the fish and they looked well although some children were small for their ages. Mohamed had three years of primary school and regretted that he did not continue with his education. His friend who started school with him went on through to University and now has an excellent job in Baghdad. His father wanted all his grandchildren to be educated and leave the village because he thought that there is no future for them there. How right he has since proved to be. He was a wise gentleman with an aristocratic face full of character and kindness.

They wanted to do some rice farming in the upland near the marshes, but there was no water for irrigation and without an irrigation canal they could not farm rice. The old man thought that there was another tribe near the upland that had cut off the water supply.

While we were talking through Dr Bassam, I was given the most delicious hot, thin and crisp rice bread. The normal bread arrived with the fish and we sat around taking the hot and rather boney bunni fish with the right hand. Apart from the fish bone problem and my difficulty in sitting without showing the soles of my feet, we had taken off our shoes on entering the house and sat on a nice carpet with bolster shaped cushions against the reed wall. I got very stiff because I couldn't sit cross-legged. One of the little boys washed our hands by pouring water from a jug, while we held our hands over a bucket. We then gave the family our oranges. The patriarch kept chasing the boys off, saying it was rude of them to sit in the presence of guests, but they always crept back again. The boldest one never moved and the old man didn't enforce his discipline.

We were offered tea but said goodbye to the patriarch and took his photo for which he posed, and then we took the boat out onto the marshes again. We were surprised by several drowned water buffalo, but when you see the distances that they swim, it is not surprising that sometimes they get exhausted.

We left our new friends in the marshes and then in Baghdad, we said a heartfelt *Shukran* to thank them for their hospitality and stimulating programme.

(*left*) Puck sitting on Sam's lap; she had already pinched his woolly cap.

(*below*) Puck with Sam's cap as her trophy; Tuck is longing to steal it from Puck.

With the Marsh Arabs, 1978. (*above*) Obeid Nasir, the Patriarch of the tribe. (*left*) Mohamed, his youngest son, who acted as our boatman. (*below*) A typical Marsh Arab village built on a floating reed bed around the large central Mudhif, where the Patriarch lived with the men on one side of a central reed screen and the women on the other side.

The following year, we lost a friend with the sudden and sad news that Dr Hassam Al Bassam had dropped dead with a heart attack. The Iranian revolution began and the wind of change would develop into a hurricane. The terrible happenings of the Iraq war against Iran were brewing ahead and I shuddered to think of our friends in the marshes with the endless fighting raging to and fro through their territories. Instead of the drowned buffalo there would be men and boys left to float bloated in the water while the villages were plundered and abandoned on their islands of reeds.

The marshes still act as a refuge for persecuted people, but with Saddam Hussein's victims being pursued by modern weapons, nowhere can be a safe haven from evil regimes. We saw Iraq before Hussein came to power, to wreak his vengeance on mankind, causing the destruction of people, flora and fauna together with the pollution of land, sea and air.

The way of life, on the marshes leading to the Garden of Eden, that we had been privileged to share for so short but unforgettable time, has gone forever.

11

Sad Losses, Happy Celebrations and More Travels: The Late Seventies

My brother Ronald who had lost his first wife Jill, from cancer, only five months after they had been married in 1961, told us the happy news sixteen years later, that he was going to marry again. Wynn, who lived in his parish of Hatfield Heath, had been suddenly widowed when her husband Dick had an unexpected heart attack, leaving her with their small son Tim, and two nearly grown-up teenagers. Ronald and Wynn decided to get married four years after Dick's death, and Wynn has since become one of my best friends. Her mother, Joan, won Sam completely at the reception after the wedding where lots of young people came with friends of Tim who was only four-and-a-half years old.

A year later in 1978 we were all shocked by the sudden death of Mimi, Monica's godmother and Sam's older sister, who was at their family holiday home in Klosters skiing over the Easter break. Unfortunately it was her two boys from her second marriage to Verduno who found her in the house. In a state of shock they shouted to their father. Guy was only twelve and Patrick fourteen, Sam and I were a godparent to each with Guy being only three weeks older than Monica. Mimi and I had been close friends for nearly thirty years and already she had suffered a terrible blow when Mariette, her daughter from her first marriage to Mario Mylius, was killed in Basel when her horse fell on her in the jumping phase of a three-day event, not even during the hazardous cross-country, but over small show jumps that usually cause few problems. That had been in 1969 when Mariette was in her early twenties and had spent a happy time during the year before at Sudgrove, riding and working with our horses and girls. She had been popular with everyone and there was always laughter and fun where ever she went. Brigadier Sir 'Jackie' Smyth vc was President of Wimbledon that year and had invited Sam and me to join himself and Lady Frances at Wimbledon the next week, but we did not watch any tennis during that sad time.

Work had to continue and Sam had organised a Ciba-Geigy seminar to be held in Cheltenham at the end of May, while I had WWF meetings at Slimbridge. Friends came to stay at Sudgrove from the WWF Board, David Ogilvy and Herter his wife, and 'Mac' Mclain Stewart from McInsey Business Management in New York. We had known 'Mac' since his firm had first helped with Geigy when Sam was made Chairman of the Board, and again with the Ciba merger with Geigy. David and Herter had invited us to stay in their Château of Touffou, when David was complaining that he had just had to pour millions of francs worth of concrete under the Chateau, to stop it from subsiding into the lovely river Vienne that runs beside it. All there was to show for this great expense was a hole in the ground through which the concrete had been poured and disappeared below. There was no beautifully renovated stone work or tiling redone, that could impress your friends, but I fear that David still had the outer and visible work to do, once the Château had been secured above the bank of the river. Both David and Mac were invaluable Trustees of the WWF with the professional advice on advertising and management they gave free while it was still emerging as a major conservation movement.

We had a lot of activity at Sudgrove with a reception on the lawn for the WWF Board of Trustees, members and benefactors, one fine evening, then a couple of days later, a Ciba-Geigy buffet lunch on the lawn, with the international business people from both functions enjoying the country and the serenity of the Cotswolds. These informal gatherings were shared by our animals, with horses looking over the wall between the lawn and the field, sheep grazing with their lambs on our banks in front of the house and dogs welcoming everyone, especially if they dropped some food, or left a full plate at a low level.

Bess, Sam's Old English bobtailed sheepdog, had once been caught proudly marching up the drive with the whole of a home-made tongue. I had also lost a Sunday lunch in Switzerland; I had prepared pieces of fillet pork, nicely seasoned and ready to pop on a hot grill pan, then I went to see how to give a special intramuscular injection to poor Sam. I returned four minutes later to see neat rounds on the board where the seasoned meat had been, so I thought the children had kindly cooked it for me. A guilty-faced whippet slunk out behind me, licking his lips. Scamper had neatly removed each piece of raw meat and left me with nothing to cook for Gilgi our cousin and doctor, and Françoise who was also Lucy's godmother, when they came to enjoy Sunday lunch with the family. I cursed these long hind legs of Scamper's, and his long and aristocratic nose telling him that only the best was good enough for a noble whippet.

1978 was also the year of my fiftieth birthday, a great occasion, as the Swiss especially celebrate any birthday with a 0 marking another decade. In 1975 when Sam was 50, Marguerite his mother had been 80, Monica and Lucy were 11 and 9 making another 20 and Catherine was 20, the coming of age in Switzerland.

Sam was one of a club of nine law students who had studied together at Basel University and obtained their doctorates at the same time. They celebrated their fiftieth birthday year and the thirtieth anniversary of their Shadrag Club with a great party at the Schauenberg Hotel near Basel. Sam was a year younger than the others and seven of the eight members still left turned up for the party in 1974. A bicycle made for five was awaiting them and in typical Basel humour and farce, they made an entertainment with a little show from each of them, pulling someone else's leg. Their rhymes were said or sung to a background of piano played by Lucas 'Cheese' Burckhardt; several of them had formed a dance band while they were students and their musical talent proved to be undimmed through the years. The music covered suitable melodies for each parody, with 'Hello Dolly,' 'Doin' what comes naturally,' 'Mac the Knife,' the 'Lambeth Walk' and Basel songs. While the men who thought they were providing all the entertainment, were wobbling off on the lengthy bicycle, we girls stole a march on them, having prepared a surprise behind their backs. Secretly the wives had been meeting once a week in a studio in old Basel, that Marisha, Cheese's wife, used for her art work. We had worked out a *Schnitzelbangg*, which is tied to the traditional Basel humour of Fasnacht, the festival at the beginning of Lent. We all sang verses about our men to the old tune of *'Z'Basel a mim Rhy'*, translated as 'Basel on my Rhine', turning each illustrated large foolscap page so that the words could be read by all in the audience.

The complete surprise of our entertainment was met with astonishment from the birthday boys, with anxiety from one, who was heard to mutter, 'and I was sure she'd gone to see Aunty on all those Wednesdays, taking the train and being away all day. Supposing she had had a lover and I would have been none the wiser!'

The thought put into the preparation of these verses and the right costume to wear, comes from the traditional Fasnacht, which is no drunken carnival, but a highly disciplined spectacle with freedom of ideas and parodies on current events and local characters carefully rehearsed. The clothes and wagons for this event and the lanterns illustrated with the rhymes, take weeks of hard work to prepare. Practising the fife and drum bands to play in complete precision is a year round exercise. The proof of the discipline and expertise comes at 4 a.m. on the first Monday of Lent, the *Morgenstreich*. All lights are extinguished in Basel, as each clique gathers at its point of departure around Basel City. On the first stroke of four, all the Clique bands start their music and march around the city by the light of their lanterns. When I hear that first sound of drums and fifes breaking the silence of the dark night I feel the back of my neck tingle.

My fiftieth birthday was also surrounded with secrecy while Sam plotted it with Mike Roberts, who had shouldered the responsibility for the organisation. I knew that we would hold a party in July, four months before my actual birthday, because we would be on holiday at Sudgrove. All I was allowed to do was to send out the invitations to about fifty couples of friends and some young people, friends of Lucy and Monica who were ten and twelve years old.

I could not miss seeing the marquee going up on the lawn, and Nicco, my uncle, and Mary Curtoys were staying at Sudgrove while on holiday from South Africa. The cars would be parked in the riding school just above the house, so that the flower bulbs along the drive would not be damaged and the way was kept free. Mike had told us that the girls wanted a disco, so both myself and Nicco felt a bit fed up and disappointed.

When I was allowed to come down in good time to greet the guests, the sound of instruments warming up in the tent made me hurry to see who was playing the music. Sam was delighted with my ecstatic reaction when I found, instead of a deafening disco, the superb seven piece dance band of the Grenadier Guards sitting there in full dress opposite the 'Koechlin Arms', where Mike's friend Bunny Brown was preparing the bottles for the evening.

The Guards had one of the round tables which were laid for supper, and could eat as much as they wanted at any time during the evening, when the guests were eating and afterwards too. The evening was a great family party with the children helping, eating and dancing along with us all. At midnight the children disappeared, while Mike called everyone out of the tent to come in front of the house. From the drive above us, lights glowed through the trees as a Pipe Band started to play, and a procession wound down the drive with the children leading the way, each one carrying a long burning Roman candle held out in front, followed by the bagpipes played by the Cheltenham Highland group.

In front of the house, the children stood in a large circle around the Pipers, with their candles lighting a girl dancer who performed the sword dance and other Scottish dances to the music of the pipers. I saw Lucy's arm tiring as she held the long candle, but Peter Scott was standing behind her and slipped his hand in support under her elbow to take the strain off her arm. Sentimental feelings were strong as the little procession lit by flickering flames marched back up into the trees with the pipe music fading as they climbed away from us. Less sentimental was the chaos created at the top of the drive when the pipers did not see the cavallettis, put across for security against gate crashers, at shin height in the shadows. Luckily their valuable instruments remained intact while they rolled around interspersed with children still clutching their Roman candles. Lucy was carried up to bed already asleep in the early hours by Ann and her husband Bob Cook.

The next day the ponies escaped through a narrow hunting gate at the bottom of our banks leading into Forest Commission land which had been left open by hikers. We were sitting on the lawn with some of our leftovers from the party for a snack lunch. We heard the children bringing the ponies back down the drive and went to meet them; Monica looked white and was walking with Anne Fitzpatrick's arm around her shoulder. Anne told us that Monica riding bareback, with only a halter on Elf, had been bucked off and had hit her head. They had not stopped to get hats or been prepared for riding when they discovered that the ponies had got out. We put Monica to bed, where she slept immediately but did not really remember her fall when she woke again.

Meanwhile Condy, my lovely 'blue' whippet, that had been bred by Dinah Nicholson, David's wife, at Condicote where they had their National Hunt training establishment came galloping to me with a bleeding tail. In the thick woods where the ponies were found, she had got under their hooves and the white tip of her tail had gone under a stray hoof. I dressed the sore tail, watched by Condy's sad gaze; it healed cleanly and well, but the white tip never came back. After our happy evening the night before, we were thankful that both daughters and animals had not come to more harm.

Another short break with the children was possible during their *Herbstferien*; the 'potato picking holiday' of the Scots and Swiss in October, although few children worked in the fields nowadays. The year before, Sam's older girls Catherine and Sibylle had left school and had their own plans for that time, but Dominik was doing his '*Matura*' exam, the Swiss entry into University where all subjects must be passed at 'A' level, so he could come with us for a week. Sam had a day or two's work to do in Athens, so he arranged for a boat with three cabins to take us sailing around some of the islands. We were to meet the yacht *Sirocco* at Piraeus.

Trouble brewed at Zurich airport, when we met Dominik and his friend Franz who was coming with us. Dominik approached Sam with a serious look, saying 'Babbe, we've got a little problem, Franz forgot his passport.' Sam, Swiss Air and the Ciba-Geigy people saved the day, and even arriving in Athens, Franz was not clapped into prison.

Lucy had run a temperature before she left, but remembering Mother's treatment of me, when I always ran a temperature before a holiday, she was wrapped up and came along, her sore throat and temperature subsiding after the first night on the boat. The girls slept in the little cabin next to us, while the boys were up in the crew's quarters, along with an Englishman, Ray, the steward, who had been in the army in Greece, and, with his Greek wife of thirty years, had only been called to help our Greek Captain and his wife on the morning we sailed.

On the first day, anchored near Kithnos, we could snorkel, but we kept clear of the jelly fish while the Captain bought red snappers, red mullet and whitebait freshly caught by a fisherman returning with his boat and catch. We lived on fresh fish and never had to resort to any reserves of frozen food or pizzas.

A strong wind from Russia hit us as we left the sheltered bay, making the boat plunge and toss about, with our Swiss pennant and Greek flag flying forwards as the waves overtook us breaking on the deck. I was worried about Lucy as she succumbed to the rolling and bucking of the boat but we hung on to both girls before we got them to lie down in our cabin below. The boys never stirred until we got to the shelter of Sifnos, where we could breakfast and snorkel in the clear sea of the bay.

After the storm the sea was cold but Sam sunned himself on the beach until he was unexpectedly joined by two nudists. His hasty retreat was recorded through binoculars by the children on the boat with much irreverent laughter.

The boys caught an octopus off one of the islands and Franz attached it to his arm as he swam back to the boat. The little medusa jelly fish could give a nasty but not dangerous sting, but they moved in shoals, so that one would only swim and snorkel where they were absent, but if they moved into the bay where we anchored, we could take the boat to find a clear stretch of water.

The boys were allowed a night on the town when we berthed at Mykonos and we knew when they returned at 4 a.m., as they must have been wearing Swiss mountaineering boots. In a more local mood, the girls had got large and smelly goatskin hats near the Temple of Aphaia, which they wore for most of the next forty-eight hours. We had enjoyed every moment and it was strange to return in the early morning to the sound of the traffic, people and planes coming in to land after the peaceful time around the islands.

The following *Herbstferien* we spent again with Dominik, in Cadaqués with my friend of nearly thirty years, Rosemary Llorens from Barcelona. Dominik had just passed his driving test and so Sam gave him the job of chauffeuring our rented car. We were shocked to see the burnt hillside as we came down to the little white town of Cadaqués nestling around its harbour on the Mediterranean. In the dry weather arsonists had waited for a wind to set alight the hills between the plain of Gerona and the sea. Poor smallholders, farmers with only a few rows of vines to make some bottles of wine and some rough grazing to keep their goats, had lost everything, often their cottages and shelter too had been burnt. Fire like any element is a terrifying destroyer when unchecked.

The Figueres museum of Picasso was a revelation to me, seeing his early delicate and superbly crafted drawings in such a contrast to his latest crude paintings with phallic symbols which were being exhibited in the Kunstmuseum at Basel, for international crowds to study. His sense of fun is very evident too.

Our plans for the next *Herbstferien* were to be made when I went with Sam for a business trip to Africa in November. It was an intensive round covering new ground for both of us, but with efficient organisation from head and local offices, it is surprising how much one can see and hear from people on the spot in a short time. I always kept a fairly detailed diary so that I could make a report for the WWF of their local interests and the needs of conservation people working there, while Sam needed a written record of people and their families that we met in conjunction with Ciba-Geigy programmes, so that he could recall his previous visits and connections when he met the same people again.

We always changed into thin sweaters to travel overnight, so that our jackets could be hung up and worn uncrumpled the next morning on disembarking. Sam was amused to see that the Aga Khan had kept his jacket on during the flight to Nairobi, while having to talk to various people, and so he emerged looking very crumpled in the early morning arrival at the airport. Later he made a welcome presentation of a horse by Crepello to the Jockey Club, no doubt having had a comfortable change of clothes in the Serena Hotel in Nairobi.

At lunch we met people involved with the Wildlife Parks and conservation programmers including Jack Block, the owner of the Norfolk Hotel, and they were depressed about the future of conservation. It was the last time that we saw Jack, who looked frail that day, because he was drowned a few months later while fishing in one of the superb lakes in Chile.

I went around the Nairobi National Park with Ellis Monks while we talked about the problems of conservation, but it was delightful to see many species of birds and animals living so close to a big city. Sam arrived soaked by a torrential rain storm after his business meeting but his wet trousers were dealt with, while he borrowed a spare pair, and my muddy boots were cleaned at the home of a friend where we had a fireside dinner.

The weather cleared as we took off from the airport early the next morning. We had to fly to Tanzania as the roads had been closed for some time over the frontier. The Cessna 310 gave us a much better view of Mount Meru, Kilimanjaro at 5,960 metres, higher than the Bernese Oberland Alps, and the smaller peak of Mawenzi, about the same height as Mount Kenya. We flew low over Tsavo West but the water holes were dry and no game was visible.

Our pilot told me of his interest in archaeology and that he had discovered an ancient Phoenician Port along the African coast. (The following year we were able to explore the pillars and walls that he had found under the encroaching jungle. That expedition was to end in myself and the children coming out in a severe nettle rash, an allergy from an unknown encounter with some poisonous plant or ivy.)

We talked of the evil influence of the so-called 'Major' Bob Astles on Idi Amin, as our pilot had trained some of Amin's pilots. In Switzerland we had helped a doctor from Uganda to get work, after he had escaped by foot over the river into Zaïre, having had a tip-off that he was next on Amin's hit list. He had sought refuge in my cousin's mission; my cousin was the Bishop of Boga-Zaïre, Philip Ridsdale. Ciba-Geigy had helped the mission with medicaments and drugs for the desperate refugees, escaping from genocide and persecution in their own districts, to the safety of church mission camps over the frontier.

There was no radio contact with Tanga airport in Tanzania, but with little sign of life there, we landed and were then told that our plane was the only one from Kenya with permission to land. Our visit started with seeing the Amboni Sisal Estates, where the plant *agava sisalana* is cultivated and we saw the whole processing of the plant from the cutting of the outside leaves to the finished factory product of binder twine and sacks made from a lower quality sisal. The plant is a native of Mexico where it has a resilience against pests and disease and was successfully introduced into Africa.

With my interest in local products from native plants, I wondered what use was made of the green part of the tough leaves washed out in the decorticating drums, leaving the long threads of white sisal. In another process with the green part, I was told that it contributed to the making of cortisone. The Mexicans would have used it for mezcal, which is refined into tequila, their excellent fire water taken with a touch of salt and a squeeze of lime. My hostess Heidi Torriani was interested in the recipe which I provided and we have been friends ever since, but I have not heard of a thriving export-earning product of 'Tanzania tequila'. I found that I was immediately allergic to the green sap of the sisal although the rash subsided after washing my hands. It was a relief that Mexican tequila had never affected me in this way.

At dusk we went fishing and although I had a bathing costume, swimming was not recommended while the Portugese Man-o-War were around, causing several people to be badly stung. At sunset I was offered a welcome sweater and a line that was being cast but unfortunately I had a pinched nerve in my shoulder that was agonising, so I could not accept the challenge. That nerve plagued me for eighteen months, making driving a car very painful together with most other activities. (One day at Sudgrove, Lini told us of a German Chiropractor who sometimes came to Cheltenham, and he put me right in five minutes with one almighty click of the shoulder and back. The National Hunt jockeys are usually the best source of information on people, qualified or not, who can help sportsmen to keep on top of neck and back problems.)

'The Boss' was then inveigled to take the line and Sam accepted diffidently after ensuring that no-one else wanted to test their fishing prowess. The next bite ran the line out at least 100 metres. After a mighty fight, with everyone offering advice and yet another run out to sea, Sam brought the fish in and landed it just in time, before its wicked teeth severed the last of the four strands of wire attaching the spinner to the line. The wahoo, weighing nineteen kilos, completed Sam's 100% game fishing success story having landed a sail fish weighing 50 kg more than that fifteen years before on his only other attempt. I could use my good left arm when celebrating his hard work and catch, when a can of beer was passed around the boat.

On the Amboni estate, all the Swiss wives ensured that they were self-sufficient for food for their families. Heidi kept cows and the milk was distributed among the Amboni wives who had children, another kept hens with the eggs and fattened chickens helping the diet all round; they baked their own delicious bread and grew all the vegetables while the men did any necessary butchering. The gardens, with cascading colour from flowering shrubs and plants, and peacocks strolling around as a further decoration, were beautiful and the warning cry of the peacocks kept thieves at bay. A unique speciality were the orchids grown with tender care in every nook and cranny. One little white star flower needed a magnifying glass to see it. I was amazed, too, at the clear beauty of the night sky with my favourite Southern Cross shining brightly for me. I always regretted losing sight of it when it slips over the horizon during a starlit flight north.

South of Tanga on Pangani and Mkwaya ranches we watched a Tanzanian expert inseminate young heifers in season from a churn of frozen semen tubes. It followed the same practice with similar problems to the Swift King Ranch in Brazil that we had seen five years before in 1973. An extra problem was caused by lion taking cattle at night.

Flying back to Nairobi, it was suggested that I flew with David, our pilot, the next morning with a consignment he had to deliver in the Rumuruti area, on the Colceccio Ranch, while Sam had a business meeting. The landing strip on the edge of the escarpment, where the Nyaso Nyiro river tumbles down to the plain below, can be very slippery and rough when wet, but we came in safely although followed closely by another little plane, an unlikely event in the wilds of Kenya. David's scowls at this crowding turned to a happy smile as he recognised a friend, Julian McKeand, who ran a camel safari trek business near Nanyuki, who came to greet us. Our meeting added to my pleasure when I found that his wife was Jane Lilley, whose father directed the Horse Show at Evesham and drove Hackney horses. I had usually competed at this fairly local show where 'Pug', Lord Ismay, was the President, in such good and welcoming company.

My short acquaintance with Rose and Jimmy Caldwell who ran the ranch made me sure that we must return here with the children for a week in the autumn of the next year. Rose did some showjumping and when I remarked on the hard dry ground, she told me that she collected elephant turds around the ranch and used the soft fibrous dung around the jumps, to make a springy take off and landing for the horses. Apart from the horses, I was interested in the camels and asked if we and the children could do a short camel safari if we came next year.

Flying back to Nairobi, David took me over Lake Nakuru to see if there was further development along the lake shore. I was relieved to see that the chemical factory had closed down but there were practically no flamingos on the lake. I had been told that with the high water there, the flamingos had migrated to other lakes, notably Lake Baringo to the north west of Colceccio.

Sam was talking business on the terrace of the Norfolk Hotel, when I got back rather late, but we talked over my plan for a future holiday and camel safari with the children when we had boarded the plane at 1 a.m. en route for Khartoum.

The Gezira cotton estates were our destination with a drive along the Blue Nile to Wad Medani passing through the ancient port of El Mesellemiva with its market, and ferry across the river. Arriving at the Barakat resthouse, the Arabic word meaning welcome, there was breakfast laid for a Chinese delegation.

We were taken out into the cotton fields with the chief entomologist, who showed us the white fly under some of the leaves where they produce a sticky substance that spoils the cotton, and we learnt about cutworm larvae and American bollworm. The crop-spraying pilots had to contend with many hazards, flying under high tension wires while spraying from only two or three metres, with the wheels of the aircraft nearly touching the crop and turning over the banks of the canals, sometimes dodging the odd camel or donkey using the track along the bank. There is no room for error in the pilot's concentration while doing this precise work in varied weather conditions. One Kiwi pilot had died hitting a high tension wire and another Bulgarian was killed when a boy lobbed a brick through the windscreen of the plane, because his water buffalo were nervous of the low-flying spray plane.

The pilots came from at least ten countries and the co-ordination of the pilots on the intercom, some with only a few words of English, was often a problem. Another big problem was boredom, as they lived together in confined accommodation with no recreational activities and flying was often curtailed by weather and wind conditions.

The rotation of crops is usually on a four year plan beginning with groundnuts to compensate the soil with nitrogen for the cotton crop, followed by sorghum or wheat, then vegetables or a year of fallow. The main sugar cane crop is grown near Khartoum.

We left at first light to fly over the 1971 El Suki scheme and then the Sennar Dam built by the British in 1925, taking in the El Suki pump and the Meina pump at Rahad before landing on the Damazine strip by Er Roseires Dam, Italian-built in 1964. As we taxied towards the hut where the two Pilatus Porters were parked, two soldiers sitting on the tin roof of the hut trained their machine guns on us. It was a sensitive area so near the Ethiopian border and Sam muttered, 'I hope they don't get stung and scratch'. We flew on in the Pilatus Porters because the Cherokee could not land on the short SEAI Co. projects strip.

Sam flew off steadily with an Australian pilot while I had the British chief co-ordinator of the pilot's programmes, who showed me the paces of the Pilatus. We kept well away from the machine-guns all along the Roseires Dam, but as we dived and twisted the pilot muttered, 'You all right?' through the corner of his mouth, while I was suspended about two inches above my seat most of the time.

We had brought stores for the people working at the Sudan Agricultural scheme camp and so they cooked sausages which we ate for breakfast, in our fingers, while we were shown the project and I admired an Abyssinian roller, a very pretty long-tailed blue bird with a buff back.

Flying to another project at Rahad, I was shown a glorious sparrow hawk that had been found sick on a sprayed field. It looked pleased with itself as its appetite had obviously returned, having devoured a quail that morning, another less fortunate patient in the bird corner of the hut. We changed back to the Cherokee to fly to Khartoum and I asked to see the Dinder National park on the return trip. Flying over the Dinder river we came in low but only saw some baboon families and a buck on the sand banks in the river. Our pilot had once landed on one of the sand banks, but flying over the deserted camp of the park, he pointed out the shell of a Twin Otter that lay near the end of the overgrown landing strip, an accident that had cost six lives a few years before, since when the strip was closed. We followed the Blue Nile north to Khartoum leaving the camel caravans below us wending their way south.

We crossed the Dinder river Syphon, where the Rahad canal is syphoned under the river. I had discussed the possible effects of this canal, in altering the habits of migratory animals, but a far larger plan and possible ecological disaster was the beginning of another drainage scheme, the Jonglei canal, aimed at draining the vast area of over 100,000 sq km comprising the Sudd marshes of the White Nile in the south of the Sudan. The canal would cut through from Bor and Jonglei, north to Malakal, changing the entire habitat and lives of marsh tribes of Dinka, the Nuer and the Shilluk, as the main ethnic groups, along with the animals living there, while cutting the migration route of a whole area. No scientific survey had been made of the Jonglei area of the Sudd before excavation to drain the area was commenced, likewise there had been no serious environmental appraisal made before the Assam High Dam was built and funded by the Russians.

The greens of the irrigated area of the Gezira were a miracle from the air, compared with the surrounding barren desert. We had been invited to lunch with the chairman and managing director of CPS, crop protection, but luckily he understood our tardiness when he had heard our programme since 4 a.m. that morning. He invited us to a welcome swim after our hot and dusty morning, before we sat down, refreshed, to appreciate his true Sudanese hospitality.

The Minister of Agriculture, that evening, was interested in my work with the WWF and arranged for me to meet the people in the Wildlife Conservation Department and the Director of the national parks. We returned to Switzerland in time for me to get to Geneva for the WWF annual meeting. I wrote my report, during the night, on the many conservation contacts with their news that I had learnt during the past two weeks in Kenya, Tanzania and Sudan. It was not the first or the last time of writing for a deadline. The greatest pleasure at the WWF meetings was the award of the WWF Gold Medal to Guy Mountford, the well known ornithologist, instigator of the scheme to save the tiger in India and one of the founders of the WWF in 1961.

A very happy year of travel and activity in 1979 started with a business trip to the

Philippines, where we found that four days work had to be condensed into three days when we were met in Manila. That night at dinner we met Ed and José Tordesillas and learnt from him that he had bought his dream island of Balesin about eight years before, 400 hectares of Paradise where he had 700 people working on the coconut plantations to make copra. Our business friends were Bob Lucas and his wife Hope, and Bob and Monica Ongpin. Hope with her special Irish gifts had seen that Ed looked exhausted from his busy schedule and took his hand, trying to revitalise him through her healing powers, so I thought I would try to help too by taking his other hand. The following day he said that he felt terrible but, as I was feeling fine I suspected that I might have passed on my jet lag to poor Ed. Bob's wife Monica became a great friend, as she was from Chile and we had much in common with mutual acquaintances.

The helicopter that arrived on the hotel roof top pad at 8 a.m. in the morning was not piloted by my old friend Jacques Castaing, but we went to inspect factory sights while during the flight we could see much of the countryside. Flying over the active volcano Taal standing in a lake, we saw another lake in the caldera of the volcano, with a tiny island in the deep emerald waters. Taal had erupted a few months before leaving black lava fields still smoking in places. We continued over the grim island of Corregidor that stands in the mouth of Manila Bay. The Americans had made their last stand there, with the guns pointing out to sea, but as with the collapse of Singapore, the Japanese had invaded from the mainland and bombarded the island from the rear, assaulting the fortress from the peninsula of Bataan.

My afternoon was spent talking to the very active Pony Club before I met Sam again at a lovely old Spanish house belonging to Swiss friends, Stephan and Jacqueline Zeullig, whose family had lived in the Philippines for many decades. Dinner was arranged outside in the floodlit garden, where mosquitoes found a way to devour my legs, in spite of my long dress. A *spirale* was brought out and lit under the table which warned off the lethal insects and allowed me to enjoy the romantic setting and dancers who flitted out of the trees, with their reflections dancing upside down in the pool while they performed the Obando dance in rural Philippine dress and carrying bright scarves. The most exciting local dance was the Tinikling where the performers feet must dance between bamboo poles without getting caught as the poles are held and snapped together at an increasingly fast rhythm. The guests were invited to try the dance and one Ciba-Geigy Filipino got up pretending not to know what to do, but he had no trouble when the bamboos were clacking at full speed.

There were flamenco dancers with castenets and Catalan *jotas* from the influence of Spanish domination mixed with Asian dances as seen in Thailand, with hand movements and fingers pointed back while the head and shoulders emphasised the rhythm of the dance. From these glorious surroundings we flew to Balesin at crack of dawn, invited by Ed and José for our last day. The grass landing-strip ran diagonally across the whole island, confirming that we had arrived on the correct island, one of 7,107 islands that make up the Philippines with only 500 of them larger than a square kilometre. Further east of the islands is the Philippine Grave, where the sea bottom drops down to 10,500 metres, but Balesin is protected by a reef and the sea was calm with no undertow.

We went to snorkel before lunch and saw parrot fish with their red snouts and yellow, black and blue stripes. Yellow butterfly fish and little cleaning fish of blue, orange and tiger stripes were the same as we had seen in Indonesia, but not so plentiful as in the Ujung Kulon reserve, because this small island had to support 700 people.

The lapu lapu fish that we lunched on later was named after the Chief who resisted Magellan and killed him as he waded ashore. A fascinating bird, like a huge kingfisher, shining blue with a long straight bill was sitting on a tree by the sea. It does not fish or dive as it is a land bird called a jungle heron. The noise of golden orioles was all around, sounding like jays and reminding me of Burg where orioles were frequent visitors, although jays were unwelcome predators of small birds and for all their colourful show, as much of a pest as magpies or crows.

Flying foxes landed ponderously on the trees around the camp at dusk, which turned to night quickly as the fireflies started flitting in the trees. We had thirst-quenching drinks of a tiny lime called *calamanzi* before eating *bakol*, a whole hot coconut with cooked fish inside. Our host had joined us for this feast with the younger four of his seven children, the older ones being at school on the mainland.

Tennis matches were being played at 6 a.m. the next morning but we had to leave the Paradise island and our generous host and his family. It was sad to leave the little brightly-coloured birds and beautiful big butterflies to return for our flight to Seattle where Sam had a day's seminar. Little did we know that we would not leave for Canada that day, as Mrs Marcos had decided that she wanted to go shopping in Australia and 'borrowed' the Philippine Airlines plane on which our tickets were booked.

Sam's business plans for Canada had to be cancelled and we were squeezed onto a Pan Am plane the next day to get to San Francisco in time for his seminar there. That gave me a free morning to see the shops in Manila and a carving of a monkey-eating eagle perched on the globe that rested on a turtle, returned with us as my shopping answer to Mrs Marcos's spending spree.

We gained a day in crossing the date line, making up for the one I had lost in 1961 when travelling to Australia. The day gained did not relieve our busy programme with Sam's meetings while I enjoyed the company of a stimulating group. An Amtrak train, the San Francisco Zephyr, then took us to Ogden, an overnight trip to get us to Salt Lake City. We saw little of the National Forest area not far from Squaw Valley in the Rockies, because a blizzard was blowing outside. At 4 a.m. we left the train in bitter cold, but our contact was not there to meet us because the train arrived early. Later we had a pre breakfast look at Salt Lake City with our Mormon of the Latter Day Saints driver who drove us from Ogden and showed us the Mormon founder's statue, Brigham Young, before we thawed out with coffee and drove to the airport. Our flight was over snowy landscapes to Dallas where I joined my cousin Jeremy Curtoys and his wife Linda, although Sam had to fly on for a business meeting in Wichita Falls. Jeremy was now Professor in Political Sciences at the University of Texas in

Stephenville and they had an adopted son David, and the next time I went to stay with them they had a second adopted son John. We went out at night with strong torches to see live armadilloes, called *tatu* in Brazil. It was sad during the day to see so many armadilloes and tortoises victims of the constant heavy traffic on the roads.

A day later I was with Sheila, Jeremy's step-sister, who has a house in Washington with her family, on the banks of the Potomac river. She took me to the Air and Space Museum to see the 'Spirit of St Louis', the plane that Lindbergh first flew across the Atlantic to Paris. The museum held a special memory of our friend John Grierson who had died there of a heart attack while lecturing on Charles Lindbergh. The first crossing of the Atlantic in a plane on 20 May 1927, was a miraculous success for the tiny wooden crate of an aircraft, with no forward visibility, because of the extra fuel tank placed ahead of the pilot. This forced him to traverse the Ocean with little aid and only side visibility for navigation. Lindbergh, exhausted from no sleep, then had to cope with the hazard of landing at night in Paris. When he wanted to look ahead he had to turn the plane sideways to see out of the small side windows. The sight of the tiny plane and the feat of Colonel Charles Lindbergh's flight, impressed me more than the Sputniks, Moon Modules, Rockets or Space Ship Laboratory. In this modern age our international flight to New York was delayed by a storm in Washington, so that we missed our plane back to Switzerland. The same thing happened when I attended the WWF meetings in Washington when Dr Richard Evans Schultes won the WWF Gold Medal in 1984. That second time I did not have Sam's hand to hold, or his resourcefulness to lean on.

During 1979 the WWF Trustees meeting was in Arles near the great marshes of the Camargue at the delta and mouth of the Rhône. Luc Hoffmann, Sam's cousin and a famous naturalist, scientist and ornithologist, owned much of the marshes around his scientific research station, Tour du Valat. We had stayed there in 1972 for a superb spring weekend with Luc and Daria his wife and their four children. It was migration time with all the birds of passage returning to Europe from Africa, while the flamingos were nesting on the lagoons. Sam, Luc and I spent eight hours in the saddle one day on his grey horses of the Camargue that are the local breed of the marshes. Most of the time we were splashing in fetlock deep water but over some stretches the water came up to the belly of the small horses. We saw no people that day but came across three families of wild boar with their litters of striped young, although we did not investigate too close to the parents as they are very aggressive with young to protect, like our wild boar in the forest around Burg. Horses do not like to go near them either, snorting and getting nervous, if they get the scent of a pig.

Peter Scott's seventieth birthday celebration dinner that September was a further acknowledgement of the enormous contribution that he had initiated in conservation. The work he started with his friends continues to expand, gaining increasing public awareness and support all the time. He was the founder of the WWF in 1961 together with Julian Huxley and Max Nicholson, mainly formed to fund the scientific body of the IUCN, the International Union for the Conservation of Nature and Natural Resources, which was started in 1948.

Just before Peter's birthday party, Sam asked me to join his management group for a night in Gruyères, where they were holding a seminar. Wives were not usually included in these tough working meetings, where everyone was tested to the core, encouraging them to be stimulated to even higher efficiency and responsibility in management. I realised that it was the last night of the seminar and usually Sam and his team thought up some light entertainment or outing as a reward for their long hours and unremitting work during the seminar.

I took to the winding road over the beautiful Passwang at 1,000 metres, in our blue Bond Equipe which we had first registered in Switzerland in 1970. With the hood open on a lovely autumn day I could enjoy the sun, the view and the crisp air, while waving to any other drivers sporting an open car. The Bond is still giving me and my girls great pleasure thirty years later, stabled now with its left hand drive in Gloucestershire and back in the land of its talented designer. Driving through the 'middleland' between the Jura and the Alps, first took me past the Schloss Bipp where Sam had spent childhood holidays with his cousins, and we had explored with our children the ruins of the castle above the Schloss with its great thick walls, draughty rooms and surely ghosts in the shadows cast by candlelight. After Bern and Fribourg, now avoided by the motorway, which was a very late development for road transport in Switzerland, I enjoyed the view along the dammed reservoir of the Lac de la Gruyères, to Bulle before winding up the lane to the little walled town of Gruyères.

My suspicions were aroused when I saw that our circus friends, the Knies had their posters up in Bulle saying that tonight was the last night of their show there. The yearly programme for the Swiss National Circus takes the Knie family all over the country with some stands of only two days. The organisation for the transport of equipment, tents, animals, people and caravans needs to be infallible, so that the performers are fit and ready for the next show, and the public will be able to watch in comfort.

Sam had long admired the discipline and thorough good management of top circus people, including the necessary psychological understanding and sympathy of temperamental artists of every nationality and sensitive animals with their own individual characters.

Most of Sam's managers at Gruyères had not been to the circus since they were boys and were surprised at the invitation. They all enjoyed the show immensely, and those who appreciated horses could admire the superb horsemanship of the Fredy Knie family. However Sam's surprise finale was to come at the end of the show, when armed with hot coffee, we watched the speed of packing up the circus 'town' at midnight. The seats were removed from the Big Top before the huge tent was lowered carefully and packed up. The canvas had to be guarded carefully against tears or rips while loading the great weight and bulk for the overnight journey.

Everyone had their job to do and miraculously the field emptied of hot dog stands, motor caravans driven by the artists, while children slept in their caravan bunks during the journey, the tents and the stables; while the horses and elephants were already on the road. They left an empty field, cleared of litter, and the night silence descended within an hour of the former scene of intense activity. The lesson in efficiency had terminated the management seminar under the moon and stars, before a good night's sleep in the quiet and beautiful mountain village.

Our next happy event of 1979 was the marriage of Catherine, Sam's eldest, and Roland Schmid. They chose a charming little church for the wedding followed by a party in the attractive local hotel. Roland had always been a favourite visitor to Steinacker, where he showed the younger children difficult dives in the swimming pool and patiently helped them to do backward dives with a clean entry into the pool, without hitting the water flat and hurting their backs. At Sudgrove the children showed him their vaulting exercises on 'Boy', our chestnut horse that patiently trotted and cantered around on the lunge rein, while everyone practised their vaulting skills on him. Our girls had been doing this sport since before they started school in Switzerland and learnt the rhythm to bounce up onto a horse when they were still very small. Roland, being athletic, soon had the feel of the rhythm needed to vault on, although he had not learnt to ride before. Vaulting is an ideal way of learning balance and relaxed confidence without hurting the horse's mouth by pulling on the reins before you can sit correctly in harmony with your mount.

Our *Herbstferien* would take us with Monica and Lucy to Africa for the first time and Dominik was able to come too, now his exams were behind him.

In Nairobi some friends met us for lunch, leaving just time for us to change after the overnight journey. First we had fruit juice, my fresh lime being delicious, but Lucy had her orange juice tipped over her clean trousers by a trainee waiter. Then we had the shashlik, but I saw to my consternation Lucy following this, at her end of the table, with a mixture of brightly coloured ice creams. We were flying to the coast that afternoon but luckily for us there was not too much turbulence that day and Lucy survived the trip.

On the Indian ocean that evening we walked on the beach seeing many varieties of waders and shore birds feeding as the tide ebbed. We took a boat in the morning to the coral reef, taking a supply of sandwiches with us. Soon we discovered, while snorkelling, that the reef dwellers were also partial to our sandwiches which attracted huge shoals of many varieties of fish that flocked around and nibbled us too, to Lucy's delight, but soon our lunch was gone. It did not worry us but it infuriated the boatman, who we did not realise had no lunch of his own. We promised, apologetically, that we would give him the best meal possible when we got back.

We explored the few ruins showing perhaps the traces of a Phoenician port beyond the mangroves growing in the Mida creek. The river Sabaki had changed its course so that coral grew across the reef because coral cannot grow in fresh water. We found a place with cobbles and some fragments of pottery near a ruined mosque and obelisk by some half-buried walls under a huge baobab tree. Cooling off back in the sea, the children were attached to a rope while they snorkelled so that they could not be carried away on the strong current that ripped around the point.

A deep sea fishing trip was not a happy experience for Lucy who was always travel sick and quickly succumbed, but Monica learnt to fish and soon brought in a lively barracuda. Dominik was the next to catch a wahoo but his triumph was his next giant fish a tewa, grouper or rock cod, which live deep on the ocean floor. He had to work hard to get it up but at last the gaping great ugly monster was heaved into the boat, and proved to be 51 kg. The men exhausted themselves getting it up the beach to weigh it. I wanted to get Lucy back before she became dehydrated from being sick, but she was fine as soon as she touched the beach.

The stone crabs amused us by grabbing a stick when Lucy put it between their claws, although they camouflage themselves under stones in the pools, with only their eyes and a tell-tale claw sticking out. I made friends with a woolly-necked stork that paraded around the pool, watching me swim. I was alone with it for nearly fifteen minutes before it slowly took off to fly into some palm trees.

Leaving the ocean with David who picked us up in his plane, we flew over Lamu where President Moi was visiting that day, then up the river Tana over the cotton project where the firm was involved. We stopped for a sandwich and drinks at Samburu, where the girls saw gerenuk feeding, standing on their slender hind legs to browse, their first sight of this antelope. Three elephants appeared at close quarters, one causing great excitement when it trumpeted at us, then we saw a herd of elegant oryx with their beautiful long and slender horns, maybe the origin of the mythical unicorn, when viewed from the side. A large eagle watched us from a tree above baboons and vervet monkeys playing nearby, scattering the pretty guinea fowl. Shaggy waterbuck and graceful reticulated giraffe cantered through a small herd of Grevy's zebra just to give our family a taste of the richness and diversity of African wildlife.

Crocodiles on the bank of the Uaso Nyiro or Black river, watched us eat our sandwiches while we observed these large fat beasts with a horrid fascination. We were careful to explain to the children just how fast these beasts could move when hunting for a kill.

Our next stop for the week was Colcheccio where after some navigation errors, we spotted the house and landing strip on the edge of the escarpment leaving Samburu in the rift valley on the plain below. Rose and Jimmy Caldwell greeted us, taking us back to the lodge where by coincidence a step-son of the Horton-Fawkes, my friends with the collection of Turner pictures in their Yorkshire house, was staying as he had business with shipping at Mombasa. When the stories that evening got around to charging buffalos, he showed on his hands and knees how to frighten a charging bull, which put everyone in the giggly mood.

We went to get the horses at 6.30 in the morning to ride over the reserve. A big warthog running from us with its tail held straight up amused the girls although they were impressed by its tusks. Two reticulated giraffe moved along un-frightened by the horses and a family of three enchanting little dik dik watched us from under a small shrub. Our Samburu guide had said that if one parent died, the other would too, from heartbreak, but they would never leave their partner while they lived and only reared one fawn at a time.

There were four big eland among a herd of Grevy's zebra, but a little foal was standing alone well away from the herd. It seemed to be sick and Lucy asked if she could take it back and nurse it, when it suddenly woke up and looked at us with its round ears pricked before galloping back to the herd bucking and kicking. Lucy would have had a job on her hands if she had caught the foal. When we got back Lucy helped Rose with a sick lamb and fed the wild bush baby which would appear out of the bush when it wanted company and food.

Sam nearly cut his finger off when feeling the blade of a spear, used by Samburu tribesmen, the tall, slim good-looking people related to the Masai tribe. The men had their hair reddened with clay and finished in a small plait behind. Rose spoke to one who had seen a man running from the road and they were going to track the man to see if he was good or bad; even tracking on the dry ground they could tell the tribe and the intention of the stranger, and deal with him if he was a poacher. The Wanderobo were a troublesome tribe on the other side of the river, but Rose spoke another tribal language, of the Gipsigis, cheerful people from the northwest of Kenya where she had been brought up. Two cheetah cubs were playing and rolling about together on the track ahead until their mother took them off into the bush and the father drew us off by loping through the bush parallel to our jeep until we were far enough away from his family, he then disappeared.

The highlight of our safari was a two day trek with the camels, spending a night in the bush where the Uaso Nyiro tumbled down the escarpment through the rocks at Crocodile Jaws. We only had three camels between us, as the others had been hired for a large party on a month's safari to Lake Rudolf. I rode the old camel Turkana with Lucy behind me, as he couldn't take a heavy load. Two other camels had been lent to us from the next ranch. Sam and Monica rode the younger riding camel, while nobody told Dominik that he was riding the salt camel, that had only been used for carting salt around and had never been ridden by a person. Dominik was kept in the dark about being the Test Pilot until we stopped for lunch, when we congratulated him for his success with his mount. The children found the five movements of a camel getting up funny at first, but the camel walk was very comfortable.

The birds and animals were not frightened of us as we loped through their territory, just as when riding in the forest one can approach deer on a horse or pony, whereas they would disappear immediately if people were on their feet.

We heard the duet of a pair of slate-coloured boubou, the male bird singing 'dong dong' with the 'tweet tweet' of the female. Our camels hated walking through puddles or marshy ground, as they are afraid of slipping on mud and doing the splits, when their muscles may never recover. We learnt to say 'Dum' for lying down, 'Ho' for getting up and 'Ho Ho' to get a move on. Maybe all camels don't speak the same language. Our old Turkana was slower than the two younger camels, but when the others stopped to wait for us, Turkana stopped too, regardless of encouraging 'Ho Hoes' from Lucy and me; he had his Union rules of 'anyone stops, I stop!' No one knew the signal that Dominik gave his salt camel, when it suddenly lay down but rose again immediately with his surprised jockey still on top.

During our midday break to loose the camels and let them browse, Lucy put on her problem face with a twenty past eight mouth. The Caldwell's small old pickup had just passed by with some iron bedsteads and mattresses loaded on the back, while we sat in the welcome shade of a tree with our sandwiches. Sam took her aside, so her problem could be sorted out in private. 'It's like the Hilton with those beds,' she tearfully told Sam, but that problem was solved by Rose saying that no-one could sleep on the ground because of snakes and scorpions; if they didn't have bedsteads above the ground in the open, they must sleep in a closed tent. All of us wanted to sleep under the stars. The camping beds were already in place near the rushing waterfall as it forced its way through the rocks at Crocodile Jaws, where we unsaddled our camels at the camping site and they were fed and watered before being left to browse.

We waited around watching the evening bird life, until the barbeque was ready, but friends who were joining us from another ranch were late, having met a lion and a porcupine on the way down to the camp and these animals took precedence on a game reserve until they had moved off the track. The girls went happily to bed later, under the stars, while stories in many dialects were re-counted around the camp fire, before we too turned in.

I heard Turkana grumbling in the morning and went in the direction of the angry noises. Turkana had his mouth open issuing camel swear words while an African tried to put the bright red nylon headcollar on him upside down. His ears were being forced through the two parts that should have been under his chin. Eventually Rose sorted out the problem in Swahili, so the light headcollars that I had brought from England for her could be put correctly and comfortably on the camels.

After the camels had got safely back to the lodge, Monica and I went for a drive, watching for David to arrive with his plane. Just before dusk a silver-backed jackal came very close to us and a big hunting dog loped over the track with his bat ears pricked sideways and the white tip to his tail showing as he merged with the darkness. Sam had especially wanted to see a wild dog, but they were rare on the ranch, and he had stayed at the lodge to wash off the two days of safari dust.

David landed before it was too dark because we were going the next day to Lake Rudolph. Flying north over Maralal and forested mountains and on over less friendly land of volcanic rock and hugh soda pans, we came to the Telekis volcano where David flew around the lava flows and we looked into the crater. Lake Turkana appeared ahead, a dark jade green with white horses which did not bode well for a calm fishing trip. The land along the lake looked very arid with just a few goat herds and camels.

Monica was sitting up with David in the co-pilot's seat and she spotted the landing strip at Kalokal near Ferguson's Gulf. The windsock was non-existent, as on many African landing strips, but we landed safely in the high wind, with

Dominik shouting at Monica 'Don't you dare to touch that stick'. We had a large icebox with us, that Jimmy and Rose hoped we would bring back full of Nile perch, as their deep freeze needed replenishing. These fish make delicious eating and can go up to 360 kg and both our men, father and son, had once landed big fish before, with Dominik's 51 kg grouper and Sam's 50 kg sailfish.

We admired the upright and proud Turkana people along the way to the river walking tall with shining jet black skin. They lived in woven grass rondavels, although their people were originally a nomadic pastoral tribe of warriors and herdsmen like the Masai. A few of them had swallowed their pride to make a living from fishing rather than cattle.

Our fishing trip was not to provide us with sustenance for the present or future. The boat had no fixed seats and I wondered how one could land a big fish in the bucking and rolling boat without disappearing overboard after the fish. Going flat out through the waves the lighter trolling lines for bait got entangled and Lucy was sick. They slowed down nearer the central island and put out the big lines to troll for Nile perch. Fishing had not been good for the last weeks and the others were feeling sick too, so we returned to the Angling Lodge and the children stayed with Sam. As we had the boat for the morning I took it along the shore around the spit and past the lagoon where flamingos and spoonbills were feeding. The boatman only had one speed which was full throttle, but with patience I got him to cut the engine while I could study the wealth of bird life.

Sam was swimming when I got back and Lucy was doing headstands in the thick green water of the lake. I joined them keeping an eye on the two mound-like islands in the lake just beyond us; we'd been warned not to swim out further than thirty yards even though the crocodiles were supposed not to be too hungry. The hippo islands sometimes surfaced with loud snorts but did not try to approach us. The green greasy water felt soft to the skin but it smelt of rotten fish and I certainly would not have put my head underwater like Lucy doing her hand stands. The green water is lush with algae which the fish and birds thrive on and the sensation of swimming in this natron lake was unique. Rivers seasonally run into the lake which has no outflow, and the big crocodiles are very dangerous; gory tales are told with relish of recent tragedies when people had been taken while bathing and then their remains found inside crocodiles slaughtered as maneaters.

The wealthy Count Samuel Teleki von Szek left Zanzibar in 1887, financed for his voyage of discovery by the Royal Imperial Highness, Prince Rudolph, who with his wife Stephanie had this lake and one to the north east, that is now nearly dried out, named after them. The exploration met with many hardships and loss of men, until in January 1887 they finally sighted the Jade Sea, naming it after the Prince. Within a year Prince Rudolph, son of Emperor Franz Joseph, had died in a suicide pact with Marie Vatsera at Mayerling.

Our holiday time was up, so Dominik took the girls back to Switzerland for school, while Sam and I had two days business in Madagascar. The children had a big laugh in the midnight plane because while Lucy, who still looked small, slept flat out in the aisle, Dominik and Monica were asked by the stewardess whether the child on the floor was theirs.

Our plane took us over the crater of Kilimanjaro to the north coast of Madagascar where the rivers were running red with the eroded soil of the island, with no trees or vegetation with roots left to hold the soil. Antananarivo is the capital, meaning the City of 1000 Soldiers in Malgashe. We were told on arrival that the dry season had nearly ended, and that night in mid October proved their point, with a fearsome thunderstorm that flooded the small roads.

In the two days I only had time to meet the WWF contact Mr Barthélémi and his wife, to give me a picture of all the work that was necessary in this unique island. The flora and fauna are more allied to Asia than Africa although it lies so near to the African coast. It reminded me of Indonesia although there are tribes with different characteristics, all touched by the French influence and language.

Lemurs are an attractive and endangered animal which encompass twenty-three species of prosimian with their inquisitive eyes and long bushy tails. Like most endangered species they suffer from the loss of natural habitat with the encroachment of human population. We did not have time to go to the north-eastern forest area where there was a chance to see them in the wild; but I was taken to have a look at the captive ones playing in the botanical gardens, studying them closely, especially the aye-aye with its long hook-like fingers that it uses like a probe. There were egrets, herons and ducks nesting on the bird island of d'Alarobia and there was so much of interest to learn and absorb that it was frustrating to have to leave so soon. In the market I found a musical instrument called a *valiha*, the local traditional type of guitar, fashioned from a bamboo of that name. It came home with me as a reminder of the hospitable and friendly Malgache people who I would like to visit again.

Riyadh was the start of our next business trip in 1980 to Saudi Arabia, where I could learn more about the history and the people of this important centre of Islam. Many of the foreign ladies had developed remarkable talents because of the strict rules limiting their freedom. They may not drive, swim or do sport in public places. At the Equestrian Club superb facilities for ladies were built separately with a swimming pool, tennis, squash courts, but just after the club was opened a high-ranking gentleman said that ladies could not be permitted to be members of the same club as men, so the ladies' side had remained empty.

While Sam was working, I went for a drive to the historical old city of Dariyyah, with two of the wives who were taking me back to Ciba-Geigy compound where they all lived. The oasis old city was surrounded by a fortification wall and became the focal point for the religious reform movement in the mid eighteenth century, supported by the ruling Saudi dynasty, before the city was destroyed in around 1819 by the invasion of the Egyptians at the instigation of the Ottoman Empire.

In the new part of the city we visited the Re-educational Centre where the Government had advisory courses in agriculture, literacy and education with classes for the normally neglected women and handicrafts for the country women.

An Egyptian lady doctor there was unveiled but wore an *abayah* over her head. She introduced us to the Saudi Director who invited us three ladies to have Arabic coffee with him. It was poured for us from a long spouted brass pot held high above each tiny cup without a drop going astray. The thin liquid is heavily spiced with *lail*, cardamom, an acquired taste that can grow pleasantly. It is polite to take three cups, but when one has had enough, you put your fingers, of only the right hand, over the empty cup and shake it, indicating that you have finished.

The display of handicrafts from classes, only started two years before, was very colourful and artistic, with knitted, crocheted and embroidered garments, baskets and rugs among other things, so I bought a prayer mat with the Arabic writing for Allah in blue on the beige wool background.

Back at the compound I met more friends, Sonya and her husband Professor William Büttiker, who is the authority on the fauna of Saudi Arabia, having written the series of scientific books on the subject. They would spend long periods of time in the desert, collecting all the data of the Saudi creepy-crawlies, while putting up with the discomforts of desert life without a thought. At the other end of Africa, they have just finished an expedition into the Namibian desert to find the southern relatives of the Saudi fauna. I learn a great deal when I can visit them in Switzerland at their house in a village not very far from Burg.

Other ladies had published books on desert flowers, Saudi Arabian birds, and a *Desert Ramblers* magazine. The wife of a medical specialist at the King Feisal Hospital had an interesting collection of birds and orphan animals like armadillos, with some especially rare little scorpions found while fossil hunting in the desert. She had to supplement the diet of some of these animals with fleas, which the chauffeurs would be asked to collect from the camel market. Another lady had taught herself to paint, when she found that she was not allowed to take photos in Saudi Arabia, just as music or artistic expression is frowned on too.

The highlight for me was a night at Abha, where the Ciba-Geigy people had a meeting. I hoped to visit the Asir National Park that was designated in 1976 and took in 450,000 hectares of this fabulous land from the mountains to the Red Sea. An unexpected honour was that we were invited to an audience or *Al-majles* with Prince Khaled Bin Feisal at Abha. The Prince, Governor of the Province of Asir, received us in a carpeted room in a small building near his stud and stables. He was sitting with his advisers and two teenage sons Bandar and Sultan and signalled to me to come and sit by him on the carpet, as we entered. We discussed sport and he said that both his boys had learnt to ride with 'Vicky' in Riyadh and they enjoyed showjumping.

Vicky Collwell, an efficient American lady ran the excellent stables containing sixty to seventy horses in the Riyadh Riding School which she had created out of a disused factory. The huge arena, divided into three parts with show jumps, cross-country fences and dressage arenas, was sprayed each year with sump oil to prevent the base of shavings from getting dusty, which had proved very effective. She had a lot of young people riding in classes and as individuals and one gathered that everyone who had learnt to ride in Saudi Arabia, had been taught by or was a friend of Vicky. The horses were in excellent condition and she told me that the Arab school horses had great patience with pupils and did not get mean or nappy with beginners. A load of Pony Club ponies arrived for a rally in an open lorry and I watched them unload. There was no ramp so to my surprise the lorry was backed against a bank and the ponies hopped off obediently.

Prince Abdullah, as he is known in the racing world, had bloodstock in England, with Final Straw by Thatch the second-best English two-year-old of that season. He had two English Thoroughbreds standing at stud nearby and arranged that we could see them the following morning. Although his sons enjoyed riding, they took their responsibilities seriously in attending audiences with their father; they were also disciplined in their education which had given them an excellent command of English. My moment of truth arrived when the Prince arose from the floor and I struggled to my feet and tried to straighten my stiff knees.

I mentioned that our mutual friend Sir Peter Scott had told me about the new Park on the Asir Mountains with the centre above Abha, so when the Prince realised that my interest lay with the WWF he was delighted to arrange for us to visit the escarpment to see the type of country where the park was sited. Peter had visited him and they had studied some of the great tract of land, which would become an invaluable area for conservation of the unique flora and fauna.

The view from the top of the rocky ridge, which rises to 3,000 metres at Al Sawdah, proved to be spectacular. We had climbed past well-terraced and fertile fields looking very green, where horses thrived, to the mountain rocks and sheer drop to the valley floor below and out to the Red Sea. Holding onto the rock face while edging to a look-out point, a huge black bird flew low over me with a terrific span of wings. I could not get my camera out in time to photo the lammergeyer or bearded vulture, but scrambling to a safer place I waited for the great bird to return but only steppe buzzards and a red kite came back to be filmed. Flocks of choughs with red bills like the flocks of dolen, the Alpine variety with their yellow bills, were ready to scavenge anything that a picnicker left discarded or unguarded. Already abandoned lemonade tins and glass bottles had been left around by people who did not appreciate how we humans can despoil nature's most beautiful sites.

The corals of the Red Sea tempted me to explore the reefs, but business did not allow us the time for this luxury. I did learn, as we returned through Egypt, that the idea of connecting the Mediterranean and the Red Sea by a waterway, through the Isthmus of Suez, dates back forty centuries. The first canal was dug under the reign of Sanausret III, Pharaoh of Egypt, about 2000 BC, joining the two seas via the River Nile and its tributaries. The canal frequently silted up, but was successfully reopened to navigation by King Darius I of Persia, Ptolemy II, Emperor Trajan and Amro Ibn El Ass, following the Islamic Conquest. The canal was finally neglected in the eighth century until it was reopened to navigation in the nineteenth century.

12

South American Experiences

Sam and I first went to South America together in 1973, when we flew into Viracopas, São Paulo. The name of the Brazilian airport came from the local village where originally a Swiss community had settled; but their drunken behaviour caused the priest to turn their wine glasses upside down, so that they could drink no more.

The South American Jumping Championships were being held there, and I could meet up with General Eduardo Yañez from Chile, whom I had known while jumping in Chile and on the international circuit. He was a great gentleman serving on the FEI, the International Equestrian Bureau, having had much experience in international jumping. The club where the championship took place had every facility imaginable for horses, riders and spectators, with sandy arenas and a big grass arena with natural obstacles, a permanent bank, waters, hedges and trees. A covered grandstand allowed spectators to see the outdoor and indoor arena and there were polo grounds as well.

The following morning we flew to Rancheria near the Mato Grosso on the Paraira river where the Swift-King Ranch Fazendas had opened the land to cattle and horse breeding. At three ranches in the district we saw magnificent Santa Gertrudis cattle crossed with Zebu cows, upgrading the calves by the generation. The semen for the AI centre was compressed and frozen in pill form, then stored in big churns, frozen in liquid nitrogen.

We were then flown to a nature reserve on the Mosquito river where the marshy jungle along the banks of the Paranapanema still held tapirs and monkeys in spite of widespread poaching and killing of any wild animal.

I was taken by a friend to the sea by Santos port, encountering the terrible pollution where the metal works were emitting thick red smoke which belched skywards for thousands of feet. It was a relief to come to the sea and great rollers breaking on superb sand. Nearby in a fisherman's bay the frigate birds were circling, using their deeply forked tails and diving down to fish where the pelicans were also waiting for any fisherman's waste from the catch.

The next day we encountered more pelicans, but on the Pacific Ocean near Lima, while we ate raw fish too, a piquant speciality called *chicha*. I had a meeting with Dr Felipe Benevides, a friend from the WWF, who had implemented a programme to save the vicuña, like a small Andean llama with a very fine wool. Felipe was an autocratic character, in whose company one was never bored. His conservation methods had to be done his way and woe betide anyone who disagreed with him; however he was a unique conservationist in Peru, who made himself heard and got results. He won a legal battle against Aristotle Onassis who had an illegal whaling fleet in Peruvian waters, catching protected whales. The Onassis fleet had to be sold after a fine of $3 million was imposed. Felipe fought for the establishment of nature reserves and parks in Peru with tenacity; his vicuña programme was also a success while he proved that vicuñas could be sheared and their soft and valuable wool marketed commercially, whereas before the only obtainable wool had come from tree stumps or fences where the animals had rubbed.

He earned many honours for his conservation work and was an International Trustee of the WWF until he resigned in 1979 over a difference of opinion in policies for vicuña conservation. In 1991 he left this life in London, where he had been educated for his future as a diplomat and businessman, soon after a very controversial television film of his had been shown on the BBC. He had had his final word and had reminded his acquaintances of his criticism of other people's work in world conservation, together with his own considerable contribution.

The ancient Peruvian Indians had believed in a Creator and Ruler of the Universe, who they worshipped under the name of Pachacamac and Viracocha, their special deity being the sun. Temples had been built in every city and town, where the altars were used for burnt offerings, to seek favours from the Sun God and his deities. The Incas acknowledged the Moon as the Sun's sister or wife with the stars as her heavenly train. Thunder and lightning were the Sun's ministers with the rainbow, the elements and the great mountains and rivers all acting as influences in the destiny of the Inca race.

Cuzco was famous for the richest temple in the land, where there was so much gold that its name of Coricancha meant the 'Garden of Gold'. The chapel dedicated to the moon was decorated with a huge plate of silver and the whole temple was filled with gold and silver plates and vases studded with gems. All these objects and riches disappeared in the hands of the Conquistadors, leaving practically no examples of the pre-conquest art, with the valuable metals being melted down and the spoils divided between the victorious Spaniards.

Sam and I left the perpetual fog blanket over Lima at dawn to fly to Cuzco high in the Andes, passing the great white faces of Ampay and Sarcantay, their peaks towering above us at over 6,000 metres. I scanned the steep rocks for an expedition that was trying to conquer these peaks, thinking back to my father's mountaineering exploits as a young man, but I saw no movement on the forbidding mountainside. Landing at Cuzco at a height of 3,326 metres is a tricky operation with the height and surrounding peaks, not an exercise to be undertaken in bad visibility or weather conditions.

As we had taken off at sea level, the captain warned us on leaving the plane, not to hurry at this height until we became acclimatised to the thin mountain air. We were met by Señor Perez who could speak Quechua, the language imposed by the Incas and used in all Indian homes. He introduced us to Dante, our most intelligent local guide who took us to the great ramparts of Sacsahuaman, the fortress of the Pre-Incas above Cuzco. No one knows the exact history of those people, but the immense stones are fantastically fitted together and earthquakes have not budged them. Unfortunately the Conquistadors wrecked many walls, taking stones for building in Cuzco, as they had destroyed most of the history and art and the records of the civilizations that preceded their conquest.

Back in the town we admired the temple of the sun and moon with more of the wonderful walls, one with a fourteen-sided stone. We had had an early start, but could get no trout for supper as the poachers had been dynamiting fish in the river. The train for Machupicchu left at dawn to zig-zag its way forwards and backwards up the mountainside above Cuzco, while alternatively one faced the front or the back of the train. Once up on the fertile plain we progressed forwards and watched the cattle, sheep and donkeys grazing. There were no alpacas or llamas to be seen on the mountains, but two groups of alpacas are kept for tourists to see at Sacsahuaman and Machupicchu.

We followed the river Urubamba all the way down the valley, while I kept my nose flattened to the grubby window, so that I would not miss any torrent ducks that I had been told might live there. My determination paid off when I saw a pair for about thirty seconds before they dived and disappeared under the fast-flowing water. There was just time to note the black and white head of the male and the orange chin and chest of the female, both sexes having very vivid colours. That alone was worth the trip, or as Michelin puts it, *vaut le voyage*. Apart from this treat there was much more of fascination ahead.

On arrival at the station in the gorge below Machupicchu, there was a stampede from the train to get places in three small mini buses. We arrived up the mountain with Dante on the roof, to the accompaniment of great cracks of thunder from across the valley, sounding like the wrath of the gods. Ignoring the elements we could wander around the ruins alone while other people stayed in the shelter of a hotel. We were spared the threatening rain and inspected the sundial by ourselves, trying to absorb the knowledge of that civilization, while the storm echoed around us with lightning hitting the dark peaks, emphasising the powers of the deities revered by the Incas.

The dignity and permanence of the old buildings contrasted favourably with the poorly patched up newer stone work from the time when Machupicchu was used as a refuge. The gateway of the Inca road could be held alone by only one or two men. In 1986, Monica and Andy, her fiancé, after they had taken their Matura exam and before starting university, backpacked along the Inca road from Cuzco, often in freezing wet mists at over 4,000 metres. They said that the great stone slab steps down the mountains were more tiring and dangerous, being wet and slippery, than the ones going up the mountainside. It had been scary camping at night with strange noises around their tent, as they were aware of the danger at that time with only two of them to camp in the mountains, so far from everywhere, but now it would be even more dangerous.

They had both been soaking wet while camping and one night Monica was shaking with fever, but the hardships of the trek were dissipated with their first sight of Machupicchu. It was dawn as they approached on the old road above the ruins to experience the perfect moment of seeing the historic city at sunrise. The mountain mists had lifted and the first warm rays touched the site of the ancient civilization, where the sun had been worshipped by the Incas and now remained with the ruin of one of their last Sun Temples.

The community had been seen once by a Spaniard on horseback but the city was too impregnable to explore further. It was left until 1911 when Hiram Bingham, the American archaeologist paid an Indian 50 cents to lead him to the lost city of the Incas, having approached from further down the river. The present zig-zag road was carved out of the mountainside and only inaugurated in 1948.

The peak across from the ruined city is Huayna Picchu, where the steep sides were terraced and probably had been used as a nursery garden for toughening crops at that height. Dante was asked how long it took people to climb the peak and replied laconically, 'Well, we've never found the last one yet'.

Our next flight took us north with wonderful views of Chimborazo and Cotapaxi, the great volcanoes south of Quito in Ecuador, then down to Bogota, capital of Colombia, and with a smaller plane up into the Andes to Medellín, where Sam had a seminar. I did not know about the drug barons and marijuana trade that has now made Medellín notorious, but I knew that the airport was a dangerous one, being high on the mountains and surrounded by peaks like Cuzco. Carlos Gardel had been killed there in a plane crash when, in his prime, he came to give a concert singing his tangos. I had many of his records that I had acquired in Buenos Aires and I had danced the tango in La Boca, the area on the River Plate with the *Acadamias* and *Bordillos* that had inspired his talent. The tango was the favourite dance of Sam and myself; where ever we were we would automatically find ourselves dancing together when the first line of a tango was played.

I had asked Dante, in Cuzco, if he had seen any condors, and he said that there were a pair in the mountains around Machupicchu, but we had not seen them. The Andes looked devoid of wildlife and apart from my luck in spotting the torrent ducks and some pairs of tiny divers in the river, unidentified but only the size of tits, there were very few birds. I saw my first condors in the Zoological Gardens in Medellín, but that was not the object of travelling in the high Andes.

Monica saw a pair of condors flying high near Lake Titicaca during her Andean trek, but then she blacked out suffering from *soroché*, the mountain sickness that often affects people at heights of over 4,000 metres.

Returning to Europe from the majestic range of mountains we saw the whole panorama of the Alps as we approached Switzerland, familiar friends that would be dwarfed by the majestic heights of the South American Andes.

Our next sight of South America was seven-and-a-half years away, but then we did not get to the high Andes on the west coast.

In June 1980 the new offices of the IUCN and WWF were opened in Gland, near Geneva. It was an important step for conservation with the scientists and researchers working under the same roof as the fund-raisers who worked to finance the necessary projects. Each programme has to be planned carefully to save the habitat of endangered species of wild animals, and protected so that the land is kept sustainable for the flora and fauna that it can support.

One finds a natural resistance between institutions and individuals to pool their knowledge because of the fear that their valuable contribution would be stolen or swallowed in an overall plan. An efficient conservation programme for this planet must utilise the complete information provided by each specialist group. Professor Mohamed Kassas from Giza University, Cairo, who was then the Director of the IUCN, made an excellent speech to highlight the urgency of the work to be carried out from the Gland centre in order to form a World Conservation Strategy.

Sam and I had witnessed some of the destruction of rain forest on an indiscriminate scale in our travels around the world. The irrevocable effects of erosion, caused by logging and slash-and-burn tactics to clear the land, was impoverishing countries that were already poor. Tribes, who had lived for centuries off the land of their region, which they had kept, like true stewards, to regenerate and sustain their usage and existence, were being invaded by greedy and ignorant people who selfishly wanted to grab everything of value with complete disregard for the future of the land or the indigenous people.

We had read about a Brazilian project in the Amazon, where the Jarí river flows into the estuary of the Amazon. Daniel K. Ludwig, a wealthy American shipping magnate had put into action an immense project which involved the destruction of a large area of rain forest, replacing it with huge plantations of fast-growing trees like eucalyptus and melina, non-indigenous species. It also involved bringing a floating pulp mill by sea from Japan, where he had built his fleet of supertankers, that had created the basis of his immense wealth.

The chance to see the effects of this enormous scheme came at the start of 1981 when Sam had business to do in Argentina and Brazil. He also made sure that we would visit Jarí on the way back and talk to the managers of the wood pulp project. First, we had to change planes in Rio en route for Buenos Aires where we found an endless queue of teenagers from Argentina waiting for our plane. They were all carrying enormous packages, but a friend remarked, 'That's what they carry, the rest is in their luggage, don't forget!' An announcement then confirmed this statement saying that our DC10 was being changed for a Jumbo because of the weight of the luggage.

At that time the Brazilians called the Argentinians the *Darmidos*, because every time they asked the price of something in a shop, they would say 'Give me two', as the Argentine was four times more expensive. In some years the Brazilians would find it cheaper to shop in Argentina when the currency fluctuated the other way.

The Hotel Plaza in Buenos Aires is a nice old-fashioned traditional hotel with high ceilings and spacious rooms. We were tired and hungry when we arrived as we had not eaten on the planes, so we ordered one steak. It arrived in our room looking as big as the usual Sunday joint, but Sam and I tackled the delicious meat from each end and met in the middle, before going to bed.

My dear old friend Violeta Tschiffely had just died in England, widow of Aimé or 'Tschiff' as he liked to be called, the hero of the ride with his criollo horses

Mancha and Gato from Buenos Aires to Washington in 1925. I was writing an article on Aimé's life, and I knew that his elder brother's son Felix Oswaldo lived in Buenos Aires. Finding him by phone at Quilmes, he also gave me the number of John Norris, who had been a pupil at St Georges school while Aimé had been a master. John's father had taught Aimé to ride during a holiday that he had spent on the Estancia with John's family.

Oswaldo and John with his wife Mary, met me in the hotel one evening. I recognised Oswaldo from the looks of his aunt Desirée, Aimé's younger sister whom he had never met. I had visited her when she lived in the Burger Spital in Bern, where 'Burgers' or old people from the family of local residents can live inexpensively in seperate rooms and eat together if they want to. Desirée had died before Violeta.

John Norris was a fit and dapper man of about seventy and soon he was talking in rapid Argentine Spanish with Oswaldo, who was about ten years younger. He recounted stories about his father who had trekked cattle over the Andes in 1904 from Buenos Aires and also sheep from Rio de Gallegos, without any maps or white men to help him. The Indians who worked for him would always be waiting to catch him off guard, so that they could make off with the herds or flocks themselves. These adventures did not make him a rich man, because after he had established the animals in Chile, the company he worked for went broke and so he got no pay.

Although he went back to England in 1908, people there treated him like a cowboy, so he returned to Argentina and established his own Estancia where he brought up his children. This was the home to which John had invited Aimé, his Swiss schoolmaster, during the holidays, giving Aimé the chance to learn to ride. The fame of Tschiff through his great ride and the success of his future books, had all depended and started with the kindness of John's family.

Tschiff had married Violeta in Buenos Aires where she had been an opera singer and played Lucy Lockett in *The Beggar's Opera*. Throughout her long life she always looked immaculate, tiny with long black hair tied neatly back from her face. Her parents were Scots who had settled in Buenos Aires and she had an attractive but prim face, which must have surprised people when she made her name in *The Beggar's Opera*.

We dined together with Carlos Delía, the Argentine Olympic rider who had been a friend since 1956. He had been Ambassador in Bruxelles, since I had last seen him, and another colleague of Sam's was Raul Salaberren, the Minister of Economy in the Province of Buenos Aires, who had been Delía's lawyer at some time, which gave us common ground for anecdotes.

I was able to learn more about Jarí when we returned to Brazil, in talking to friends who knew the set up of the project. We visited *fazendas*, farms, in Minas Geraís, a province as big as France, to see programmes of maize, the main crop, then sorghum and soya beans, which have a delicate balance with germination problems. We were flown to Lagoa de Sevra to be shown the alcohol sugar factory 'Santa Elisa' where the cars are all run on alcohol taken from the sugar cane grown in the area. Brazil should have produced 4.1 billion litres of alcohol that past year, each billion representing an economy of one fifth of the gasoline being consumed there, but the results did not justify undue optimism.

In the same area is the immaculately kept insemination station, where the car and oneself must be disinfected on entry, and people change into white coats and plastic boot covers. We could then inspect the grass enclosures for the 36 bulls; the magnificent Zebu bulls with their huge hump, the cupim, which is a delicacy when roasted, are relatively easy to handle as are the Nelore, Guzzera, Gir and Hindu Brazil, a cross between Indian Zebu and Brazilian indigenous cattle, that have formed a breed like the Guzzera with long floppy ears.

The dangerous breeds used to take semen are Holstein (one bull had killed a man that past year), Simmenthal and Charolais. Forty receiver cows were kept to plant the embryos in them, to produce well-bred calves, while the pedigree cows produce new embryos for transplantation.

Driving through a tropical thunderstorm, the cars had to stop for a while until the rain stopped torrenting down before we could proceed to a little town of Brazilian skyscrapers, which seemed to me incongruous when built in such a vast country, as it loomed out of the murky sky. Arriving at the inn, we found that the plate glass entrance door had shattered, caused by the element's disrespect of modernisation, with a sudden change of temperature during the storm.

Early next morning we flew to see two more *fazendas*, where my eyes strayed from the corn crops to the brown and white buzzards and the collaro, a tiny black collared bird that hopped up and down on the ripening rice; on the dam, a heron fished for tilapia, an introduced fish that we had often eaten in Africa. The busy and interesting morning terminated in a *churrasco*, a barbecued lunch, with invited local authorities and prominent people.

The cook, or *churrascieiro*, was a great character and looked like an Indian cowboy with his hat. He held a fern leaf to sprinkle salt and water on the pieces of meat as he put them on the grill, our first delicacy being cupim, the Zebu hump. Meat followed meat and more meat until a stormy wind brought heavy rain just when the speeches were about to begin. Disregarding the soaking wet blowing over us, the speeches ran their full course.

The speech maker who stole the thunder was the local dentist, apart from his many other activities, but he was not accompanied by his wife. His speech finished with the Laotse Chinese subtlety, 'I can see the heights, I may not reach the peaks but I will try to climb the mountain, and if I fail and cannot shake your hand, I will throw my heart up to you so that we can contemplate the world together.'

Flying to Salvador, the next flight, Sam had to keep his briefcase under his chin while his neighbour who overlapped his seat, cleaned his nails. I was writing on my knee and a big arm hung back over the seat in front of me, the hand dangling over my notebook. I wonder if later he noticed the faces that his fingernails had acquired during the journey.

When Sam and Walter Benz departed for business early, Frankie, Walter's wife and I profited from seeing the delightful town. The monastery of San Francisco was founded in 1635, one of the oldest orders in Brazil which exercised a great influence on the cultural, social and religious lives of the people. In the cloisters are lovely tiled scenes showing Lisbon before the earthquake of 1775, perhaps the only record of the original city. A shanty town had grown on stilts in the lagoon where above on the hill is the old slave market. There were slave stories attached to the old sugar mill with round arches on the sea front, a grim reminder of those days, but our time was too limited to sample the food in the mill, now restored as a restaurant, the Solar do Unhao.

In the market I found a little sandstone *tatu* or armadillo for Sam, before we met up with the men to fly together to Belém, with a stop at Recife where every seat was filled. Hopping on north along the coast in the dark, I was sad not to get a view of the towns where we landed, Fortaleza, San Luis and Rio Amazones, before flying at dawn to the northern side where the Rio Jarí forms the boundary of the provinces of Amapá and Pará. The trip across the extensive mouths of the Amazon from Belém to Monte Dourado was 520 km in a full two-propeller Heller plane.

Coming to the red landing strip, we could see the new trees of the plantations that had replaced the old rain forest. We came straight in to land smoothly, a luxury after some of the rough and bumpy grass 'runways', that we had to inspect, making low passes in the air before choosing the least rutted and safest place to land on the *fazendas* that we had visited during the previous days.

Ludwig had forseen a world-wide paper shortage with increasing necessity for communication and the wood pulp for production of paper. He had planned to buy cheaply and then develop roughly 1.4 million hectares of the eastern Amazon in a project financed by his company. His main object was to clear the ancient rain forest and create a silvi-cultural plantation of pulpwood trees for the wood pulp mill, that would bring income into this unexploited region. He was replacing the natural forest with fast growing trees like eucalyptus and *gmelina arborea*, a quick growing species of Asian origin. Research had not been thorough before the whole scheme was put into action, with the introduction of non-indigenous species. There was the question of changes to the soil and especially the danger of pests and diseases to the plantations of a single species of tree, with insects, caterpillars and other pests including fungus. All these had already been noted on the plantations, the worst being atta, the leaf cutter ant which could kill *pinus* seedlings up to two years old. The plantation experiment could prove to be a disaster, leaving the land impoverished and stripped of indigenous forest. (In Gloucestershire, when I got back, I asked the naturalist John Hughes, the conservation and wildlife specialist, if there was another technical term for forestry mono-culture, with plantations of only one species of tree. He assured me that foresters had another name, but unfortunately it is unprintable.)

The whole Jarí complex also included a smaller area for mechanized cultivation of rice, with the Amazon flood plain dyked and bulldozed. The other sideline was the world's largest herd of water buffalo, but it was said that these cattle were not a financial success and that the herd was being dispersed for slaughter. It is not the first time that the jungle has proved more competent of looking after itself than when man interferes with its natural balance, in trying to exploit its resources.

The whole complex of Monte Dourado had been built for the 35,000 people who worked there, including families and contracted labour. We saw the bank, the gymnasium, hospital, school and houses on our way to the pulp mill and generating plant. Each of these two floating giants had been built in Japan and towed by two of the strongest tugs in the world for eighty-seven days at sea to Jarí. Once they had arrived at the river the tugs left them to be towed into place on the lock system by huge tractors.

We were taken up the ninety metal steps to the top platform of the mill, with deafening noise and heat from the machinery until we entered the sound-proofed control room at the top. The whole process of turning wood into paper was explained to us and one floor down the pulp was going through enormous rollers, being mixed with kaolin which whitened the grey pulp. The kaolin was mined over the river where bauxite was discovered too, that had not yet been exploited. All the effluent went through a scrupulous process to be discharged as clean water into the river. Sam had always specialised in this necessity in the chemical industry.

We met a botanist engaged in identifying the edible and inedible fruits of the forest, among other botanical work. Strips of primary forest had been left along the river banks at intervals between the plantations of quick-growing trees for pulp. The trees of the primary forest were of every variety and being left in strips without the protection of a dense forest, they were easy to examine. It was obvious that these trees could not sustain the needs of fruit-eating animals, as movement would be difficult for wildlife between the strips in order to find different kinds of fruits as they ripened.

At the tree nursery a programme had just been completed to raising 24 million eucalyptus seedlings for planting out. The seedlings when ready, were individually pricked out into little plastic bags of soil, then later the young trees were pruned and planted out in the plantation. Apparently the women were best at the transplanting of seedlings, being quick and deft at their work. To see those vast plantations of one species of tree growing on land that had always supported so many varieties, was a worrying thought as one species could be wiped out by one disease. The rain forest held such diversity of tree and plant life, sustaining so great a range of fauna, from forest floor to the tree canopy more than 30 metres above; this the wonderful cycle of nature with its complex bio diversity, would be broken with the destruction and replacement of the primary forest.

The managers of the Jarí project were all top men with excellent qualifications who were employed to carry out the scheme. In spite of responsible research they realised that the whole project was changing the character of the land. The lugubrious dugongs swimming in the Jarí river, supposed to be one of the fish species that originated the myth of the mermaid, also made good eating and were easy to catch, so their numbers were being quickly depleted to feed the thousands of hungry and poor families that had suddenly found themselves moved into this wilderness. New roads and developments had also interfered with the balance of nature that had thrived for centuries, yet the ever increasing population explosion forced more land to be stolen from nature to satisfy the demands of man.

Returning home in the plane, I tried to sort out the experience of the past ten days and write up my notes. Dawn over Africa was spectacular, then there was clear sun and snow over France. We were warned that the temperature was −6°C in Frankfurt, our destiny, having left Rio with 37° in the shade. We had covered more than 35,000 km during that trip before we saw the children at home, who were in great form and intrigued by our tales of South America. We did not know then that this was to be our last trip together in health.

13

Major Fences: The Eighties

Christmas at Sudgrove followed an established pattern with family Communion at Miserden Church, followed by presents under the Christmas tree in the hall, with the wood fire blazing up the chimney and warming the house with its heat. Our Christmas dinner was always a superb turkey, a present from Frank and Cynthia Haydon, followed by a home-made Christmas pudding made the year before, when everyone in the house had stirred it while making a wish. The lights were turned out as the brandy was lit over the pudding and then I doled out tiny pieces for the family, because they found it too rich, making sure that there was a wrapped charm hidden on each plate. Those who could manage larger portions had more pudding to search through for the charm. Crackers were pulled and hats were donned while the same riddles were solved, resurrected from years of cracker jokes.

Our children's meet of the Cotswold hounds was usually between Christmas and New Year, when lots of children and ponies of every size arrived, sometimes on the leading rein, or with a parent in tow. The Master would talk to the children telling them about the work of hounds and how the riders should behave, showing courtesy and thanks to the farmers and people who owned the land that they rode over. Good manners should come before the thrill of galloping and jumping, a basic courtesy often forgotten by the grown-ups.

Our fireworks display before the New Year has been held for nearly three decades. Local people and friends with children are all welcome for this after-Christmas attraction. Mike Roberts is always the expert chief of the show, buying and setting up the display for us, having already organised the village Guy Fawkes display in November, when we were not at Sudgrove. Mike usually found one top attraction among the bevy of colour, flashes and stars that he ignited with a glowing cigar butt. Most popular with the children was a rocket that was strung on a line that the spectators could not see. When Mike lit it, he would run away, but the rocket would chase him, then he would double back and run the other way, but the rocket too, would turn at the end of the line and chase him back, before it exploded.

Mamama, Sam's mother, came with us from Basel to Sudgrove regularly for Christmas. During the holiday, she would give a supper for everyone who worked with us in the house, stables and farm, at the Highwayman Pub nearby. Sadly, that special evening in 1979 was the last year that Mamama, then aged eighty-four, could come to Sudgrove, as her health and failing sight did not allow her to travel abroad again, although she lived in Switzerland for another ten years. She still enjoyed the cartoon book each year that Carl Giles always signed and sent her, for the family to enjoy.

She had a Christmas party at her home in Basel every year, where all the family was summoned. This family gathering got everyone together once in the year and was the great occasion that no-one was allowed to miss. We organised her party at Steinacker once when she was not fit enough to hold it, then Sam's elder brother Harty took on the organisation of the Koechlin Christmas party in Basel, where it is still an annual gathering.

A month after our look at the Jarí Amazon scheme in 1981, Monica was confirmed in the church at Fluh near her school, on Sam's birthday, 29 March. March was a busy month with Dominik's and Monica's birthdays just passed and Marguerite's the following day, so the lunch that followed the confirmation was also a family birthday celebration, which we held at our Bad Burg village restaurant. The pub lies on the Swiss side of the frontier, beside the French customs post, but the word Bad did not refer to outlaws at this crossing or the quality of the food, but rather to the healing properties of the bath water.

Our party consisted of the five children, Sam's eldest Catherine with her husband Roland, and Mamama came from Basel. Paddy and Mike had come over from Sudgrove as godparents of Monica, Mimi's stepdaughter Greger came to represent Monica's godmother who had died, but my brother Ronald could not leave his church where he had Sunday services to take. Margrit Diem our neighbour and friend, whose son Hans-Joggi was in Lucy's class also made up the gathering on a sunny spring day.

Exactly two months later, Sam had his left lung removed with cancer. The awful discovery had happened because for two nights I had been worried as Sam's left lung was making squeaky singing noises while he slept. On the second morning as he left early for an important board meeting, I asked him if I could tell our cousin and doctor friend Gilgi about the noises I had heard. He said that I could if I wanted to, but he would only be available at a hotel in the hills where the meeting was held, during the half-hour lunch break.

I knew that Sam had business commitments in Spain and the USA during the following two weeks, but I phoned Gilgi with trepidation and told him the facts and Sam's programme. Gilgi immediately put into action a series of tests to be done on Sam. I drove him for these sessions at hospitals, but we were not told anything definite except that his immediate travel plans were to be cancelled. I had the twentieth anniversary conference of the WWF at Wembley from 26–28 May where Prince Philip would take the Chair as the new President. Originally this time had coincided with Sam's USA visit and so as a Trustee of the WWF I could attend the conference while he was away.

Sam had another test to be done over those two days in the hospital, so we decided I would run him to Basel and go to Wembley by plane, only one hour's flight from Basel, while he was being examined. On the second morning when I phoned him, he told me, 'They've decided to operate tomorrow'. I left immediately and arrived in Basel to spend the evening with him.

I went riding while Sam's operation was in progress, on a black horse Pablo, a rather nappy animal that played up if it met farm vehicles or deer in the forest. I needed the challenge of riding him, rather than just sitting waiting. I remembered the day that Mariette was killed in a fall, I had lost my wedding ring during the time waiting to hear what had happened. The time still dragged when I got back until Gilgi phoned. He told me in clinical French that Sam's lung had been removed and the growth was malignant. The next morning I phoned the intensive care unit, and to my delight I was able to speak to him, although the tube damage to his throat from the operation made his voice unrecognisable. He croaked 'They got the so and so out', so I realised that he must know too that the growth was malignant.

Sam, with the sportsman's disregard of pain and determination to get back to normal life, recovered quickly enough for me to bring him home after twelve days. He never mentioned to anyone that the surgery had left him in great pain with damaged nerves in the shoulder, which plagued him until the end. He went through the radiation treatment travelling from home, until that was finished at the end of July, when we could come back to Sudgrove.

England was celebrating the Royal Wedding of Prince Charles and Lady Diana just at that time. We came back again to Sudgrove for the autumn holiday at the end of September, and Sam seemed much better. Dominik was with us too, with his friend Reto who during the holiday visited Slimbridge with us and fed Peter Scott's favourite néné Hawaian geese. Reto also tried voltige on our patient horse 'Boy' while Dominik improved quickly at this vaulting exercise. Another of Dominik's friends, Daniela, had also been a welcome guest and she had become good at voltige with us, although she had never ridden before. Back in Switzerland it was a great joy when Catherine's first child Rebecca was born, at the end of October, to give Sam his first grandchild.

In spring 1982 Sam was working again and we went together to New York in March, but he was not well and ran frequent temperatures. We had a friend Felix Lejeune who had nearly died on the Russian front during the war, so he had been sent to Switzerland by the Red Cross to recover. Before the war his father managed a huge estate and stud farm on East German land that had been taken by the Russians. Felix survived his wounds and made friends with Sam, starting to earn his living by teaching riding and training horses in Switzerland after the war. More riding accidents had not improved his small and battered body, but he rode young horses with great sympathy and calm. He would stay with us once a week, while he took lessons for people in our vicinity, when we would chat about horses and people.

On one of those evenings Sam went to bed and I talked a little longer with Felix before he retired. When I went to our bedroom I had a shock, finding Sam on the floor not able to communicate properly or move. I quickly fetched Felix and then our girl groom, and they helped me, with a blanket, to get Sam back on the bed. After a couple of hours I knew that the fall had been caused by more than drugs, although Sam could talk again in the morning. Gilgi arranged for an ambulance to take him to the Kantonspital. My replaced hips had turned blue and sore from the efforts of the night before, but that was a minor problem and the hips had stood the test.

It was on the second day that I visited Sam in hospital, when he told me that Dominik had phoned him in a terrible state, because he had just heard that Reto and Daniela, who had been driving together to the South of France, had been killed. Their car had hit a tree in the early morning and it seemed likely that the driver had gone to sleep. They must have been driving all night from Basel, to see a friend before returning for Monday morning. We were shattered.

When Sam came home, nothing definite about his health had been found. He still ran temperatures and a month later went back to a more friendly hospital, the Clara, where a specialist worked on the problem. He found the trouble on the fourth day. Infection had got into the left lung cavity where an abscess had formed and a drainage pipe would have to be inserted into Sam's back. That operation was done and I learned from the nurses how to manage and treat it when Sam came home.

The quality of life had badly deteriorated for Sam, but he was so brave that after another operation in London where Dr John Batten put a larger drainage tube in his back, he came straight to Sudgrove. That day Anne Fitzpatrick and Tim Clarke were married at Miserden Church with Monica and Lucy among the bridesmaids. Sam appeared in the churchyard carrying a camera, like a reporter, as they came out of church as a married couple. He had been operated on that morning in the Brompton Hospital in London but Anne's wedding party at Sudgrove had been arranged in advance, and Sam refused to change her plans.

Another day Sam wandered up to the field where I was doing a 'Maestro' programme for HTV with Frank Keating. It was a wonderful support for me, while I persuaded Lucy on Squirrel to do another round over some jumps for the cameras. How I valued his help and appreciated the effort he had made to walk up the hill, especially as he hated publicity and cameras.

In September another operation was done in Basel to clean out his lung cavity and close the drainage exit. This caused more pain and a month of agonising physiotherapy, but at least the daily dressings with the tube were over.

During this time Sam had announced his retirement as Chairman, first at lunch at Steinacker to his personal secretary Herr Gerney with whom he always had a special relationship and trust, and Heidi Müri, his secretary. I brought the lunch outside, where the flycatchers were nesting and the blackcap sang lustily from the bushes under our tulip tree. Both of them were stunned when he broke the news, but apart from myself and Gilgi, few people knew how Sam was suffering. Sam told the Board that the plan that he had made, in case of emergency or alternatively on the date of his sixty-second birthday, was put into immediate action. His forward planning meant that his retirement caused hardly a ripple in the whole organisation and I was relieved that we could concentrate now on the best way to regain his health.

I had kept in touch with my WWF contacts and had been to Sutton Place where Max Nicholson was justly rewarded with his WWF Gold Medal. The following year, 1983, Sam came with me when Dr Norman Myers received his Gold Medal at Aigle, an ancient castle on the Lake of Geneva.

Lucy had been confirmed that year and in the summer she came to Badminton with me, where we had bought a Jack Russell puppy from Masters' Beaufort Hunt Kennels. Master was there when we came and was delighted when Mary, the Duchess of Beaufort who was already ill, suddenly recognised me and showed her delight that the puppy, Daisy, was going to Sudgrove.

We had chosen the pup together, before it had its eyes open during the Easter holidays while Master and Major Gerald Gundry were sorting out the best hounds to send to the big hound shows. It had been an education to hear the two experts discussing hounds, kindly asking for our opinion too in their deliberations. We also learnt that we were lucky not to have lost Daisy before she was ready to leave her mother. During an 'open day' when Master generously invited the public to enjoy his park and see hounds, two dog siblings from Daisy's litter had been stolen, probably by a thief putting the tiny pups in his pocket.

We had often been to Badminton for social and charity occasions and once at a piano recital, we had an Austrian guest who talked to Mary about Vienna, where Mary had been educated. They showed us the portrait gallery, where Ronald, my brother and a history scholar, told me some of the lesser known facts about the aristocratic characters hanging on the walls. Master also recalled the evening when Dame Nellie Melba came for an overnight stay at Badminton. The old Duke, Master's father, had been out hunting all day and the hounds had given the field some good and strenuous runs. When the Duke had bathed, he had decided to go to bed instead of entertaining Dame Nellie at dinner.

Dame Nellie was not put out, but connived with the family and mounted the Ducal staircase to sing at the Duke's bedroom door. Her coloratura echoed around the guest hall and landing, with the melody and adjusted words:-

'Hark the Herald Angels sing,
Beechams Pills are just the thing.
Three for a Duke and four for a King
Beechams pills cure everything'

Master would recount these stories when we went to relax in the sitting room, with Mary first shooing the many dogs from the chairs, in order to turn over the cushions to the guest side, although the dogs were back on the cushions as soon as one rose from a chair.

One Christmas I was invited to Badminton, while I was on crutches after a hip operation, to meet an old friend of Mary's, Horatia, of the same family as Nelson. She was going to have a hip operation and wanted to be reassured that it was a wise move. I asked if I could bring Paddy along with me to drive, as Sam was away working, and so Paddy and I arrived at the front entrance, as I would not have any steps to negotiate, whereas the back way in was much more complicated. We rang the bell several times, after hearing no footsteps crossing the hall to let us in. The door was eventually unlocked by Mary looking harassed, who told us 'Everyone has gone down with 'flu, so Master and myself have to do the table, but the chef is still all right.'

We crossed the hall, where the game of Badminton originated, the dimensions of the hall giving the measurements for a Badminton court, and we went to sit with Horatia, who was a great character. When lunch was served, Master acted as butler and brought around the plates with the carved meat, and then the vegetables which he held at a dangerous angle about a yard from one's plate, leaving a big gap between the dish and the plate. The gravy nearly went for a Burton when it slid across the silver salver, but I just caught the boat in time, before it spilled its contents.

We laughed a lot and then after lunch Mary said she was going to do the washing-up. Paddy offered to help and Mary gratefully accepted her help, saying that they would wash up in the ladies loo, as the kitchens were miles away. The loo had several basins, so the dishes could be soaked, washed and rinsed in different ones. On the way home Paddy said as a joke, that she had not expected to have kitchen duties to perform with a Duchess. Once she had been invited to Government House in Australia, before the war, and there too, she had been delegated the job of handing round the coffee, as a member of the staff had not turned up.

During the war, Queen Mary had descended on Badminton with her household, while Mary Beaufort was given a tough time, to keep her authority over her house and home.

In 1982 there was an attempt to bring the Royal International Horse Show back to the White City. I was asked to perform the opening ceremony which was magnificently staged, but the whole stadium looked neglected and shabby, a shadow of its former glory. The RIHS moved to Birmingham National Exhibition Centre the following year, where it held its own in excellent surroundings and comfort for competitors and public, leaving the White City to the gypsies until the stadium was demolished.

Sam and I were able to attend a very interesting Arab seminar at Exeter University, as we had a plan to go to Arabia, for Sam's new work as consultant. I had a moment to slip into the early communion service at Exeter Cathedral on that Sunday, where the Dean spoke with a twinkle in his eye, quoting a past Principal of the University who had held the view that, 'Jesus taught us compassion, but the Greeks taught us everything else.'

On our twentieth wedding anniversary in Steinacker, we were sitting reading in the sun when visitors arrived, Sir John Batten with his wife Anne, the sister of David Attenborough's wife Jane, and Hans Hug, a great friend of Gilgi, who had first seen the signs of trouble in Sam's lung. There was no better excuse to open a bottle of champagne and watch the sun go down over the Swiss Jura, with the setting rays colouring the Vosges mountains in France and the Schwarzwald of Germany.

Lady Eleanor Glover had become a friend before she lost her second husband Sir Douglas. She had been the widow of Conrad Hurlimann the Swiss financier, and was famous for her hospitality at Freudenberg, the country house and superb gardens that he had built looking out over the lake of Zug. Water fowl and reed warblers, nested in the haven of unspoilt shoreline.

Mrs Thatcher used to take her holiday there with Sir Denis until the press became too aggressive, having found out the calm and beautiful residence well after she had become Prime Minister. Sam and I were occasionally invited for a family lunch when Mrs Thatcher was there. The Prime Minister was always very interested in how things were run in Switzerland, with the system of government starting at the bottom of the pyramid, from the elected head of each commune who represented their town or village. The wise Swiss politician Kurt Fürgler was sometimes present at these lunches too.

Once I had a long discussion with Mrs Thatcher on the subject of the World Conservation Strategy that the WWF and IUCN had launched, when I explained that Belize was a unique country for the strategy. As an unspoilt area, it contained every sort of habitat from above the treeline on high mountains descending through the natural scrub and grass land to the humid rain forest, and down to the sea and coral reefs along the coast with their rich marine life. If the neighbouring country of Guatemala had been allowed to march into Belize, this country of superb bio-diversity would be destroyed and ruined, so that scientific research on the environment would become impossible. I happily noted in a newspaper some weeks later that our troops were not going to be withdrawn, leaving Belize defenceless.

Maurice Strong gave the World Conservation lecture that year at London University. As Sam had meetings in Manchester that day, he would fly back to London for a night at the Cavendish Hotel, where Ciba-Geigy had a room available. He offered to give some of our WWF friends dinner there·after the lecture, with Peter and Phil Scott, Guy Mountford, Tim Walker and Sir Arthur Norman, the past Chairman of WWF UK and the Director George Medley.

Maurice had been a friend of Sam's and had visited us over several years. His brilliant intellect always threw up top ideas, which is why he is so much in demand in business and in environmental problems. The lecture of one hour had enough content for twice that time. As Maurice started out reading at rapid speed, I felt my heart try to beat his record rate of speech. I did not know what to do, as it would have upset the proceedings if I had dropped unconscious at the front of the podium. As I sat very still I worried about the dinner, that I had organised. I needed to be fit enough to help Sam host it, as he was not well and would be tired. My heart recovered just in time, but it had given me a shock.

We were back in Switzerland the next morning and then left for the USA where we both had a busy programme. In New York I did fit one afternoon in at the Madison Square Horse Show, the first time I had been in the newer building. Bill Steinkraus spotted me and came to chat, telling me, 'You're the one that changed this show for the better thirty years ago when you criticised our courses'. I said that I hoped I hadn't been rude. 'The word you actually used was "Prehistoric"!' Apparently that had really put the cat among the pigeons. Sam and I laughed about it when we flew back that night; he had been working in New York when I was in our team there in 1953, and remembered the newspaper headlines. When I got home I did have an ECG done but my heart was behaving.

At the beginning of 1984, Sam had meetings in the Arabian peninsula and felt that he could manage to cope with the business trip which he had hoped to achieve earlier. At that time, a scheme being monitored by Ralph Daly in the Sultanate of Oman, had initiated the reintroduction of the Arabian oryx into the central desert, where the wild herds had become extinct. The released gazelle were genetically diverse, with some animals from founder lines bred outside the US captive herds. The animals were put under the watchful eye of the local Bedouins, who were proud to protect their herd from poachers, with the Harasis rangers. Drought for four years slowed down reproduction at first, but the present-day picture after less than a decade is one of rapid growth with many young animals.

We left for Oman with a meeting in Abu Dhabi, United Arab Emirates, on the way, before arriving at Muscat, where we were shown the harbour with the two Portugese forts. The colours of the Arabian twilight lit the sky before our early supper of grilled hammour, the local Gulf fish. Flying along the coast one saw that it would be easy to selectively mine the Straits of Hormuz, which have a very narrow channel for laden ships.

Nizwa, with its fort, mosque and busy market place, was our overnight stop, where we toured the Institute Farm at Nerwa. Sam stayed at the motel to rest while I joined the others to find our way to Bahla, where pottery is still made by ancient methods. Our driver found where one old plotter lived by his kiln. We were helped by a good-looking young man, a neighbour of the potter, who worked for the Ministry of Labour and Social Affairs. He showed us a store of pots, some already burnt and others waiting for the next burning which is done with special wood. The process would take two days for the 4,000 pots that could fit into his kiln.

The old man started to work on a square of clay, using a wooden foot wheel, turned by his right foot. While he sat working in the corner of the cave the pot began to take shape, aided by his hands and muscular arms. As the pot grew bigger above the base, he wound some string around to support it, then when the lip cracked he wet the crack and squeezed it together. Within ten minutes the pot was finished, he slipped a piece of string underneath to separate it from the wooden base and put the pot aside to dry.

Once the old potters have died, factories will be provided by the government for the trade to be carried on, but not by the methods that have been used for centuries. Water cools when kept in these pots, while hot coffee or tea retains its heat in the closed pots.

The air flight to Salalah, took us close to the Ar Rub Al Khali, the empty quarter, which did not look friendly for travellers. Salalah in contrast had fertile and irrigated farms, which we would be shown by some of the highly qualified managers of the Royal Family Farms. We were each offered a drink from a whole coconut, brought in fresh, with the top sliced off with a machete, allowing us to sip the delicious clear milk, before touring the fields and plantations of various grasses, red, green and yellow bananas, papaya and tomatoes.

The sea is just as productive, with local rock lobster that have no claws, but are quite big. Along the coast I saw areas of drying sardines, both red and silver; now was the height of the harvest time in February. This fish became a necessary protein, fed to the cattle and camels during the dry season. Nearby we drove through a herd of camels and saw a new born baby, with its coat still wet and curly. The anxious mother pushed it to its feet and it staggered on long legs to the Land Rover, with its big friendly eyes looking at us.

Before I left that night, I went to bargain in the Suq for myrrh and frankincense. Friends in Switzerland were violin makers and they needed some of the resinous frankincense to put a finish on the violins. Salalah was said to be the place from where the three Wise Men had travelled to Bethlehem, bringing their gifts. The frankincense trees and myrrh bushes grew on the mountains there, but no-one was able to show me the source of the incense.

Flying back to Muscat in the dark, we had to leave again for the airport at 4.30 a.m. Meanwhile I started to shiver as I was being briefed about the people and programme ahead in Saudi Arabia. I could not concentrate and shivered my way from Muscat to Bahrein. We changed to another packed plane for Riyadh where I was impressed by the new Riyadh airport with fountains and water falls, but not impressed by control delays, where no lady could go through without her man, or she would suffer insuperable difficulties.

Arriving at the hotel, I retired shivering to bed, not seeing the sun again for five days, as there are no hotel windows, only slits, preventing us from looking out and outside people from looking in. It was difficult for ladies to get medical attention in Riyadh, but a retired German doctor, a friend through Ciba-Geigy, came to see me; he soon asked anxiously about my heart. I explained that the irregular beat was caused by my diphtheria when I was four. He cancelled my trip alone to Abha the next day where I'd arranged to meet the research people from the Asir National Park. Two days later he told us to cancel the North Yemen programme; Sam did not seem as disappointed as I was, because he may not have felt up to that trip, so my illness may have been a blessing in disguise. We had planned for a short but energetic programme in North Yemen, from the heights of Sana'a to the Red Sea coast.

I watched the great camel race, after working on a little TV set in my sunless room. The event of the 10th Annual Royal Camel Race at Riyadh had attracted most of the Arab Royalty with visiting Princes and Sheiks from many countries of the Arab world. The men greeted each other with three kisses, one on each side and one in the middle. The customary kissing ceremony changes from country to country; here the robed gentlemen kissed again at the end of the day's sport before they departed to the airport.

The camel jockeys were tiny, the youngest aged eight years. In 1980, in the race that we had just missed, a nine-year-old jockey had won the first prize of about £15,000 for the owner of the camel and a 2,000 gallon water tank, of much more practical use than a cup.

The start of the 22 km race was riotous, with some of the camels starting off in the wrong direction in spite of desperate efforts by their minute jockeys. The thousand Saudi camels were racing for prizes of money for the first 200 camels, a Range Rover, a Diahatzu Jeep, a tent, 1,000 bags of barley and the small winning jockeys received gold and silver *djambia's*, daggers from the King. They told the King the names of their camels in piping voices, the winner having an English name of Harvest Moon. The King and his special guests followed the hour's race in a Royal bus, dodging the forlorn camels that had lost their riders.

One loose camel enthusiastically went the whole way of the race and finished with the leaders. The winners were not distressed but several unfit camels had to give up along the course, with one or two couching, lying down on strike and refusing to rise until the race was finished.

My only other diversion in the hotel room had been a *Daily Telegraph*, but I found the leader page removed by the Saudi censor.

I was very disappointed that we had to miss the four days in North Yemen, because without Sam, it would have been almost impossible for me to enter the country. The land held such a diversity of habitat, from the high mountains to the corals and marine life of the Red Sea.

These journeys that Sam and I did together were a real bonus to both our work programmes. Although instability of governments, causing unrest and even civil wars were usually negative in saving the environment and creating National Parks one always hopes that any seeds of interest will germinate and develop into a national consciousness of the rich heritage each nation holds and its need to be protected in their country.

Sam rarely allowed himself more than one or two days that were not connected to business, but he always supported me in my conservation work and often discussed the confidential reports that arose through our travels.

I was able to meet some of his contacts in industry, while during our excursions to see field projects, we met key people in the field and could experience their working conditions. It was then more productive to talk to local administrators who could influence the programmes on saving the environment to protect the local species in their district. It was most important to reassure the local helpers that the scientists and fund raisers would listen to their troubles, in head office, and see where active help could be provided. Often a vehicle was a top necessity to patrol the area designated for protection.

Many workers in the field feel very isolated and lacking in support, sometimes with their Rangers and local helpers in danger from murderous opponents and poachers. Man's greed which leads him to grab anything that is profitable in the land, has often left it barren and bare of habitat and resources. He does not think ahead about the sustainable use of the land so that it can continue to offer its bounty.

Originally tribal life was ruled by sustainable living, with birth control administered by mixing certain plants of the forest, so their area of forest and jungle would not become over populated beyond the capacity of the land resources.

I hope that my contacts have helped to bridge the gap between the field work and administrators, so that we can work once more towards sustainable use of the land.

We left on a Swissair flight, one of the first foreign airline planes that was allowed to fly direct to Riyadh. Before that, one always had to change planes at Jeddah, as only Saudi planes were allowed to land at the capital. The same day arriving in Switzerland, I had an electro-cardiogram with Gilgi, and he told me that I had had a near heart attack and that I could not go with the girls to Wengen for the ski week holiday. The girls were not sad to look after themselves and cope with the mountain climb up to the chalet, while Sam and I stayed less energetically at Steinacker. I said a quiet prayer of thanks that I was all right and could still care for Sam.

In May 1984, Sam and I had a work plan for a week in New York and Washington, where he had meetings, while I had the annual WWF Council conference in Washington. Two weeks before we left, Sam started coughing and on medical advice he cancelled his trip. We changed my ticket too so that I would only do the three-day conference, travelling alone.

My programme was very full, with seeing my cousin Sheila and her family, also some of Sam's friends who had hoped to see him. The conference programme included a delightful evening when we were invited by Vice-President Bush for a barbecue, in the parkland of the imposing naval house where he and his wife greeted us all as we trooped in. Some of our American WWF members were already friends and acquaintances of George and Barbara Bush.

The presentation of the WWF Gold Medal Award was held in Washington, for the winner, Professor Richard Evans Schultes from Boston. His great-grandfather had been a forester from near Zurich but then the family emigrated and became American. Dick Schultes, as a biologist, had worked for fifteen years in the Amazonas rain forest, living with the Indians and learning their languages. He studied their knowledge of the medicinal qualities and uses of the plants growing in the forest and eventually helped to set up a laboratory in Manaus, where leaves could be analysed while they were still fresh, rather than sending the dry leaves to the States, as often the medical properties of the fresh plant were lost when dried, giving a negative analysis.

Dick and his wife Dorothy were great friends with our neighbours at Burg, Dr Albert and Anita Hofmann. They came to retire to our remote village, building a house with a wonderful view, on the Rittimatte, by the frontier track above us leading to the top of the mountain, with a lookout tower on the Remel at 1,000 metres. Albert's biological work in Mexico had been during the same time as Dick was working in the Amazonas.

I had an exhausting return trip to Basel, with the Washington–New York plane being nearly three hours late due to storms and other factors. I missed my Swissair connection and was left to cope alone at midnight in the dark and empty J. F. Kennedy airport. My heart stood the stress of hurrying in the dark from place to place in search of a seat on a plane for Europe, while all the desks and lounges were unattended and closed. Eventually I found only one Arab line plane that was crossing the Atlantic. The journey did not give me any comfort, as women travelling alone were ignored by the stewardesses. As the plane refuelled in Vienna, I disembarked in the rural airport, to start another search for transport to Switzerland. After two more plane journeys and contact with home, I got back to Sam where he had waited as anxiously as myself.

The following month was taken up with Sam's hospital visits, and although no more cancer was diagnosed, the lung cavity was still poisoning him, so yet another operation was arranged. Catherine's second child Sarah was born, a happy event to help us through the medical preparations.

The operation was a big one and took a long time, but I had Paddy Bury over from Sudgrove to help me through the waiting time. As soon as I could see Sam in intensive care, I donned the sterilised gown and opened the door with foreboding. 'Good, you've come at last, they've got no phone in here, so I couldn't tell you all the things that I need immediately. Have you got a pen and paper?'

I could not believe my eyes, as he had been unconscious not long before. He was lying propped up in the bed full of awful tubes and machines recording his heart, but that was not the first time I had visited him in intensive care. I quickly put a pad of paper, that I usually carried, on his knees and a pen into his hand, and he started to make completely illegible notes. Before I left, he had relaxed and realised that I would see him again in the afternoon. When I saw Gilgi over the lunch break, he could not believe that Sam was trying to write, in fact he had been afraid to let me into his consulting room in case I would blame him for Sam's condition.

He needed a month in hospital before I could bring him home after the long and complicated operation but he was only forty-eight kilos, ten less than me, and he stood over six feet tall. I learnt to give him a series of injections to help his weight, but it is an unpleasant ordeal to have to hurt someone who is so close to you. Two months later he was strong enough to come for the autumn holiday at Sudgrove.

Sam's great friend Niggi Hodel, one of the seven law students who had passed their law degree together in Basel, and formed the Shadrag Club, was celebrating his sixtieth birthday at the Romerbad in Badenweiler in November. We were all invited to spend the night there, and Sam was determined that we would go. We carefully chose the smoothest roads along the Rhine valley, as I did not want to drive him over the rough zigzag mountain roads of the Black Forest. We even danced once that night to my joy, while I feared for his courage.

Before Christmas I was installed as an Honoury Liveryman in the Worshipful Company of Farriers. At the beginning of the year, when Princess Anne became the Master of the Farriers, there had been a Court Dinner, where we both had to propose a toast. This dinner in December was before she terminated her term as Master of the Company. I had first received the Honoury Freedom of the Farriers Company on 28 November 1955, with the 600th anniversary of the Company in the following Olympic year 1956. I learnt that the Company was placed 55th in precedence, which meant the places allotted each Guild on State occasions. At that time there were 200 members of the Company and the Duke of Beaufort,

'Master' was an Honoury Freeman as Master of the Horse, while I was the first woman to be honoured.

We had a more social Christmas than usual with the family arriving in time to decorate the tree, the hall and the living room with our own holly and mistletoe. The weather was kind so our friends could visit us without the worry of ice and snow. During the holiday we entertained General Sir 'Monkey' Blacker and his wife 'Zulu', whose son Philip Blacker is a well-known sculptor of horse bronzes. Monkey was the Chairman of the British Team Jumping selection committee that I served on, but we had jumped on teams together in countries as far away as Chile.

American friends, Walt and Priscilla Avery, came down for the day. Walt and Sam had worked together as lawyers while Sam was in New York in 1953, since then Walt had retired and was living in London.

Sam and I went to our old haunt of Miserden House, where we had first been together thirty-five years before. Dodo and Johnnie Ormiston now lived there, with their superb sporting pictures and furniture gracing the lovely old Dower House. Looking about twenty years younger, Johnnie had celebrated his eight-ieth birthday, an occasion that Sam thought would merit a pair of longhandled bellows, in order to save his back when lighting the fire. Anne and Tim Clarke came with Emily, Monica's godchild, Frank and Cynthia Haydon called and Valery brought David and Richard, Mamama's great-grandchildren, the son's of Robert, Mimi's eldest son. Even Barbara came with the twins, John and Nick from South Africa and we saw the likeness to his Grandpa Nicco in young Nick, whereas John was taller and unlike his sibling. Barbara had told me the difficult-ies of bringing up twin boys, because anything naughty that one thinks of doing, the other may think up something even worse. The boys were so different that they did not have the doubtful advantage of pretending that they were each other, but they had fun together.

On the last day of the year I had a midday sports show on HTV in Bristol, then the holiday was over, with New Year's Day spent back at Steinacker. The girls went off to school in Basel the next day while Sam was at the office making plans for his working year ahead.

We both lunched with Marguerite, and although her sight had nearly gone, she remarked that Sam had eaten better than for some time. He had always dis-ciplined himself to be a light eater, but while he was ill during those last years, he could hardly face any food at all.

Two weeks later Sam had a sore throat and an x-ray disclosed pneumonia. That weekend we had planned to go to Gilgi's birthday party at Adelboden with all his friends at a family hotel where he had spent a lifetime of holidays. We stayed at home while Sam had a course of antibiotics, and Gilgi left his middle son, Olivier, also a godson of Sam's, and a doctor, in charge of his own and his father's practices in Basel.

A few nights later at midnight, Sam had a crisis and I thought that I would lose him; phoning Olivier, he told me to try and prop him up, which I did with a big cushion. In the morning Sam was able to tell me the extraordinary dream he had during the night. When Gilgi returned that afternoon, he organised the ambulance to take Sam to the Clara Spital. It was snowing and foggy with ice on the roads and I followed the ambulance in Sam's car, because it had 'spikes', studded wheels, which helped us get up our steep and icy hills in winter, but were banned on motorways. The route taken by the ambulancemen flashing their lights, was onto the motorway at high speed. I risked everything to follow them and got boxed in by huge German juggernauts that covered my little car with slush. I got to the hospital, scared from the drive, and went into 'emergency' with Sam on the stretcher bed.

As soon as we arrived, I asked that he should have oxygen. He was also put on a drip and I held his hand, while yet another needle was stuck into his arm. His mind was very active and he gave me a list of things to bring to the hospital in the morning, as our departure had been so rapid. I promised that I would return at 8.30 a.m. and I would bring a fresh crispy bread roll for his breakfast from the bakery in our next village of Metzelen.

I returned home in the fog and snow and saw the girls before they went to bed. The phone rang just as I got out of the bath around 11 p.m.; it was Gilgi. 'Come immediately to the hospital.' I asked 'Has he died?' His voice hesitated, 'No, but come immediately.' When I got there through the snow and ice, Gilgi was pacing up and down outside the hospital. He told me what had happened. Sam had rung his bell at 9.20 p.m. but when the nurse came in his heart had stopped. The heart was artificially started and he was rushed to intensive care, but Gilgi suspected that it had been too late.

I stayed with Sam, talking to him, but seeing no reaction or change of heart rhythm. I left early in the morning for a little sleep before returning to the hospital. The children returned from school at lunchtime as Wednesday was a half-day, so I went back to tell them what had happened.

In the afternoon while I sat with Sam, the door opened and Monica came in. She had come with Andy her boyfriend, who stayed outside, while Monica talked bravely for a few minutes to her father. I was deeply touched that she should have come on her own initiative. That evening they took Sam out of intensive care, as there was nothing further to be done, so an empty room had been found for him.

Our chaplain from the English Church in Basel, Canon Tom Roberts, is a very understanding friend, so we arranged to meet the next morning at 7.30 a.m. in Sam's room at the hospital. That night I did not risk returning to Burg in the snow, but Niggi and Elizabeth Hodel let me stay at their house near the hospital. Tom said communion in the morning with Sam and me, after which Sam seemed to be breathing more peacefully. A month before we had all made our Christmas communion at Miserden.

Gilgi came to see Sam with me that night and I slept again with the Hodels. At about 3.30 a.m. in the morning I heard the phone, and Niggi took it in their room. I knew before he told me that Sam had died.

Niggi helped me through the awful formalities that follow a death, taking me to sign the necessary papers in unfriendly civil offices, he filling in the correct answers to a myriad of German questions. Sam had written in his will that he wished his last resting place to be in Miserden churchyard. In Basel the services were taken by Tom Roberts, and Rupert Forbes sang the hymn 'Lord Jesus Christ, you have come to us'. Rupert's tenor voice filled the St Martin's Kirche, before Louis von Planta, President of Ciba-Geigy, spoke of his friend and colleague. They had worked together for twenty years through the Geigy reorganisation before the merger with Ciba to form the present international company. Louis told me later, at the lunch that Ciba-Ceigy had arranged at the Schlüssel, a traditional Guild building in the old city of Basel near the market place and the Church, that he and Sam had never had a major disagreement through their years of business partnership.

The finality of death in this life, was brought home to me that week, when dozens of baskets were delivered to Steinacker with all Sam's files and papers. His personal furniture and pictures were sent back from the office in the same load. I finished addressing the hundreds of envelopes with the family's thanks and acknowledgement for condolences in German, French and English, that it is customary to send, apart from personal letters. I left for England while Sam's ashes had been brought over from Basel with Mike and met at Heathrow by Walt Avery, to bring them home. The internment was held with just our Sudgrove friends on St Valentine's Day in the snow.

It was a critical time for the girls, as Monica was preparing for her *Matura* exams, similar to the French *Baccalauréat*, with all subjects taken at this advanced level. Lucy who had been working with a theatre group, had the first performance of the play they were producing. She had the part of the frontier officer who gets drunk while guarding *The Bridge*, the name of the play written by the Austrian Odon von Morvath.

I was very proud of them both when Lucy performed her part well, managing to separate theatre from real life and Monica achieved her *Matura*, showing her strength of character at this time. Both girls had moved into Basel, to be near their friends and school during the bad weather to avoid the difficult journey to Burg. Lucy was staying in her brother's apartment while Dominik was studying law in Basel University, which was a happy arrangement as it was just across the river from her school.

In March came the sale of half our farm at Througham, an event that Sam had put into motion during our last autumn holiday, as though he had forseen that there was no way that I could finance the whole farm if I lost him.

Colonel Sir Mike Ansell, the architect of post-war jumping and the International British Showjumping team, celebrated his eightieth birthday at a great gathering of many of his friends in the Cavalry Club, where we could show our appreciation of all he had done for our sport and for the blind during many years of dedicated work. Sam would have had his sixtieth birthday a few days later, but on 9 April, Easter Monday, we held a service of thanksgiving for him at Miserden and afterwards about seventy-five of our friends and family came to lunch at Sudgrove.

My involvement with conservation thankfully kept me busy, while as President

(*above*) The release of a year old eagle owl in Basel Land. The parents had been damaged on the roads and rescued by farmers who kept them for breeding in huge pens. The young are only handled once, when they are measured, weighed, ringed and then released at dusk.

(*below*) Oman, 1984. At Bahla we saw the nearly extinct work of the craftsman potters, with pots fired in their ancient kilns. This method of production is now giving way to factory modernisation.

(*above*) Rhino at Hluhluwe, Natal and (*below*) giraffe at Sabie Sand 1989.

of the British Showjumping Association I had the chance to meet younger riders away from their horses, when they won awards or sponsorship, celebrated in London. The WWF had an attractive London programme to encourage sponsors too, after the annual meeting held in Divonne on the Swiss border. A banquet at the Fishmonger's Hall and a reception at the Duke of Wellington's Apsley House, brought many interested people from abroad. The Duke of Wellington reminded me that he had been President of the BSJA for the term preceding mine, so that we had the two interests with the WWF at heart.

Two good friends who I had originally met skiing had their memorial services at this time. The first was Chappie Snowdon, who with Viv his wife were both great skiers who we met at Wengen every year, and fellow Saddlers. Chappie had been Master of the Worshipful Company of Saddlers, the Livery Company with twenty-fifth precedence and his family had been long involved with the Guild. I had been made a Yeoman of the Worshipful Company of Saddlers in 1963 and had attended many of their functions.

The service for Sir Max Aitken was three days later at St Clement Danes. He, too, was a great skier whom I had first met at Wengen, where the stories of his skiing adventures were legendary.

A great friend of his had been Chris Mackintosh, who had been to the local Wengen school during the Great War, and spoke Swiss dialect with his Wengen friends. Chris had skied for Great Britain and both he and Max were dare devils; a gully on the Tschuggen run is still called Mack's leap, where Chris had once cleared it at speed. Whenever the two were together there was leg-pulling and laughter.

Max was in the Battle of Britain from 1939 when he flew the first engagement as Squadron Leader with Blenheim's in November, then commanding the 601 Squadron. He was awarded the DFC in May 1940 and two years later won the Czech Military Cross and the DSO. In 1944 he commanded a wing of Beaufighters and also Strike Mosquitoes, retiring as Group Captain in 1946. It was only then that he was able to return to Wengen.

His Swiss friends gave him a hero's welcome, arranging that the next morning they would take the Jungfraujoch railway up to the tunnel stop, where skiers could go through the wall onto the Eismeer. This glacier has now receded, so that one cannot ski there, but then even good skiers had a tricky start with a quick turn on the steep glacier, to avoid the gaping crevasses waiting to devour unwary people in their depths.

Max strapped his skis on and cheerfully took off down the frozen glacier, when to the horror of his Swiss friends, he missed his first turn, speeding on over the open crevasses to the other side of the gully where he could stop. Everyone breathed again, while he found a less hazardous descent, suppressing thoughts of newspaper headlines, 'Distinguished Air Ace survives war only to perish in Swiss crevass'. The guides knew that they would have been held responsible for taking such a risk before Max had tried his skis after years away at war. He was also son of Lord Beaverbrook, the influential owner of the *Daily Express*.

The *Express* newspaper sponsored the Foxhunter Competition, for young horses with a potential to become international show jumpers. Many good horses gained experience through these classes, named after Sir Harry Llewellyn's great international horse, one of the three in the showjumping team event that won Great Britain the Olympic Gold Medal at Helsinki in 1952.

Once I had the thrill of sailing in *Drumbeat*, Max's racing yacht, together with Uffa Fox and I could observe the team discipline and hard work needed from a top crew. Sam had bought a horse, Drumbeat, from Janet Kidd, Max's older sister, who sold several of her horses to Swiss friends.

All sportsmen have to cope with tough conditions in training and competing often disregarding any discomfort or injury. I was able to meet many of the top people, especially at the celebration in the Savoy for the *Daily Express* Sportsman of the Year. I was writing on showjumping and skiing for the *Express* at the time and so I knew the journalists as friends, rather than as spies into your private life, as several famous people have found to their discomfort. The sports crowd were all good company and although they knew how to enjoy themselves, they were usually very generous and thoughtful to those less well off than themselves, especially with children and the disabled.

It is hard to understand why gifted, athletic and generous people like Sam should die before a useful retirement, having suffered illness and pain rather than having the reward of health to enjoy activity in the later years of life. Max, although much older suffered too as did Dorian Williams, who died later that year. He was a friend over forty years and the first television commentator to bring showjumping into people's homes, among his many other facets.

My girls, Monica and Lucy, both learnt to drive with me during Sudgrove holidays, as in England they could have a provisional licence at seventeen rather than aged eighteen in Switzerland. Our steep and narrow Gloucestershire lanes gave them good experience in control of the car and the use of the gears to break the speed in steep places. I never found it difficult to change to the other side of the road when on the continent, because the driving seat would be on the outside, unless one had an English car abroad. Whenever I drove English left-hand drive horse boxes on the continent I quite liked having the kerb of the road on my side, as long as I had a good passenger who could tell me when to pull out to pass slow vehicles.

Lucy was seventeen by July when she drove me on L-plates to the Royal Welsh Show at Builth Wells, experiencing the hills of the Forest of Dean, some dual carriageway and then the lovely route through the Black Mountains along the upper reaches of the River Wye. Sir Harry Llewellyn was the President of the show and we stayed with Harry and Teeny that night at Llanarth, which broke our journey home to Sudgrove. Lucy also drove me to lunch with Tim and Rosemary Walker near Bradford-on-Avon. Tim had taken over the chair of the WWF UK from Sir Arthur 'Gerry' Norman. On the land around his lovely home he had some endangered species of animals which he was breeding, with vicuñas from Peru and Przewalski horses (the original ancestors of the modern day horse), the species that had last survived in the wild in Mongolia. There is now an

Earthwatch project to return some wild horses from the world herd of 962 animals to their original habitat in the Mongolian Altai Gobi, where the Mongolian Government is designating a new reserve.

Monica shared the next longer drive with me when she had her Swiss licence and we were invited to spend a long weekend with David and Herter Ogilvy at their Château of Touffou. We took Sam's Scirocco and only stopped once or twice when we saw an interesting old church in the small towns on the route to Poitiers, Touffou standing on the banks of the Vienne river that joins the Loire after passing the great Château of Chinon.

David had told Sam and myself, when we visited them some years before, that the first great expense he had suffered when he acquired Touffou, was to pour thousands of gallons of cement under the Château, to stop it from sliding into the river as the bank subsided. Now it was the roof that was covered with scaffolding and I had despairingly thought that the upkeep of Sudgrove was more than enough.

That evening we dined outside on the round tower approached along the castle wall, overlooking the river and the rich expanse of countryside, with the gardens down below us. The morning we returned meant an early start to get back in one day, but I was not sleeping well. During the short night before we left, David did not sleep well either, and he clonked around their bedroom above mine all night. He and Herter kindly came to see us off at 6 a.m. and I asked him why he had kept falling out of bed all night. He paused, before saying 'She pushed me.' We waved goodbye, all of us laughing as we drove off.

My worries partly stemmed from a cardiologist, who I had been recommended to see by a good friend Dr Mervyn Emrys-Roberts, who was now retired, but had worked in Africa and Canada since he left Stratford-on-Avon, from where he visited Miserden occasionally. He was friends with all our Sudgrove people and often stayed when we were there for holidays. He had known that I had a heart problem but had not pursued the subject while I was looking after Sam. I was not well while at Sudgrove and, because I could not see my Swiss doctor, he suggested firmly that now Sam did not need me, I should see a heart specialist that same week. The result from the appointment was the following statement from the cardiologist. 'Well I expect you will say "naturally" if I tell you that you are very rare.' My heart dropped into my boots and I had no illusions of being a Walter Mitty. 'You have a rare condition but you are lucky because one surgeon has performed an operation for your problem, it was done two years ago for the first time, and you must have an open heart operation.' I made a quick calculation and said I would be in England for Christmas and could come to hospital then, and could he tell me what was my condition. 'You have Hypertrophic Obstructive Cardiomyopathy and you won't be here at Christmas.'

My mind concentrated quickly as I did not want the girls to lose both parents in the same year, with so much that was still left to be sorted out. I was *Chéf d'Equipe* for the British Team at St Gallen CSIO and I had to clear our Wengen apartment in the Chalet Tschingel that had been built at the same time as Steinacker. It was being sold to Henry and Alberta Strage with their four children who were around the same ages as our two and were all friends. There was then an HTV programme 'At Home' with Bruce Hockin, which took care of the four September weeks. A week into October I spent the first evening of the Horse of the Year Show at Wembley and moved into St Thomas' Hospital for the operation the next day.

Bryn Williams, the only heart surgeon who had performed the HOCM operation in Europe, came to see me in the evening before the operation. He slightly nodded his head as I said when he left, 'Please let me go if at any time I cease to be there. The girls have already had that trauma in January.'

He had given me valuable advice that I might be on a life support machine when I came to and not to panic. My first thought as I regained consciousness was relief as I found that I was breathing by myself. The next, when I could speak, was to ask the nurse the time, so that I could work out how many hours I had been out. It was 2 a.m. and the operation had started at 10 a.m. the day before. The next job was to wiggle my toes and my fingers, as I had learnt when I had my other big operations. I was surprised how little my chest hurt although my heart was thumping. Then I was allowed to put a foot to the floor when changing onto a trolley during the morning, to be wheeled back to my bed.

I wanted to get home as soon as possible and decided to have almost no visitors, so that I could set myself a training programme. I started to time myself so that on each turn of the hour during the day, I would get out of bed and take one step, at the next hour two steps and so on. When I was taken by wheel chair for my post-operation check ups, I found that the porters would leave me in the draughty corridors, shivering and alone, when they found that I was in a private ward, although my Swiss insurance was paying the National Health account.

Eight days after the operation I had to have an ECG, X-rays and another check up before I got the all clear to go home. That day I did not bother the porters, because I walked to all the departments in the vast hospital without help and arrived back to my bed exhausted but triumphant. After that proof of my state of health, no-one could stop me going home that evening when Emrys came to rescue me. The nurses were wonderful and always on my side, approving of my efforts to get fit. After I left, a lot of the staff and patients went down with a bad 'flu epidemic, but I was already in the pure air and sunshine of the Cotswolds.

Condy, my blue whippet, who was bred by Dinah Nicholson, wife of 'the Duke,' at David's training establishment in Condicote, was as faithful to me as whippets are famed to be. She gave me an ecstatic welcome when I returned from hospital; she had missed Sam when he had not returned with me after Christmas, maybe she feared that I would not return either. She had not been well and the vet thought that she had arthritis in her back, but for the next three weeks she shadowed my every movement and lay as close as she could to me when I was sitting inside or outside in the late October sunshine. Suddenly she died in the night and the cause was found to be cancer.

After Christmas, Ronald and Wynn came for a short holiday, when one evening I got an excruciating pain in my side and sweated and shivered in agony all night until the doctor came and sent me straight to Cheltenham General hospital with a suspected embolism, the most stabbing pain possible. The heart operation had only caused discomfort but an embolism is in another league. I realised that my acute shoulder pain, after the operation when Monica was born must also have been an embolus or blood clot. The cure was to thin my blood with warfarin and I have been on rat poison ever since.

There were many sick people brought to the emergency ward, with poor patients, mostly elderly, dying night and day; distressing work for the nurses, while I could only talk or listen to help people who wanted to communicate. One young mother had suffered a stroke and could not speak or feed herself. Her husband and three young boys visited her every day to feed her and chat about their school and sports events, while the mother would often cry with frustration that she was so helpless. To see that family give their mother so much support, made me appreciate once again the good things in one's own life.

I had a fright at 6 a.m. on New Year's Day morning when I hoped to be allowed home. A temporary nurse came to take my temperature and asked me my date of birth, I replied 22, 11, 36, and I checked myself because my year was 28. I realised I had dysphasia, but the nurse had not noticed so I managed to hide the fact. I carefully chose my words to be sure I could speak them when the Sister came to take my blood, then the Doctor came to tell me that the warfarin level was correct and I could go home.

Dysphasia is caused by a small blood clot passing through the brain. I knew what I wanted to say but another word came out. At home that evening I was talking on the phone when it hit me again, so I used another word and took a pen to write down the word I wanted; my brain was alert but my hand could only do illegible baby writing. I had experienced dysphasia once before at Steinacker, before Sam died, when I gave him his early morning tea and took mine to the kitchen to give Felix his breakfast before he left for his teaching appointment. My tea spilled on the carpet as I opened each door and again on the kitchen table with my right hand not working properly. On that Monday morning the *Putzfrau* came to clean, but as I greeted her I heard myself speaking Kindergarten Swiss to this intelligent lady. A short time later I apologised to the lady, when my speech was normal; however she told me that she had not noticed anything unusual, which brought home to me that my use of Swiss dialect was not impeccable.

This first experience with dysphasia in Switzerland was the reason why I talked to Sam, while he was in a coma, because perhaps the brain can receive messages, even if the person cannot communicate outwardly.

Everything I did required a lot of effort, which disappointed me in that my recovery rate was not faster. At Steinacker I noticed the difference of height on the Jura, twice as high as at Sudgrove on the Cotswolds, but the increased effort was good training. At Lucerne we had our team at the Horse Show; Mamama had ceased to travel there and have her party at the Eichstutz for the riders in the delightful setting of the chalet in the lake, with the boats kept under the living room, but the hospitality of Victor and Wy Hauser at their Schweizerhof Hotel was always superb for our team and the hub of the show organisation.

At Bern, Sibylle and Mathu were married, with the children that Sibylle taught at school arranging a special display for her outside the church. Now she has three boys, David, Julian and Benjamin, while Catherine's children are Rebecca, Sarah and Salome. Two years later Dominik and Stephie married at the ancient Kirche Ringgenberg built on a rock above the Lake of Brienz, followed by a boat trip across the lake to the wedding party at the Giessbach Hotel built close to the spectacular torrent that roars down the mountain and into the lake. Their two little children Helen and Samuel make up the eight grandchildren, cousins who are all within nine years of each other.

A Trustee and old friend from the WWF, Pepe Mayorga, aided my recuperation from the past year's events, by inviting me to join his party for the Granada Music Festival. His daughter María and Alicia, one of her daughters, were both in the party, which especially delighted me, as María and her daughters, who are around the ages of my two, visit Sudgrove and I stay with them in London. It gave me an excuse to go to Spain again, see old friends in Madrid and feast on the magical music in the historical town of Granada. The magic was enhanced by a full moon coming to its splendour over the Generalife Gardens during two nights of ballet – Giselle, on the second night, when the harvest moon rose behind the cypresses, in its full glory at 12.30 a.m., an hour later than the night before. The huge yellow disc shone down on the Wilis as they danced out of the woods in pale green to join Giselle's ghost in the weird and beautiful natural surroundings.

I sat practically at the feet of Rostropovich when he played his two concerts and escaped alone into the courts of the floodlit Alhambra during the intervals, when few people were there. No hordes of tourists blocked the graceful arches framing the Albaicin and floodlit churches on the horizon of the hill beyond. In silence, the stalactite decorations of the arches and ceilings cast shadows to remind Arabs of Mohamed's abode in a cave. I sat in the window arch looking out over nighttime Granada, with the soothing sound of the twelve lions of the fountain dribbling water while the bats fanned me as they winged past from their haven amongst the stalactites. People were crowding back into the theatre as I returned to hear Manuel de Falla's dances of the Three Cornered Hat.

The Mayorga family had many local friends in Granada and knew Plácido Domingo who was performing the Anthology of Zarzuela another night, under the direction of José Tamayo, a son of Granada. The performance was for the Mexican Earthquake Fund as Plácido was born and raised in Mexico. First José Tamayo received the Medal of Honour from the Foundation Rodriguez-Acosta on the patio of their house. He had lost his power of speech, a decade before, during a breakdown, but with patience he had recovered. Now, with an emotional speech, amongst his childhood friends applauding his honour, the evening ahead with his friend Plácido, and the Generalife Gardens overflowing with admirers for the Zarzuela, his nerves held well to complete a memorable night. An unrehearsed finale, after the orchestra and company had left, delighted the tenacious faithful who remained applauding and calling for Plácido, when he returned to sing 'Granada', to the accompaniment of some chords on one guitar.

My other highlights happened during the birthday celebrations for the Queen at the British Embassy in Madrid where Lord Nicholas Gordon Lennox was Ambassador. First Lady Mary gave me the good news that the lady-in-waiting to Princess Alexandra, Mary Fitzalan Howard, had just married; the following week I would see her at the Royal Show. I had been friends with the family when I stayed at Arundel for the many shows that Lavinia, Duchess of Norfolk had run with the help of the family. As I sat in the Embassy garden listening to the Scots Pipers with the fountain playing I realised that Andrés Segovia himself was sitting by me at the same table.

Segovia had been my hero since 1949 when he was in the room next to me in the charming little Villa Lorraine in the *Bois*, while I was jumping in the British team at *Le Jumping de Bruxelles*. I had kept my ear to the wall to hear his blissful guitar playing before a concert. It had been my first chance to meet the great man, while another first was recorded when I won the *Grand Prix de Bruxelles* on Nobbler, a horse kindly lent to me at the last moment by Mary Whitehead. The Italian d'Inzeo's and Spaniard Paco Goyoaga objected to a girl winning a Grand Prix, but no rule could be found to substantiate their objection, so they took the minor places. Now Segovia was ninety-three years old and after he kissed my hand when he left, it was with reluctance that I washed that hand again.

Wengen staged an excellent Music Festival in September, another mountain setting that I had known for forty years. Grenada, Wengen and Basel brought me back to the pleasure of music, which had never been a priority for Sam, who was not influenced by the musical talents of his Alsation relative Charles Koechlin, the composer who is now gaining more recognition than during his lifetime.

Climbing up the steep streets and mountainsides in Granada and Wengen prepared my heart for Assisi. The 25th anniversary of the WWF in 1986, held at La Cittadella in Assisi, launched a new initiative in establishing a conservation dialogue with five of the world's major religions. Assisi was chosen because of the example of St Francis. After his religious conversion he preached the need to live in harmony with nature and during the Crusades, he crossed all boundaries by working and preaching with both Christians and Muslims.

The culminating Interfaith Ceremony was held at the Basilica of St Francis. The Pilgrims, from many corners of the earth, had converged on Assisi, walking the last days in bad storms. They arrived at the ceremony on time, their spirits undampened, to provide a colourful spectacle dancing outside the Basilica, with the flags fluttering in the strong wind and sunshine.

The five religions represented in the service were Buddhism, Christianity, Hinduism, Islam and Judaism. The Franciscan choir sang and the family of Franciscans helped to plan the ceremony in the Basilica. The emphasis was on the fact that from ancient times people have always cared for and been inspired by nature, with cultures, traditions and religions usually based on the need to live in balance with nature.

Appropriately it was a Founder of the WWF, Sir Peter Scott, who was awarded the WWF Gold Medal at Assisi that year, also his birthday on 14 September fell on the anniversary of the day in 1224 when St Francis had preached to the birds on Mount Subasio. I found that I was sitting next to Peter and Phil Scott in the

Basilica, when during the celebration, Prince Philip, the President of the WWF emphasised that the conservation of nature has a desperate need for the interdependance of faith, which would be symbolised by the tieing on of *rakshas*. We were each given a silver ribbon with a panda badge to perform this Hindu custom, when sisters tie these bracelets onto the arms of the man in the family who protects them. It means that while you protect me physically, I protect you spiritually.

When we tied a *raksha* onto our neighbour's wrist, and received one in return, we expressed the message that the conservation of nature depends on the cooperation of all people. Peter and I exchanged our *rakshas* and he tied mine with a firm nautical knot, while I secured his with a sheet bend, just to show that I had been a Sea Ranger at school, a small gesture to lighten the emotional impact of the ceremony.

The three Presidents of the WWF had all been at Assisi, Prince Bernhard the Founder president, John Loudon, also from Holland but from a family of Scottish origin, who is a wise and sympathetic conservationist and Prince Philip who had been President for five years and still is the efficient and energetic head of the WWF. I was surprised and overjoyed when John invited me as his guest with David and Herter Ogilvy for an October weekend on his yacht the *Ivara*, a sea shell, sailing in the Mediterranean off the South of France, an experience where I felt really spoilt. It was fascinating to hear, too, these brilliant and successful businessmen recount with much humour, some of their experiences with the many top people of the century that they had met.

I changed into my equestrian hat as President and selection committee of the BSJA, finding myself on a plane to Aachen with Major Malcolm Wallace and General Jack Reynolds, the three Presidents of the horse disciplines, on the way to the World Show Jumping Championships. Ladies had not been allowed to compete in this event while I was riding, but the point was taken this time when a lady, Gail Greenough from Canada, was the only finalist who rode four clear rounds on her own Mr T, a German-bred horse, and the other three horses of the finalists, with Conrad Homfeld on Abdullah and Nick Skelton on Apollo second and third.

A gathering of the International Bureau of the FEI, with Prince Philip as President, brought the International officials in horse events to London for a meeting before the end of the year. We were entertained royally at Buckingham Palace with a buffet supper, where I learned how good pheasant could be when casserolled, instead of the fiddly job of carving the roast birds to go round one's guests without waste. My friends from the Southern Hemispheres then returned to their summer, while I prepared Sudgrove for Christmas.

There was a tough spring ahead in 1987 when it became obvious that I could not keep 'Im Steinacker,' now that my children were settled at their studies in Basel and the older children did not want the responsibility of a country house. Our home of twenty-two years was put on the market. That was a lonely time, with little help from people that Sam had trusted and no-one else to turn to, during the loss of our beautiful home in Burg. I had planted the 150 trees around the house, and now they had come to their glory, with the maples and the red oak, with tulip trees flowering and walnut trees loaded with nuts, the fruit trees bearing wonderful crops and the garden in good order producing vegetables, currants and herbs.

The three older children had spent holiday time with us while our two had grown up in Burg, starting with primary school, all five classes being in one school room with the teacher. From there they took the exam to find their level for the secondary school in Flüh. Burg was in Kanton Bern, but Flüh is in Solothurn and to do their *Matura* they had to change their Kanton again to Basel Stadt. At that time the Kantons had independent curriculums, but at least the *Matura* in Basel qualified them for university there.

Steinacker had been built with good cellars for storage, necessary for our large household. One big cellar had the ping-pong table, where many matches had been fought out, and also a chimney fire where Sam would make raclette, toasting a large cheese and scraping off the toasted layer with the back of a knife. This was the rumpus room where the children could have parties too.

The accumulated goods and chattels of nearly a quarter of a century had to be cleared out, a shattering and depressing job. My one comfort in my despair was the arrival of Paddy from Sudgrove to share that last week with me at Steinacker. When the moment of leaving Steinacker came, and we followed the removal van to Oberwil to unload there, she gently goaded me into making the rented place into a small home. Mike Roberts came over too and was a tower of practical help, putting shelves where I had none and taking furniture apart for the move and reassembling it at Oberwil. I could not have survived without their support.

April Fool's Day was the takeover date, when the move was made to a small housing estate, which at least was just off the road and had a forest behind the row of houses. A suburban vixen barked outside my window on the first night I slept there, while it ripped the rubbish bags put ready for collection in the early morning, looking for scraps. I saw her fox cubs, a few days later when I was walking in the woods one evening. They did not see me as they played, but I could smell their strong foxy scent while I watched them play. A buzzard sat on a branch outside my window in the early morning, so I could imagine my wildlife friends from Burg had sent a message to their Oberwil cousins that I was a friendly settler.

One big problem was to find a place for books, which we all loved and kept carefully. Monica and Lucy had a bedroom each but bookshelves took up some of the valuable space, while many of our books that I needed for research remained in their boxes to be stored in the attic, a space we were lucky to have available, but uncomfortable and cold when one needed information from probably the bottom book in a cardboard carton. I spent a lot of time pulling the attic ladder down from the ceiling and clambering up and down to retrieve or search for something.

It depressed me to have no animals at Oberwil and I escaped to Sudgrove at any excuse, where I had acquired a companion for Daisy, a whippet collie cross. My friend had told me that her whippet bitch was going to be mated with an exclusive dog to produce expensive whippet puppies. It turned out that the children had left the kitchen door open, after the society whippet marriage, and the bitch had slipped off with her local collie boyfriend. The boyfriend won and the puppies when they arrived were two mixed up dogs and a bitch, which were 'going cheap'. The bitch ran to me, with its happy tail curled up over its back instead of the sad tucked in tail look of a proper whippet. Her name was immediately Wollie and she came home.

During the Hickstead Shows I used to stay with Janet Kidd at Slythehurst, where she had a small indoor pool, that I enjoyed when returning tired from a day at the show. She had taken up painting quite late in life, when Rachel Carpenter, my friend from teenage days, gave her a box of oils and brushes. Rachel was Janet's right hand help to the end. Janet had offered us an open invitation to her home at any time in Barbados, Holders, where Sam and I had once spent a night many years before. Janet was not well, so I asked if I could join her for the first two weeks of February 1988 to make a break from winter.

I found the people there delightful and hospitable, living in a lush environment that was fed by warm rains and sunshine. All the water sports were available with coral reefs for scuba diving, and equestrian activities with polo and racing that Janet had encouraged and contributed to largely during her many years on the island. Several wise people had retired in this peaceful haven, as I found when I visited Scobie and May Breasley, bronzed and fit on the cool terrace of their home on the beach. Unfortunately Janet was very immobile although she organised and watched the activities at Holders and entertained many of her friends.

She asked me a surprising question, when I went to her bedroom by the swimming pool, to thank her and say farewell, before I left for the airport. Comfortably propped up on pillows in the big bed, where I sat on the side, she fired at me, 'Who have you loved most in your life?' I answered without hesitation, 'Sam'. She thought for a moment and told me, 'That doesn't often happen in marriage.' 'Well it did happen to me,' I replied, 'only the time together was cut short too soon.'

> The years they are not mine that time has taken from me
> the years they are not mine that still perhaps might be.
> You moment, you are mine, and if I treasure thee,
> then He is also mine, who made time and eternity.

This poem written during the baroque period by the German, Andreas Gryphius (1616–1664), is quoted in Dr Albert Hofmann's book *Insight Outlook*.

During the summer I stayed with Janet when I had meetings at Hickstead, being there on her eightieth birthday, but she sadly died in November, when her Bajan friends came over for her funeral bringing a local steel band to play the music and drums that she had so enjoyed.

I had decided to sell most of my cups in aid of the WWF that spring, and had talked to Tim Walker, the dynamic Chairman of WWF UK, about arranging the sale. He scared me when he said he had to have a small operation on his throat to remove a nodule. The worst fears were realised when he died at Easter, aged only forty-six. Conservation lost a valuable friend too, which made his loss even more poignant.

Lucy passed her *Matura* exams before Easter, but did not want to go straight to university as she was not sure which subjects to study. Anton Rupert of Stellenbosch, a longstanding friend and Trustee of the WWF, also President of the South African Nature Foundation, told me that his Director could give Lucy a job for six months, as assistant co-ordinator of Flora '88, the famous wild flower show held in Cape Town. She arrived there six weeks later to help with the liasion between Cape Town and its sister city of Nice in the south of France, and to learn about the wonderful flowers of South Africa, with her first office work in the gardens of Kirstenbosch. She also met Mary and her daughters Sue and Barbara, my cousins, and their children.

In the autumn I went to visit them, first being invited to Sun City Horse Show, the fabulous centre for gamblers and sportsmen, with a stadium and a companionship golf course. The complex was built in the bush of Bophuthatswana to give work while creating income for the homeland. Outside the tourist hotels and sports facilities the Pilanesberg National Park has been created and restocked with African wildlife, which are thriving there. A research station for conservation education also interested me greatly, as it was situated in an ideal place to observe and study the wildlife. Education is a most important part of conservation, as the younger generation are those who would become leaders in the future.

During the show I was called to present some of the prizes and could meet up with some old friends like Anneli, who I'd known since she was three when I lived with the Drummond-Hays. Gonda Butters had come to jump in England when she was only fourteen after I had met her in South Africa during an invitation visit to Pretoria to open the show and jump a couple of horses in the competitions. She showed remarkable talent and I recommended her to the BSJA as a first-class rider to compete for a season in England. Two more couples at the show had their daughters jumping, and they invited me to Natal which would be new country to me. I wanted to visit the University of Pietermaritzburg where a new Chair had been created for the Institute of Natural Resources under Professor Charles Breen, helped by John Hanks, at that time working in the WWF & IUCN at Gland.

First I flew to Cape Town to see Mary, and check on my younger daughter. We had dinner together at the Vineyard in Claremont, a suburb of Cape Town, close to where she had found digs. She discussed enthusiastically her new job; the next day was the big opening of Flora '88, and Lucy would have her work cut out. I need not have worried as she had settled in like an old hand. The girls in the office had not approved when they heard that a Swiss girl was coming as assistant coordinator, they had imagined a superior society girl arriving wearing the newest European fashion, with high heels and an elevated opinion of herself. Lucy had turned up in her jeans and gym shoes, trailing her anorak behind her, and with a cheeky look introduced herself, 'Hi. I'm Lucy, what d'you want me to do, because I haven't a clue.' They all laughed with relief and became friends.

It was freezing cold walking against the gale to the great building in Cape Town where the banks of wild flowers from all the regions in South Africa were set out in their own type of habitat and background. I had been told that Cape Town was like a baby, 'wet and windy', but I soon warmed up seeing the banks of flowers, many of them being proteas and everlastings. There was a stir after the opening speeches and when the crowd parted, Mrs Botha appeared in an astounding dress covered with pink ostrich feathers, it was sensational.

The layout of the exhibition was superbly done and many top botanists were there from Kew Gardens, the IUCN and experts on native flora. The following day I spent outside in the unique garden of Kirstenbosch. Friends took me too, to visit a private stretch of land at Buck Bay, north along the Atlantic shore. Some sheep grazed there, with wild deer, birds, tortoises and so many coloured wild flowers underfoot that there was no way one could avoid treading on them with each step. Often one fell into mole holes while the horse flies were ferocious, but the surrounding arum lilies, alysum, blue felica and wild carpets of colour, made up for any discomfort.

I met the friends I had made at Sun City in Durban. Sue Armstrong took me back to Rosetta to their home at Danesfort where Graham farmed and kept polo ponies for himself and his son. On the way I was able to stop at the University of Natal in Pietermaritzburg, where luckily Professor Breen had time to tell me about the education work with the Institute of Natural Resources.

Sue took me to see Colonel Jack Vincent at Mooi river where Peter Scott had visited. Peter had painted a watercolour for him of a nyala, one of the most attractive of the antelope family. Jack had known Peter and Guy Mountford since he worked in Morges at the IUCN office before the WWF and IUCN were united in the same building at Gland. He was an expert on rhinos and had been in contact with Professor Ruedi Geigy and Ruedi Schenkel and his wife Lotte, from Basel, with the establishment of the Ujung Kulon Javan rhino reserve in Indonesia. He had very definite ideas of how one should go about conservation and quoted a statement by 'Monty' during the war, 'Throughout my life and conduct my criteria has not been the approach of others nor of the world; it has been my inward conviction, my duty and my conscience,' adding himself, 'it's often necessary, not only to look back in anger but also forward with fury.'

Giant's Castle, the reserve in the Drakensberg, was our destination that afternoon where we met Paul and Eve Miles, again a small world with conservation and showjumping our mutual interests. Paul took us up the mountain in a four-wheel drive vehicle, from where we could see the range of the Drakensberg with Injusuti at 3,459 m and the flat topped Giant's Castle. We were lucky to find the hide on the edge of the escarpment empty. It was thrilling to see so many big raptors, with my first sight of a pair of black eagles before a young black eagle settled on a rock close by, only to be buzzed by a brave Lanner falcon. The huge lammergeyer, bearded vulture, cruised by, and below us the enormous Cape vulture settled on a rock, using the vantage point as a lookout post.

A damp and misty morning restricted the view off the mountains when we walked along the Bushman's River to the caves where one could study their paintings. The colour red was made from iron oxide, black from manganese and charcoal, white with clay and birdlime, yellow with limonite, mixed with binding vegetable oils and juices like latex and resin. The bearded vultures rub their chests in red clay which stains them, while captive lammergeyers stay with white chests, because they have no accessible clay. Genuine red-tailed and streaky chested jackal buzzards are spectacular with the chestnut below turning to dark upper parts.

While we admired the bird life and pretty rippling river, from behind a rock a serval cat appeared. I quickly put up my camera to take a shot of this usually shy animal, but I did not need to hurry as the cat joined us as company on our walk. It dashed off once to hunt and catch a rat, which it proudly brought back to us, playing with it and eventually eating it. We heard that it was one of two abandoned kittens that someone in the camp had rescued and brought up, but always leaving them free to do their own hunting as they got older. Now they would occasionally appear in a friendly way before going off again into the wild. It would be interesting to see if their kittens would also have no fear of man.

My other Natal friends were Geoff and Isabel Cleasby and their daughter Caroline, who was a contemporary of Elizabeth Armstrong. Isabel and Caroline had time to take me up the coast to St Lucia where we were taken by boat into the estuary to see the bird life, with the next day spent in the Umfolozi reserve. The following year we went to the adjoining reserve of Hluhluwe, with the HL pronounced like the Welsh LL. This was perhaps the most beautiful countryside and reserve that I had seen, putting it in the same category as the Rwindi in Zaïre. The animals could roam from one to the other park, but the most spectacular sight was the quantity of rhinos, of every age, in Hluhluwe.

Without time to change from my gym shoes I flew back to Johannesburg where Cecily Niven, in her nineties, was having tea with Barbara, and both of us were staying for the night. Cecily is a respected and knowledgeable person in conservation and was going to a meeting that evening. She had a camp in the Kruger Park and one was very privileged when invited to her stamping ground that she had known since childhood.

I bought an air ticket for Nelspruit, to fly there the next day, and was surprised to hear Barbara's lady friend in the Agency ask her, 'Does she qualify?' 'Yes, I think she qualifies,' Barbara replied. I enquired what qualification I needed and was delighted to hear that I got a half-price ticket for being a VOP, very old person.

Sam and I had been to Sabie Sand for a couple of nights in 1973, to see the wildlife during a business trip. There we had met up with a friend who skied in Davos every year; I had just met him while I competed at the International Horse Show in the 1950s. George Turner and his mother Helen, called 'Ning' by her friends, came to meet us and we had excellent game viewing and a lot of laughter over some tall tales. His mother had since died when she was eighty-eight but I was invited to the lovely family house of Bedford, White River.

I had visited Bedford once in 1957, when I was jumping in Pretoria, after which the committee arranged for me to visit the Kruger Park to spend two nights in Skukuza Camp, which was small and personal then, not like the town it has become today. Melo McRoberts and his wife had driven me from Pretoria and I mentioned that a friend I had met skiing lived in White River, and he and his mother had asked us to tea at Bedford. It turned out that Melo and George had been through the war together.

I now heard the sad news that Melo had died shortly after Ning. Helen had been the eldest of six sisters, daughter of Sir George Farrer, and she married Basil Turner. George's father was flying during the Great War with Pilot's Licence no. 39. He had been present and seen the crash of the Cuffley airship in September 1916; he had taken a fragment of the aluminium frame to make into a box, which was still in the house.

George spoke most of the native languages fluently having been brought up among the people, spending a lot of time in the Kruger Park before it was enclosed, and having exciting adventures with wild animals as a boy. The language at White River was Swazi, but in Sabie Sand Shangaan is spoken, the holiday camp called Mala Mala being Shangaan for Sable Antelope.

The first evening we dined on fish, fresh from the Crocodile river that George, being an expert fisherman, had caught that afternoon. This was followed by the best fresh fruit salad, Robert's speciality, Robert having been with George for thirty years. Robert brought some of his fruit salad with us the next day when we went to Sabie Sand to George's camp and reserve of Othawa. When the river Sand is too high, the dam cannot be crossed to the camp. We took all our stores with us to stock the fridge and there were plenty of tins for reserves, so that no-one could be caught starving. The drive down there is through the Kangwane homeland where Chief Enos Wabuza was a friend of Mrs Thatcher's.

I tried to learn some Shangaan words at supper that night, because I felt cut off when I could not talk with the local people. In most of the world one of the European languages will carry one through, but I was missing the delightful sense of humour and play on words of the rich African languages. Another native language that had been compiled in a dictionary before it was lost was that of the South American Indians of the Ono tribe who lived in Tierra del Fuego. Their language was much richer in descriptive words than any European language, but the tribe has died out since it had contact with the white man and his diseases.

Othawa camp was perfectly placed above the river to see the game come to drink and sometimes wade across the river. Sitting under the M'Jomo tree, even if it did sometimes spit, while a purple-crested loerie shouted 'krook krook,' from a high branch, one could watch for hours, animals, birds, insects, the trees and flowers and always the river, and the sky. The light changes through every phase of the day, with spectacular sunrises and sunsets reflected in the water of the dam. This is one of my favourite places to sit with binoculars and perhaps a pad of paper to jot down observations on the life of the wild.

I had the choice of being more active so I was asked if I would like to go on a game count. I took the wildlife on the left side and the Ranger watched the other side as he drove and said the numbers of each species, the sexes and young or adult, while I wrote down our information. He could tell at a glance the numbers in a herd of antelope, while I tried to count in twos, before they disappeared but practice helped me to speed up. I saw a pair of woolly-necked storks and remembered the friendly one that had watched me swimming when we were in Kenya with the children on our one African holiday as a family.

Observing game in a wild reserve without tourists, gives a more natural picture, with the animals less habituated to vehicles, but always being alert and on their guard against other predators, essential for basic survival in the wild. I learnt from the lifetime of experiences of people born and bred in these surroundings, and could get information from Makalash, the head man, or George, who would immediately know the right answers.

In Kangwane homeland I was invited to the Teacher Training College, where twenty-five student teachers were encouraged to each give a short lecture on a specific subject of their choosing. The thoughts that emerged in each talk were individual and all related to nature. Among the subjects chosen were a waterfall, a butterfly and microbes, producing wonderful ideas that would stimulate their pupils in subjects that they related to and understood. There was a nature trail too, where students and visitors were encouraged to identify wild rock jasmin, a plant growing like mint for making tea, another plant used for poultices in treating chest problems and a bush that made good brooms that would last a long time.

I regret each time I leave Africa; I arrived back early at 5.30 a.m. in Heathrow, and as I had only asked Helen Whitehouse, who helped me with everything at Sudgrove, to come at 7 a.m., I sat down to drink an orange juice in the empty arrival hall. I recognised Tim Liversedge from Botswana who had been on the same Jumbo. We had been with Tim and June in the Okavango and I had been trying to contact him for a long time. Tim had gone to the smoking section and found three seats free where he lay and slept all night. I had been in the non-smoking without another free seat, so felt tired and stiff. He was coming to Bristol for the Wildlife film competition which he won that year with his documentary on the Okavango.

At Sudgrove the children joined me for my sixtieth birthday party, not on the scale of my fiftieth party that Sam had given me, but a good evening with 'Mike's surprise', the pipers again piping their way down the drive to the front of the house and then plenty of dancing, with the young waiting for their sort of dance music, when the oldies had given up.

The New York show had asked me to be Appeal Judge at Madison Square Gardens; as it turned out, this was the last show to be held in New York, the cost of staging it in the City having grown out of proportion. Having only competed twice in the '50s at the old Madison Square, when I was occupied with my horses more than the social side, I had forgotten how formal the evening performance was for the officials. Evening dress was mandatory which required a lot of packing for the five nights. These were evenings of atrocious weather with the wind and rain howling up the avenue, which had to be crossed in evening dress with smart shoes getting soaked in the flooded gutters and no chance of carrying an umbrella without taking off like Mary Poppins. After leaving the hotel looking immaculate, one arrived through the hazards of the weather and traffic on 8th Avenue looking like a bedraggled wreck, with hair and make-up streaming down and no chance to do the repair work. It was a great week meeting old friends and making new ones, with an after midnight party every evening. I felt very privileged to participate in that last Madison Square show, my first having been in 1953.

In December after the Koechlin Christmas party in Basel with all the children, as Lucy had returned after her job in South Africa, I went to Bruxelles for the fortieth anniversary of *Le Jumping de Bruxelles*. Several of my old friends and rivals turned up for this event, with Pierre Jonquères d'Oriola, Paqui d'Orgeix and Guy Lefrant of France, Piero and Raimondo d'Inzeo of Italy and José Hoffmann the indefatigable organiser and also competitor from the past, meeting again for the Gala. Four veterans also rode again on four different horses, all jumping clear rounds on each, to show that age had not diminished their skill. Riding is a wonderful sport; providing one is still physically fit enough and that the nerve is still steady, there is never a reason to hang up one's boots.

(*above*) Sir Peter Scott (second from left) and Philippa his wife, with Max and Toni Nicholson, when they lunched at Sudgrove on 18 August 1989; only ten days later Peter died, just before his eightieth birthday.

(*below*) November 1991: surveying the Oravango Delta by makoro and elephant with young.

(*right*) Lucy on holiday in
Sweden with friends.

(*below*) Monica with Eureka and Charm, young great-granddaughters of Tosca, 1991.

14

Into the Nineties:
Renewing Friendships around the World

There were more changes ahead for me, when I decided that I could not rent a Swiss place now that the children had their own apartments and my work was increasingly centred in England, where some of my close friends were too busy or not fit enough to stay with me in Switzerland. We had known the sporting artist Michael Lyne and Jessie his wife, over many years especially while he painted Sudgrove and the first two sons of Tosca for us. When he died, it left another gap in our Gloucestershire community, but at Kempsford I could say farewell at his funeral, because I had a happier event soon after at Sudgrove, the wedding of my goddaughter Jocey Frenkel to the bowls champion Tony Allcock. The reception was held in a marquee on our lawn after their service at Bisley church. Tony had often come to our Miserden church when he lived in the district, and so they both felt at home at Sudgrove.

In August of 1989 Max Nicholson telephoned to say he would be in Gloucester-shire the next day and would like to drop in for lunch. I suggested that I might ask Peter and Phil Scott to join us, an idea that delighted Max. The Scott's were very busy with fund raising and preparations for Peter's eightieth birthday, but decided to drop everything and come to lunch with Max and Toni. A perfect day dawned which we celebrated with champagne, sitting on the lawn among the many birds that came to show themselves to two of the founders of the WWF. Toni approved of the Swiss flag flying with the Union Jack, as Max's wife is Swiss too. The gathering was the happiest time and I was sure that this last-minute arrangement was something to remember especially when Peter kissed me goodbye.

Ten days later Peter died of a heart attack with his faithful Phil and the family at his side. It was two weeks before his eightieth birthday, an event that he had dedicated to raising money for the Wildfowl and Wetlands Trust; he had lived a positive life until the end.

The day I happened to see an English paper with the headlines of Peter's death, I was the *Chêf d'Equipe* of the British Team in St Gallen. It was the fiftieth anniversary of the outbreak of World War II. Our last rider John Whitaker had to have less than 2 faults to win the Nation's Cup, but his had been the surprising discard score of 14 faults in the first round. The German team were thinking that they had won although their team had been caught rapping their horses the night before to make the horses jump higher in the Nation's Cup. Rapping is forbidden, but the Swiss watchmen in charge of the stables, did not have the authority to convict them, and the horses had no numbers on, breaking another regulation, and had been quickly hidden by the riders after being seen.

I was in a state of shock having just read about Peter, who had been a war hero and very competitive in sport. I ran to John, our last rider, and told him 'the stakes' for the Nation's Cup in no uncertain terms, as he came down the funnel to the ring, emphasising the fact of this fiftieth anniversary of the outbreak war. He had to get less than two faults for time with no fences down. He went calmly into the ring and jumped clear with one-and-a-half time faults. I nearly fainted with relief, and thought that maybe Peter too was helping him over the fences and pushing him through the finish.

At St Paul's I was sitting with Max and Toni Nicholson among the enormous gathering of Peter's friends for his Memorial Service. Peter would have approved of the service and the excellent tribute to him by Keith Shackleton. In 1913 a service had also been held there for those who died with Robert Falcon Scott, the leader of the 1912 Antarctic Expedition. He was Peter's father, who had written in his last letter to his wife, 'make the boy interested in natural history'. How well his last wish had come true.

One of Peter's dearest wishes was that Antarctica should be made into a protected World Conservation continent so that it would remain unexploited with no pollution. His wish is nearer to fulfilment with the recent moritorium on mining in the Antarctic, scene of the fatal expedition to the South Pole by Peter's father.

Our lawn at Sudgrove has heard many interesting conversations and another special meeting was with Dr Albert Hofmann, who was staying with me for a week with Anita, and Max Nicholson joined us for two days with Toni, to meet the Swiss couple. It was the first time that the scientists had met and they had many topics to discuss. I think that Peter's presence was felt, because he would have enjoyed the great men expounding their views on science, ecology, the future course to take for saving the bio-diversity in the world and the control of pollution.

Albert, at eighty-six, had worked in the mountains of southern Mexico as a research chemist, studying with the Indians the properties that they had found, generations before, in plants, leaves, mushrooms and ergot. At the same time, his friend Dick Schultes, had studied in the Amazon forests for fifteen years with the Indians, learning the properties of plants that they had used in their tribes for generations. Their forebears had been the great explorers and pioneers of medicine, and they had discovered how to use and blend the plants to treat people for birth control, fertility, the production of male or female babies, and cures for many illnesses, all from natural products of the forest. These early scientists, who would have been termed 'savages' by the white conquerors, received no acclaim with medals, degrees or money.

Max, a little senior in age to Albert, had worked with Aldous and Julian Huxley and was involved with the founding of the IUCN in 1928 and WWF in 1961. These gentlemen showed that their intellects were still razor sharp and neither had ever contemplated retirement from their life's work. Albert and Anita had built their home in Burg, up the mountain, just after we had moved into Steinacker in 1965.

The 1989 WWF Annual Council was held in Montreux and I must have caught pneumonia from sitting under a cold air conditioning vent, my place during the meetings. My move from Switzerland followed immediately and the temperature dropped to $-10C$, while door and windows were kept open for the removal of everything at Oberwil. This must be the last 'moving of house' that I could ever take mentally and physically.

On my last day in Basel I went to see Marguerite and sat with her for a long time. She was happy that the Koechlin Christmas party had been such a success and that all her twelve grandchildren and twelve great-grand children had come to see her. Harty, her eldest and only living child, had celebrated his seventieth birthday in September before arranging the yearly December party and both had been happy occasions. Mamama said to me before I left, 'The family must be kept together, that is the most important thing for them.' I kissed her goodbye and promised that we would keep and respect her traditions. As I parted, I confirmed that I would be back to see her in the New Year; she replied 'Goodbye'.

I shivered my way back to England and was put almost immediately in the emergency ward again at Cheltenham Hospital. While I was ill with pneumonia, Mamama died peacefully, ten days after I had been with her. I realised that she had been tired of life for a long time, being immobile in bed but as Matriarch of the family she was determined that all the family should see her and talk to her about her Christmas party, before they left with happy memories of seeing Mamama. At ninety-four years her passing took with her an era of Basel life, from the turn of the century.

It saddened me too that my expected visits to her bedside would be no longer necessary, because that had been one reason for staying on near Basel. Switzerland had been my home for nearly three decades, but now I would concentrate on Sudgrove and remake my life there, so the children could have another happy home in England for their holidays.

The Koechlin family had its roots in the Alsace, that much fought-over land that changed its nationality three times over the years preceeding the turn of the century, where people had been schooled in French as their first foreign language or instead German as the school language, depending on whether the French or the Germans occupied their land at that time. Meanwhile they had all spoken Alsation in their homes, which neither the French or the Germans understand, although this dialect is understood in Basel and along the Alsace border with Switzerland, as in our village of Burg.

Charles Koechlin, who died in 1950, was a musician and composer who had studied with Fauré and Massenet and had orchestrated Fauré's *Pelleas et Mél-isande*. He taught Poulenc, Tailleferre, Milhaud, among other French composers, and he helped Cole Porter to write the ballet 'Within the Quote', in the 1920s. His fascination with movie stars in the early days of the screen had him writing musical portraits of Lilian Harvey, Douglas Fairbanks, Marlene Dietrich, Greta

Garbo and Charlie Chaplin. Some of his music has come into vogue in recent years.

The family was also responsible for Maurice Koechlin, the architect of the 300-metre metal tower in 1884, that became the Eiffel Tower, a revolutionary design in metal, double the height of the Washington Monument, at that time the tallest nineteenth-century construction. The World Exhibition was scheduled for Paris in 1889, and Mr Eiffel realised the brilliance of the spectacular design and bought the plans from Maurice Koechlin for a song, before breaking the clause in the contract stating that Maurice Koechlin's name should be used in the construction of the Tour Eiffel, that could well have been called the Tour Koechlin.

In Basel the Koechlin's were involved with the dye stuff industry, an important international commercial business with Geigy, a firm founded in 1758. They specialised in dyes for ribbons, famous in Basel, then progressing from dye stuffs and gradually expanded in the chemical industry. The Geigy family business became a public company in 1947, as it increased its international markets, especially in the United States. Sam was already Chairman of the Geigy board from 1965 which led to the merger with Ciba, when he took the Chair of the Ciba-Geigy board from 1972.

There was time ahead to devote to conservation work for as long as I was fit. The first opening to extend my horizons came with the invitation to join the board of Earthwatch Europe. The organisation, centred on bridging the gap between science and the community, in doing research work for conservation, interested me greatly.

Volunteers can choose from a wide range of projects to go and work with a team under an expert while paying for the privilege of two weeks experience in gaining top information and knowledge on their chosen subject with the scientist. The volunteers are well briefed beforehand, so that they have a basic background to the project they have chosen. Their health, accommodation and travel documents are all checked, the objectives of the project in terms of the environment are carefully explained as well as the social and historical background to the country where the research work is progressing.

The first project that I visited was the S'Albufera, a wetland in Mallorca, where the delicate black-winged stilts had nested and were sitting on their eggs. Along the shaded paths planted with local bushes and trees, making dry communication routes between the marshes, so many nightingales sang that one lost count. The value of the popular and successful bird habitat was obvious, for the wide variety of species that thrived there; this wetland must be saved from the encroaching concrete jungle, that seems to be endemic to Spanish seaside resorts. Migrating birds desperately needed the haven for rest and food, during their long journeys between Europe and Africa.

Among the Albufera Earthwatch team, were two young people sponsored by the Prince's Trust, who were working with enthusiasm on their allotted research projects – they had applied to join and were finding satisfaction in science and nature rather than the 'anti' riots that had previously occupied their time.

Up on the rugged mountain chain where my friends Enrique and Heidi Gildemeister lived, 7 km from the road, there were black vultures that soared and sometimes sat on a rocky pinnacle to observe. Another successful project had succeeded in reintroducing these magnificent birds that enhanced the craggy heights rising straight up from the sea.

For the next Earthwatch project I joined Max Nicholson, to survey the Guernsey cliffs with the intention to reintroduce choughs, that were declining in number in Wales and had become extinct in many of their old habitats. Erosion of the cliffs could also be helped by some replanting and have protected areas, preventing new paths from forming gullies where top soil would be washed down by heavy rain. I spent a delightful evening and night on Lihou Island, joined at low tide by a causeway to the main island, with Robin and Patricia Borwick. Robert, Lord Borwick, Robin's elder brother, had found his bride Babbins at Miserden House, where they had been in my guest house, while Robert studied at the Royal Agricultural College. I was godmother to Mary-Anne, their second daughter. Lihou Island, with only the Borwicks living permanently there, is a paradise for nesting seabirds and I saw many Adonis blue butterflies and gatekeepers. The excavation of the Priory on Lihou was another Earthwatch project that we discussed, sitting on the spring turf surrounded by the sea, with herring gulls, black-backed gulls and oystercatchers among the rocks, while linnets and Dartford warblers sang from the windswept bush covering and protecting part of the treeless and rocky shore. Walking on the shingle the cries of the oystercatcher echoed off the stones as they buzzed me, while guarding their nests. Lichens and scarlet pimpernel found crannies to grow in, when suddenly overhead a boom in the clear sky signalled the arrival or departure of the New York–Paris Concorde going through the sound barrier. The wild birds did not stir at the rude sound breaking the peace, but I jumped out of my skin.

Showjumping had a highlight during the summer of 1990 when the first World Equestrian Games were held in Stockholm. The jumping was held in the same arena where we had jumped in the 1956 Olympic Games, the only difference being that an all-weather arena surface had been laid for the event. The fibre and sand mixture needed regular watering and rolling, with the best going for the horses that followed this treatment. The hot sun meant that the process had to be regularly repeated, but some of the horses found the going 'dead' and missed the spring of proper turf, although it was the same for everyone.

The French were brilliant throughout and well deserved their team Gold and Individual Gold with Eric Navet riding the four finalist horses with sensitivity and talent. Milton, our team's sensational grey with John Whitaker, did not show his usual brilliance although our team won the bronze behind a little known German team, and John on Milton finished with the Silver Individual. The favourite ride of the four finalists was on the other grey, Gem Twist, ridden by Greg Best from America, that finished as the best horse after the other riders had all jumped clear rounds on him.

Stockholm had rekindled memories of my ambitions in my first Olympics with Flanagan. Another 'first' was his double clear rounds in the Hickstead Derby of

1962 which was celebrated that year. Douggie Bunn had asked me to lead the
Hickstead Derby Parade on the thirtieth anniversary. I was the first living Derby
winner, on Flanagan in 1962, because Seamus Hayes who won in 1961 on
Goodbye, had died not long before. He was our Irish friend who competed with
me from the 1940s. I enjoyed my tour of the arena, seeing once more the Derby
course while sitting on a horse that was as surprised as me to get such an
unaccustomed ovation. After I dismounted I was very happy to watch the
competition from the sidelines and applaud the victory of Nick Skelton on Apollo.

Conservation interests needed my concentration on travel arrangements in order
to attend conferences that were being held in the autumn around the world. The
four organisation's events in where I participated were at Boston, Mass, the
Headquarters of Earthwatch, the ICBP 20th World Conference in Hamilton
Waikatu University, New Zealand, the WWF International Council Meeting in
Sydney, Australia, followed by the IUCN 18th General Assembly at Perth.

The sequence of meetings followed the route to the west, that would fit the
conditions for a round-the-world air ticket. The time between could be spent in
seeing other projects with the help of friends, also interested in conservation, who
had local contacts to advise me on programmes. One finds an international circle
of friendship in both conservation and sport, where one contact leads to another.
I was wary of relying on this unscheduled way of travel, because of my age and
health. That had not bothered me when I made journeys around the world
showjumping on very haphazard plans before I was married, and travelling with
Sam had spoiled me; he being a chief executive had the complete infrastructure in
any country to make his local arrangements, while I only had my personal and
WWF contacts to organise.

The tempo for my seven weeks away was set from the beginning. My day
started at 4 a.m. with Lucy driving me to Heathrow. Flying into Boston after
crossing the Atlantic, the local time was midday. I was flying with the sun, which
intends to make your travel hours long, but physically one is supposed to adjust to
the time change more quickly. Sam and I had always geared ourselves to adjust to
local time on arrival as soon as we boarded a plane. I had turned down a BA steak
offered for lunch on the flight, as it would have been 7 a.m. Boston time. At the
airport I was met by a lady from Earthwatch who told me that we were going
straight to the office for a sandwich lunch with the board. I had many new people
to meet, well-known in their own work, but giving their time as well to help
environmental issues with Earthwatch. Brian Rosborough had a good team and
office staff who showed me the head office organisation, one innovation being a
software computer game on world ecology, which could answer nearly any
problem if you knew how to use it.

The evening at home that Brian and his wife Lucy had arranged brought many
friends, with Muffie Coolidge, widow of Harold who had been involved with the
IUCN and WWF for so many years and had set up the Coolidge Centre for
Environmental Leadership. It was good to talk to Dick Schultes and Dorothy and
to find him really fit again. He was now chairing an important commission in

Venezuela and perhaps had culled some leaves from the Rain Forest to regain his full health, following the medical knowledge that he had gained during his fifteen years with the Indians of the Amazon.

Flying to San Francisco from Boston in daylight gave me a new experience of the North American Continent and its range of land and water. As I changed planes at Chicago, the flight path was not too high for identifying the geographical layout, with a clear view of the north end of the Appalachian chain before the great Hudson River. Ahead I saw a line of cloud, it fulfilled the description of a 'front', with a straight line from north to south from clear visibility to solid cover, over the Great Lakes. The next leg took me over the Mississippi from Illinois to Iowa and then the Missouri at Sioux City. I had not seen these places from the air, since Ralph Beermann had taught me to fly his Piper and then a Bonanza in 1953, when I was staying with the family in south Sioux City. The next river was the Green River and from the air the colour of the water was pure green. The only other really green water I'd seen was the stretch of the Rhône where it cascades from Switzerland into France beyond Geneva.

The desertification as we approached the Rockies made the land look barren, while flying over the ridges of the Rockies the land seemed very saline, shining white around the lakes. California was suffering from a four year drought. In this short space of time I had left a dry England in October with hose pipe bans, to a wet Boston, that had plenty of water, to a parched California where only irrigation had produced pockets of green. Even a wealthy developed country needs co-operation from the elements, but they cannot always perform their natural functions when pollution by mankind and acts of deforestation can change the natural ecology and flow of water from previously protected sources.

The innovation of driving up and down the terraces of San Francisco was an amusing delight. My hostess Doris Magowen, whose husband had been a Trustee of the WWF for many years, was an experienced driver in the fascinating city. Doris gave me a good insight into the remaining marvels of nature on that coast. We crossed the Golden Gate Bridge to the Muir Woods National Monument and walked in awe among these mighty Redwood trees that had been growing for centuries along Redwood Creek. Further south along the coast the extensive Monterey Bay Aquarium displayed the rich ocean life of the Pacific coast. A seven-finned shark was the largest, against the smaller Leopard sharks and the great variety of fish that were being fed together in the huge aquarium. The sea otters had their own living space and never stopped playing together their big sleek bodies gracefully entwining as they rolled over on the surface of the water before diving down into rocky caves.

Down the coast at Cypress Point, sea lions were basking on rocks shared by a colony of pelicans and gulls. The big males in the sea lion colony were silhouetted against the surf and spray of the impressive Pacific breakers, while sleek sea otters gambolled in the waves. Cormorants flew in at sunset, black against the red sky in the west on the ocean horizon. This wild coast was the setting for Pebble Beach and Cypress Point golf course, where players had to brave shots over the Pacific breakers, to reach holes built on rocky headlands, while being distracted by the wonderful shore wildlife.

Sylvia Earle, another longstanding friend from the WWF Council and expert oceanologist came to spend the evening and give us the good news that she had been made President and Chief Executive Officer of NOAA, National Oceanic and Atmospheric Administration. She would be in Washington for at least two years, which disrupted her own Deep Ocean Engineering company in San Leandro; but she was the right person for the big Governmental responsibility in NOAA.

From the local paper I saw that the zoo had a young douroucouli, the rare South American nocturnal monkey, from the prosimian family like lemurs, a link between leaf-eating insects and mammals, from pre-primate ages. Good zoos are excellent for student research into rare and endangered species of wildlife; we were able to see these facilities before the zoo opened in the morning and talk to the scientists working on various projects. One's eyes had to become habituated to the dark room where the douroucouli's were kept, in rain forest conditions, before making out the baby riding on his father's back. The male cares for the young while the mother only nurses it when it is hungry and then returns the baby to the male. They are not easy to see being small and dark in colour with long prehensile tails to help them through the trees.

Other study projects included siamangs with young and orang-utans: the last time I had seen these primates was in the wild at Bohorok, Sumatra. Families of lowland gorillas were thriving in an area with trees and rocks where they played and claimed bits of territory.

A performance of *Cappriccio* with Dame Kiri te Kanawa as the Countess came as a surprise bonus before I left San Francisco for the Dame's native New Zealand. I broke the long journey at Honolulu to see some projects on Hawaii Island with its great diversity of habit from sea coast through rain forest up to the volcanic heights of Mauna Loa and Mauna Kea at over 4,000 metres.

My contact with Hawaii had been through Haku Baldwin, the lady who came from the old-established family of Damon. Her grandfather had been given land, from Honolulu up into the mountains above, by the king. As a child she remembered riding her pony up the mountain to their house, followed by the famous soprano Galli-Curci riding behind her, who had been invited by Haku's father while she was singing at the Honolulu Opera House. She burst into song as she happily rode with the surprised child, who remembered that the birds reacted to her singing complimenting the lovely voice echoing around the mountains.

We had been introduced by Laurie Morgan, the Australian three-day event Gold Medallist, in Rome during the 1960 Olympic Games. She invited me to stay on my way to Australia the following year, where I was invited to ride at the Sydney Royal Easter Show. Thirty years later she had attended the Stockholm World Equestrian Games, although our paths had not crossed there but now I could make my second visit to these wonderful islands. I discovered that Haku meant locally the 'Boss' or Master, and her friendship was much valued especially her enthusiasm in supporting the equestrian activities of the Islands, also her Club and Centre with excellent stables built around an indoor school.

Haku told me that I would go straight to Hilo at dawn, the place on Hawaii, the largest island, where 'horses would shy at people not carrying an umbrella'. The rain came down in buckets to prove the point about umbrellas. Peering through the misty dawn from the little plane overshadowed by the 4,000 metre volcanoes, I noted that the streams and rivers were swollen with white water cascading down the waterfalls around the high cliffs.

Hilo was my bed and breakfast pad for the three-day excursions with Ida and Lorna, both amateur botanists who knew and could show me the people and projects in nature conservancy. They were very involved in stopping endemic plants from taking over and smothering the indigenous flora. After centuries of 'settlers' there were many introduced species that had thrived in the islands.

Ida, Haku's friend, welcomed me at Hilo, with a Lei Plumeria and frangapani, which each of us wore on our heads, like a victor's laurel wreath. The flowers kept fresh from the frequent rain showers that make the vegetation so lush, while my showerproof anorak was soaked through in a moment, up in the Rain Forest Volcanoes Native Park at Kilauea, where we walked along the sandalwood trail, smelling the sulphur from the fields of steaming lava.

There were many new things to learn about plants; one being the delicious ohelo, with red berries, related to the huckleberry and blueberry. Another plant the akla wikstroemia stunned fish when thrown into the water; it was poisonous to cold-blooded fish but leaving them edible for humans. On the coast noni trees with big green fruit had healing powers and were used for medicine, dyes and in times of famine the fruit, stem and root were all edible. Squashed noni fruit could be made into a paste to kill nits on your head, but as the nits left you, it was said that your friends would go too. This *morinda citrifolia* was a prehistoric tree that had come with the Polynesian immigrants. So many of the indigenous or native plants and trees had medicinal and special qualities and although some of the endemic vegetation also had some useful qualities, other introduced plants had taken over, with unwelcome effects on the local flora and fauna.

Many introduced species of animal have desecrated the natural balance of indigenous wildlife all over the world. Rats, cats, mongoose and mink are some of the worst eradicators of ground nesting birds and their eggs. Hawaii had almost lost the néné, the Hawaiian goose and emblem of the country through the mongoose that preyed on their eggs. There were signs on the mountain roads with a picture of néné and the warning 'Go Slow'. Peter Scott had reintroduced a lot of geese that had bred at Slimbridge to help with their re-establishment. While I was on the crater of Haleakala caldera at 10,000 ft on Maui, I sent an arrow prayer to Peter asking to see some of his néné, that were now resident on the volcano. I started to call 'néné, néné' just as Peter used to call them at Slimbridge and a pair of néné appeared from behind a big black rock of lava, answering me 'néné, néné'. They stayed around me until I left.

The colourful birds had pretty local names; we called in to a Game Management Camp at 2,300 metres on Mauna Kea where tiny birds called amakihi were being checked and ringed, some of the species being indigenous only to Hawaii, others to the group of Islands. Back at Hilo we had six inches of rain in the night.

In New Zealand, my next port of call, I still had friends from my 1961 three weeks of riding and lectures before I had ridden at the Sydney Royal Easter Show. Other friends had stayed at Miserden with me in the 1950s, so we could check back on years of news. One highlight was seeing the gannet sanctuary on Cape Kidnapper where the gannets were sitting on their eggs in their colony, their nests built within centimetres of each other. When the birds came in to land among this dense nesting area, they got a rough reception if they landed a few feet off course by another bird's nest. Pilots had studied the gannets and their landing techniques, as they were heavy birds with an immense wing span, yet could make an accurate drop landing.

Nearby at Tuki Tuki I visited Malcolm and Judy Coop, where I had swum in the river with their grey jumper Rajah and a pet deer, thirty years before. Malcolm had been Master of the Hawke's Bay Hounds, a pack originating from hounds brought to Hawke's Bay a hundred years ago by Dick Roake, the son of the Pytchley huntsman in Leicestershire. Malcolm had just retired from the Mastership and had bred the Tukidale sheep that have been established world-wide. His present enterprise was with red deer which had the velvet from their antlers harvested each year, a valuable crop for the market in the Far East, that finds medicinal properties in the velvet. The deer were very tame along with the many coloured donkeys and their foals which had been in residence over a long time.

I had no time to visit the South Island, but could telephone Thady Ryan, a friend from my Limerick days in the 1940s, who had retired from the Mastership of the Scarteen Hounds, to live at Prebbleton in New Zealand, where he had an Irish Draught stallion standing at his stud.

I had time for a quick visit to lovely Lake Taupo, where the fish population had declined drastically since my last visit, although the hospitality had certainly not diminished. I stayed with Elizabeth Harker, a friend of 'Bee' and met Anne and Walter McKinnon, great friends of Sir Mike Ansell.

My reason for going to New Zealand was for the ICBP XXth World Conference, the International Council for Bird Preservation, as I am on the Achievement Board. This was being held at Hamilton University and the day before it started I could stay nearby with Jeff and Vicki McVean at the Glen Oaks Stud, surely one of the most superb studs that I have seen. The paddocks were double fenced to eight foot high, with thick hedges planted between for isolation and weather protection. A girl of twenty-four was working there, from Miserden, where she had known Monica and Lucy when they went for a short time to the village school, while I was having a hip operation: the world seemed very small.

Jeff and Vicki had lived in Gloucestershire near Stow-on-the-Wold while he had been show jumping internationally. He was then offered the job as manager of the Glen Oaks Stud and had taken it; although he is Australian, his wife is from New Zealand. Hamilton was nearby, but I found that the accommodation in the Waikatu University fell far short of the luxury at Glen Oaks. Only one bathroom with shower, basin and toilet was available for six student rooms, with no lock on the door. Another lady and myself were outnumbered by the four gentlemen who shared the bathroom. The hail came in the fixed open window and one blanket on the bed left me shivering in spite of using sweaters to sleep in. I recalled my student days at the end of the war.

The Conference started with a Maori Marae with a choir and a warrior, who nearly did not arrive in time. The Maori Queen was there for the dignified ceremony which included the warrior challenging the strangers on their arrival and then the welcome to us all. Many of the top conservationists were there, whose books I had read or knew through other acquaintances. There was a great deal to hear and learn from the speakers and participants.

My birthday brought me the treat of a mini bus trip to Miranda, on the estuarine area east of Auckland, where we walked along the shell ridges, watching flocks of waders feeding at low tide. We spotted the New Zealand Wrybill, sweeping the mud flats with its sideways turned bill curved to the right, the New Zealand and the banded Dotterel and a long list of everything else.

That day brought Mrs Thatcher's resignation, also the date of President Kennedy's assassination but I never read a newspaper during the whole trip. I left my University room, that by then had no light in my cell or hot water in the bathroom because the bulb and the boiler had broken.

Dr Luc Hoffmann and I had to fly to Sydney for the three days of the WWF International Council which was held at a comfortable hotel. There was a park and open ground near the hotel with many lovely birds of the parrot family and other Australian species. Walking early in the morning, before the ubiquitous flies began to bite, it was fascinating to hear and study these exotic and colourful galahs and cockatoos, before returning to breakfast and the first meeting. As the sun got up, it was easy to understand the Australian greeting, with a flick of the hand past the face, an automatic gesture to remove the persistent biting flies.

At the WWF conference, I was among many friends, all dedicated to the cause of conservation, before the environment would become irremediable. I have been involved, as a Trustee or on the Nominating Committee before being invited to join the International Council of the WWF, from the early days when the head office was in Morges and before the 1001 club was formed to finance the organisation, so that all donations would go directly into helping conservation projects.

The 1990 WWF Gold Medal was presented at our Sydney Conference to Professor Edward Wilson, a friend of Dick Schultes, the 1983 winner whom I had first seen in Boston. His speciality and favourite work in his wide scientific field, was the way that ants communicate and organise their communal lives together. This is done by various chemical changes in their bodies from which the discipline and organisation is understood by the other ants. I would have liked to learn a great deal more about his research and conclusions.

When Prince Philip's celebration dinner finished, we were able to continue our fascinating conversation of the table, when we found ourselves in the same coach returning to the hotel.

At the end of our conference a trip was arranged with a special bus to the Blue
Mountains. The colour comes from the oil moisturising in the gum tree leaves,
which makes a diffusion of blue light. Up in the forests were the lyre bird, the
power owl and many rosellas and parrots, while grey kangaroos and wallabies
grazed in the clearings.

From the superb day in the mountains, a few of us flew north to the southern
end of the Barrier Reef on Heron Island, now a nature reserve with laboratories
and the research station. The island had originally been used by a factory for the
products of the green turtle. We boarded the ferry from the mainland and had to
face a rough sea, but we were so lucky that no cyclone or typhoon left us
marooned or unable to enjoy our short time. The low trees were full of noddies
nesting and sitting on eggs, their favourite tree being the fig, but the nests were
built everywhere. Brown noddies with their white caps raise only one egg and
chick, and if it falls from the nest, they will not feed it.

As we walked around the island, we were warned not to fall into the sandy
burrows that the wedge-tailed shearwater's make for their underground nest. If
your foot does make a burrow collapse, you must dig the passage again so that the
broody female can come out to feed at night. The shearwater, also called the
mutton bird because of its taste, make a weird banshee howl at night, sometimes
very disturbing if they have burrowed just under your hut. If you mimic their cry
they will reply to you. The males fly in as it gets dark and they need a good clear
runway for their rather clumsy landing, with long wings outstretched to balance
them. If you walk into their landing path they cannot manoeuvre so they crash
into you. Then they must find their correct burrows and feed their mate and
young. After a noisy night with their cries, they will launch themselves into the air
for another day's food gathering, leaving the island before dawn.

We were very lucky with the timing of our visit; the phase of the full moon
meant the tides were right for the green turtle to leave the water at midnight, dig
their nests up on the beach and then return to the water after laying their eggs and
covering the nest with sand. We were asked not to carry torches on the beach in
the dark, because the artificial light could disorientate the turtles. After one full
night's vigil watching the turtles digging and laying their eggs by the full moon,
with the Southern Cross lying on its side under Orion, I took photos of an
incredibly lovely dawn and sunrise, which all seemed to happen in a passing
moment.

The coral reefs were full of many fish and varieties of coral, and we could see
where the delicate reef had coral torn away by ship's anchors causing much
damage to the marine habitat. The manta rays had a great sense of fun; although
they lived on the sea bed, they would sometimes come to the surface and leap in
and out of the water, playing with each other. The reef shark did not disturb us
while we snorkelled, but walking on the reef at low tide, the clams would snap
closed, at prying fingers, sending a jet of water spraying in your face.

In the evenings we could learn a great deal about reef ecology at the research
station and also check on one's own discoveries during the day. After another
dawn walk seeing the turtle tracks and more photos of herons and turnstones at

sunrise, the ferry came to take us away from our island on the Tropic of Capricorn, with my head and notebook full of the experiences of three wonderful days.

My clock went back another three hours on the 3,300 km journey to Perth, where the IUCN was holding its immense World Conference with 1,800 delegates at the excellent Burswood Centre. It was a relief to find some people I knew so that I could talk with Max Nicholson and Dick Estes of Earthwatch, with David Munro, past Director-General of the IUCN there too. Martin Holgate, the present Director-General was chairing the final day and the consensus was positive about progress during the conference. Other people I had hoped to meet had left already but my short time at Heron Island had been worth the detour and had given me a unique experience.

Cousins of Paddy Bury, Frank and June Craig, who lived near Perth, took me generously under their wing to show me West Australia for the first time, in the few days that I had left. Down south we went through forests of red gums and saw the Gloucester tree, an impressive size with a high fire look-out on top. The Duke of Gloucester had been there in 1946 while the tree was being pegged, for climbing up to the look out.

Great stretches of sandy beaches followed the coast line and at Bunbury there were dolphins that had come in to join children swimming off the beach. I was taken for a day at Ascot races and used my binoculars, not only for the horses, but to see the varieties of shags, coots, ducks and the smart chestnut breasted shelduck or mountain duck, swimming on the lake that makes a decorative centrepiece to the race course.

The worst plague of locusts to hit those parts within living memory was approaching Perth. We drove to the Craig's son's farm, where the locusts had just appeared, which gave me a new experience of nature gone crazy. I had seen the army worm strip miles of vegetation on my uncle's farm in South Africa, leaving nothing after passing through fields of high maize, and crossing the roads in masses, which stopped cars and lorries in their tracks as they could get no purchase on the roads. Before driving to the farm, a fine mesh metal shield was tied across the radiator, so that the locusts could not block the engine as they hit the front of the car. The day became dark as we approached the millions of locusts that were flying in a never-ending cloud. We continued driving steadily, having to stop and clear the windscreen and radiator mesh at regular intervals. The cloud of milling grasshoppers never let up for hours of driving and when we arrived at the farm, they were thick on the ground, with the small children running around barefoot on the lawn, that would soon be stripped of grass, sending up more clouds of locusts to join their flying friends.

Among the great trees of peppermint, blackbutt and white 'wando' gums, 10,000 merino sheep lived on the 1,200 hectare property, but world sheep prices had hit Down Under too. Sheep that had sold for 35 dollars last year, were down to 3 dollars, a desperate state for the farmers.

Prince Charles had been to Perth, and during his visit had congratulated June Craig on being the first lady to become a minister. Frank had added, that, finding things not going too well on the farm, he had had to find her the best paid job going.

My homeward journey was interrupted by the flight returning to Singapore in a new British Airways plane, where we got the full treatment of fire engines and ambulances, as we landed after flying for three hours, to jettison our fuel over the sea; I was sorry for the fishes.

Many hours later we were loaded back for our return to England. Keeping well north of the troubled Gulf zone, all went well until we had the lights of London ahead. The Captain's voice suddenly told us that we had to divert to Gatwick because our fuel was too low to wait for permission to land at Heathrow. He made it, perhaps gliding, directly into Gatwick, which was closing for the night with ice forming rapidly outside. The plane tried to put into a bay to unload the hundreds of weary passengers, with some old and infirm and many babies and young children. The connection between the bay and the plane did not work, so eventually we were towed backwards onto the open tarmac. A ladder arrived with narrow and icy steps for everyone to descend onto the freezing ground below. It seemed a long way from Perth.

During the icy drive on the M25, by taxi to Heathrow, not knowing if anyone was still waiting for me, I looked back on my way of travel over half a century before. Then our only transport had been Pixie and the Ralli trap, clip-clopping happily along the top of the Cotswolds, with the sacks of fresh cut garden vegetables, until seeing the Devil's Chimney, a rock column at the top of Leckhampton Hill, where I would get down and hold the trap back as Pixie went carefully down the steep pitch. Returning up the hill from Cheltenham, with the rations paid for with the cabbage and lettuce money, I would push the trap to help Pixie. It was downhill then to Crickley Lodge, our wartime home, nestled below the Devil's Table, a huge split rock, with the ancient British Camp above and the view over the Severn vale, with the Black Mountains on the horizon beyond Gloucester and the sharp outline of the Malverns beyond Tewkesbury. There were no travel worries then worse than Pixie losing a shoe, which I could easily nail on again if I found the shoe undamaged.

These thoughts were interrupted by the taxi leaving me alone and shivering with my 'round the world' baggage at the big and almost empty building of Terminal 4 after midnight. Helen, my right hand in running Sudgrove, was still waiting for me at Heathrow to my immense relief. The worry caused by a lack of direct communication over the past two days of journey trouble was eased by Helen's calm acceptance of the situation, in spite of her worry and discomfort while waiting. She drove me home in the small hours to arrive at Sudgrove with a great welcome from the dogs and the log fire still warm and smouldering.

The accumulated post brought me up to date with the international showjumping results. The challenge ahead lay in the build up of our team for the 1992 Barcelona Olympic Games as a priority for our planning committee. Since the pre-war standards, with only military teams, showjumping has developed into a top international sport and big business through sponsorship. The overall standard of riders and horses has improved as prize money increased making thrilling competitions with fractions of a second dividing the conqueror and the conquered. Spectators follow the fortunes of their favourite horses and partnerships; with a horse such as Milton, a spectacular grey Emperor among showjumpers, attracting a full house wherever he appears. Like people, only certain animals have this charisma to project their character and influence their followers. I appreciated that my top horses had this special attribute.

I do not regret any of my time spent competing during the tremendous changes in the sport after the war. It was an uphill battle with no financial support or big prizes while competing against 'amateurs' who were being financed behind the scene, or otherwise had come from a wealthy background. The positive advantage of those years was that people were more honest and trustworthy at home and abroad. When Paul, one of the only girl grooms on the international circuit, a tough man's world, and myself travelled alone, we never got robbed or molested. The 1950s were fun years and life was very stimulating.

The preparation of a good horse has not changed since then. The priority has always been to produce a fit and healthy horse and rider partnership able to perform their best on the vital day. The will to win, and to win fairly, is another essential and constructive ingredient with sport building the character of participants in the best way.

To win a team medal, the riders must work together with trust in each other and the trainer or manager. When the top riders are competing together regularly in international team events, an unwritten understanding can grow between them in giving each other support that creates the true team spirit. This preparation will produce the best results in the supreme test of the Olympic Games. Brilliant individuals put together at the last minute to form a team can never give the consistent standard of excellence in the results that a well-established and proven team can give; they know each other's strength and weakness over years of competition.

The Sudgrove team that has always helped me so much for many years are still around me living in the Sudgrove hamlet. Betty Morgan was the first friend from the 1950s, who helped us when sewing our clothes, while there was still clothes rationing; then when I came to Sudgrove she was there, with her husband Leslie, living in the cottage, having started work at Sudgrove for the Mills family at the age of fourteen. They still had no bathroom or inside toilet, which priority we remedied immediately when I moved to Sudgrove. She loved and cleaned the house especially silver and brasses, and made the curtains.

When Sam and I married and we built Steinacker, she came to Switzerland with Paddy and made the curtains there, and also for our flat at Wengen, the Tschingel, with the wonderful view of the Bernese Oberland. She is still my right hand, coming every morning, with her seventy-fourth birthday this year. Paddy is still with me since 1955 and keeps herself involved with all that goes on, with her seventy-fifth birthday celebration in July. The other cottage has Duncan and Betty Boyd, now retired here, having cared for our sheep since soon after Sam and

I were married when Duncan became our Farm Manager. He is a respected speaker on sheep and farm affairs.

Mike Roberts, now an Art Blacksmith with international connections, celebrates his fiftieth birthday, having come to Mother and me as one of our first guests at Miserden, when only six-and-a-half years old. In spite of his age, we found that his grandfather had left him to make his home with us. Later he spent a time at Steinacker while recuperating from an illness, where he and Sam would have energetic ping-pong matches. Mike learnt industrial metal work as an apprentice in the Ciba-Geigy school in Basel, but taught himself art blacksmithing.

Sadly we have now lost two of our little community with the deaths of Betty's husband Leslie, and Lini, Ollo's widow, who lived in our cottage, where Paddy joined her, for nearly twenty years. The hospitality at their homes is again undiminished, with their superb cooking.

Cirencester is still represented by the Agricultural students who have stayed over forty-four years, on their various courses, with changes of generation. The house is fully occupied with activity at most times, which I enjoy especially when any of the children drop in for a holiday. I've returned to home in Gloucestershire while retaining my worldwide interests.

My contact with four of the top conservation movements had brought home to me the devastation caused by the loss of habitat and natural resources, but also gave me hope that people around the world were getting their act together. We had discussed the importance of immediate action and co-operation that are essential to deal with the threatening ecological disasters due to interference with nature's bio-diversity creating each link in the life cycle.

Although three decades have passed since the WWF was formed emphasising the desperate need for conservation and care of our unique planet, it is a relief that at last the word is spreading and interest in the problems we face is growing rapidly.

Industrial pollution has worked havoc on land, sea and in the air with increased health hazards especially to the very young. The destruction of habitat leading to soil erosion has increased the risk of desertification and climate change caused by man's misuse of natural resources. For many years this knowledge has been preached by certain scientists and dedicated conservationists, whose voices fell on deaf ears. Now, at last, people are becoming concerned about the way this world is being treated, leaving mountainous problems that our misuse has created.

The selfishness and greed of man, combined often with unforgivable ignorance, has been apparent everywhere. Some of the wealthiest people or businesses have put their money where most harm can be done. This, for instance, is justified by calling a project 'sustainable' logging, which on inspection proves to be complete rape of the forest, even around the headwaters of great rivers in South America and other continents, changing the whole ecology of the land. Finance put into mining of natural resources has also caused the opening of forest areas and pollution from the mining works poisoning the rivers together with all life that depends on those waters. While this is happening, the financiers, making a quick turnover on their investment, sit comfortably in their ivory towers and offices, turning a blind eye to the consequences caused by their profit apart from leaving the land of no further value to anyone.

A problem that is stretching earth's resources beyond the limit has been the population explosion during this century, which increases at an uncontainable rate. Nature, left to itself without the interference of man, has had its own way of arranging sustainable resources. If too many lions breed successfully and deplete their food source, usually the antelope, they will starve and die when the meat runs out, leaving the few antelopes that escaped to breed in peace and replace their numbers. Homo Sapiens, with his superior brain, still needs to learn the discipline to curb desire and greed, or the human race will no longer be supported by the earth.

I have been impressed to see that some industries are now taking a more positive attitude in helping with conservation. I have always tried to encourage liaison with industry, rather than adopting a negative, 'anti', position. There is often the danger of a fanatical element in a body of people, even if it is 'green' and a matter of passionate believe. A fanatical stand can be self-destructive if it alienates the people who are in a position to give positive help financially and materially. We must recognise that certain industries can be of great help towards solving some of the problems that have been created.

The pharmaceutical industry usually has an infrastructure of educational programmes for their promotion of the safe use of drugs in the Third World. This working set-up can also be used for conservation programmes, if the right approach is arranged with the company. Another important part of the big chemical companies is the investment needed to set up modern and one hundred per cent efficient machines for the complete destruction of toxic waste. It is better to give this essential work a trial, rather than the project being condemned by people who offer no alternative methods or money to get rid of dangerous substances, and are objecting merely on principle.

Now that the conservation movement has attracted the public's attention, there is a danger of people wanting to promote themselves while the going is good. This can not only harm our cause but can also upset local people and governments of the countries, who are often working in very difficult conditions.

We must live with industry, without it there would be a howl of protest, but we should have liaison with those responsible for the vast enterprises that are part of our way of life. We must all take a closer interest in the world around us and help where it is possible. Everyone needs to become involved with conservation, starting with their homes and waste disposal, using biodegradable products, recycling paper and bottles and generally using thought in the care of our Earth, especially in preventing further pollution.

We have gained so much in technical advancement in only the past century and yet it is doubtful if this 'progress' fully compensates for the land we have already spoiled and the species of flora and fauna that have been lost. The population explosion has caused famine and desertification of land overgrazed by domestic animals, while wars have intensified these problems of homeless families suffering in poverty. So many of the tribes lived better lives before they were 'discovered' by the more wealthy west, who then exploited their land. We cannot turn the clock back, but we must work for the future to help the peoples of the world to have a better quality of life in a habitat that can sustain them. Everyone must co-ordinate their efforts and take responsibility for attaining this goal because without each person and family contributing to the achievement of a better future, there can be no comprehensive plan. Thousands of species of flora and fauna have already become extinct with many more on the brink of extinction.

Without the efforts of the WWF, IUCN and all conservationists we would already have lost more species of animals in the last thirty years, perhaps even averting the final breakdown point in the essential and natural cycle of nature. The action taken, only just in time, has reprieved unique species like the tiger, the oryx, the vicuña, the néné, the Javan rhino, the gorilla, among so many others.

Now that people are becoming aware of the urgency to save our beautiful world, my hope is that the younger generation will help the gathering momentum for conservation and care of our inheritance. They are the people that can show their parents the mistakes that have been made in the past and the relevant values needed for a better quality of life for everyone. I am confident that my girls will continue to care and work for a better world, when they launch out from their Swiss University studies where Monica has completed her law finals *Cum Laude* and can now write her thesis for a Doctorate, while working as assistant to Dr Wildhaber, the Principal of Basel University, who is also a Judge at the Court of Human Rights in Strasbourg. Sam would have been so proud that both his son Dominik and now Monica had qualified, as he did, in Law. Many of their generation realise the importance of sustainable living and the value of the world's flora, fauna and natural resources, a subject that was never mentioned in my schooldays.

Our education came from living and working closely with nature, learning the habits of wildlife and the occasional poaching for the pot. Peter Scott gained his great knowledge of wildfowl and wetlands through his original love of wildfowling. Once converted, the poacher can be the best gamekeeper and guardian of wildlife because he has an instinct for the ways of the wild.

I am thankful for all this life has offered me and would like to be spared a little longer to contribute any small part in the conservation programme. There is so much to be done while time passes quickly, with every moment counting. These precious moments are there to treasured and turned to effective use, so that future generations may be able to appreciate some of the wonders of nature and life on this planet.

Life is a great and fascinating challenge with many obstacles and heartbreaks to be encountered on the way. The courage and skill needed to leap safely to the other side can enable us to anticipate the next, and maybe tougher, problem fence

ahead. Now determination, without losing accuracy on the approach, can generate the enthusiasm and confidence that nothing is insurmountable – the joy and
achievement of soaring clear over the new obstacle reinforces the courage we need
to achieve a better future.

Index of People

Index of Important Horses